AF371845

Investment Arbitration and State-Driven Reform

Investment Arbitration and State-Driven Reform

New Treaties, Old Outcomes

WOLFGANG ALSCHNER

OXFORD

UNIVERSITY PRESS

OXFORD
UNIVERSITY PRESS

Oxford University Press is a department of the University of Oxford. It furthers the University's objective of excellence in research, scholarship, and education by publishing worldwide. Oxford is a registered trade mark of Oxford University Press in the UK and certain other countries.

Published in the United States of America by Oxford University Press
198 Madison Avenue, New York, NY 10016, United States of America.

© Oxford University Press 2022

Library of Congress Cataloging-in-Publication Data
Names: Alschner, Wolfgang, author.
Title: Investment arbitration and state-driven reform : new treaties, old outcomes / Wolfgang Alschner.
Description: New York : Oxford University Press, [2022] | Based on author's thesis (doctoral - Graduate Institute of International and Development Studies (Geneva, Switzerland), 2015) issued under title: State-driven change in international investment law and its (uncertain) impact on investor-state arbitration. | Includes bibliographical references and index.
Identifiers: LCCN 2021061260 (print) | LCCN 2021061261 (ebook) | ISBN 9780197644386 (hardback) | ISBN 9780197644409 (epub) | ISBN 9780197644393 (updf) | ISBN 9780197644416 (online)
Subjects: LCSH: Investments, Foreign—Law and legislation. | Investments, Foreign (International law) | International commercial arbitration. | International and municipal law.
Classification: LCC K3830 .A424 2021 (print) | LCC K3830 (ebook) | DDC 346/.092—dc23/eng/20220325
LC record available at https://lccn.loc.gov/2021061260
LC ebook record available at https://lccn.loc.gov/2021061261

DOI: 10.1093/oso/9780197644386.001.0001

Note to Readers
This publication is designed to provide accurate and authoritative information in regard to the subject matter covered. It is based upon sources believed to be accurate and reliable and is intended to be current as of the time it was written. It is sold with the understanding that the publisher is not engaged in rendering legal, accounting, or other professional services. If legal advice or other expert assistance is required, the services of a competent professional person should be sought. Also, to confirm that the information has not been affected or changed by recent developments, traditional legal research techniques should be used, including checking primary sources where appropriate.

(Based on the Declaration of Principles jointly adopted by a Committee of the American Bar Association and a Committee of Publishers and Associations.)

You may order this or any other Oxford University Press publication
by visiting the Oxford University Press website at www.oup.com.

Für Friedi

Contents

Figures and Tables — xv
Preface — xvii
Acknowledgments — xix
Abbreviations — xxi
Table of Cases — xxiii

Introduction — 1

PART I. STATE-DRIVEN REFORM

1. Treaties as Data — 23

2. Change as Gap-Filling — 47

3. Evolution as Americanization — 81

PART II. NEW TREATIES, OLD OUTCOMES

4. Reversing Innovation through MFN — 123

5. Overriding Differences through Custom — 153

6. Perpetuating Mistakes through Precedent — 183

PART III. NEW TREATIES AS ANCHOR POINTS

7. Forward-Looking Interpretation — 219

8. Data-Driven Renegotiation — 245

9. Tax-Style Multilateralization — 269

Bibliography — 293
Index — 311

Detailed Table of Contents

Figures and Tables   xv
Preface   xvii
Acknowledgments   xix
Abbreviations   xxi
Table of Cases   xxiii

Introduction   1
   A New Hope: A New Generation of International Investment
      Agreements   3
   Hope Disappointed: New Treaties, Old Outcomes   6
   What's Going On?   8
   Toward a Map of the Investment Treaty Universe   11
   Reading New Treaties Like Old Ones   14
   Reading Old Treaties Like New Ones   16
   Blind Spots   17
   How to Read This Book   19

PART I. STATE-DRIVEN REFORM

1. Treaties as Data   23
   I. INTRODUCTION   23
  II. THE EMERGING FIELD OF COMPUTATIONAL LEGAL
     STUDIES   24
  III. WHAT WE KNOW AND DON'T KNOW ABOUT THE
     DESIGN OF IIAS   27
    A. Uniformity vs. Diversity across States' IIA Practice   27
    B. Continuity and Change across Time   29
  IV. LETTING INVESTMENT TREATIES SPEAK FOR
     THEMSELVES   31
    A. The EDIT Dataset   31
    B. Text-as-Data Analysis of IIAs   33
    C. Robustness Checks   37
   V. THE PUZZLE: NEW TREATIES, OLD OUTCOMES   39
    A. The Rise of New-Generation Treaties   40
    B. Current Trajectory: New Treaties, Old Outcomes 41
  VI. CONCLUSION   46

2. Change as Gap-Filling   47
   I. INTRODUCTION   47
   II. CONTRACT THEORY   47
      A. Complete and Incomplete Contracts   48
      B. Curbing Opportunism and Seizing Regret   49
      C. Relationship between Ex Post Flexibility and Ex Ante
         Commitments   50
      D. Credibility through Effective Enforcement   50
      E. Strategies to Overcome Incompleteness   51
      F. Relation between Gap-Filling Strategies   52
   III. CONTRACT THEORY AS META-FRAMEWORK FOR
        UNDERSTANDING IIA DESIGN CHANGE   53
      A. Quest for Optimal Design Rather Than Policy Space   54
      B. Precision as Comprehensive Gap-Filling over Time   55
      C. Taking Back Control by Rewriting Terms of Delegation   57
   IV. EVOLUTION TOWARD MORE COMPLETE IIAS   58
      A. Mimicking the CCC Design—More Comprehensive and
         Detailed Contracting   58
      B. Seizing Regret—Adding Escape Clauses   69
      C. Relational Contracting   73
      D. Managing Delegation—Curtailing Judicial Gap-Filling   77
   V. CONCLUSION   80

3. Evolution as Americanization   81
   I. INTRODUCTION   81
   II. ORIGINS: FCN TREATIES AND BITS AS COMPETING
       MODELS OF INVESTMENT PROTECTION TREATIES   83
      A. FCN Treaties as Part of Symmetrical North–North Relations   84
      B. BITs and Asymmetrical North–South Investment Relations   86
      C. FCN vs. BITs   89
   III. THREE WAVES OF INNOVATION   95
      A. Wave 1: 1982—The United States Joins the BIT Universe and
         Incorporates FCN Heritage   95
      B. Wave 2: 1992—The NAFTA Moment   98
      C. Wave 3: 2004—The Revised US and Canadian Model BITs   105
   IV. GLOBAL DIFFUSION OF AMERICAN TREATY DESIGN   108
      A. New Symmetry in Investment Relations   109
      B. Increasing Domestic Politicization of Investment Law   112
      C. Embracing American IIA Design   114
   V. A NEW DIVERSITY   119
   VI. CONCLUSION   120

PART II. NEW TREATIES, OLD OUTCOMES

4. Reversing Innovation through MFN   123
   I. INTRODUCTION   123
   II. ROLLING BACK TREATY INNOVATION THROUGH MFN   125
     A. MFN Is Frequently Used to Import More Favorable Substantive Clauses   126
     B. Rolling Back Clarifications of Protective Standards   128
     C. Bringing Back Phased-Out Protective Standards   129
     D. Bypassing Exceptions   131
   III. FROM NONDISCRIMINATION TO MULTILATERALIZATION   132
     A. The Dual Nature of MFN in ISDS   133
     B. Emergence through Case Law, Amplified through Scholarship, Entrenched through Practice   135
     C. Putting the Genie Back in the Bottle   139
   IV. THE LIMITS OF MFN   142
     A. Limitations Based on the Scope of the Base Treaty   143
     B. Limitations Based on the Scope of the MFN Clause   144
   V. CONCLUSION   151

5. Overriding Differences through Custom   153
   I. INTRODUCTION   153
   II. ROLLING BACK INNOVATION THROUGH CUSTOM   155
     A. Increasing Commitments through Custom   155
     B. Lowering Flexibilities through Custom   159
   III. TREATIES AND CUSTOM: A HISTORY OF LINKING AND DELINKING   166
     A. Phase I: Codifying Custom   166
     B. Phase II: Rise of Arbitration and the Delinking of Custom   169
     C. Phase III: Arbitral Self-Correction and the Return of Custom   172
     D. Phase IV: Codifying Custom More Explicitly   175
     E. Phase V: Custom Confused   176
   IV. RECOGNIZING WHEN IIAS CONTRACT ON CUSTOM OR GO BEYOND IT   176
     A. Contracting on Custom: When to Lift Up Incomplete Agreements   176
     B. Going beyond Custom: How to Avoid Rolling Back Innovation in More Complete Agreements   178
   V. CONCLUSION   180

6. Perpetuating Mistakes through Precedent   183
   I. INTRODUCTION   183
   II. ROLLING BACK INNOVATION THROUGH PRECEDENT   185
     A. Interpreting More Complete Treaties Like Incomplete Ones   185
     B. Circumventing Corrective State Interventions through Precedent   192

III. THE STICKINESS OF PRECEDENT   198
   A. Normative Preference for Following Precedent   199
   B. Institutional Incentives for Following Precedent   201
   C. Lack of Effective Controls to Police Precedent   202
   D. Self-Reinforcement of Precedent   206
IV. BREAKING THE PATH   210
   A. Policing Precedent through Annulment and Set-Aside   212
   B. Shepardizing Precedent   213
V. CONCLUSION   215

PART III. NEW TREATIES AS ANCHOR POINTS

7. Forward-Looking Interpretation   219
   I. INTRODUCTION   219
   II. CONTRACT THEORY AND INTERPRETATION   221
      A. Arbitral Tribunals as the Interpretive Agents of the Contracting
         Parties   221
      B. The Degree of Contractual Completeness Determines Tribunal's
         Approach to Interpretation   226
      C. Reading Incomplete Treaties in Light of More Complete Ones   230
   III. USING SUBSEQUENT AGREEMENTS AND PRACTICE TO
        MODERNIZE INCOMPLETE IIAS   231
      A. Explicit Interpretative Gap-Filling Ex Post—VCLT Article 31(3)a
         and Article (3)(b)   233
      B. Implicit Interpretative Gap-Filling Ex Post—VCLT Article 31(3)c
         and Article (1)   237
      C. Supplementary Means—VCLT Article 32   243
   IV. CONCLUSION   244

8. Data-Driven Renegotiation   245
   I. INTRODUCTION   245
   II. MISSED OPPORTUNITIES: WHY RENEGOTIATIONS ARE
       RARELY AND POORLY USED   247
      A. Renegotiations Are Rare, Concentrated, and Driven by the
         Wrong Reasons   247
      B. Reasons Why Renegotiations Remain Rarely Used   250
   III. A DATA-DRIVEN APPROACH TO RENEGOTIATIONS   251
      A. What Treaties to Prioritize for Renegotiation?   251
      B. How to Renegotiate?   257
   IV. PLURILATERALS: REPLACING OR EXACERBATING THE
       SPAGHETTI BOWL?   264
      A. The Benefits of Layering   265
      B. The Costs of Layering   267
      C. Using Plurilaterals as Renegotiation Tools   268
   V. CONCLUSION   268

9. Tax-Style Multilateralization   269
    I. INTRODUCTION   269
    II. THE EVOLVING UNCITRAL PROCESS   271
    III. MOLDING THE REFORM AGENDA ON TAX-STYLE
         MULTILATERALISM   273
         A. Shaky Assumptions   273
         B. Record of Procedural Successes and Substantive Failures
             Colored Perceptions   275
         C. Trade Analogies Exacerbate Perceptions   276
         D. Switching Frames to Tax-Style Multilateralism   278
    IV. REFORMING INVESTMENT MULTILATERALISM
         TAX-STYLE   281
         A. Bulk Update through Soft Law: Emulating the OECD Model
             Convention and Commentary   282
         B. Bulk Upgrade through Hard Law: Emulating the OECD's MLI   286
    V. CONCLUSION   292

Bibliography   293
Index   311

Figures and Tables

Figure 1.1 Main design variation of IIAs over time (with dotted trend line) 36

Figure 1.2 Main design variation of IIAs over time based on UNCTAD's mapping data 38

Figure 1.3 Variance explained by the first fifteen principal components based on UNCTAD's mapping data 39

Figure 1.4 Breakdown of ISDS cases with final award until 2020 42

Figure 2.1 The major content variation of IIAs (y-axis) 59

Figure 2.2 Average word length of BITs with standard deviation 60

Figure 2.3 Average mentions of "for greater certainty" or "for the avoidance of doubt" per IIA over time 61

Figure 2.4 Clarifying scope of protective obligations 64

Figure 2.5 Phasing out unclear or redundant protective obligations 67

Figure 2.6 Proliferation of public policy and security exceptions 70

Figure 2.7 Rise of economic coordination exceptions and exclusions 71

Figure 2.8 Provisions situating investment protection in broader fabric of investment relations 75

Figure 3.1 The evolution of IIAs 82

Figure 3.2 Evolution of Canadian BITs 103

Figure 3.3 Evolution of Mexican BITs 109

Figure 6.1 Average age of cited precedent (in years) 193

Figure 6.2 Share of unique citations from ISDS awards to SGS Pakistan and SGS Philippines per year 204

Figure 8.1 Renegotiations by year and type 248

Figure 8.2 Selected content elements in Australian BITs color-coded for their presence 258

Figure 8.3 Counts of IIAs with umbrella clauses or public policy exception by year of signature 259

Figure 8.4 Comparison of IIA practices of Turkey and Japan 261

Table 1.1 EDIT full texts included in the analysis 32

Table 1.2 Example of a document-term matrix depicting term frequencies 33

Table 1.3 New-generation IIAs (i.e. treaties with a principal component score above 30) that have produced merits decisions (NAFTA omitted) 43

Table 2.1 Highest and lowest ranked BITs by PC1 score 61

Table 4.1 IIAs connected through the fifty-six awards with MFN claims that sought to import substantive treatment and their success and rejection frequency 126

Table 4.2 Clauses that have been successfully imported via MFN 127

Table 4.3 Assuming that MFN can incorporate by reference third-treaty provisions, its operation leaves most of the state-driven treaty design innovations of Part I intact 150

Table 6.1 Share of 4,531 citation connections between ISDS awards by IIAs' level of contractual completeness 186

Table 6.2 Outward citations by litigated treaties with highest principle component scores in the dataset 187

Table 6.3 Treatment of voided passages of the *Metalclad* award in subsequent decisions until 2019 196

Table 8.1 Number and type of BIT renegotiations by top five parties 249

Table 8.2 EU treaties replacing overlapping BITs 253

Table 8.3 Regional IIAs overlapping with concluded BITs 254

Table 8.4 Computer-generated transfer of funds clause 263

Table 9.1 Matrix of MLI reforms and their application in tax and investment 291

Preface

It was a landmark decision. *Gold Reserve v. Venezuela* began as a textbook dispute on foreign investment. The Canadian company Gold Reserve had acquired two mining concessions in southeastern Venezuela in the 1990s. Venezuela, under President Hugo Chavez, then began to nationalize the country's extractive industries. In 2008, Venezuela's Ministry of Mines revoked Gold Reserve's concessions, citing environmental grounds. Gold Reserve reacted by making use of investment law's most potent remedy: it initiated investor-state dispute settlement (ISDS) proceedings before an international arbitration tribunal against Venezuela based on the Canada–Venezuela bilateral investment treaty (BIT). The case would have been unremarkable was it not for the treaty in question.

Since the early 2000s, scholars and international organizations have heralded the emergence of a "new generation" of international investment agreements (IIAs). Whereas early BITs were short, relatively vague, and focused exclusively on investment protection, this new generation of agreements was different. The treaties were longer, more complex, and included explicit clauses that balanced the protection of foreign investment with the host state's right to safeguard public health, to protect the environment, and to regulate in the public interest. The Canada–Venezuela BIT signed in 1994 was the first treaty with such novel public policy exceptions to be litigated. This turned *Gold Reserve v. Venezuela* into a test case on how the new generation of IIAs would play out in practice.

The stakes were high. Since the early 2000s, investment arbitration had increasingly come under fire for privileging the interests of investors over those of host states. Billion-dollar awards against developing countries, coupled with high-profile challenges against public policy legislation in developed countries, created a perception that the regime was tilted in favor of powerful multinational enterprises. The tribunals settling these ISDS cases came under scrutiny, too. Investment arbitrators were viewed by some as unaccountable profiteers with a financial stake in the continuous expansion of this one-sided regime.

With the legitimacy of ISDS cast in doubt, the regime was in crisis mode. An attempt to rescue the investment law system lay in changing the design of investment treaties.

Gold Reserve v. Venezuela is a landmark case because it disappointed these hopes and expectations. The tribunal did not use the novel public policy exception in the BIT to rebalance the interests of investors with those of host states. In fact, the award does not even mention the clause. In deciding the case, the tribunal instead borrowed from precedents rendered under older investment treaties that lacked exceptions to make sense of Venezuela's environmental defense. In short, the tribunal read the new investment treaty like an old one. Not only did the tribunal thereby ignore the innovations introduced in the BIT, in doing so, it cast doubt on the promise that the recent generation of agreements with novel features would address and alleviate the imbalance between investment protection and host state sovereignty that characterized earlier investment treaties.

Gold Reserve v. Venezuela may be a poster child of a missed opportunity, but it is not alone. From *Eco Oro v. Colombia* to *Bear Creek v. Peru* to *Copper Mesa v. Ecuador* and others, this book examines awards that have been rendered under newly designed investment agreements. They all point in the same direction: new treaties produce old outcomes as the new generation of IIAs is interpreted like the old one. The much-celebrated treaty design innovations have done little to address the regime's legitimacy crisis. This bodes ill for the future of international investment law that hinges on successful reforms to regain public trust and confidence in the system.

This book does three things. It shows how we got here, what is wrong with where we are, and what we can do about it. The book draws on legal data science to present new empirical evidence at a yet unseen scale. It uses diverse interdisciplinary and comparative international law methods to shed new light on old debates. Perhaps most importantly, it provides the reader with a new map to navigate the investment law system and to charter a course for its successful reform.

Acknowledgments

The idea for this book first emerged in 2010 in the cafeteria of the United Nations in Geneva. During an internship at the UN Conference on Trade and Development (UNCTAD), a colleague, Jan Knoerich, suggested that it would be a good idea if somebody wrote an empirical account of the evolution of investment treaty design. I thought so, too, and started my PhD at the Graduate Institute a year later. Much of the first part of this book stems from my PhD research. During my years in Geneva, I benefited greatly from the stimulating academic environment of the Graduate Institute and the proximity to international institutions. However, it was friends, colleagues, and mentors who made those years truly special. A deep-felt gratitude goes to my PhD supervisor Joost Pauwelyn for his unwavering support. He provided constant inspiration on what analytical and creative research, intellectual curiosity, and dedicated, question-driven teaching looks like at its best. I am also grateful to my friends and colleagues at the Institute, especially at the Centre for Trade and Economic Integration, and at UNCTAD for the innumerable conversations, acts of kindness, and support that I benefited from. A special thanks goes to Lisi Tuerk for her mentorship at UNCTAD and to my friends Julia Seiermann and Chris Thornton for many memorable Ferney moments. I also owe a depth of gratitude to Dmitriy Skougarevskiy, who first introduced me to text-as-data research. The subsequent collaboration with him marked the most productive phase of my academic life. Thanks, Dima!

This book also benefited from comments, encounters, and conversations during research stays at other institutions. I am grateful to Lauge Poulsen, whose PhD dissertation influenced my thinking about the investment regime like no other work, and who hosted me at Oxford, where I was able to bounce ideas off other aspiring international investment law scholars who later became friends, such as Taylor St. John, who also reviewed part of this manuscript. At Stanford, I benefited from the guidance of Alan Sykes, inhaled Deborah Hensler's enthusiasm for empirical research, and learned how to code and conduct text-as-data research from Justin Grimmer (thanks to Justin's Teaching Assistant Franny for patiently explaining the basics of Python to me). I greatly enjoyed my time at Stanford, and I am deeply grateful to Sergio Puig, who encouraged me to apply in the first place, and to my SPILS mentors and colleagues. In addition, much of this book would have been impossible without my postdoc work at the World Trade Institute in Bern. I am indebted to Manfred Elsig for his support and mentorship over the years and to the always kind and cheerful Rodrigo Polanco for his unmatched dedication to the EDIT project.

Finally, I am grateful to my friends and colleagues in Canada, where most of the second half of this book took shape. I would not be here but for the advice, support, and encouragement from Nicholas Lamp. I am grateful to my University of Ottawa colleagues, especially Debra Steger, Tony VanDuzer, Céline Lévesque, and Parick Dumberry, for their warm welcome and for their input on my work in progress. I am also indebted to my friend Cam Vidler, who helped me hash out the main argument of the book over beers after a *Star Wars* movie and for everything he and his family have done to make my family feel at home in Ottawa. Last but not least, I want to thank my uOttawa students and research assistants for their hard work and dedication. In particular, I am grateful to Bin Cheng, Gregory Landry, and Claudia Lach for the data they helped to collect and analyze for this book and the many others who assisted with the EDIT project.

During my research I immensely benefited from the comments I received from other scholars. Stephan Schill and Thomas Schultz served on my PhD Thesis Committee and provided detailed comments that encouraged me to look deeper at the impact of treaty design on arbitration outcomes. I also owe gratitude to the teams at PluriCourts and iCourts, whose dedication to empirical work has been motivating and whose conferences provided important opportunities to get feedback on emerging ideas and to meet other scholars. A heartfelt thank-you goes to Anthea Roberts for her mentorship and friendship. Anthea's avant-garde scholarship, intellectual curiosity, and breadth of interests are a continuous source of inspiration to me. Finally, I am extremely grateful to everyone who took the time to engage with my work in one way or another over this past decade, be it over coffee, via email, at conferences, in corridors, or via Zoom.

Aside from the individuals and institutions who shaped this book's journey, I also owe a depth of gratitude to those who have funded my PhD and research. I gratefully acknowledge the support of the Canada Foundation for Innovation, the Canadian Social Science and Humanities Council, the Ontario Early Researcher Award, the Swiss Network of International Studies, the Swiss Science Foundation, the Gallatin Fellowship, and the Europaeum Oxford-Geneva Scholarship. I am also grateful to the team at Oxford University Press and the anonymous reviewers for their role in turning this manuscript into a book.

In closing, I want to thank my family for their love and support. My parents and grandparents prepared me for this journey, and my wonderful daughters delighted my days as I approached the finish line. Above all, I am grateful to my wife, Friederike, to whom this book is dedicated. She stoically endured enumerable conversations about investment treaties and offered her love, encouragement, and wisdom in return. Without her kindness, understanding, and support, this book would not have been written.

Wolfgang Alschner, Chelsea, Canada, October 31, 2021

Abbreviations

AB	*Appellate Body*
ASEAN	*Association of Southeast Asian Nations*
BIT	*Bilateral Investment Treaty*
CCC	*Complete Contingent Contract*
CETA	*Comprehensive Economic and Trade Agreement*
COMESA	*Common Market for Eastern and Southern Africa*
CPTPP	*Comprehensive and Progressive Agreement for Trans-Pacific Partnership*
CSR	*Corporate Social Responsibility*
EDIT	*Electronic Database of Investment Treaties*
FCN	*Friendship, Commerce, and Navigation Treaty*
FDI	*Foreign Direct Investment*
FET	*Fair and Equitable Treatment*
FTA	*Free Trade Agreement*
FTC	*Free Trade Commission*
GATS	*General Agreement on Trade in Services*
GATT	*General Agreement on Tariffs and Trade*
ICJ	*International Court of Justice*
ICSID	*International Centre for Settlement of Investment Disputes*
IIA	*International Investment Agreement*
ILC	*International Law Commission*
ISDS	*Investor-State Dispute Settlement*
MAI	*Multilateral Agreement on Investment*
MFN	*Most Favored Nation*
NAFTA	*North American Free Trade Agreement*
OECD	*Organisation for Economic Co-operation and Development*
PCA	*Principal Component Analysis*
RCEP	*Regional Comprehensive Economic Partnership*
REIO	*Regional Economic Integration Organization*
TPP	*Trans-Pacific Partnership*
TRIMs	*Trade-Related Investment Measures*
TRIPS	*Trade-Related Aspects of Intellectual Property Rights*
UNCITRAL	*United Nations Commission on International Trade Law*
UNCTAD	*United Nations Conference on Trade and Development*
VCLT	*Vienna Convention on the Law of Treaties*
WTO	*World Trade Organization*

Table of Cases

INVESTMENT ARBITRATION CASES

Adel A Hamadi Al Tamimi v. Sultanate of Oman, ICSID Case No. ARB/11/33,
Award, 3 November 2015 [*Al Tamimi v. Oman*] 44–45

ADF Group Inc. v. United States of America, ICSID Case No. ARB(AF)/00/1,
Award, 9 January 2003 [*ADF v. USA*] 148, 193–94

Aguas del Tunari, S.A. v. Bolivia, ICSID Case No. ARB/02/3, Decision on
Respondent's Objections to Jurisdiction, 21 October 2005 [*Aguas del
Tunari v. Bolivia*] 234–35

Asian Agricultural Products Ltd. v. Sri Lanka, ICSID Case No. ARB/87/3,
Final Award, 27 June 1990 [*AAPL v. Sri Lanka*] 123, 136–38, 240

Bear Creek Mining Corporation v Republic of Peru, ICSID Case No ARB/14/21,
Award, 30 November 2017 [*Bear Creek v. Peru*] 7, 42–44, 162–63,
165–66, 178–79, 180

Bilcon of Delaware et al v. Government of Canada, PCA Case No. 2009-04,
Award on Jurisdiction and Liability, 17 March 2015 [*Bilcon v. Canada*] 157,
176–77, 193–94

BG Group Plc. v. Republic of Argentina, UNCITRAL, Award, 24 December 2007
[*BG Group v. Argentina*] 66–67

Canadian Cattlemen for Fair Trade v. United States of America, UNCITRAL,
Award on Jurisdiction, 28 January 2008 [*Canadian Cattlemen v. USA*] 236

*CC/Devas (Mauritius) Ltd., Devas Employees Mauritius Private Limited and
Telecom Devas Mauritius Limited v. India*, PCA Case No. 2013–09,
Award on Jurisdiction and Merits, 25 July 2016 [*CC/Devas v. India*].........161–62

Chemtura Corporation v. Government of Canada, UNCITRAL (formerly
Crompton Corporation v. Government of Canada), Award, 1 August 2010
[*Chemtura v. Canada*] 148

Chevron Corporation (U.S.A.) and Texaco Petroleum Corporation (U.S.A.) v.
Republic of Ecuador [I], PCA Case No. AA 277, Partial Award on the Merits,
30 March 2010 [*Chevron v. Ecuador*] 67–68, 129–30

CME Czech Republic B.V. v. Czech Republic, UNCITRAL, Final Award,
14 March 2003 [*CME v. Czech Republic*] 206

CMS Gas Transmission Company v. The Republic of Argentina, ICSID
Case No. ARB/01/8, Award, 12 May 2005 [*CMS v. Argentina*] 132, 144, 157,
160–61, 164–65

CMS Gas Transmission Company v. The Republic of Argentina, ICSID Case No.
ARB/01/8, Decision of the ad hoc Committee on the Application for
Annulment of the Argentine Republic, 25 September 2007
[*CMS v. Argentina*]...161–62

Copper Mesa Mining Corporation v Republic of Ecuador, PCA No 2012-2,
Award, 15 March 2016 [*Copper Mesa v. Ecuador*] 7, 42–44, 163

Crystallex International Corporation v Bolivarian Republic of Venezuela, ICSID
Case No ARB(AF)/11/2, Award, 4 April 2016 [*Crystallex v. Venezuela*]..... 7, 180, 191

*David R. Aven, Samuel D. Aven, Giacomo A. Buscemi and others v. Republic of
    Costa Rica*, ICSID Case No. UNCT/15/3, Award, 18 September 2018
    [*Aven v. Costa Rica*] 44–45
Deutsche Telekom v. India, PCA Case No. 2014–10, Interim Award,
    13 December 2017 [*Deutsche Telekom v. India*] 161–62
Duke Energy Electroquil Partners and Electroquil S.A. v. Republic of Ecuador,
    ICSID Case No. ARB/04/19, Award, 18 August 2008
    [*Duke Energy v. Ecuador*] 67–68
Eco Oro Minerals Corp. v. Republic of Colombia, ICSID Case No. ARB/16/41,
    Decision on Jurisdiction, Liability and Directions on Quantum,
    9 September 2021 [*Eco Oro v. Colombia*]. 7, 42–44, 163–66, 178–79, 180
*EDF International S.A., SAUR International S.A. and León Participaciones
    Argentinas S.A. v. Argentine Republic*, ICSID Case No. ARB/03/23,
    Final award, 11 June 2012 [*EDF v. Argentina*]. 130, 138, 147–48
Electrabel S.A. v. Republic of Hungary, ICSID Case No. ARB/07/19, Award, 25
    November 2015 [*Electrabel v. Hungary*] 188
Emilio Agustín Maffezini v. The Kingdom of Spain, ICSID Case No.
    ARB/97/7, Decision of the Tribunal on Objections to Jurisdiction,
    25 January 2000 [*Maffezini v. Spain*] 123, 137–38, 148–49,
                                                            184, 206–7, 208–9
Enron Corporation and Ponderosa Assets, L.P. v. Argentine Republic, ICSID
    Case No. ARB/01/3, Award, 22 May 2007 [*Enron v. Argentina*] 160–61, 164–65
Enron Corporation and Ponderosa Assets, L.P. v. Argentine Republic, ICSID Case No.
    ARB/01/3, Decision on Annulment, 30 July 2010 [*Enron v. Argentina*] 161
European American Investment Bank AG (EURAM) v. Slovak Republic, UNCITRAL,
    Award on Jurisdiction, 22 August 2012 [*EURAM v. Slovakia*] 135
Fraport AG Frankfurt Airport Services Worldwide v. Republic of the Philippines,
    ICSID Case No. ARB/03/25, Dissenting Opinion of Mr. Bernardo M.
    Cremades, 16 August 2007 [*Fraport v. Philippines*] 215
Gas Natural SDG, S.A. v. The Argentine Republic, ICSID Case No. ARB/03/10,
    Decision of the Tribunal on Preliminary Questions on Jurisdiction,
    17 June 2005 [*Gas Natural v. Argentina*] 234–35
Glamis Gold, Ltd. V. The United States of America, UNCITRAL, Final
    Award, 8 June 2009 [*Glamis v. USA*] 173, 214–15
Global Telecom Holding S.A.E. v. Canada, ICSID Case No. ARB/16/16,
    Award, 27 March 2020 [*Global Telecom v. Canada*] .44, 177–78
Gold Reserve Inc. v. Bolivarian Republic of Venezuela, ICSID Case No.
    ARB(AF)/09/1, Award, 22 September 2014 [*Gold Reserve v. Venezuela*] 42–44,
                                                            180, 190, 195, 212
Hochtief Aktiengesellschaft v. Argentine Republic, ICSID Case No. ARB/07/31,
    Decision on Jurisdiction, 24 October 2011 [*Hochtief v. Argentina*] 146–47
İçkale İnşaat Limited Şirketi v. Turkmenistan, ICSID Case No. ARB/10/24, ICSID
    Case No ARB/10/24, Award, 8 March 2016 [*İçkale v. Turkmenistan*] . . . 141, 157–58
Infinito Gold Ltd. V. Costa Rica, ICSID Case No. ARB/14/5, Award, 3 June 2021
    [*Infinito v. Costa Rica*] 7, 45–46, 180
Kilic Insaat Ithalat Ihracat Sanayi ve Ticaret Anonim Sirketi v. Turkmenistan, ICSID
    Case No. ARB/10/1, Award, 2 July 2013 [*Kilic v. Turkmenistan*] 214–15
Loewen Group, Inc. and Raymond L. Loewen v. United States of America, ICSID
    Case No. ARB(AF)/98/3, Award, 26 June 2003 [*Loewen v. USA*] 193–94, 206

Marion Unglaube v. Republic of Costa Rica, ICSID Case No. ARB/08/1, Award,
  16 May 2012 [*Unglaube v. Costa Rica*] 189–90, 191
*Menzies Middle East and Africa SA and Aviation Handling Services International
  Ltd. v. Senegal*, ICSID Case No ARB/15/21, Award, 5 August 2016
  [*Menzies v. Senegal*] 141
Merrill & Ring Forestry L. P. v. Government of Canada, UNCITRAL,
  ICSID Administrated, Award, 31 March 2010 [*Merrill & Ring
  v. Canada*] 157, 193–94
Mesa Power Group, LLC v. Government of Canada, UNCITRAL, PCA
  Case No. 2012–17, Award, 24 March 2016 [*Mesa v. Canada*] 144, 193–94
Metalclad Corporation v. The United Mexican States, ICSID Case No.
  ARB(AF)/97/1, Award, 30 August 2000 [*Metalclad v. Mexico*]........ 172, 174, 195,
                                                               205–6, 208–9
Methanex Corp. v. United States of America, UNCITRAL, Final Award of the
  Tribunal on Jurisdiction and Merits, 3 August 2005 [*Methanex v. USA*]..... 174–75,
                                                               193–94, 233
Mobil Investments Canada Inc. v. Canada, ICSID Case No. ARB/15/6, Decision on
  Jurisdiction, 13 July 2018 [*Mobil v. Canada*]................................236
Mondev International Ltd. v. United States of America, ICSID Case No.
  ARB(AF) 99/2, Award, 11 October 2002 [*Mondev v. USA*]......... 156–57, 193–94
MTD Equity Sdn. Bhd. and MTD Chile S.A. v. Republic of Chile, ICSID Case No.
  ARB/01/7, Award [*MTD v. Chile*]........................... 123, 137–38, 170
National Grid P.L.C. v. Argentine Republic, UNCITRAL, Decision on
  Jurisdiction, 20 June 2006 [*National Grid v. Argentina*]....................233–34
Noble Ventures, Inc. v. Romania, ICSID Case No. ARB/01/11, Award, 12 October
  2005 [*Noble Ventures v. Romania*] 68
Parkerings-Compagniet AS v. Republic of Lithuania, ICSID Case No.
  ARB/05/8, Award, 11 September 2007 [*Parkerings v. Lithuania*]............133–34
Planet Mining Pty Ltd v. Republic of Indonesia, ICSID Case No. ARB/12/14 and 12/
  40, Decision on Jurisdiction, 24 February 2014 [*Planet Mining
  v. Indonesia*]... 199–201
Pope & Talbot Inc. v. The Government of Canada, UNCITRAL, Award in Respect of
  Damages, 31 May 2002 [*Pope & Talbot v. Canada*] 128–29, 156, 170,
                                                       172–73, 184, 192–94, 203, 208–9
*Quiborax S.A., Non Metallic Minerals S.A. and Allan Fosk Kaplún v. Plurinational
  State of Bolivia*, ICSID Case No. ARB/06/2, Decision on Annulment,
  18 May 2018 [*Quiborax v. Bolivia*] 212–13
Railroad Development Corporation v. Republic of Guatemala, ICSID Case No.
  ARB/07/23, Award, 29 June 2012 [*RDC v. Guatemala*] 44, 197
*Renta 4 S.V.S.A, Ahorro Corporación Emergentes F.I., Ahorro Corporación Eurofondo
  F.I., Rovime Inversiones SICAV S.A., Quasar de Valors SICAV S.A., Orgor de
  Valores SICAV S.A., GBI 9000 SICAV S.A. v. The Russian Federation*, SCC No.
  24/2007, Award on Preliminary Objections, 20 March 2009
  [*Renta 4 v. Russia*] 134
*Rumeli Telekom A.S. and Telsim Mobil Telekomunikasyon Hizmetleri A.S. v. Republic
  of Kazakhstan*, ICSID Case No. ARB/05/16, Award, 29 July 2008
  [*Rumeli v. Kazakhstan*] 157, 170
Rusoro Mining Ltd v Bolivarian Republic of Venezuela, ICSID Case No
  ARB(AF)/12/5,0 Award, 22 August 2016 [*Rusoro v. Venezuela*]..........42–44, 180

Saipem S.p.A. v. People's Republic of Bangladesh, ICSID Case No. ARB/05/07,
Award, 30 June 2009, [*Saipem v. Bangladesh*] 172
Saluka Investments B.V. v. Czech Republic, UNCITRAL, Partial Award, 17 March
2006 [*Saluka v. Czech Republic*] 175, 190
Sanum Investments Limited v. Lao People's Democratic Republic, UNCITRAL,
PCA Case No. 2013–13, Award on Jurisdiction, 13 December 2013
[*Sanum v. Lao*] 233–34
Sempra Energy International v. The Argentine Republic, ICSID Case No.
ARB/02/16, Award, 28 September 2007 [*Sempra v. Argentina*] 160–61, 164–65
Sempra Energy International v. The Argentine Republic, ICSID Case No.
ARB/02/16, Decision on Annulment, 29 June 2010 [*Sempra v. Argentina*] 161
*Sergei Paushok, CJSC Golden East Company and CJSC Vostokneftegaz Company v.
Government of Mongolia*, Award on Jurisdiction and Liability, 28 April 2011
[*Paushok v. Mongolia*] 128–29
Siemens A.G. v. The Argentine Republic, ICSID Case No. ARB/02/8, Decision on
Jurisdiction, 3 August 2004 [*Siemens v. Argentina*] 131–32, 149, 172
SGS Société Générale de Surveillance S.A. v. Islamic Republic of Pakistan,
ICSID Case No. ARB/01/13, Award on Jurisdiction, 6 August 2003
[*SGS v. Pakistan*] 68, 203
SGS Société Générale de Surveillance S.A. v. Republic of the Philippines,
ICSID Case No. ARB/02/6, Decision on Jurisdiction, 29 January 2004
[*SGS v. Pakistan*] 68, 203
Société Générale v. The Dominican Republic, LCAI Case No. UN 7927, Award on
Preliminary Objections to Jurisdiction, 19 September 2008 [*Société Générale
v. Dominican Republic*] 143
Tecnicas Mediambientales Tecmed S.A. v. the United Mexican States, ICSID
Case No. ARB (AF)/00/02, Award, 29 May 2003 [*Tecmed v. Mexico*] 143, 172,
204–5
Telefónica S.A. v. The Argentine Republic, ICSID Case No. ARB/03/20, Decision
of the Tribunal on Objections to Jurisdiction, 25 May 2006 [*Telefonica v.
Argentina*] 235–36
*Urbaser S.A. and Consorcio de Aguas Bilbao Bizkaia, Bilbao Biskaia Ur Partzuergoa
v. The Argentine Republic*, ICSID Case No. ARB/07/26, Award, 8 December
2016 [*Urbaser v. Argentina*] 188
Venezuela US, S.R.L. (Barbados) v. Bolivarian Republic of Venezuela, PCA Case No.
2013–34, Dissenting Opinion of Professor Marcelo G. Kohen, 26 July 2016
[*Venezuela US v. Venezuela*] 141
Vladimir Berschader and Moïse Berschader v. The Russian Federation, SCC Case No.
080/2004, Award, 21 April 2006 [*Berschader v. Russia*] 138
White Industries Australia Limited v. The Republic of India, UNCITRAL, Final
Award, 30 November 2011 [*White Industries v. India*]......... 129–30, 138, 147–48

OTHER CASES

The Ambatielos Case, 1953 ICJ Reports 10, Judgment, 19 May 1953
[*Ambatielos*] 135–36, 137–38
B-Mex, LLC and Others v. United Mexican States, ICSID Case No. ARB(AF)/16/3,
Judgment of the Ontario Supreme Court, 20 July 2020 [*B-Mex*] 236–37
Cargill, Incorporated v. United Mexican States, ICSID Case No. ARB(AF)/05/2,
Ontario Court of Appeal, Decision on the Application to set aside award,
4 October 2011 [*Cargill*] 236–37

Danish Preliminary Ownership Cases, CJEU (Joined Cases C-115/16, C-118/16, C-119/16, C-299/16), 26 February 2019 284

Dispute Regarding Navigational and Related Rights (Costa Rica v. Nicaragua), Judgment of 13 July 2009, ICJ Reports 2009 241

Government of the Lao People's Democratic Republic v. Sanum Investments Ltd [2015] SGHC 15, 20 January 2015 233–34

Appellate Body Report, *Japan – Taxes on Alcoholic Beverages*, WT/DS8/AB/R, WT/DS1O/AB/R, WT/DS11/AB/R, 4 October 1996 [*Japan-Alcohol*] 235

Kasikili/Sedudu Island (Botswana/Namibia), 1999 ICJ Reports 1045, Judgement, 13 December 1999 233

United Mexican States v. Metalclad Corporation, ICSID Case No. ARB(AF)/97/1, Reasons for Judgment of the Honourable Mr. Justice Tysoe, Supreme Court of British Columbia, 2 May 2001 195

Introduction

A textbook summary of how international investment law developed over the past fifty years may go something like this. States signed thousands of largely similar international investment agreements (IIAs) to protect the property of their investors abroad. Most of these IIAs allowed foreign investors to sue host states via investor-state dispute settlement (ISDS) for treaty breaches. ISDS was barely used until the late 1990s. When ISDS claims finally surged, states realized that their treaties offered greater investment protection than intended. States reacted by narrowing the commitments offered in newly concluded agreements. This backlash against investment arbitration resulted in a "new generation" of IIAs that rebalanced investment protection and host state regulatory autonomy.

This traditional account gets two things wrong, which this book will set right. First, new-generation IIAs, while promising on paper, have failed to rebalance investment protection and host state sovereignty in practice. This book reviews the first series of ISDS awards rendered under new-generation treaties and finds that these disputes reproduce old interpretive outcomes. While recent IIAs do contain new clarifications, omit controversial investment protections, and include new exceptions to safeguard policy space, these innovations have had little effect in practice, because new agreements are interpreted like old ones. ISDS tribunals are only partly to be blamed. The ultimate reason why new treaties reproduce old outcomes is that older IIAs continue to dominate interpretive reasoning in ISDS, including in cases based on new generation agreements.

That the coexistence between new and old IIAs is potentially problematic is nothing new. The UN Conference on Trade and Development (UNCTAD) has urged states to shift attention from negotiating new agreements to renegotiating older ones.[1] In UNCTAD's view, older bilateral investment treaties (BITs) pose heightened litigation risks due to their lack of public policy safeguards. What has remained underappreciated, however, is that older IIAs are not only a problem per se. Instead, they also undermine the impact and innovations of newer treaties. States that focus reforms on concluding new agreements thus bet on the wrong horse. Only if the stock of older agreements is updated, too, will new treaties lead to new outcomes.

---

[1] UNCTAD, *Phase 2 of IIA Reform: Modernizing the Existing Stock of Old-Generation Treaties*, IIA Issue Note, Issue 2, June 2017.

Investment Arbitration and State-Driven Reform. Wolfgang Alschner, Oxford University Press. © Oxford University Press 2022. DOI: 10.1093/oso/9780197644386.003.0001

The second aspect the traditional account gets wrong is states' backlash against investment arbitration.[2] States tend to be viewed as reactive litigants that change their treaties in response to interpretations by tribunals rather than proactive lawmakers who direct the interpretation of their treaties on their own initiative.[3] What is more, when states contract out of arbitral precedents in new treaties, they are often perceived as sore losers escaping earlier commitments rather than the masters of their treaties correcting past arbitral mistakes.[4] This perception fuels a systemic imbalance where the judiciary (ISDS tribunals) and not the legislator (contracting states) is viewed as the primary engine for normative development in the investment regime.[5] The tail is wagging the dog.

This book presents an alternative account of the interaction of states and tribunals that sees these roles reversed. The evolution of IIAs is a history of continuous state-driven change. Treaty design shifts commonly attributed to states reacting to rising ISDS claims predate the surge in ISDS cases. Moreover, much of the innovation in recent treaties has not been about escaping but about expanding commitments that benefit investors. Conversely, tribunals rather than states are often the reactive party. In response to state-driven change, tribunals have been rolling back normative innovation in new IIAs. New exceptions are ignored or watered down by equating them with preexisting customary international law flexibilities, omitted clauses are brought back via most-favored nation (MFN) provisions, and clarifications are blunted by reviving decades-old investor-friendly precedents. Investment law's evolution is thus best understood as proactive state-driven change that is being challenged by an arbitrator backlash.

Correcting the account of international investment law's past and present matters for shaping its future. Reforms of investment law that are ongoing at the national and international level grapple with fundamental questions. How can changes in treaties translate into changes in practice? How can states delegate power to adjudicators to resolve disputes without handing over the reins on interpreting their legal obligations? Answering these questions not only helps

---

[2] THE BACKLASH AGAINST INVESTMENT ARBITRATION: PERCEPTIONS AND REALITY (Michael Waibel ed., 2010).

[3] José E. Alvarez, *The Return of the State*, 20 MINN. J. INT'L L. 223 (2011).

[4] Charles H. Brower II, *Investor-State Disputes under NAFTA: The Empire Strikes Back*, 40 COLUM. J. TRANSNAT'L L. 43 (2001); Todd Weiler, *NAFTA Investment Law in 2001: As the Legal Order Starts to Settle, the Bureaucrats Strike Back*, 36 INT'L L. 345 (2002); Stephen M. Schwebel, *The United States 2004 Model Bilateral Investment Treaty: An Exercise in the Regressive Development Of International Law, in* JUSTICE IN INTERNATIONAL LAW (2011).

[5] STEPHAN W. SCHILL, THE MULTILATERALIZATION OF INTERNATIONAL INVESTMENT LAW 268 (2009) ("the institutional position of investment tribunals is, therefore, favorable to increasingly displace States as the primary rule makers in international law."); Catharine Titi, *The Arbitrator as a Lawmaker: Jurisgenerative Processes in Investment Arbitration*, 14 J. WORLD INVESTMENT & TRADE 829–851 (2013) (identifying instances of judicial lawmaking and tracking how states responded by changing their treaties).

guide investment law reform but improves our understanding of change and contestation in investment law and international law more generally.

This book provides a holistic account of how states have changed the investment regime through their evolving treaty practice, how ISDS tribunals have rolled back changes by interpreting new treaties like old ones, and how states and tribunals can successfully modernize the investment regime by reading and reforming old treaties in light of new ones. This book tackles these issues by adopting a systemic, evidence-based, and interdisciplinary perspective. It leverages new data that comprehensively reflects regime dynamics, employs state-of-the-art technology including legal data science to treat legal text as data, and draws from a range of theoretical frameworks spanning from law and economics to complexity science. The result is a new and authoritative empirical account of the evolution and current state of the international investment regime.

A New Hope: A New Generation of International Investment Agreements

The international investment regime is at an inflection point. Calls for reform are ringing from every corner. Today, international investment law is easily the most controversial field of international law. Why is that so? Critics point to two deficiencies of the international investment regime.

The first criticism concerns the way investment disputes are being settled. Most IIAs allow foreign investors to bring claims directly against host states for treaty breaches to win monetary damages. These disputes are litigated before international arbitration tribunals. More than 1,100 such ISDS disputes have been launched to date.[6] Critics point out that ISDS cases are essentially public-law disputes, but they are decided by a private-law litigation mechanism modeled on commercial arbitration that wields considerable power without meaningful oversight.[7] Moreover, investment arbitration practitioners have allegedly been "profiting from injustice."[8] Arbitrators have a financial interest in reappointments and have made money by acting in revolving roles as counsel, arbitrator, and legal expert in different proceedings, which creates potential conflicts of interest.[9] These, in addition to other concerns from costly litigation to inconsistent decisions, have made ISDS extremely controversial.

---

[6] UNCTAD, WORLD INVESTMENT REPORT 2021: INVESTING IN SUSTAINABLE RECOVERY 129 (2021).

[7] GUS VAN HARTEN, INVESTMENT TREATY ARBITRATION AND PUBLIC LAW (2007).

[8] Pia Eberhardt & Cecilia Olivet, *Profiting from Injustice: How Law Firms, Arbitrators and Financiers Are Fueling an Investment Arbitration Boom*, CORPORATE EUROPE OBSERVATORY (2012).

[9] Malcolm Langford, Daniel Behn, & Runar Hilleren Lie, *The Revolving Door in International Investment Arbitration*, 20 J. INT'L ECON. L. 301–332 (2017).

A second criticism suggests that the field gets the balance between investment protection and host state sovereignty wrong. Already in 2002, a US documentary informed the general public that investors have been using investment treaties to recover lost profits by challenging general regulations, such as bans on environmentally harmful substances, where domestic law provides no comparable remedies.[10] Since then, commentators have feared that investment law risks chilling countries from regulating in the public interest[11] or that multimillion dollar awards cripple a host state's finances.[12] These worries came to a head in the mid-2010s when negotiations over the Comprehensive Economic and Trade Agreement (CETA) between Canada and the European Union almost failed when thousands of Europeans took to the streets to protest against ceding regulatory sovereignty for the benefit of multinational companies. Later, a veto by the Belgian regional parliament of Wallonia against the deal could only be averted at the last minute after the contracting parties agreed to an authoritative interpretation that confirmed that CETA preserves states' right to regulate economic activity in the public interest.[13]

Aware of these procedural and substantive concerns, states have begun concluding a new generation of investment treaties. On the procedural side, recent IIAs have added transparency, publication, and participation requirements as well as arbitrator codes of conduct alongside other procedural innovations to reform ISDS.[14] In addition, spear-headed by the European Union, some treaties have replaced ad hoc arbitration with a standing tribunal and appeal instance.[15] These efforts are accompanied by multilateral reforms. In 2017, the Mauritius Convention on Transparency in ISDS entered into force to insert transparency

---

[10] PBS Documentary, *Politics and Economy: Trading Democracy*, February 1, 2002, transcript available at https://nsarchive2.gwu.edu/NSAEBB/NSAEBB65/transcript.html (last accessed October 15, 2021).

[11] Stephan W. Schill, *Do Investment Treaties Chill Unilateral State Regulation to Mitigate Climate Change?*, 24 J. INT'L ARB. (2007); Tienhaara Kyla, *Regulatory Chill and the Threat of Arbitration: A View from Political Science*, in EVOLUTION IN INVESTMENT TREATY LAW AND ARBITRATION 606–628 (Chester Brown & Kate Miles eds., 2011); Julia G. Brown, *International Investment Agreements: Regulatory Chill in the Face of Litigious Heat*, 3 W. J. LEGAL STUD. (2013).

[12] Martins Paparinskis, *A Case Against Crippling Compensation in International Law of State Responsibility*, 83 MOD. L. REV. 1246–1286 (2020).

[13] *See* the Joint Interpretative Instrument on the Comprehensive Economic and Trade Agreement (CETA) between Canada and the European Union and its Member States, October 27, 2016, available at https://data.consilium.europa.eu/doc/document/ST-13541-2016-INIT/en/pdf/ (last accessed October 15, 2021).

[14] Jack J. Coe Jr., *Transparency in the Resolution of Investor-State Disputes—Adoption, Adaptation, and NAFTA Leadership*, 54 U. KAN. L. REV. 1339 (2005); J. Anthony VanDuzer, *Enhancing the Procedural Legitimacy of Investor-State Arbitration Through Transparency and Amicus Curiae Participation*, 52 McGILL L.J. (2007).

[15] *See, e.g.*, CETA (2016), arts. 8.27–28 or EU–Vietnam Investment Protection Agreement (2019), Chapter 3.

obligations into existing IIAs.[16] Since 2017 broader multilateral negotiations to reform ISDS are ongoing under the auspices of the UN Commission on International Trade Law (UNCITRAL).[17]

On the substantive side, the new generation of IIAs introduced innovations to balance investment protection and host state policy space.[18] These include, among others, preambular language mentioning the right to regulate, clarifications of protections to carve out policy space, and general exceptions.[19] It is these substantive changes and their effect that this book will focus on.

Scholars and international organizations have placed much hope in these substantive innovations. UNCTAD declared that "a new generation of foreign investment policies is emerging . . . [that] place inclusive growth and sustainable development at the heart of efforts to attract and benefit from investment."[20] According to Suzanne Spears, these "new-generation IIAs provide arbitrators with new analytical devices for adjudicating disputes involving competing policy objectives."[21] Spears believes that these new agreements

> will embolden investor-state tribunals to consider host states' rights and obligations to regulate in the public interest more frequently than they have in the past and that this should alleviate some of the concerns that have been raised in recent years about the potential for IIAs and investor-state arbitration to unduly fetter states' regulatory power.[22]

New-generation IIAs have thus emerged as one of the main reform instruments to remedy the shortcomings of the international investment regime and to regain legitimacy and public trust. In that vein, James Zhan, Director of UNCTAD's Investment Policy Division, likens the new generation of treaties to electric cars

---

[16] United Nations, United Nations Convention on Transparency in Treaty-based Investor-State Arbitration (Mauritius Convention on Transparency), 2014, available at https://uncitral.un.org/en/texts/arbitration/conventions/transparency (last accessed July 6, 2021).

[17] Report of the United Nations Commission on International Trade Law (UNCITRAL), Official Records of the General Assembly, Supplement No. 17. (A/72/17), Fiftieth Session (July 3–21, 2017), para. 264.

[18] UNCTAD, Investor-State Dispute Settlement and Impact on Investment Rulemaking 87 (2007) ("New generation IIAs have become more sophisticated, attempting to define 'investment' more precisely, clarifying certain key standards of protection, specifying in greater detail ISDS procedures and promoting a balance between investment protection and liberalization and other key public policy objectives.").

[19] S. A. Spears, *The Quest for Policy Space in a New Generation of International Investment Agreements*, 13 J. Int'l Econ. L. 1037–1075 (2010).

[20] UNCTAD, World Investment Report 2012. Towards a New Generation of Investment Policies xxiii (2012).

[21] Spears, *supra* note 19, at 1044.

[22] *Id.* at 1045.

that will slowly but surely replace the outdated vehicles of a different era and lead the world to a more sustainable future.[23]

Hope Disappointed: New Treaties, Old Outcomes

The new generation of IIAs indeed looks promising on paper. But thus far, it has disappointed in practice. Empirical research conducted by Tarald Berge has found that agreements with more flexibilities or more precisions are not associated with lower risks of investment claims.[24] Furthermore, the first wave of ISDS disputes launched under new agreements suggests that new IIAs have failed to change how ISDS tribunals balance investment protection with states' regulatory autonomy. In fact, new-generation treaties are being interpreted just like old ones. This is most obvious when it comes to novel general public policy exceptions that have been "missing in action."[25]

To many observers the inclusion of general public policy exceptions into investment agreements looked like a big deal. These clauses absent in earlier IIAs promised to shield measures for the promotion of public health or the conservation of the environment from liability (albeit under strict conditions). If the trade regime was any guide, the existence of policy exceptions would end the dominant practice in investment law to assess competing policy objectives exclusively under primary protection obligations and shift the balancing of economic and noneconomic values, at least in part, to the exception.[26] Commentators speculated whether such a change would enhance or narrow the policy space states enjoyed, but they were in wide agreement that including exceptions would change how investment treaties would be litigated.[27] They were wrong.

---

[23] James Zhan, Remarks at the Roundtable: The Future of International Investment Regulation, SIEL Conference 2021, July 7, 2021.

[24] Tarald Laudal Berge, *Dispute by Design? Legalization, Backlash, and the Drafting of Investment Agreements*, 64 INT'L STUD. Q. 919–928 (2020).

[25] Wolfgang Alschner & Kun Hui, *Missing in Action: General Public Policy Exceptions in Investment Treaties*, in YEARBOOK ON INTERNATIONAL INVESTMENT LAW AND POLICY 2018 (Lisa E. Sachs, Jesse Coleman, & Lise Johnson eds., 2019).

[26] Nicholas DiMascio & Joost Pauwelyn, *Nondiscrimination in Trade and Investment Treaties: Worlds Apart or Two Sides of the Same Coin?*, 102 AM. J. INT'L L. 48–89 (2008); Bradly J. Condon, *Treaty Structure and Public Interest Regulation in International Economic Law*, 17 J. INT'L ECON. L. 333–353 (2014).

[27] Andrew Newcombe, *General Exceptions in International Investment Agreements* 12; Céline Lévesque, *The Inclusion of GATT Article XX Exceptions in IIAs: A Potentially Risky Policy*, in PROSPECTS IN INTERNATIONAL INVESTMENT LAW AND POLICY: WORLD TRADE FORUM (Roberto Echandi & Pierre Sauve eds., 2013); JÜRGEN KURTZ, THE WTO AND INTERNATIONAL INVESTMENT LAW: CONVERGING SYSTEMS 5 (2016); Amelia Keene, *The Incorporation and Interpretation of WTO-Style Environmental Exceptions in International Investment Agreements*, 18 J. WORLD INVESTMENT & TRADE 62–99 (2017); Caroline Henckels, *Should Investment Treaties Contain Public Policy Exceptions Essays: Substantive and Procedural Reforms*, 59 B.C. L. REV. 2825–2844 (2018).

The arbitral jurisprudence on these general public policy exceptions to date can be put into three equally discouraging boxes of exceptions confused, ignored, and misconstrued. First, in *Infinito Gold v. Costa Rica*, the respondent raised an exception argument but cited the wrong paragraph relying on an interpretive clarification rather than the neighboring general exception and lost the case without the tribunal commenting on the mistake or the exception.[28] Second, in a series of cases against Venezuela, the underlying new-generation treaty contained a public policy exception and the facts of the cases warranted its discussion, but the exception was ignored.[29] Third, in *Copper Mesa v. Ecuador*, *Bear Creek v. Peru*, and *Eco Oro v. Colombia*, the tribunals confused the flexibility states enjoy under customary international law with the complementary flexibility that states acquire under a general exception, which dulled the effect of the exception.[30] As a result, IIAs with general public policy exceptions have been interpreted and litigated just like IIAs that lacked such clauses.

These cases do not necessarily suggest a coordinated attempt by investment tribunals to thwart state-driven change. Indeed, in most of these disputes the respondent state (or the international law firm hired to represent it) bears much of the responsibility for the ultimate outcome. Venezuela seems not to have raised the exception, Costa Rica picked the wrong provision to make its argument, and Peru presented general exceptions as a specific manifestation of a customary law doctrine presaging the interpretive path the tribunal later took. But nor should these cases be seen as poorly argued accidents or a couple of awards getting things wrong. Instead, they are part of an emerging pattern.

Across the board, new international investment agreements are interpreted like old ones, and crucial treaty design innovation aimed at rebalancing investment protection and state sovereignty is being rolled back. States have phased out controversial provisions such as effective means and umbrella clause in their treaties, which are being brought back through MFN treatment in litigation. States have sought to reaffirm the role of customary international law as a ceiling for protections and a floor for flexibilities in newer IIAs only to see custom being transformed during dispute settlement into an elevator of investment protection and a cap on flexibilities. Respondents find their conduct assessed against

---

[28] *Infinito Gold Ltd. v. Costa Rica*, ICSID Case No. ARB/14/5, Award, June 3, 2021, paras. 755–781. Particularly disconcerting is that the tribunal discussed every exception in the same provision, but the public policy exception, as part of its interpretive reasoning. It staunchly avoided mentioning the clause the respondent should have invoked.

[29] *Gold Reserve Inc. v. Bolivarian Republic of Venezuela*, ICSID Case No. ARB(AF)/09/1, Award, September 22, 2014; *Crystallex International Corporation v. Bolivarian Republic of Venezuela*, ICSID Case No. ARB(AF)/11/2, Award, April 4, 2016; *Rusoro Mining Ltd. v. Bolivarian Republic of Venezuela*, ICSID Case No. ARB(AF)/12/5,0 Award, August 22, 2016.

[30] *Copper Mesa Mining Corporation v. Republic of Ecuador*, PCA No. 2012-2, Award, March 15, 2016, paras. 6.58–6.67; *Bear Creek Mining Corporation v. Republic of Peru*, ICSID Case No. ARB/14/21, Award, November 30, 2017, paras. 459–474.

"zombie precedent" that had been previously set aside by domestic courts or rejected through treaty design changes. In consequence, reading new treaties like old ones has emerged as a systemic challenge.

What's Going On?

There are three ways to make sense of what is happening. Optimists may treat these developments as the growing pains of a field in transformation.[31] Many of the features in recent IIAs, like general public policy exceptions, are indeed new and untested. It is not unusual that conflicting interpretations abound as investors, states, and tribunals make sense of these new provisions. Investment arbitration has been said to be "in listening mode and ready to adapt."[32] Give it time, optimists may say, and the system will find its footing. That is especially true since new-generation IIAs are only beginning to be litigated. Ninety percent of all ISDS disputes have been brought under IIAs signed prior to 2000.[33] This trend is only slowly changing. Out of sixty-eight ISDS disputes launched in 2020, 65 percent were based on treaties signed in the 1990s or earlier and 97 percent were brought under IIAs signed before 2011.[34] New IIAs have therefore barely started to make their mark on ISDS practice.

Yet, the promise of gradual adaptation is no guarantee for it. The expectation that, given time, the investment regime will organically self-correct has been around for some time.[35] On the one hand, there is empirical evidence that the regime has morphed in unexpected and sometimes dramatic ways.[36] Investment arbitrators have evolved too and have been responsive to criticism.[37] On the other hand, the regime has also been progressively entrenching rather than gradually resolving existing deficiencies. Good awards have not chased the bad ones as some commentators had hoped.[38] Instead, inconsistent state- or investor-friendly interpretations are perpetuated as litigants cite and tribunals endorse

---

[31] Silvia Constain, *11 ISDS Growing Pains and Responsible Adulthood*, *in* Reshaping the Investor-State Dispute Settlement System 344–350 (2015).

[32] The Backlash Against Investment Arbitration, *supra* note 2, at xxxix.

[33] UNCTAD, *Phase 2 of IIA Reform: Modernizing the Existing Stock of Old-Generation Treaties*, *supra* note 1.

[34] UNCTAD, *supra* note 6, at 130.

[35] J. Paulsson, *International Arbitration and the Generation of Legal Norms: Treaty Arbitration and International Law*, *in* 3 International Arbitration 2006: Back to Basics?, 889 (Albert Jan van den Berg ed., 2007) ("We are in an early phase of dramatic extension of investment arbitration [...] good awards will chase the bad").

[36] Joost Pauwelyn, *At The Edge of Chaos: Foreign Investment Law as a Complex Adaptive System, How It Emerged and How It Can Be Reformed*, 29 ICSID Rev. 372–418 (2014).

[37] Malcolm Langford & Daniel Behn, *Managing Backlash: The Evolving Investment Treaty Arbitrator?*, 29 Eur. J. Int'l L. 551–580 (2018).

[38] Paulsson, *supra* note 35, at 889.

precedents that favor extreme positions.[39] Structural obstacles embedded in the regime are an important impediment for organic self-correction.

This brings us to a second view shared by a diverse group of commentators who consider the current mode of dispute settlement as the main structural obstacle for change.[40] Seen in this light, the backlash of arbitrators against a new generation of investment agreements marks yet another setback in states' attempts to rein in ISDS tribunals. ISDS has morphed from a cost-effective, low-key, depoliticized resolution of individual investment disputes into an expensive, convoluted, and politicized machinery with a mind of its own whose decisions produce externalities that affect litigants in unrelated disputes.[41] Past efforts by states to regain the interpretive reins, for example, through authoritative inter-pretations have largely failed.[42] New treaties whose innovations are rolled back merely mark another defeat in the struggle to control the ISDS machinery.

What is needed, then, is to fix dispute settlement once and for all by rewriting the terms of delegation between contracting states and adjudicators in interna-tional investment law. Current multilateral negotiations at UNCITRAL to re-form ISDS may achieve just that. According to the European Union, for example, a standing multilateral investment court with appeal instance would do a better job than ad hoc arbitrators at providing a correct and consistent reading of IIAs, including of the most recent vintage.[43] Such an institutional reset would not only correct currently misaligned incentives of arbitrators. It would also likely lead to an "interpretive reset"[44] that would allow new-generation IIAs and their novel features to be read without the baggage of the arbitral precedents from past decades.

By themselves, however, procedural investment law reforms are insufficient to comprehensively address investment law's legitimacy crisis and may even

---

[39] Wolfgang Alschner, *Correctness of Investment Awards: Why Wrong Decisions Don't Die*, 18 THE LAW & PRACTICE OF INTERNATIONAL COURTS AND TRIBUNALS 345 368 (2020).

[40] This heterogenous group includes both principled opponents to ISDS and those who believe it is deficient in some form and requires reform. *See, e.g.*, Susan D. Franck, *The Legitimacy Crisis in Investment Treaty Arbitration: Privatizing Public International Law through Inconsistent Decisions*, 73 FORDHAM L. REV. 1521 (2004); G. Van Harten & M. Loughlin, *Investment Treaty Arbitration as a Species of Global Administrative Law*, 17 EUR. J. INT'L L. 121–150 (2006); Jason Webb Yackee, *Controlling the International Investment Law Agency*, 53 HARV. INT'L L.J. 391 (2012); Colin M. Brown, *A Multilateral Mechanism for the Settlement of Investment Disputes. Some Preliminary Sketches*, 32 ICSID REV. 18 (2017).

[41] Yackee, *supra* note 40; Geoffrey Gertz, Srividya Jandhyala, & Lauge N. Skovgaard Poulsen, *Legalization, Diplomacy, and Development: Do Investment Treaties De-Politicize Investment Disputes?*, 107 WORLD DEV. 239–252 (2018); Anna Herranz-Surrallés, *"Authority Shifts" in Global Governance: Intersecting Politicizations and the Reform of Investor–State Arbitration*, 8 POL. & GOVERNANCE 336–347 (2020).

[42] SCHILL, *supra* note 5 at 268–275.

[43] European Commission, Staff Working Document on multilateral reform of investment dispute resolution, COM(2017) 493, September 2017.

[44] I am grateful to Nicolas Lamp for suggesting the term.

exacerbate existing imbalances. If new adjudicators interpret new treaties in new ways, investors will simply divert claims to older IIAs where balancing language is absent. Even the most talented adjudicators will then struggle to read old, vague IIAs to the satisfaction of all stakeholders. Ultimately, only states' substantive reforms can balance investment protection and host state sovereignty in new and old treaties alike. In addition, the investment regime is already imbalanced with the judiciary playing an outsized role in lawmaking. Strengthening dispute settlement further without concurrently engaging in broader substantive reforms will further disempower states as lawmakers and place ever more authority and responsibility on adjudicators.

This book therefore advocates a third perspective. Yes, growing pains and procedural shortcomings of ISDS contribute as proximate causes to new treaties producing old outcomes. However, it is ultimately the regime's substantive bifurcation into reformed treaties sitting alongside unreformed ones that stifles change and that needs fixing.

Older agreements affect the application and interpretation of their modern counterparts in a myriad of ways. Older IIAs can divert litigation away from newer ones as they often exist in parallel with investors, for example, channeling their cases from a recent regional IIA with exceptions to an old BIT that lacks sovereignty-preserving clauses.[45] In litigation, *a contrario* arguments can attribute significance to language variation between earlier and later agreements producing surprising or undesirable interpretations.[46] Most importantly, however, the content of outdated IIAs can directly undermine innovation in new IIAs. MFN treatment, customary international law, and precedent create a direct link between the interpretation of new and old treaties that cannot be easily severed. As this book will show, they together explain to a large degree why new treaties result in old outcomes.

Fortunately, the side-by-side of new and old agreements presents opportunities as well as challenges. The string of recent awards that interprets new treaties like old ones illustrates the downside of the regime's bifurcation. These decisions

---

[45] Wolfgang Alschner, *Regionalism and Overlap in Investment Treaty Law: Towards Consolidation or Contradiction?*, 17 J. INT'L ECON. L. 271–298 (2014).

[46] *See* TARCISIO GAZZINI, INTERPRETATION OF INTERNATIONAL INVESTMENT TREATIES 125 (2016) ("the choice not to use any given terms or expressions or different ones was a deliberate one and may reveal the meaning the contracting parties wanted to attach to the provision. The presumption is even stronger when the contracting parties were aware—or could reasonably have been aware—of different terms or different expressions used in other similar legal instruments."). *See also* Catharine Titi, *Book Review: Commentaries on Selected Model Investment Treaties. By Chester Brown (ed)*, 84 BRIT. Y.B. INT'L L. 361–364, 363 (2014) (noting, for example, that "it is unclear whether textual changes in new model BITs will be perceived as clarifications of how the party understands standards also included in earlier BITs or whether, with an argumentum a contrario, the new rules will be considered not to apply to earlier treaties."). *See also* David A. Gantz, *The Evolution of FTA Investment Provisions: From NAFTA to the United States–Chile Free Trade Agreement*, 19 AM. U. INT'L L. REV. 679, 688–689, 766 (2003).

advance interpretations that entrench the status quo and maintain consistency where states seek change. On the upside, however, states can leverage the regime's bifurcation to produce lasting and systemic change. By reforming their most recent treaties states have already done the heavy lifting. All that remains is to complete the job and modernize old IIAs in light of new ones.

The key insight guiding investment law reformers should thus be that old and new IIAs do not exist in silos. They affect each other in procedure as well as substance. States then have a choice. Will they let tribunals read new treaties like old ones or will they use modern treaties to reform outdated ones?

For certain is that new-generation IIAs are not the electric cars of the investment regime that promise to replace the combustion engine of old treaties to initiate a more sustainable future. Instead, we should think of the universe of investment agreements as an armada of fast steamships and slow sailboats forming a fleet that can only travel as quickly as the slowest ship. Old investment treaties are dragging down the progress and innovation achieved in new treaties. Rather than celebrating the speed of steamships that only exists on paper or replacing the engineers to ensure that the fastest ships run on full steam, investment reformers need to shift attention to the slowest vessels. Only if old and outdated IIAs are modernized will new agreements yield new outcomes. Conversely, as long as reformed and outdated treaties coexist, investment law's legitimacy crisis will persist.

Toward a Map of the Investment Treaty Universe

But what does it really mean for an agreement to be "modern" or "reformed"? UNCTAD has attempted to put a timestamp on the transition from an "old" to a "new" generation of agreements in the early 2010s.[47] But a treaty's age is an imperfect proxy to differentiate treaty content. Some treaties concluded in the 1990s mirror the design of the treaties UNCTAD would describe as new-generation IIAs. Conversely, some of the treaties concluded in the 2010s do not look much different from the agreements signed in the 1970s or 1980s.

Nor is it particularly accurate to limit the differences between agreements to specific content features. For example, scholars have characterized the evolution of IIAs as a progression toward more policy space,[48] but empirical research has found that IIAs have increased in substantive commitments at the same time

---

[47] UNCTAD, in recent publications, uses the year 2012 as dividing line between old- and new-generation treaties. *See* UNCTAD, WORLD INVESTMENT REPORT 2019: SPECIAL ECONOMIC ZONES 109 (2019). This date appears arbitrary from a treaty content point of view, is inconsistent with earlier UNCTAD reports, and is arguably motivated by UNCTAD's Investment Policy Framework for Sustainable Development (IPFSD), which was published in 2012.

[48] Spears, *supra* note 19; CATHARINE TITI, THE RIGHT TO REGULATE IN INTERNATIONAL INVESTMENT LAW 72 (2014); Alexander Thompson, Tomer Broude, & Yoram Z. Haftel, *Once Bitten,*

as they included new flexibility elements.[49] Other accounts depict IIAs as becoming longer and more precise,[50] or note that new agreements tend to take back control over interpretation from arbitrators.[51] These narratives capture important aspects of treaty design change but they do not offer a meta-narrative that describes the evolution of IIAs in all its diversity.

Rather than imposing a theoretical mold to tell outdated and modern IIAs apart, this book lets treaties speak for themselves. Chapter 1 uses natural language processing to treat the texts of more than three thousand IIAs as data. Coupled with statistical analysis this allows to inductively discover the single most important design difference that runs through the IIA universe. What emerges is a map of sorts that tracks the design evolution of IIAs over time. Treaties that score high tend to be new, long, and comprehensive and include novel reform features such as general exceptions. Treaties that score low tend to be old, short, and focus exclusively on investment protection and generally lack flexibility features such as exceptions. Text-as-data analysis thus allows to systematically distinguish between old- and new-generation design of IIAs. Using this distinction, Chapter 1 reviews how new-generation IIAs have fared in ISDS practice and concludes that new IIAs have produced old outcomes.

Chapter 2 then unpacks the distinction between old and new generation IIAs. It argues that the major design difference of IIAs is one of contractual completeness. The concept comes from contract theory, a branch of law and economics. It posits that a contract is necessarily incomplete as contracting parties find it either impossible or inefficient to agree on contractual solutions for every future scenario. To get around that problem, contractors employ four strategies for closing contractual gaps. They (1) draft more precise and comprehensive contracts, (2) include escape clauses, (3) add new relational components to ensure ongoing cooperation, and (4) delegate gap-filling to third parties.

The evolution of IIAs mirrors that progression toward more contractual completeness. States have concluded more detailed agreements by including clarifications, exceptions, and new preambles to structure ongoing relations (strategies 1–3) and by delegating interpretation to treaty-based institutions including inter-state committees and arbitral tribunals (strategy 4). The main difference between new- and old-generation IIAs is thus their level of contractual

Twice Shy? Investment Disputes, State Sovereignty, and Change in Treaty Design, 73 Int'l Org. 859–880 (2019).

[49] Berge, *supra* note 24.

[50] Mark S. Manger & Clint Peinhardt, *Learning and the Precision of International Investment Agreements*, 43 Int'l Interactions 1–21 (2017); Caroline Henckels, *Protecting Regulatory Autonomy through Greater Precision in Investment Treaties: The TPP, CETA, and TTIP*, 19 J. Int'l Econ. L. 27–50 (2016).

[51] José E. Alvarez, *The Evolving BIT*, Transnat'l Disp. Mgmt. (2010).

completeness, that is, the varying extent to which treaties make use of these four gap-filling strategies.

Chapter 3 then explains how IIAs have evolved toward ever greater levels of contractual completeness and motivates where to draw a line between old- and new-generation design. The IIA regime experienced three bursts of innovation that are closely associated with changes in North American treaty practice. First, when the United States launched its BIT program in the early 1980s, it incorporated many elements from earlier Friendship, Commerce, and Navigation (FCN) treaties, such as an investment liberalization component, that contemporary European BITs lacked. Second, the conclusion of the North American Free Trade Agreement (NAFTA) in the early 1990s marked the introduction of new exceptions and more detailed terms of delegation to ISDS that were subsequently widely copied in other agreements. It is at that point that the first new-generation IIAs emerged. Third, around 2004, following the first wave of ISDS claims, Canada and the United States inserted additional targeted clarifications in their agreements to reassert original intent and correct arbitral misinterpretations. As ISDS claims surged thereafter, features from these three waves of innovation progressively spread to the treaty practices of other states, fueling a trend toward more complete IIAs around the globe.

The comprehensive account of treaty design evolution in Part I of this book thus provides a more nuanced picture of what sets new- and old-generation IIAs apart and tells the story of how we got here. In the process it debunks two widely held views about the changing content of IIAs. First, the book shows that states have been proactive lawmakers all along rather than reactive litigants. Contrary to the prevalent view that state-driven change occurred in form of a backlash against developments in investment arbitration, Part I shows that innovation peaked in NAFTA, arguably the first "new-generation" IIA, and then spread globally in recent decades as comprehensive and detailed IIA design came to dominate treaty practice. Treaty design innovation therefore largely predates the surge of ISDS claims.

Second, Part I shows that the evolution of IIAs cannot be equated with a gradual lowering of investment protection.[52] American-style IIAs instead strive for an optimal balance between commitments and flexibility. Aside from including new exceptions, these treaties also contain new commitments, for example, protecting investors from performance requirement that involve the obligatory use of local goods or services. The evolution toward greater contractual completeness in IIAs is thus about neither under- nor overprotecting investors, but about getting investment protection just right.

---

[52] Schwebel, *supra* note 4.

Part I of this book also notes that major changes are underway in the last five years of observation that point to a growing diversity in gap-filling strategies. American-style IIAs place emphasis on more detailed contracting and escape clauses (gap-filling strategies 1 and 2). Brazil, in contrast, has launched a new treaty program that prioritizes relationship-building through new investment cooperation treaties (gap-filling strategy 3), and the European Union has enhanced the importance of delegation by introducing a permanent investment tribunal (gap-filling strategy 4) in recent IIAs. What unites these diverse gap-filling strategies, however, is a proactive effort on the part of states to close contractual gaps and conclude ever more complete agreements.

Reading New Treaties Like Old Ones

Part II of the book then uses this deeper understanding of the evolution of IIAs to evaluate the first wave of ISDS awards that have been rendered under more complete IIAs. Based on the observation that tribunals' reasoning under new-generation agreements mirrors that under old-generation ones, Part II asks how and why new treaties produce old outcomes.

Contract theory, again, helps frame the analysis. Gap-filling strategies can be in competition when they provide divergent answers on how gaps should be filled and by whom. Incomplete IIAs delegate gap-filling almost exclusively to adjudicators. As Charles Brower put it, "when treaty drafters intentionally use ambiguous phrases to gloss over differences, they effectively grant the competent judicial body a quasi-legislative power to formulate specific rules of conduct."[53] In contrast, when states write more complete agreements ex ante and fill gaps through more precise drafting or explicit balancing, they seek to displace gap-filling by adjudicators ex post. The evolution toward more contractual completeness is thus also about curtailing the "quasi-legislative power" of arbitrators and to substitute arbitral lawmaking with state-driven lawmaking as the dominant gap-filling mechanism.

In practice, however, this reallocation of gap-filling powers in more complete IIAs away from tribunals toward states has met resistance and triggered an arbitrator backlash. Showing impressive foresight, Jose Alvarez asked a decade ago "if . . . international investment law is driven by the jurisprudence produced by investment arbitrators, does that jurisprudence provide a firewall to protect foreign investors against [treaty] trends in favor of 're-balancing'?"[54] The first wave of ISDS cases under more complete IIAs provides a resounding "Yes!" Tribunals

---

[53] Brower, *supra* note 4, at 56; SCHILL, *supra* note 5, at 263.
[54] Alvarez, *supra* note 3, at 241.

have created a "firewall" against interpretive change, rolled back innovation in new-generation IIAs, and reasserted their gap-filling authority by reading new treaties like old ones.

The chapters in Part II discuss the three instruments that enable and underpin this "firewall": MFN treatment, customary international law, and precedent. These instruments will be well-known forces to investment law scholars and practitioners, but they have not received the attention they deserve for rolling back innovation in new, more complete treaties and for linking the interpretation of new-generation treaties to old-generation ones.

Chapter 4 describes how MFN clauses have been used to import substantive provisions from older agreements that have been phased out or narrowed in new-generation treaties. While a minority of IIAs has limited the scope of MFN, most treaties still contain clauses that can be interpreted as allowing the incorporation-by-reference of ostensibly more favorable substantive protections. Phased-out clauses can be brought back into these new agreements via a double expansion. First, a particularly investor-friendly interpretation, which was corrected in subsequent treaty practice, is activated to turn a neutral reading of a protective standard into a more-favorable one. Second, the clause is imported via MFN into an IIA that lacked the provision. Although in theory most recent design innovations are shielded from their operation in one way or another, MFN clauses in practice remain a potent instrument for rolling back state-driven change.

Chapter 5 turns to customary international law as a second technique for rolling back innovation. Most more complete IIAs seek to use custom as a ceiling for (some) investment protection and as a floor for (some) flexibilities. In practice, however, these roles have been reversed. References to highly incomplete treaties have served as proof of an evolving custom that is then used to ratchet up the floor of investment protections in recent IIAs. At the same time, custom is reconceived as a ceiling rather than a floor for interpreting flexibilities in more complete IIAs as tribunals have read policy exceptions as codifying or substituting custom instead of complementing it. As tribunals fail to honor how and when states contract on or out of custom, part of the innovation in recent IIAs is being reversed.

Both readings of MFN and custom are underpinned by a third technique for rolling back state-driven change: the extensive reliance on precedent that roots today's interpretation of new treaties in yesterday's reading of old agreements. As Chapter 6 explains, cited precedents in ISDS are becoming progressively older. Furthermore, existing arbitral interpretations are also incredibly resilient to state-driven change. Zombie precedents can even survive the set-aside by domestic courts. The stickiness of precedent means that states face a constant uphill battle to displace prior arbitral interpretations. The excessive reliance on precedent, including where underlying treaties differ fundamentally, such as when a highly complete IIA is interpreted through awards rendered under highly incomplete ones, creates consistency between past and present arbitral practices in instances where states sought change.

In combination, MFN treatment, customary international law, and precedent result in a de facto lowering of contractual completeness of new treaties. Arbitral gap-filling displaces other gap-filling tools, such as more precise drafting or escape clauses, and rolls back innovation by rooting the interpretation of new treaties in the reading of old ones. Although the impact of each of these three techniques can be mitigated, the ultimate problem consists of the large stock of incomplete and outdated IIAs. These unreformed agreements are the argumentative quarry that is being mined for ostensibly more favorable provisions or a progressive evolution of customary law toward more investment protection. Furthermore, the continued dominance of unreformed treaties in litigation further entrenches extreme interpretations as precedents. The most sustainable way to ensure that new treaties result in new interpretive outcomes thus lies in reforming the stock of incomplete IIAs.

Reading Old Treaties Like New Ones

Part III of this book illustrates how investment law reformers can shift the interpretive center of gravity from old, unreformed to new, reformed treaties. States can leverage the bifurcated structure of the IIA regime to propagate innovation from more complete agreements to older incomplete ones. Investment treaties have evolved in a deeply path-dependent manner. Most investment protections included in old generation IIAs are still found in new-generation IIAs. While the norms have remained the same, their precision has increased drastically, and targeted additions have been introduced. As a result, the way contracting states have closed interpretive gaps in more complete IIAs can help states and adjudicators to fill gaps in incomplete ones. Three avenues to modernize the outdated stock of IIAs with the help of more complete IIAs are open to states.

Chapter 7 describes how states and tribunals can use interpretation to read old agreements in light of new ones. The way contracting states close gaps in recent treaties provides interpreters, including ISDS tribunals, with the best guess of how states would have wanted their past agreements to be understood with the benefit of hindsight. Public international law provides ample justification (within bounds) for such a forward-looking reading of old IIAs. Tribunals can endorse a forward-looking interpretation to propagate rather than thwart state-driven change. Contracting states, in turn, can facilitate the forward-looking interpretation of tribunals through explicit means such as joint interpretative declarations and implicit means such as their consistently evolving treaty practice. While interpretation remains confined to clarifying vague and ambiguous meaning, it holds immense promise where states have filled gaps by adding precision to terms used extensively in past practice.

Chapter 8 explains how states can leverage renegotiations to amend incomplete treaties in light of more complete ones when interpretation alone does not suffice. Renegotiations are rare, underused, and often dismissed out of hand as a costly and haphazard way to remedy the shortcomings of thousands of existing treaties. A data-driven approach to renegotiations, however, promises to change that. Selecting regional agreements for revision that would replace hundreds of incomplete agreements in one stroke can alleviate criticism related to the inefficiency of renegotiations. The ongoing renegotiation of the Energy Charter Treaty is a case in point. The treaty overlaps with and affects the interpretation of more than six hundred BITs. Its modernization could thus reform the reading of a quarter of the BIT stock in one stroke. Furthermore, data science makes it easier to identify areas of normative convergence between contracting parties and can even propose draft texts, which reduces the strain on administrative resources and turns renegotiations into a low-hanging fruit for updating old treaties in light of new ones.

Finally, Chapter 9 explains how current multilateral reform efforts under the auspices of UNCITRAL can modify the entire existing stock of outdated IIAs to lift incomplete treaties to the level of more complete ones. It suggests that investment law reformers can learn from the neighboring tax regime to multilateralize IIAs in novel and creative ways in both substance and procedure. The tax regime's focus on continuous but informal rule-making can correct the systemic imbalance between the judiciary and legislature in investment law, putting states back into the driver's seat of the field's normative development. In addition, the tax regime's successful hard law reform that recently modernized thousands of outdated bilateral tax treaties in substance and procedure provides a useful template for achieving harmonization through mandatory minimum standards, while accommodating states' diverging preferences through flexibilities that allow states to contract out or into all other reforms. Tax-style multilateralization thus promises to end the bifurcation of the regime into new and old treaties and would converge IIA practice around reformed, recent, more complete agreements.

Blind Spots

Like any academic work, this book suffers from a couple of blind spots. First, when treaties speak for themselves, we tend to hear the voices of developed states. The investment regime suffers from deep power asymmetries.[55] Empirical research has shown that investment treaties are predominantly the product of capital exporting countries imposing their treaty template on capital importing countries that sign at the dotted line.[56] Since this book focuses on state-driven change *as manifested in treaty design*, the choices by developed countries typically take center stage. This does injustice to developing countries that have engaged in state-driven change through other means, such as UN resolutions and the termination of agreements, and that are exerting more agency in recent negotiations at the bilateral, regional, and multilateral level.[57] In short, this book presents only part of a larger story of state-driven change and focuses particularly on the role developed states have played in shaping the investment regime.

Second, the investment regime is changing quickly. Some of the findings of this book need to be revisited as the regime's transformation progresses. Three trends are particularly important to watch. First, recent treaty practice by Brazil, for example, deviates markedly from earlier IIAs and differs from the otherwise prevalent impact of North American practice.[58] These new treaties barely register yet in the data used for this book's analysis, but this may change if alternative treaty models become more widespread. Second, no disputes have yet been launched under IIAs with permanent investment tribunals concluded by the European Union. It thus remains an open question how these adjudicators would approach the interpretation of recent IIAs and whether these new treaties also reproduce old outcomes. Third, the ongoing UNCITRAL reform process may result in instruments that affect the reading or litigation of past treaties. In short, the book's conclusions need to be re-evaluated against future reforms and developments.

[55] A rich and extensive scholarship probes these asymmetries especially between developed and developing states. M. SORNARAJAH, THE INTERNATIONAL LAW ON FOREIGN INVESTMENT (3rd ed. 2010); K. Miles, *International Investment Law: Origins, Imperialism and Conceptualizing the Environment*, 21 COLO. J. INT'L ENVTL. L. & POL'Y 1–557 (2010).

[56] Wolfgang Alschner & Dmitriy Skougarevskiy, *Mapping the Universe of International Investment Agreements*, 19 J. INT'L ECON. L., 576 (2016).

[57] Wolfgang Alschner & Dmitriy Skougarevskiy, *Rule-Takers or Rule-Makers? A New Look at African Bilateral Investment Treaty Practice*, Special Issue on international arbitration involving commercial and investment disputes in Africa TDM (2016); Makane Moïse Mbengue & Stefanie Schacherer, *The "Africanization" of International Investment Law: The Pan-African Investment Code and the Reform of the International Investment Regime*, 18 J. WORLD INVESTMENT & TRADE 414–448 (2017); Olabisi D. Akinkugbe, *Reverse Contributors? African State Parties, ICSID and the Development of International Investment Law*, 34 ICSID REV.—FOREIGN INVESTMENT L.J. 434–454 (2019); Makane Moïse Mbengue, *Africa's Voice in the Formation, Shaping and Redesign of International Investment Law*, 34 ICSID REV.—FOREIGN INVESTMENT L.J. 455–481 (2019).

[58] Vivian Gabriel, *The New Brazilian Cooperation and Facilitation Investment Agreement: An Analysis of the Conflict Resolution Mechanism in Light of the Theory of the Shadow of the Law*, 34 CONFLICT RESOL. Q. 141–161 (2016); Prabhash Ranjan & Pushkar Anand, *The 2016 Model Indian Bilateral Investment Treaty: A Critical Deconstruction*, 38 NW. J. INT'L L. & BUS. (2017).

Third, the insights that this book presents are driven but also limited by the data used. The map of the IIA universe relies on the Electronic Database of Investment Treaties (EDIT)—the most complete dataset of IIA full texts to date, which covers almost all treaties in force.[59] Data on investment awards and citation patterns is less comprehensive, while still covering a large portion of the ISDS universe. Hence while this book offers the most comprehensive empirical account of the investment universe to date, even better or more comprehensive future data especially on awards may further nuance some of this book's findings. Moreover, readers should remain attentive to the difference between empirical findings and their interpretation. For example, the map of how IIAs differ presented in this introduction is a robust empirical fact. Anyone conducting the analysis of Chapter 1 will be able to replicate the same findings. The insight that the map depicts a move toward greater contractual completeness, in turn, is an interpretation that one can disagree with.

How to Read This Book

Ideally, the book should be read cover to cover. But with the main arguments summarized, busy readers may choose to focus their attention. Those less familiar with the evolution of the investment regime should start with Part I. Chapter 1 is also crucial for those who want to learn more about the computational analysis of legal texts, which can be applied to study international law more broadly. Others may only want to skim Chapter 1 and the beginning of Chapter 2 to get the gist of what is meant by complete and incomplete treaties. Those interested in how and why new treaties are read like old ones should focus on Part II. Finally, Part III is especially valuable to practitioners, policymakers, and negotiators who want to reform the investment law regime through interpretation (Chapter 7), by drawing on new technologies and their use in renegotiations (Chapter 8), or by modeling procedural and substantive bulk reform on the international tax regime (Chapter 9).

---

[59] Wolfgang Alschner, Manfred Elsig, & Rodrigo Polanco, *Introducing the Electronic Database of Investment Treaties (EDIT): The Genesis of a New Database and Its Use*, 20 World Trade Rev. 73–94 (2021).

PART I
STATE-DRIVEN REFORM

1
Treaties as Data

I. Introduction

The investment treaty universe is vast. By 2020, UNCTAD recorded 2,943 bilateral investment treaties (BITs) and 417 treaties with investment provisions in existence.[1] Its large size makes the international investment agreement (IIA) universe difficult to navigate for all stakeholders. As UNCTAD put it, "[w]ith thousands of treaties, many ongoing negotiations and multiple dispute-settlement mechanisms, today's IIA regime has come close to a point where it is too big and complex to handle for governments and investors alike."[2]

Size and complexity pose problems for researchers, too. Traditional legal analysis thrives in small data environments but struggles to make sense of big data. Manual analysis of thousands of agreements treaty by treaty is costly, time-consuming, and involves challenging trade-offs between scale and detail. Crowd-sourcing efforts can help mitigate these limitations but come with their own shortcomings. They are challenging to administer, difficult to validate, and do not easily permit recoding efforts. In part, for these reasons, many scholars turn to the much smaller set of national model investment agreements to make sense of global treaty trends.[3]

Data science offers an alternative approach to investigate the IIA universe in all its breadth and depth. Computational methods are designed for big data environments and open the door to a world where size and complexity do not matter. A rule of thumb in computer science says that whenever a manual task is unpleasantly time-consuming, costly, and repetitive, there is probably a way to automate it. This chapter shows how natural language processing, a branch of computational linguistics, helps to automate treaty content analysis. The analysis yields a unique bird's-eye view that permits the comprehensive study of thousands of investment treaties over decades.

---

[1] UNCTAD, WORLD INVESTMENT REPORT 2021: INVESTING IN SUSTAINABLE RECOVERY 123 (2021).

[2] UNCTAD, WORLD INVESTMENT REPORT 2011: NON-EQUITY MODES OF INTERNATIONAL PRODUCTION AND DEVELOPMENT xvi (2011).

[3] *See, e.g.,* Mark A. Clodfelter, *The Adaptation of States to the Changing World of Investment Protection through Model BITs*, 24 ICSID REV. 165–175 (2009); CHESTER BROWN & DEVASHISH KRISHAN, COMMENTARIES ON SELECTED MODEL INVESTMENT TREATIES (2013).

Investment Arbitration and State-Driven Reform. Wolfgang Alschner, Oxford University Press. © Oxford University Press 2022. DOI: 10.1093/oso/9780197644386.003.0002

Data science comes with a second advantage, too. It lets treaties speak for themselves. Traditional content analysis is typically deductive and theory-driven. Content features are selected at the outset based on their theoretical relevance. Scholars interested in regulatory space look for features indicative of regulatory space; those interested in treaties' increased precision focus on features indicating precision; and so on. Trends in the data unanticipated by theory, however, remain unknown. An inductive approach, in contrast, turns this process on its head. It first explores variation in the data and only then tries to rationalize the findings from a theoretical perspective. Inductive, data-driven approaches can thereby reveal patterns that researchers did not expect nor actively look for.

This chapter pursues such an inductive data science approach. It lets the treaties speak for themselves to reveal the major content evolution of more than 3,300 IIAs. The chapter begins with a brief introduction to the emerging field of computational legal studies. It then argues that investment law scholars and stakeholder still lack an empirically grounded meta-account of the design evolution of investment agreements. The chapter proceeds to create such an account through an original computational legal analysis that treats treaty texts as data to uncover the latent, hitherto unknown, major content change running through the IIA universe. The resulting map of treaty design evolution forms the centerpiece of this book and will be used in the final section of this chapter to show that new IIAs have produced old outcomes in investor-state dispute settlement (ISDS).

II. The Emerging Field of Computational Legal Studies

Scaling empirical research used to be difficult. It was cumbersome to gather data, content analysis was done mostly manually, and researchers used theory to narrow down a myriad of possible explanations about how the world works to a manageable set of hypotheses. These hypotheses were then tested against a small sample to draw statistically significant inferences about larger populations. Advances in computing power, the increased availability of large, machine-readable datasets, and new methods for their analysis now allow researchers to move past these limitations.

Under the umbrella of "big data," "data science," "computational legal studies," or "digital humanities," legal scholars and social scientists have begun using computer science techniques to empirically study legal phenomena.[4]

---

[4] *See, e.g.,* Law as Data: Computation, Text, and the Future of Legal Analysis, (Michael Livermore & Daniel Rockmore eds., 2019); Computational Legal Studies: The Promise and Challenge of Data-Driven Research, (Ryan Whalen ed., 2020).

Legal text is processed as data rather than read; the entire corpus of cases and treaties and not mere subsamples are investigated; and instead of testing pre-defined hypotheses, researchers "can let data speak for itself"[5] to reveal new insights.[6] As computers increasingly do the heavy lifting, legal researchers today can analyze more data, with less effort, and at less cost, which renders empirical legal research scalable.[7]

In addition to scalability, computational research also promises an entirely new perspective. "Using all the data lets us see details we never could when we were limited to smaller quantities," write Viktor Mayer-Schönberger and Kenneth Cukier about big data research.[8] Not only can scholars uncover patterns, trends, and correlations that they did not expect or actively looked for, but they can detect systemic structures that can only be seen in the aggregate.

The wave of data-driven, computational research has recently reached international law where it supports doctrinal, applied, and empirical scholarship.[9] Computational linguistics assists in treaty interpretation, natural language processing maps normative trends, and network analysis traces the operation of international precedent at scale.[10] In the process, computational legal research contributes to every subfield of international law and informs everything from macro questions on international law's fragmentation or the role of precedent[11] to micro questions relating to the litigation of individual legal disputes.[12] Urška Šadl and Henrik Palmer Olsen summarize the contributions of computational scholarship as follows:

> [Computational methods] ensure the reproducibility, generalizability, and
> empirical validity of doctrinal studies. They add to the transparency of legal

[5] Viktor Mayer-Schönberger & Kenneth Cukier, Big Data: A Revolution That Will Transform How We Live, Work, and Think 14 (reprint ed. 2014).

[6] Wolfgang Alschner, Joost Pauwelyn, & Sergio Puig, *The Data-Driven Future of International Economic Law*, 20 J. Int'l Econ. L. 217–231 (2017).

[7] Wolfgang Alschner, *The Computational Analysis of International Law*, in Research Methods in International Law: A Handbook (Rossana Deplano & Nicholas Tsagourias eds., 2021).

[8] Mayer-Schönberger and Cukier, *supra* note 5, at 13.

[9] *See generally* Ashley Deeks, *High-Tech International Law*, 88 Geo. Wash. L. Rev. 80 (2020); Tilmann Altwicker, *International Legal Scholarship and the Challenge of Digitalization*, 18 Chinese J. Int'l L. (2019).

[10] Alschner, *supra* note 7.

[11] Damien Charlotin, *The Place of Investment Awards and WTO Decisions in International Law: A Citation Analysis*, 20 J. Int'l Econ. L. 279–299 (2017); Niccolò Ridi, *The Shape and Structure of the "Usable Past": An Empirical Analysis of the Use of Precedent in International Adjudication*, 10 J. Int'l Disp. Settlement 200–247 (2019).

[12] Fabien Tarissan & Raphaëlle Nollez-Goldbach, *Analysing the First Case of the International Criminal Court from a Network-Science Perspective*, J. Complex Networks (2016); Amanda Potts & Anne Lise Kjær, *Constructing Achievement in the International Criminal Tribunal for the Former Yugoslavia (ICTY): A Corpus-Based Critical Discourse Analysis*, 29 Int'l J. Semiotics of L. 525–555 (2016).

methodology while substantially clarifying the legal method. They can provide empirical evidence to validate hunches and prove legal intuitions correct. Furthermore, they effectively address the limitations of traditional legal scholarship, including a lack of precision, subjectivity, a surplus of anecdotal evidence, and a tendency to succumb to herd behavior.[13]

At the same time, computational legal methods have shortcomings. A focus on data and methods may come at the expense of theory or risks losing touch with normative international law debates.[14] Moreover, computers process data, but do not understand it. Researchers can thus let the data speak but should not let it think for itself.

That is why legal scholarship is at its best when it combines traditional and computational tools and builds on their complementary strengths. Computational legal research is about a "distant reading" of legal texts: it leverages computing to provide a bird's-eye view that renders large amounts of legal information accessible. Traditional legal research is about a "close reading" of texts: it leverages interpretation to assess the legal meaning of defined text passages.[15] Computational methods therefore often form the starting point but rarely the end point of the analysis.

In short, computer and data science expand the toolkit of lawyers. They shed new light on old questions and open the door to new explorations. To be done well, computational legal research must be methodologically sound, pursue relevant questions, be integrated with traditional legal research techniques, and be grounded in theoretical, conceptual, and normative debates. This book strives to do just that.

How investment treaties have changed over time and how this change impacts investor-state dispute settlement are empirical questions of a big data nature where computational legal methods can make significant contributions. Even after several decades of intense study, investment law scholars and practitioners still lack a meta-narrative to comprehensively describe the content evolution of investment treaties. This chapter develops the empirical basis for such a meta-narrative and provides investment law stakeholders with a map chartering the field's normative evolution.

---

[13] Urška Šadl & Henrik Palmer Olsen, *Can Quantitative Methods Complement Doctrinal Legal Studies? Using Citation Network and Corpus Linguistic Analysis to Understand International Courts*, 30 LEIDEN J. INT'L L. 327–349, 330 (2017).

[14] Huaxia Lai, *The Unfulfilled Promises of the Data-Driven Approach to International Economic Law, in* PLURALISING INTERNATIONAL LEGAL SCHOLARSHIP 173–189 (Rossana Deplano ed., 2019).

[15] That distinction goes back to the pioneering work of the computational literature scholar FRANCO MORETTI, DISTANT READING (2013).

III. What We Know and Don't Know about the Design of IIAs

The investment law literature is full of seemingly contradictory claims about the design variation and evolution of investment treaties. When comparing national treaty programs, commentators oscillate between emphasizing the uniformity across all IIAs[16] while stressing the diversity of national treaty practice.[17] Similarly, when looking at treaty change over time, they note a continuous presence of "core elements" in IIAs[18] but also point to areas of normative evolution.[19] At the outset, it is therefore helpful to summarize what we know and what we don't know about the meta-design structures that describe the IIA universe (A) across states, and (B) over time.

A. Uniformity vs. Diversity across States' IIA Practice

Empirical research has revealed a set of meta similarities and differences that describe treaty design variation between national IIA programs as a function of (1) shared principles, (2) power asymmetries, and (3) varying meta-approaches to treaty design.

First, IIAs are indeed remarkably similar to each other. Common normative ancestry has produced a degree of commonality across national treaty practices that is manifested both in shared principles and in shared language.[20] Early model

[16] Schill contends that a multilateral system of international investment protection has emerged on the basis of bilateral treaties. STEPHAN W. SCHILL, THE MULTILATERALIZATION OF INTERNATIONAL INVESTMENT LAW (2009). Montt sees the BIT universe as a global network of treaties with largely uniform provisions. SANTIAGO MONTT, STATE LIABILITY IN INVESTMENT TREATY ARBITRATION: GLOBAL CONSTITUTIONAL AND ADMINISTRATIVE LAW IN THE BIT GENERATION (2009).

[17] Chaisse and Bellak have coded 1,498 BITs and 158 FTAs across seven core investment treaty categories capturing whether a clause provides high or low investment protection. J. Chaisse & C. Bellak, *Navigating the Expanding Universe of International Treaties on Foreign Investment: Creation and Use of a Critical Index*, 18 J. INT'L ECON. L. 79–115 (2015).

[18] Researchers and international organizations have developed typologies for virtually all core investment treaty provisions based such differences and have gone to great lengths to manually code treaties for such variation. UNCTAD's mapping project, the most extensive manual content analysis to date, uses one such typology to code over a hundred features in more than 2,500 IIAs. UNCTAD, *IIA Mapping Project*, available at http://investmentpolicyhub.unctad.org/Upload/Documents/UNCTAD%20IIA%20MAPPING%20PROJECT%202013-2014.pdf (last accessed October 15, 2021). Using the mapping, UNCTAD could then trace whether states heed its policy recommendations. UNCTAD, WORLD INVESTMENT REPORT 2016. INVESTOR NATIONALITY: POLICY CHALLENGES 113–114 (2016).

[19] José E. Alvarez, *The Evolving BIT*, TRANSNAT'L DISP. MGMT. (2010).

[20] Dolzer and Schreuer identify common principles of international investment law. RUDOLF DOLZER & CHRISTOPH SCHREUER, PRINCIPLES OF INTERNATIONAL INVESTMENT LAW (2nd ed. 2012). Salacuse argues that the treatification of investment law created a global regime for investment characterized by common principles, norms, rules, and decision-making processes. JESWALD W.

conventions by international organizations consolidated investment standards, which were then included, albeit in varying textual guises, in subsequent investment agreements.[21] These clauses on "expropriation," "national treatment" or "fair and equitable treatment" will be well known to international investment lawyers. In addition, some national practices produced signaling effects for other states contributing to a latent similarity in treaty language within subgroups. Great Britain's treaty practice, for example, strongly influenced the BIT programs of several other states including Israel, India, and a handful of Eastern European countries.[22] Later, NAFTA served as a template especially for states in Asia and Latin America, which borrowed its language profusely.[23] As a result, there are significant cross-cutting and often global similarities in IIA design.

IIA design, however, also varies in systematic ways across states. In part, this is due to underlying power asymmetries. Empirical research has found that developed states are the predominant rule-maker in investment law.[24] Capital exporting states sign internally consistent agreements (often using a model treaty) with their (mostly) capital-importing counterparts. Great Britain, for example, has signed over one hundred BITs over a period of thirty-five years that on average share 75 percent of text. Conversely, developing countries are the system's rule-takers. They tend to opt in to the treaty templates proposed by their developed state counterparts, producing a patchwork of differently designed agreements. The result is an investment treaty universe that is marked by stylistic uniformity (within rich states' IIA networks) and stylistic diversity (between rich states' IIA networks).[25]

Finally, commentators have identified meta-differences on how states approach IIA design. But these accounts tend to either focus on specific provisions or remain underdeveloped from a theoretical or empirical standpoint. On the one hand, scholars have distinguished IIAs by content features. For example, researchers have classified agreements based on their dispute settlement design, distinguishing between "weak" IIAs (without ISDS clauses) or "strong" IIAs (with ISDS clauses).[26] While meaningful, such typologies bypass other important content variation that differentiates IIAs.

SALACUSE, THE LAW OF INVESTMENT TREATIES (2010); J. W. Salacuse, *The Emerging Global Regime for Investment*, 51 HARV. INT'L L.J. 427–553 (2010).

[21] SCHILL, *supra* note 16 at 39–40.

[22] Wolfgang Alschner, Manfred Elsig, & Rodrigo Polanco, *Introducing the Electronic Database of Investment Treaties (EDIT): The Genesis of a New Database and Its Use*, 20 WORLD TRADE REV. 73–94 (2021).

[23] Wolfgang Alschner & Dmitriy Skougarevskiy, *Convergence and Divergence in the Investment Treaty Universe—Scoping the Potential for Multilateral Consolidation*, 8 TRADE, L. & DEV. (2016).

[24] Wolfgang Alschner & Dmitriy Skougarevskiy, *Mapping the Universe of International Investment Agreements*, 19 J. INT'L ECON. L. (2016).

[25] *Id.*

[26] *See* JASON WEBB YACKEE, SACRIFICING SOVEREIGNTY: BILATERAL INVESTMENT TREATIES, INTERNATIONAL ARBITRATION, AND THE QUEST FOR CAPITAL (2007); Jason Webb Yackee,

On the other hand, more comprehensive classifications of IIAs that cut across design features tend to lack empirical grounding or are undertheorized. Distinguishing IIAs based on whether investment protection norms are found in a bilateral investment treaty or in a free trade agreement, for example, makes little sense, because content-wise, investment chapters are "no more than a BIT dropped into a free trade agreement."[27] Other typologies are underdeveloped. For example, according to UNCTAD "looking from the perspective of developing countries, there are two BIT models: (a) 'protection only' BITs mostly with European countries and other developing countries; and (b) liberalizing BITs concluded mainly with the United States and Canada, and more recently, with Japan."[28] Yet preliberalization provisions are, in fact, only one of several differences between traditional European BITs and North American treaties.[29] In addition, new meta-approaches that challenge existing treaty design paradigms have yet to be properly situated in global practice. For example, Brazil's new IIAs that focus less on investment protection and more on inter-state cooperation and investment facilitation are hard to place among existing models.[30] In short, while the systematic similarities and stylistic differences between national IIA practices are well understood, meta-approaches that further aggregate these practices are lacking.

B. Continuity and Change across Time

The picture is even more complicated when it comes to similarities and differences over time. On the one hand, the investment universe is characterized by a strong path-dependency producing continuity in treaty design.[31] States have been "locked in language": the same set of investment protections found

---

Conceptual Difficulties in the Empirical Study of Bilateral Investment Treaties, 33 Brook. J. Int'l L. 405 (2007); *see also* Joost Pauwelyn, *At the Edge of Chaos: Foreign Investment Law as a Complex Adaptive System, How It Emerged and How It Can Be Reformed*, 29 ICSID Rev. 372–418 (2014) (drawing a distinction between first-generation investment treaties without ISDS and second-generation treaties with ISDS).

[27] *See The Canadian Cattlemen for Fair Trade v. United States of America*, UNCITRAL, Award on Jurisdiction, January 18, 2008, para. 163. For an in-depth empirical comparison of investment protection norms in BITs and FTAs, *see* Wolfgang Alschner, *Heading for Divorce?: Investment Protection Rules in Free Trade Agreements*, in The Shifting Landscape of Global Trade Governance: World Trade Forum 325–358 (Gabriele Spilker, Manfred Elsig, & Michael Hahn eds., 2019),

[28] UNCTAD, The Role Of International Investment Agreements in Attracting Foreign Direct Investment to Developing Countries 20 (2009).

[29] This is well documented through Lauge Poulsen's interviews with negotiators that point to differences in precision and detail rather than just pre-establishment. *See* Lauge N. Skovgaard Poulsen, Bounded Rationality and Economic Diplomacy: The Politics of Investment Treaties in Developing Countries 280 (2015).

[30] Catherine Titi, *International Investment Law and the Protection of Foreign Investment in Brazil*, 13 Transnat'l Disp. Mgmt. (2016).

[31] Pauwelyn, *supra* note 26 at 411.

in early treaties continues to dominate current practice.[32] Indeed, the degree of continuity in treaty practice is remarkable. Recall that Great Britain signed virtually identical treaties over the span of thirty-five years, notwithstanding major intervening changes such as the end of the Cold War or the rise of ISDS.[33] The United Kingdom is not an outlier. In fact, until recently, few states have significantly innovated their treaty practice.[34]

On the other hand, scholars rightly point to areas of change. A growing number of states have innovated their treaty practice in response to legal developments, such as rising ISDS claims (e.g., the United States adjusting its BIT practice in 2004 after having faced ISDS claims under NAFTA),[35] economic ones (e.g., China moving from a capital importing nation safeguarding its own policy space to a capital exporting nation ensuring the protection of its own investors abroad),[36] and political ones (e.g., the election of Donald Trump as US president prompting a renegotiation of NAFTA).

Scholars, however, have struggled to fit these patterns of continuity and change under a meta-narrative. Some, like Suzanne Spears see a "quest for policy space in a new generation of international investment agreements,"[37] as contracting states have included new preambular language, more clearly defined protective standards, and general exceptions in their treaties to balance investment protection with host state sovereignty.[38] Others speak of a trend toward greater legalization or precision as states add new footnotes and explanatory annexes to their

---

[32] Wolfgang Alschner, *Locked in Language: Historical Sociology and the Path Dependency of Investment Treaty Design*, in RESEARCH HANDBOOK ON THE SOCIOLOGY OF INTERNATIONAL LAW 347–368 (Moshe Hirsch & Andrew Lang eds., 2018).

[33] Alschner & Skougarevskiy, *supra* note 24.

[34] *See* Cree Jones & Weijia Rao, *Sticky BITs*, 61 HARV. INT'L L.J. 357–406 (2020); Wolfgang Alschner, *The Impact of Investment Arbitration on Investment Treaty Design: Myth Versus Reality*, 42 YALE J. INT'L L. (2017). Surprisingly, for example, the wave of South-South IIAs concluded in the 1990s and 2000s mirrored the design of earlier North-South BITs. *See* Lauge Poulsen, *The Politics of South-South Bilateral Investment Treaties*, in THE POLITICS OF INTERNATIONAL ECONOMIC LAW (T. Broude, M.L. Busch, & A. Porges eds., 2011).

[35] G. Gagné & J. F. Morin, *The Evolving American Policy on Investment Protection: Evidence from Recent FTAs and the 2004 Model BIT*, 9 J. INT'L ECON. L. 357–382 (2006). On changes in treaty design in response to ISDS, *see* Alexander Thompson, Tomer Broude, & Yoram Z. Haftel, *Once Bitten, Twice Shy? Investment Disputes, State Sovereignty, and Change in Treaty Design*, 73 INT'L ORG. 859–880 (2019).

[36] Stephan W. Schill, *Tearing Down the Great Wall: The New Generation Investment Treaties of the People's Republic of China*, 15 CARDOZO J. INT'L & COMP. L. 73 (2007); Congyan Cai, *International Investment Treaties and the Formation, Application and Transformation of Customary International Law Rules*, 7 CHINESE J. INT'L L. 659–679 (2008); Axel Berger, *China's New Bilateral Investment Treaty Programme: Substance, Rational and Implications for International Investment Law Making*, in THE POLITICS OF INTERNATIONAL ECONOMIC LAW: THE NEXT FOUR YEARS, WASHINGTON, DC, NOVEMBER 2008 14–15 (2008); Chunbao Liu, *The Evolution of Chinese Approaches to IIAs*, in IMPROVING INTERNATIONAL INVESTMENT AGREEMENTS 59–74 (Armand de Mestral & Céline Lévesque eds., 2011).

[37] S. A. Spears, *The Quest for Policy Space in a New Generation of International Investment Agreements*, 13 J. INT'L ECON. L. 1037–1075 (2010).

[38] *Id.*

agreements.[39] Again others emphasize how states have reformed their approach to ISDS, often in an effort to take back control from arbitrators or to correct arbitral misinterpretations.[40] While these different accounts are not mutually exclusive, they also do not naturally aggregate to form an overarching narrative. The first part of this book will therefore let treaties speak for themselves to inductively arrive at a meta-narrative that comprehensively describes the design evolution of IIAs across space and time.

IV. Letting Investment Treaties Speak for Themselves

All investment treaties differ, but some differ more than others. Data science allows researchers to quantify these treaty design differences and to prioritize large design variations over smaller ones. The result is a map of treaty design meta-variation that describes the evolution of investment treaty design.

This section conducts an inductive, computational data analysis of IIAs in three stages using a new and comprehensive dataset of treaty full texts. First, IIAs are "datafied," that is, they are brought into a form amenable for quantitative data analysis through natural language processing. Second, a statistical analysis of the data's principal components reveals the most significant variation in treaty design. Third, robustness checks using UNCTAD's hand-coded mapping of IIAs ensure that the derived results are valid and reliable. Busy readers are welcome to skip the technical explanation and go directly to the map of IIA design variation toward the end of this section.

A. The EDIT Dataset

The recently completed Electronic Database of Investment Treaties (EDIT) provides the most comprehensive full text database of the IIA universe to date.[41] In a five-year effort, EDIT researchers have been painstakingly collecting IIA full

---

[39] Caroline Henckels, *Protecting Regulatory Autonomy through Greater Precision in Investment Treaties: The TPP, CETA, and TTIP*, 19 J. INT'L ECON. L. 27–50 (2016); Mark S. Manger & Clint Peinhardt, *Learning and the Precision of International Investment Agreements*, 43 INT'L INTERACTIONS 1–21 (2017); Tarald Laudal Berge, *Dispute by Design? Legalization, Backlash, and the Drafting of Investment Agreements*, 64 INT'L STUD. Q. 919–928 (2020).

[40] Jones & Rao, *supra* note 34 (showing how states have changed their treaties to correct controversial ISDS awards); on the "return of the state," *see* José E. Alvarez, *The Return of the State*, 20 MINN. J. INT'L L. 223 (2011); RODRIGO POLANCO, THE RETURN OF THE HOME STATE TO INVESTOR-STATE DISPUTES: BRINGING BACK DIPLOMATIC PROTECTION? (2019).

[41] The EDIT database is freely accessible at https://edit.wti.org.

texts from a diversity of sources and have digitized, standardized, and translated them into English. The dataset includes the texts of BITs, BIT models, post-1950s Friendship, Commerce, and Navigation (FCN) treaties, and other IIAs, such as multiparty investment treaties like the Energy Charter Treaty or investment chapters in free trade agreements (FTAs). With a coverage of 99.75 percent of all IIAs in force (only nine full texts of IIAs in force are missing from the dataset), the EDIT corpus enables a holistic analysis of the IIA universe. In January 2021, the EDIT database comprised 3,617 IIAs concluded between 1950 and 2021.

To compare apples to apples in treaty design variation, small adjustments are made to the EDIT data.[42] In the case of FTAs, where the full treaty text is available in EDIT, only the text of investment chapters is used to make FTAs comparable to BITs that deal exclusively with investment.[43] FTAs that only ancillary cover investment protection—for example, ones that include less than a chapter or section on investment—have been excluded from the analysis. All treaties with incomplete texts in EDIT were discarded as well. For each treaty included, the full text contains the preamble (except for investment chapters) and the body of the text, including footnotes. Annexes have been included except when they contain exchange of letters or schedules of concessions. The resulting corpus includes 3,366 full texts of IIAs and a total of 10,803,214 words. Table 1.1 summarizes the included full texts by type and by earliest and latest year of signature.

Table 1.1 EDIT full texts included in the analysis (extracted January 2021)

Bilateral Investment Treaties (BITs)	Model Bilateral Investment Treaties (Model BITs)	Other IIAs (FTAs with investment chapter or multiparty agreements)	Friendship, Commerce, and Navigation (FCN) Treaties
3,114 (earliest: 1959) (latest: 2021)	75 (earliest: 1984) (latest: 2021)	137 (earliest: 1965) (latest: 2020)	40 (earliest: 1950) (latest: 1976)

[42] Despite these adjustments, there is a small risk of comparing apples with oranges. FCN treaties contain many investment protection provisions but also deal with commercial and diplomatic matters. FTAs deal with investment-related matters, such as tax or exceptions, also outside the investment chapter. However, as the following robustness checks indicate, a feature rather than text-based analysis presents similar patterns.

[43] As the United States argued in one investment dispute, investment chapters are "no more than a BIT dropped into a free trade agreement." *See The Canadian Cattlemen for Fair Trade v. United States of America*, UNCITRAL, Award on Jurisdiction, January 18, 2008, para. 163.

B. Text-as-Data Analysis of IIAs

To let treaties speak for themselves, IIA full texts have to be transformed into data. Mayer-Schönberger and Cukier call this process "datafication." As they explain, "datafy[ing] a phenomenon is to put it in a quantified format so it can be tabulated and analyzed."[44] Since law is primarily text-based, computational analysis of law often requires natural language processing (NLP), which translates text into data.[45]

1. Natural Language Processing of IIAs

The simplest and most widely used representation of text as data is a so-called unigram term-frequency model that records the frequency by which each word occurs in a document (Table 1.2 exemplifies a resulting document-term matrix).[46]

Reducing texts to their word frequency may make some readers uncomfortable. The natural language processing literature has shown, however, that, despite its simplicity, unigram models perform surprisingly well in information-retrieval tasks, making more contextual models of language typically unnecessary.[47] Furthermore, as Justin Grimmer and Brandon Stewart suggest, the fact "that all automated methods are based on incorrect models of language also implies that the models should be evaluated based on their ability to perform some useful

Table 1.2 Example of a document-term matrix depicting term frequencies

	TERM			
DOCUMENT	"fair"	"equitable"	"treatment"	...
NAFTA (1992)	1	1	5	...
TPP (2015)	2	1	3	...
	...	...	...	...

---

[44] MAYER-SCHÖNBERGER & CUKIER, *supra* note 5, at 78.

[45] Justin Grimmer & Brandon M. Stewart, *Text as Data: The Promise and Pitfalls of Automatic Content Analysis Methods for Political Texts*, POL. ANALYSIS, 6–7 (2013).

[46] CHRISTOPHER D. MANNING, PRABHAKAR RAGHAVAN, & HINRICH SCHÜTZE, INTRODUCTION TO INFORMATION RETRIEVAL 240 (1st ed. 2008). There are more sophisticated forms of language model, but there is a trade-off between computational complexity and the capture of context and meaning. Language models in the social sciences do not aspire to be perfect but to be useful. Most applications work well with simple language models, but ultimately the choice of language model depends on the task at hand. For discussion, *see* Grimmer & Stewart, *supra* note 45; Alschner, *supra* note 7.

[47] MANNING, RAGHAVAN, & SCHÜTZE, *supra* note 46, at 240.

social scientific task"—or here, some legally meaningful task—and not based on how perfectly they represent meaning.[48] To develop a bird's-eye view of the evolution of treaty design, a simple language model suffices. Frequency counts of treaty terms such as "health," "labor," or "environment" may not capture the nuances of a legal text, but in the aggregate, they reveal trends in treaty design.

Furthermore, in line with standard practices in natural language processing, the analysis preprocesses IIA full text to remove conceptually irrelevant variation.[49] Punctuation, numbers, standard stop words ("and," "is," "it," etc.), and words with two characters or less are deleted. In addition, only words that appear in at least three documents and at least five times in the corpus are retained. The latter step accounts for errors from EDIT's optical character recognition process when scanned treaty images are imperfectly converted to digital texts (e.g., an "i" may be falsely recognized as an "l"). Next, all words are lowercased. The ultimate corpus contains 8,056 unique words. Finally, the frequency of words is weighted by document length to ensure that treaty length does not drive results.

2. Tracing Treaty Design Evolution through Principal Component Analysis

In its datafied form, the IIA universe is represented as a spreadsheet that tabulates the frequency counts for all 8,056 terms for each treaty. That spreadsheet can then be analyzed using the normal toolkit of statistics. Although treaties vary in their term-frequency, some agreements will be more alike than others, and many terms co-occur in predictable patterns (e.g., "fair" co-occurs in similar frequency as "equitable"). The data in the spreadsheet can therefore be reduced and condensed without losing too much information on how treaties vary. In statistics, this process is known as "dimensionality reduction." Principal Component Analysis (PCA) reduces the dimensionality of data by finding the patterns—the principal components—that underlie the data's variance.[50]

The first principal component explains the most pervasive difference along which the data varies. That is because principal components are ordered with each explaining a progressively smaller and uncorrelated portion of the differences in the data. One way to think about what the first principal component represents

---

[48] Grimmer & Stewart, *supra* note 45, at 4.

[49] *See* MANNING, RAGHAVAN, & SCHÜTZE, *supra* note 46, at 27. This analysis only deviates from standard natural language processing preprocessing by omitting stemming. Stemming reduces words to their core or stem, which can cause problems in the legal domain. The Lancaster Stemmer, for example, stems "arbitrator" and "arbitrarily" to the common stem "arbit," while the Porter stemmer is able to distinguish between "arbitrary" (stems to "arbitrary") and "arbitrator" (stems to "arbitr"). Hence, stemming (and the choice of stemmers) can significantly affect ultimate results.

[50] For an accessible explanation of PCA, *see* https://georgemdallas.wordpress.com/2013/10/30/principal-component-analysis-4-dummies-eigenvectors-eigenvalues-and-dimension-reduction/ (last accessed May 18, 2015).

is to imagine asking an investment law expert: "If you had just one scale along which to group all IIAs and you want to group similar agreements together and different treaties apart, how would you place them along that scale?" Of course, this is a difficult task for a human to perform, but it is exactly what the PCA does. The first principal component draws a line through the data and situates every treaty along that line.

Arthur Spirling, for example, used the PCA of treaty texts to find the main difference along which US treaties with Native Americans differed to understand how these agreements had evolved. Based on treaty text variation along the first principal component, he concluded that treaties differed in "harshness."[51] US treaties with Native Americans had grown progressively stricter over time as the power of the United States expanded and that of Native Americans decreased. Importantly, however, what the first principal component means in substantive terms will vary from one dataset to another and is not known ex ante. It always needs to be interpreted by the researcher ex post.

3. A Map of IIA Design Evolution

The first principal component scores summarize the content of the more than three thousand IIAs along a single dimension. Plotted over time in Figure 1.1, they produce a map of sorts that visualizes the main design evolution of investment agreements. The absolute principal component scores are not meaningful per se. What counts is how the scores situate agreements in relation to each other. Treaties with similar PCA score share common design features. Treaties with different PCA scores diverge in design.

The map depicts a gradual evolution from low-scoring early BITs to high-scoring recent IIAs. Chapters 2 and 3 will unpack the map in detail. Yet a few preliminary observations are worth highlighting.

- *Higher PCA scores correlate with longer, more comprehensive, and detailed treaties.* If one looks at the IIAs that score high and low, stark differences appear. Agreements with low scores are short, often only a few pages in length, and tend to deal exclusively with investment protection. IIAs with higher scores are longer and more comprehensive, including not only provisions on investment protection but also on investment liberalization, explicit sovereignty-preserving flexibilities, and more detailed language generally.
- *The trend toward higher scores is increasing, though not universal.* On average, treaties score higher in the past decade than they did in the 1960s through 2000s. The trend toward longer, more comprehensive agreements

---

[51] Arthur Spirling, *U.S. Treaty Making with American Indians: Institutional Change and Relative Power, 1784–1911*, 56 Am. J. Pol. Sci. 84–97 (2012).

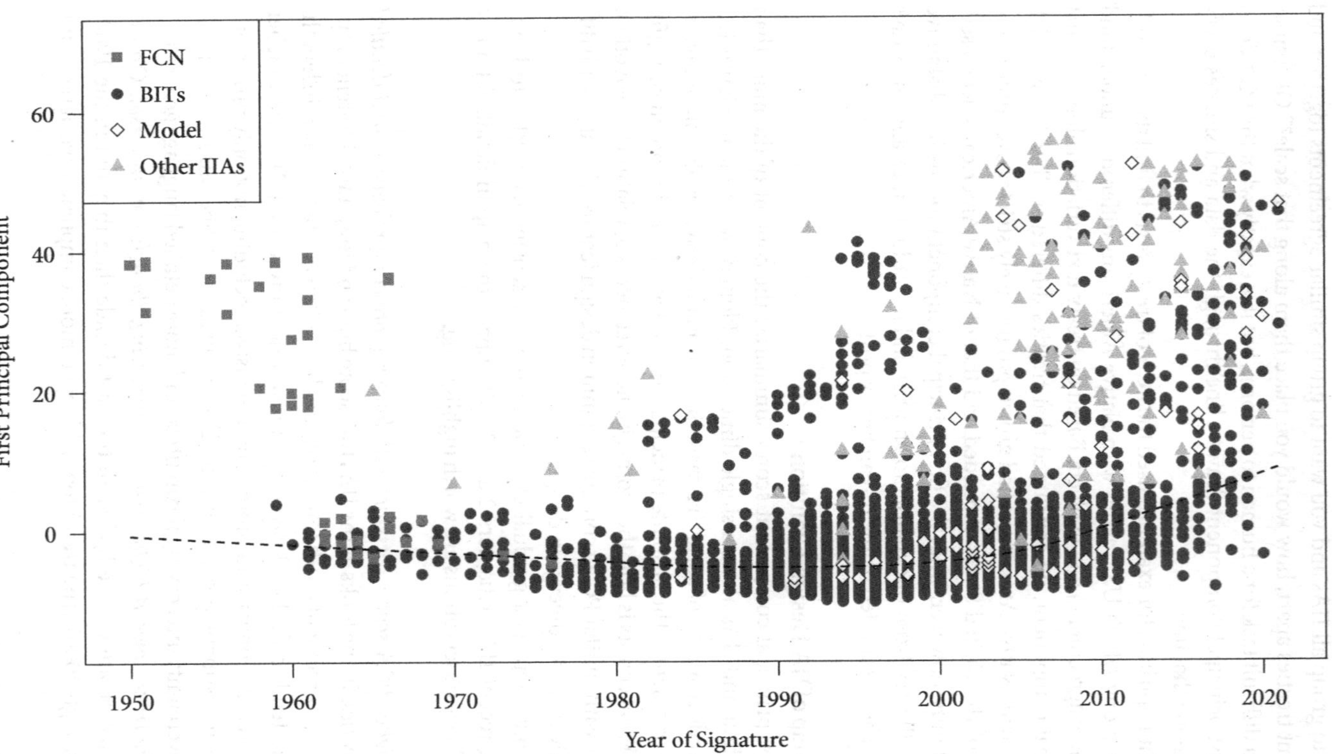

Figure 1.1 Main design variation of IIAs over time (with dotted trend line)

extends around the globe but is particularly pronounced in American and East Asian treaty networks. Short IIAs with low scores have turned from the majority to a minority of agreements but continue to be concluded.

- *The trend toward progressively higher scores is shared across BITs, BIT models, and other IIAs, but early FCN treaties predate that trend.* All modern IIA types have become progressively longer and more comprehensive. Early FCN treaties have significantly higher scores than early BITs and score closer to recent BITs and FTA investment chapters.
- *The evolution toward higher scores occurred in phases.* Following an initial decline as high-scoring FCN treaties were phased out in favor of low-scoring BITs, scores first jumped in the early 1980s, then again in the mid-1990s, and finally, but less drastically, in the early 2000s. These phases coincide with changes to North American IIA practice.

Chapters 2 and 3 will develop each of these insights further. Chapter 2 is dedicated to unpacking the y-axis arguing that the first principal component represents varying levels of contractual completeness of IIAs. Chapter 3 focuses on the x-axis and argues that the evolution of IIA treaty design is a history of gradual state-driven change inspired by North American practice. At the end of Part I, readers will have a solid understanding of how IIAs changed over time and how to use Figure 1.1 to navigate the IIA universe.

While this map of treaty design change is the centerpiece of this book and will be referenced throughout, it only makes sense to study the variation it depicts in depth if its findings are robust. Small changes to the modeling process should not drastically alter results. This section therefore concludes with robustness checks to ensure that the design variation found is real and meaningful.

C. Robustness Checks

To ensure that the previous findings represent a true depiction of the most important design variation characterizing IIAs, the same analysis will be repeated with data from UNCTAD's mapping project. UNCTAD's mapping data is the result of a comprehensive, crowd-sourced manual content analysis along 205 content features of 2,577 IIAs (both BITs and other IIAs) that have been concluded between 1959 and 2016. While EDIT's full text data is necessarily full of "noise"—differences between British and American spelling, for instance, create variation in the data—UNCTAD's content mapping only captures variation that humans considered legally meaningful.[52] If the main design variation

---

[52] While full text analysis is overinclusive, capturing variation that is not legally meaningful such as spelling differences, manual content analysis is almost necessarily underinclusive. Some legally

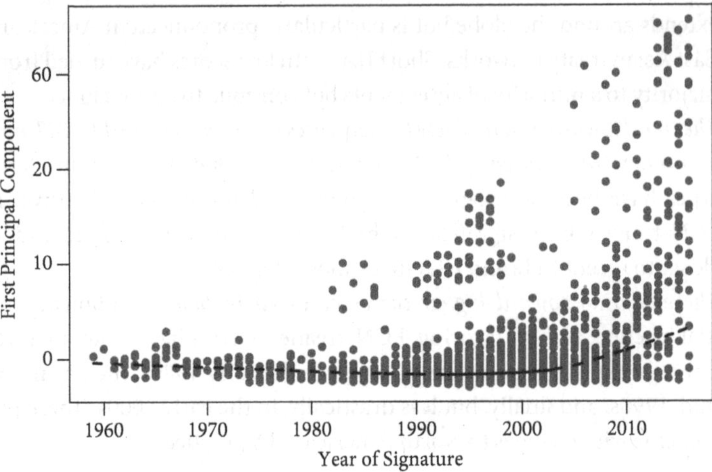

Figure 1.2 Main design variation of IIAs over time based on UNCTAD's mapping data

discovered earlier is indeed a meaningful way to differentiate between differently designed agreements, then this variation should be present in the smaller, but more curated UNCTAD data as well.

When the principal component analysis is repeated with UNCTAD's mapping data, the results validate the foregoing findings. Figure 1.2 plots the principal component scores based on UNCTAD data over time. The same phased evolution with three increases in the early 1980s, the 1990s, and the 2000s is visible in the graph. Again, these three phases coincide with changes to North American IIA practice, and again, longer treaties that include more clarificatory language, new sovereignty-preserving flexibilities, and additional investment liberalization components score high, while older, shorter BITs that focus exclusively on investment protection score low.

Particularly encouraging is that the variation captured by the first principal component amounts to 12 percent of the overall variation in the UNCTAD data (but only 2 percent based on full-text data). Each additional principal component only contributes marginally to describing the variation in the dataset. That is important, because it justifies focusing exclusively on the first principal component to describe the evolution of IIAs. Figure 1.3 depicts the variance explained by the first fifteen principal components, showing an L-shaped curve, which means that the first principal component alone describes a significant portion of the

relevant differences between agreements are not accounted for in UNCTAD's codebook. Indeed, it is probably impossible to code every single difference between three thousand texts by hand. Hence, neither dataset is perfect, but when they reveal the same dominent pattern, then researchers can be confident that the analysis captures a real and meaningful distinction between agreements.

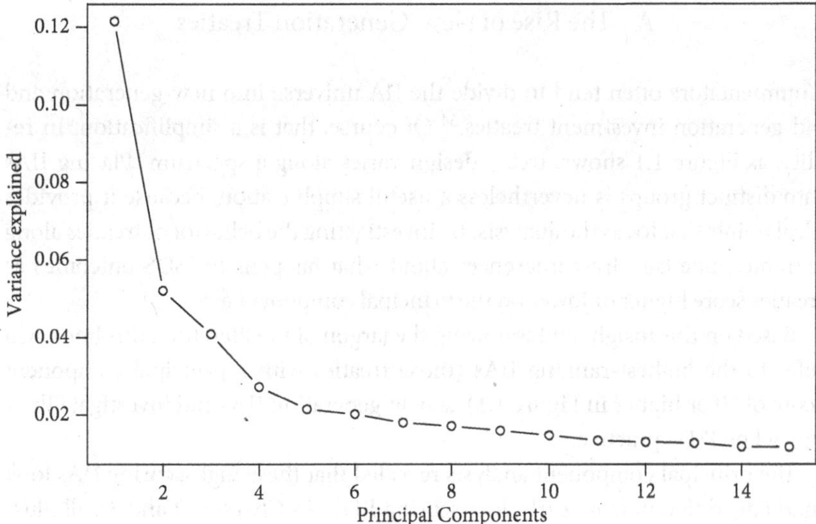

Figure 1.3 Variance explained by the first fifteen principal components based on UNCTAD's mapping data

variation in the IIA data and that the remaining components provide little added value in explaining the structure of the data.[53]

Therefore, the robustness check confirms and strengthens the initial findings. If we let treaties speak for themselves and ask for their most significant design dimension that distinguishes agreements, a map in the shape of Figures 1.1 and 1.2 emerges.

V. The Puzzle: New Treaties, Old Outcomes

The map of investment treaty design allows us to differentiate between agreements on a solid empirical basis and to investigate to what extent these design differences matter in ISDS practice. This final section uses the map to set up the puzzle that will guide the rest of the book. On the one hand, the IIA universe is increasingly divided into older, low-scoring agreements and more recent, high-scoring treaties that differ starkly in design. On the other hand, the first wave of cases under high-scoring treaties suggests that treaty design changes have thus far mattered little in ISDS practice as new, reformed IIAs are read like old, unreformed ones.

---

[53] In the worst case, many principal components are needed to describe the data. Visualized as a graph that shows the variance explained by each component, it would look like a line with constant slope that steadily declines.

A. The Rise of New-Generation Treaties

Commentators often tend to divide the IIA universe into new-generation and old-generation investment treaties.[54] Of course, that is a simplification. In reality, as Figure 1.1 shows, treaty design varies along a spectrum. Placing IIAs into distinct groups is nevertheless a useful simplification, because it provides ideal points that focus the analysis. By investigating the behavior of treaties along extremes, one can draw inferences about what happens to ISDS outcomes as treaties score higher or lower on the principal component axis.

Based on this insight and following the jargon of the literature, this book will refer to the highest-ranking IIAs (those treaties with a principal component score of 30 or higher in Figure 1.1) as new-generation IIAs and investigate their impact on ISDS practice.

The principal component analysis revealed that these high-scoring IIAs look markedly different from early, low-scoring BITs. As Chapters 2 and 3 will illustrate in greater depth, these new-generation IIAs abound with reform features that the literature associates with state-of-the-art investment agreements such as greater precision and detail, exceptions to balance investment protection and host state sovereignty, and more detailed delegation to allow the contracting states greater control over investment arbitration. Conversely, lower scoring treaties, even if they have been recently negotiated, lack some or all of these reform features.

New-generation treaties are rapidly taking over contemporary treaty practice. The share of annually concluded IIAs with low scores (< 10 on the principal component axis) has decreased from 100 percent in the 1970s to roughly 10 percent in 2020. Medium-scoring IIAs (30 < and > 10 on the principal component axis) and high-scoring treaties (> 30 on the principal component axis) now form the bulk of newly concluded treaties. High-scoring, new-generation IIAs accounted for half of all newly concluded IIAs in the late 2010s, up from only around 5 percent in the mid-1990s.

In terms of the treaty stock, however, high-scoring, new-generation treaties only make up a minority, albeit a growing one. Most low-scoring IIAs concluded in the 1970s through the 2000s continue to exist and are only gradually phased out, if at all.[55] As a result, the IIA universe is increasingly dominated by extremes.

---

[54] *See, e.g.*, John Beechey, *New Generation of Bilateral Investment Treaties: Consensus or Divergence?*, CONTEMP. ISSUES IN INT'L ARB. & MEDIATION: THE FORDHAM PAPERS (2008) 5–25 (2009); Spears, *supra* note 37; UNCTAD, WORLD INVESTMENT REPORT 2012. TOWARDS A NEW GENERATION OF INVESTMENT POLICIES (2012); Catherine Titi, *Most-Favoured-Nation Treatment: Survival Clauses and Reform of International Investment Law*, 33 J. INT'L ARB. 426 (2016).

[55] UNCTAD, WORLD INVESTMENT REPORT 2019: SPECIAL ECONOMIC ZONES 112–113 (2019).

The vast majority of IIAs in force have a principal component score below 10. Half of the remaining agreements have a principal component score above 30. Most of the IIA universe is therefore divided into low- and high-scoring treaties.

In sum, the IIA universe is increasingly divided as treaties with old-generation design coexist with those of new-generation design.

How does this bifurcation of IIA design impact ISDS outcomes? Conventional wisdom suggests that the bifurcation of IIA design would lead to a bifurcation also of ISDS practice. Disputes under new- and old-generation agreements would then differ in their outcomes with new treaties producing new outcomes. As noted in this book's introduction, most commentators and international organizations appear to subscribe to this view. That does not necessarily mean that respondent states would win cases that they would have formerly lost, but that the interpretation of high-scoring, new-generation treaties differed from the reading of older, low-scoring ones. New-generation IIAs with high principal component scores and explicit general public policy exceptions would thus be interpreted differently than low-scoring IIAs that lack such exceptions. Similarly, clarifications inserted to high-scoring treaties would prevent those past misunderstandings that had arisen due to the vagueness and brevity of older, low-scoring IIAs. In short, the change of design from low to high-scoring treaties would have been accompanied by an interpretive reset in ISDS. But do new-generation treaties indeed produce new outcomes?

B. Current Trajectory: New Treaties, Old Outcomes

Admittedly, new-generation IIAs are just beginning to be litigated.[56] However, the cases that have been decided under high-scoring treaties seem to defy conventional wisdom and suggest a different trajectory: new treaties reproduce old outcomes. Figure 1.4 unpacks ISDS decisions rendered until 2020. Out of 484 disputes with final award, only 64 cases or 13 percent have been litigated under high-scoring, new-generation IIAs (i.e., with principal component scores above 30). The majority of those 64 cases fall under NAFTA (thirty-eight awards). Although, as will be explained in Chapter 3, NAFTA, is the first IIA of new-generation design, reformed IIA practice, and had a lasting imprint on the IIA universe. It was also the petri dish in which ISDS litigation first emerged, and it produced a relatively self-referential caseload.[57] NAFTA awards are therefore

---

[56] Furthermore, not all decisions under high-scoring IIAs are pertinent for studying the impact of treaty design change as they deal with matters in which old and new treaties are alike.

[57] Suha Jubran Ballan, *Investment Treaty Arbitration and Institutional Backgrounds: An Empirical Study*, 34 Wis. Int'l L.J. 31–91 (2016); Suha Jubran-Ballan, *How Institutions Matter: On the Judicial Reasoning of Investment Treaty Arbitration Awards*, 41 Hous. J. Int'l L. 57–106 (2018).

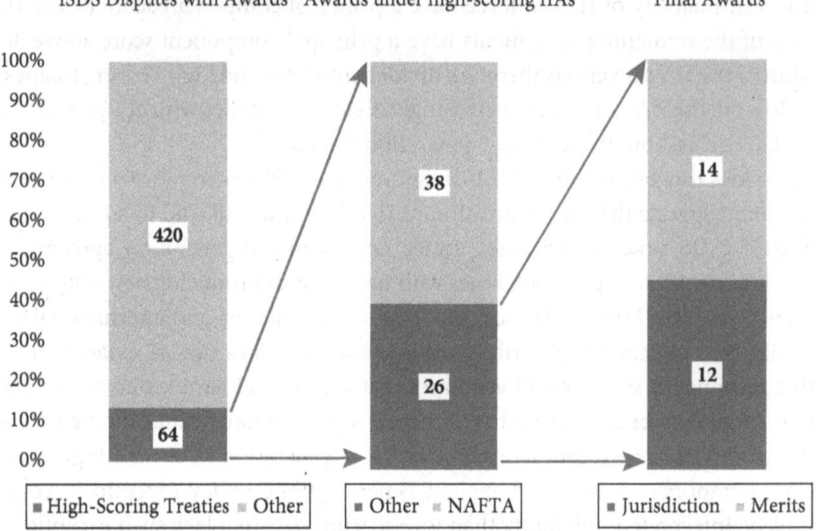

Figure 1.4 Breakdown of ISDS cases with final award until 2020 (source: UNCTAD Investment Policy Hub)

important but also of limited guidance for studying the impact of agreements with new design features. Out of the remaining twenty-six non-NAFTA awards, twelve were dismissed at the jurisdiction stage. Hence, up to 2020, only fourteen merits decisions have been decided under high-scoring IIAs, and all have been rendered under North American treaties (Table 1.3). Let us take a look at these awards to gain a first impression of how new-generation IIAs fare in practice.

A summary analysis of the awards rendered under high-scoring IIAs with reform features suggests that these decisions are not much different from those decided under other lower scoring IIAs that lack reform features. Consider first the five merits decisions that out of those fourteen awards dealt with general public policy exceptions. In *Copper Mesa v. Ecuador* and *Bear Creek v. Peru*, the respondent states invoked the general exceptions in their respective treaties with Canada. These exceptions were thought to provide additional policy space to shield the host state from liability for treaty violations.[58] Yet, the tribunals conflated the treaty-based defense with the police powers doctrine rooted in customary law, which is thought to be available to defendants even in the absence of an exception.[59] This conflation of treaty and customary law defenses has since been exacerbated with the 2021 *Eco Oro v. Colombia* award that equated a public

---

[58] Amelia Keene, *The Incorporation and Interpretation of WTO-Style Environmental Exceptions in International Investment Agreements*, 18 J. WORLD INVESTMENT & TRADE 62–99 (2017).

[59] *Copper Mesa Mining Corporation v. Republic of Ecuador*, PCA No. 2012-2, Award, March 15, 2016, para. 6.58, and *Bear Creek Mining Corporation v. Republic of Peru*, ICSID Case No. ARB/14/21, Award, November 30, 2017, paras. 472–473. *See* Chapter 5 for an in-depth discussion.

Table 1.3 New-generation IIAs (i.e. treaties with a principal component score above 30) that have produced merits decisions (NAFTA omitted)

High-Scoring IIAs	Count of Merits Decisions	Cases
Canada–Venezuela, Bolivarian Republic of BIT (1996)	4	Vannessa Ventures Ltd. v. Bolivarian Republic of Venezuela (ICSID Case No. ARB(AF)/04/6); Rusoro Mining Ltd. v. Bolivarian Republic of Venezuela (ICSID Case No. ARB(AF)/12/5); Crystallex International Corporation v. Bolivarian Republic of Venezuela (ICSID Case No. ARB(AF)/11/2); Gold Reserve Inc. v. Bolivarian Republic of Venezuela (ICSID Case No. ARB(AF)/09/1)
Dominican Republic–Central America–United States FTA (CAFTA-DR) (2004)	3	TECO Guatemala Holdings, LLC v. Republic of Guatemala (ICSID Case No. ARB/10/23); Railroad Development Corporation (RDC) v. Republic of Guatemala (ICSID Case No. ARB/07/23); David R. Aven, Samuel D. Aven, Giacomo A. Buscemi and others v. Republic of Costa Rica (ICSID Case No. UNCT/15/3)
Canada–Ecuador BIT (1996)	2	EnCana Corporation v. Republic of Ecuador (LCIA Case No. UN3481); Copper Mesa Mining Corporation v. Republic of Ecuador (PCA No. 2012-2)
Barbados–Canada BIT (1996)	1	Peter A. Allard v. The Government of Barbados (PCA Case No. 2012-06)
Canada–Croatia BIT (1997)	1	Mr. Nedjeljko Ulemek v. Croatia (not public)
Canada–Egypt BIT (1996)	1	Global Telecom Holding S.A.E. v. Canada (ICSID Case No. ARB/16/16)
Canada–Peru FTA (2008)	1	Bear Creek Mining Corporation v. Republic of Peru (ICSID Case No. ARB/14/21)
Oman–US FTA (2004)	1	Adel A Hamadi Al Tamimi v. Sultanate of Oman (ICSID Case No. ARB/11/33)

policy exception with customary international law conditions precluding wrongfulness, finding that even if a measure falls under an exception, a state still has to pay compensation.[60] In three other cases brought by Canadian mining investors against Venezuela, the respondent sought to justify its conduct by pointing to

---

[60] *Eco Oro Minerals Corp. v. Republic of Colombia*, ICSID Case No. ARB/16/41, Decision on Jurisdiction, Liability, and Directions on Quantum, September 9, 2021, paras. 830, 835.

the environmental protection rationale of the measure.[61] But the treaty-based exception in the applicable IIA designed to mediate between investment protection and environmental concerns was not invoked by Venezuela, and the tribunals decided the cases by following precedent rendered under low-scoring investment treaties instead. In short, general public policy exceptions have been "missing in action."[62] ISDS tribunals have treated new-generation treaties with general exceptions much like old-generation treaties that lacked such novel clauses.

A second set of merits decisions involving clarifications to correct past arbitral misinterpretations relating to the fair and equitable treatment (FET) standard provide a similar impression. In *RDC v. Guatemala*, the tribunal did not give effect to the explanatory annex of the investment chapter of DR–CAFTA (2004) that directs interpreters toward an analysis of state practice and *opinio juris*.[63] Instead, the tribunal based its interpretation of FET on past arbitral decisions rendered under agreements that lack such a clarification. Similarly, in *Global Telecom v. Canada*, the tribunal disregarded historical evidence and Canada's consistent practice in linking FET to customary international law and rooted the award in past interpretations.[64] Again, new agreements were read like old ones.

The only set of cases where novel language mattered, at least at first sight, concerned novel right-to-regulate provisions that allow states to regulate investment to protect the environment as long as states do so in manner otherwise consistent with the treaty. In *Al Tamimi v. Oman*, the tribunal constituted under the United States–Oman FTA (2004) noted that its interpretation of FET "must be guided by the forceful defence of environmental regulation and protection provided in the express language of the Treaty."[65] Similarly, in *Aven v. Costa Rica*, litigated under DR–CAFTA (2004), the tribunal considered that such a right-to-regulate clause "essentially subordinate[s] the rights to investors [under the treaty] to the right of Costa Rica."[66]

---

[61] *Gold Reserve Inc. v. Bolivarian Republic of Venezuela*, ICSID Case No. ARB(AF)/09/1, Award, September 22, 2014; *Crystallex International Corporation v. Bolivarian Republic of Venezuela*, ICSID Case No. ARB(AF)/11/2, Award, April 4, 2016; *Rusoro Mining Ltd. v. Bolivarian Republic of Venezuela*, ICSID Case No. ARB(AF)/12/5, Award, August 22, 2016. *See* Chapter 6 for an in-depth discussion.

[62] Wolfgang Alschner & Kun Hui, *Missing in Action: General Public Policy Exceptions in Investment Treaties*, *in* YEARBOOK ON INTERNATIONAL INVESTMENT LAW AND POLICY 2018 (Lisa E. Sachs, Jesse Coleman, & Lise Johnson eds., 2019).

[63] *Railroad Development Corporation (RDC) v. Republic of Guatemala*, ICSID Case No. ARB/07/23, Award, June 29, 2012, para. 219.

[64] *Global Telecom Holding S.A.E. v. Canada*, ICSID Case No. ARB/16/16, Award, March 27, 2020, para. 484.

[65] *Adel A Hamadi Al Tamimi v. Sultanate of Oman*, ICSID Case No. ARB/11/33, Award, November 3, 2015, para. 389.

[66] *David R. Aven, Samuel D. Aven, Giacomo A. Buscemi and others v. Republic of Costa Rica*, ICSID Case No. UNCT/15/3, Award, September 18, 2018, para. 412.

Yet even though the new clause ostensibly "greened" the interpretation of protective standards, this ultimately mattered little in practice, given that under the clause regulatory measures have to be otherwise consistent with the treaty. The *Aven* tribunal therefore added that such "subordination is not absolute" but bounded by international law and the terms of the treaty. In both *Al Tamimi* and *Aven*, the tribunal ultimately considered that the conduct did not rise to the level of an FET violation, casting doubt on whether the new clause made a difference.[67] The subsequent 2021 *Infinito Gold v. Costa Rica* award furthermore confirmed that a similar right-to-regulate clause in the Canada–Costa Rica BIT (1998) differed from a general exception and could not save a measure from liability once a treaty violation was found.[68] The impact of these right-to-regulate clauses thus appears modest at best.

In sum, a cursory analysis of the first series of awards rendered under high-scoring treaties appears to challenge the conventional wisdom that new treaties result in new interpretive outcomes. It seems that most of these cases would have been similarly reasoned and decided, if they had been rendered under old, low-scoring agreements. We are thus left with a puzzle. While IIA design has changed remarkably in recent decades, the interpretative outcomes in ISDS, including under these new treaties, seem to remain unchanged and unaffected. What is going on?

The first wave of awards under high-scoring treaties provides preliminary clues as to why the interpretation of new agreements appears to remain rooted in the reading of old-generation IIAs. First, each of the awards under new-generation treaties that produced old outcomes heavily relied on precedent. Since around 90 percent of existing awards have been rendered under older, lower scoring treaties, the reliance on yesterday's ISDS case law anchors new treaties in past practice. Precedent thus creates continuity where new treaties seek change.

A second device surfacing across these awards and rolling back treaty design innovation is customary international law. In the first set of cases on exceptions, custom emerged as a ceiling to limit the flexibility that new exceptions provide by equating exceptions with preexisting customary law flexibilities. Conversely, in the cases involving clarifications, custom was used to elevate the floor of protection by grounding the meaning of FET in past arbitral interpretation rather than state practice and *opinio juris* as the agreements had called for. Custom thereby overrides treaty design differences and converges the interpretation of new agreements with that of old ones.

Finally, in *Infinito* and *Gold Reserve*, the claiming investor sought to use most-favored nation (MFN) treatment to replace innovative provisions in the high-scoring base treaty with ostensibly more favorable terms in the older low-scoring

---

[67] *Al Tamimi v. Oman*, Award, para. 390 and *Aven v. Costa Rica*, Award, para. 585.
[68] *Infinito Gold Ltd. v. Costa Rica*, ICSID Case No. ARB/14/5, Award, June 3, 2021, para. 777.

treaties.[69] While ultimately rejected, similar arguments have succeeded before other tribunals.[70] MFN clauses appear therefore as a third normative device that risks rolling back innovation in recent agreements by importing language from older treaties. Each of these three strategies results in new-generation, high-scoring agreements being interpreted like old-generation, low-scoring ones. Part 2 of this book will look at this practice in-depth with chapters on MFN (Chapter 4), custom (Chapter 5), and precedent (Chapter 6).

Although the small number of awards rendered under high-scoring IIAs to date makes the preceding conclusions tentative and preliminary, these awards paint a worrying emerging picture. The fact that new-generation treaties have produced old outcomes calls into question decades of state-driven change and treaty design innovation. It suggests that concluding new agreements—states' main strategy to alleviate investment law's legitimacy crisis—has been ineffective, at least up to now. The remainder of this book will investigate this puzzle of new treaties producing old outcomes in-depth and suggest a path forward for shifting the interpretive center of gravity in investment law from old- to new-generation treaties.

VI. Conclusion

Using text as data tools, this chapter inductively traced the evolution of investment law by letting IIAs speak for themselves. It revealed the main design variation running through the IIA universe and created a map of the evolution of treaty design. That map showed that IIAs are increasingly bifurcated into newer, long, more detailed, and comprehensive agreements and older, shorter, often vague treaties that focus exclusively on investment protection. The next two chapters will study the results revealed in Figure 1.1 in depth. Chapter 2 will unpack the y-axis and answer the question what the first principal component represents in theoretical and normative terms. Chapter 3 then shifts attention to the x-axis and provides a narrative to describe, contextualize, and explain the evolution of IIAs over time. The remainder of the book in Parts 2 and 3 then unpack and resolve the puzzle identified in this chapter that new-generation, high-scoring IIA lead to old outcomes.

---

[69] *Infinito v. Costa Rica*, Award, paras. 720–754. *Gold Reserve v. Venezuela*, Award, paras. 624–632.
[70] *See* Chapter 4 for an in-depth discussion.

2
Change as Gap-Filling

I. Introduction

In inductive, computational analysis, theory comes in through the back door. Rather than generating empirically testable hypotheses ex ante, theory explains the patterns observed ex post. While Chapter 1 let treaties speak for themselves, this chapter uses theory to interpret what they are saying. It argues that the main content variation running through the IIA universe—the y-axis of the map of treaty design evolution in Figure 1.1—is a difference among treaties in their levels of contractual completeness.

The concept of contractual completeness is part of contract theory, a branch of law and economics that seeks to better understand contract design. Contract theory asks why contractors design agreements in the way they do in light of the contracting challenges they face. Contract theory thereby focuses attention on the treaty drafters and their efforts to write better, more complete treaties. Furthermore, contract theory provides a conceptual umbrella framework that unites different existing meta-narratives of IIA design change, from a quest for policy space, for precision, or for control, as states' drive to progressively fill contractual gaps and to conclude more complete agreements.

This chapter is structured as follows. Section II introduces contract theory and its central concepts. Section III explains how contract theory accommodates and links existing narratives on treaty design change. It also places gap-filling strategies in a broader perspective arguing that the shift in the relative importance of different gap-filling strategies has worked to empower contracting parties at the expense of adjudicators who used to serve as default gap-fillers. Section IV shows how the four gap-filling strategies developed in contract theory help describe and contextualize the treaty design variation and changes observed.

II. Contract Theory

Contracts are "enforceable commitments over time."[1] Due to the time difference between a contract's conclusion and its performance, contractors have to foresee

---

[1] Simon A. B. Schropp, Trade Policy Flexibility and Enforcement in the World Trade Organization: A Law and Economics Analysis 28 (2009).

Investment Arbitration and State-Driven Reform. Wolfgang Alschner, Oxford University Press. © Oxford University Press 2022. DOI: 10.1093/oso/9780197644386.003.0003

various contingencies that may arise in the future, from the nonperformance of contractual obligations due to unforeseen circumstances to the resolution of contractual ambiguities. Contractors want a contract that is not only optimal ex ante, that is, at the time of writing, but also ex post, that is, at the time of performance.[2] Treaty negotiators face similar challenges. They too want to secure optimal levels of cooperation over time in the face of uncertainty. Contract theory can therefore inform the understanding of treaty design.[3]

A. Complete and Incomplete Contracts

Central to contract theory is the notion of contractual incompleteness. Incomplete contracts are defined in contradistinction to a "Pareto-efficient complete contingent contract" (CCC).[4] The CCC corresponds to the "ideal of a contract that completely informed, perfectly rational parties would write in absence of any contracting imperfection."[5] The CCC is the perfect contract. It details all contractual rights and obligation for all possible contingencies at all times. As a result, it does not require ex post adjustments in light of changing circumstances, because it is already welfare maximizing. It is thus the first best outcome of any negotiation and a useful benchmark for comparison.

In real life, unfortunately, it is impossible to achieve a CCC for several reasons. First, it is simply impossible to foresee all prospective contingencies in a contract as the future is fraught with uncertainty. Second, even if contractors could foresee all future contingencies, transaction costs would prevent them from writing the rules to address them. Contracting is costly. These costs quickly outweigh the benefits of designing a contract that seeks to deal with contingencies of even the smallest probability.[6] It is hence efficient for contractors to leave contractual gaps. Third, to prevent a failure in negotiation, contracting parties often wrap contentious issues in deliberately vague language as an "agreement to disagree," creating intentional gaps.[7] Finally, contractors make mistakes. According to the assumption of bounded rationality, contractors may lack foresight and

---

[2] ROBERT E. SCOTT & PAUL B. STEPHAN, THE LIMITS OF LEVIATHAN: CONTRACT THEORY AND THE ENFORCEMENT OF INTERNATIONAL LAW 61 (2006).

[3] For applications of contract theory to investigate the design of international treaties, *see, e.g.,* Jeffrey L. Dunoff & Joel P. Trachtman, *Economic Analysis of International Law*, 24 YALE J. INT'L L. 1, 28–30 (1999); Anne van Aaken, *International Investment Law Between Commitment and Flexibility: A Contract Theory Analysis*, 12 J. INT'L ECON. L. 507–538, 520 (2009).

[4] For further explanation of the concept, *see* SCHROPP, *supra* note 1, footnote 103; van Aaken, *supra* note 3, at 515–516.

[5] SCHROPP, *supra* note 1, at 56.

[6] Richard A. Posner, *The Law and Economics of Contract Interpretation*, 83 TEX L. REV. 1581, 1582 (2004).

[7] *Id.* at 1583.

may use "rules of thumb" rather than engaging in more sophisticated analysis.[8] Because of all these reasons, all real-life contracts are necessarily incomplete and imperfect.

B. Curbing Opportunism and Seizing Regret

While the CCC does everything right, that is, it imposes commitments where necessary and leaves flexibility where needed to maximize the joint welfare of the contracting parties, incomplete contracts contain gaps. These gaps mean that a contract provides either too much flexibility or too much commitment, which gives rise to two central contracting challenges: curbing opportunism and seizing regret.

Curbing opportunism. Opportunism occurs when the contract is too flexible. It fails to prevent acts by one of the contractors (the injurer) that are geared toward maximizing its own welfare rather than the parties' joint welfare, thereby harming the other contractor (the victim).[9] Opportunism undermines the credibility of commitments undertaken ex ante and may lead to a breakdown of cooperation.[10] To maximize their joint welfare, contractors will thus want to write a contract that prevents opportunistic behavior. This is especially important when contractors contract under a veil of ignorance, that is, they do not know ex ante who will be the injurer and who will be the victim ex post.[11]

Seizing regret. A contract that allows opportunistic behavior is underinclusive as compared to the ideal CCC: it fails to regulate behavior that would have been disciplined in the CCC. Contracts, however, can also be overinclusive: they can constrain behavior that would have been left undisciplined in the CCC.[12] Differently put, a contract can be overly constraining. In contract theory, that problem is referred to as regret.[13] Contracts are welfare enhancing when they provide flexibility where needed to seize ex post regret.

The imperatives of curbing opportunism while seizing regret create a tension in contract design. On the one hand, contracts need to be rigid enough to prevent opportunism. On the other hand, they have to be yielding enough to avoid regret. Getting that mix just right is the central challenge for any contractors, including for states negotiating investment treaties.[14]

---

[8] Schropp, *supra* note 1, at 59.
[9] *Id.* at 29.
[10] *Id.* at 9.
[11] *Id.* at 130.
[12] *Id.* at 54.
[13] *Id.* at 2.
[14] *See particularly* van Aaken, *supra* note 3.

C. Relationship between Ex Post Flexibility and Ex Ante Commitments

The tension between flexibility and rigidity ex post affects contractors' propensity to agree on commitments ex ante.[15] Contractors will agree more readily to tie their hands to an obligation, if they can be discharged from it when performance becomes inefficiently burdensome.[16]

The World Trade Organization's (WTO's) Safeguards Agreement is a case in point. The Agreement allows WTO members to escape from their WTO obligations temporarily if a surge in imports threatens to cause serious injury to the like domestic industry. The Agreement heeds considerations of domestic politics enabling politicians to make more liberalization concessions ex ante knowing that they can be temporarily withdrawn ex post should the political necessity arise.[17]

At the same time, if contractors can use escape clauses not to seize regret but to opportunistically escape from commitments, these clauses will undermine the credibility of commitments ex ante and may well prevent the conclusion of the contract in the first place. Maximizing commitment ex ante is then contingent on the contracts ability to distinguish between welfare-enhancing permissible intracontractual flexibility (seizing regret) and welfare-depreciating impermissible extracontractual flexibility (opportunism).[18] Yet if contractors get it right, somewhat counterintuitively, contracts with more flexibility can contain higher levels commitments than a contract without such flexibility.

D. Credibility through Effective Enforcement

Even if a contract successfully distinguishes between regret (allowing flexibility) and opportunism (imposing commitment), it may still fail to secure welfare maximizing behavior. Asymmetric information between the parties can make it difficult for one party to assess whether the other party is acting intra- or extracontractually, which in turn creates a moral hazard problem.[19]

To overcome this problem, contractors rely on third-party adjudicators to police the terms of the contract ex post. Effective enforcement, however, requires that information on the behavior of the parties is readily observable

---

[15] SCHROPP, *supra* note 1, at 9.

[16] KRZYSZTOF J. PELC, MAKING AND BENDING INTERNATIONAL RULES: THE DESIGN OF EXCEPTIONS AND ESCAPE CLAUSES IN TRADE LAW 2 (2016).

[17] ALAN O. SYKES, THE WTO AGREEMENT ON SAFEGUARDS: A COMMENTARY (2006).

[18] Van Aaken, *supra* note 3, at 516–517.

[19] SCOTT & STEPHAN, *supra* note 2, at 70–71.

and verifiable for the adjudicator.[20] The clearer the rules are ex ante, the easier it will be for the adjudicator to verify contractual compliance ex post, creating an additional incentive to write more complete contracts.[21] Contracts that fail to specify such rules merely defer the problem to the dispute settlement stage where adjudicators risk confusing intracontractual acts to seize regret with extracontractual opportunism.

E. Strategies to Overcome Incompleteness

While contractors will not be able to write a complete contract that achieves optimal levels of ex ante commitments and ex post flexibility, which, on top of that, can be effectively policed, they can draft the second-best alternative: a cost-efficient incomplete contract. When negotiation costs are high and the benefits of more completeness are low, it will be efficient for parties to leave contracts incomplete. In contrast, when expected benefits and attended costs warrant it, contractors can make use of four gap-filling strategies to write more complete contracts.[22]

More complete contracting. Contractors can seek to minimize the degree of contractual incompleteness by mimicking the design of the CCC. Put differently, they can engage in complex and comprehensive contracting approximating, yet without ever achieving, the ideal CCC. Aside from raising the costs of contracting, this strategy brings about its own pitfalls. As contractors close ever more gaps through specific rules, new contractual language gives rise to new gaps and ambiguities.[23] So this strategy can all but mitigate incompleteness.

Escape clauses. Contractors can also draft flexibility mechanisms. In contrast to comprehensive contracting that seeks to mirror the content of the CCC, flexibility mechanisms seek to replicate its outcome.[24] They either specify concrete contingency measures that allow nonperformance in predefined circumstances or take the form of general escape clauses.[25] As highlighted earlier, the challenge there lies in determining verifiably what constitutes legitimate (intracontractual) nonperformance, that is, seizing regret, and what is considered illegitimate (extra-contractual) nonperformance, that is, opportunism.

Relational contracting. Alternatively, contractors can engage in precaution limiting the room for misunderstandings and tensions. Through diligent drafting

---

[20] *Id.* at 71.
[21] *Id.* at 72–75.
[22] This list is based on SCHROPP, *supra* note 1, at 83–94.
[23] *Id.* at 89–91 (providing a more detailed account of possible pitfalls).
[24] *Id.* at 86.
[25] *Id.* at 86–92.

and upfront research, they can strive to write the most thorough (as opposed to the most complete) contract possible. Furthermore, they can engage in relationship building, for example, by using preambular language to set out the spirit of the contract, which can serve as reference point both for good faith performance and for third-party interpretation of the contract.[26]

Delegation. The final and perhaps simplest strategy to close contractual gaps is for contractors to delegate the task of completing the contract to courts or tribunals.[27] The tribunal then wears two hats: that of a gap-filler and that of an adjudicator. On the one hand, as "norm experts," the members of the tribunal will resolve contractual ambiguities.[28] On the other hand, they will police the contractual terms as adjudicators, verifying whether the contractors' conduct represents a permissible use of intracontractual flexibilities or an impermissible opportunistic breach of the contract.[29]

F. Relation between Gap-Filling Strategies

These different strategies are typically employed together. Yet they can also substitute each other. More detailed contracting ex ante, for instance, alleviates the need for courts or tribunals to close gaps ex post allowing them to concentrate on their policing role.[30] Conversely, less complete contracting necessitates more active gap-filling by adjudicators. One of the key insights of contract theory, discussed in depth in Chapter 7, is therefore that contract drafting and contract interpretation by adjudicators are interconnected. The more contractors invest at the contract negotiation stage, the more deference they expect at the interpretation stage.[31]

In practice, however, this division of labor between gap-filling strategies gives rise to tensions.[32] When contractors take it upon themselves to close contractual gaps through more complete contracting, they take gap-filling power away from

---

[26] *Id.* at 92–94.

[27] This strategy is available both where contractors assume (as in inadvertent incompleteness) and where they know (as in foreseeable incompleteness) that contractual gaps exist, *see* Alan Schwartz, *Relational Contracts in the Courts: An Analysis of Incomplete Agreements and Judicial Strategies*, 21 J. LEGAL STUD. 271–318, 281 (1992).

[28] Anne van Aaken, *Delegating Interpretative Authority in Investment Treaties: The Case of Joint Commissions*, 11 TRANSNAT'L DISP. MGMT. 6 (2014).

[29] *Id.* at 6.

[30] SCOTT & STEPHAN, *supra* note 2, at 72–75.

[31] Richard A. Posner, *The Law and Economics Contract of Interpretation*, John M. Olin Law & Economics Working Paper No. 229, November 2004, at 5.

[32] For an insightful analysis of the distinction between state-driven gap-filling and judicial gap-filling, *see* Harlan Cohen, *International Law's Erie Moment*, 34 MICH. J. INT'L L. 249–308 (2013).

adjudicators.[33] Much then depends on how third-party adjudicators view their role. Are they agents of the contracting parties who fill contractual gaps only if they have to and otherwise defer to the choices of the contractors? Or do they act as trustees on behalf a separate community and have an independent authority to close contractual gaps as they (rather than the contractors) see fit?[34] In short, different gap-filling strategies can empower different actors and can give rise to tensions on how gaps should be filled and by whom.

III. Contract Theory as Meta-Framework for Understanding IIA Design Change

Applied to IIAs, contract theory provides a meta-narrative to make sense of treaty design change. As noted in Chapter 1, scholars have portrayed the evolution of IIA design variably as a quest for policy space, as an attempt to add precision to vague treaties, and as an effort to take back control over treaty interpretation from arbitrators. Contract theory accommodates these different accounts under one umbrella. The quest for policy space is about seizing regret. The attempt to write more precise investment agreements is about mimicking CCC design. And the attempt by states to take back control from arbitrators is about getting the interplay between gap-filling strategies right.

In addition, contract theory helps understand the interaction of these existing narratives and adds nuance to them. More policy space and more precise contracting, for example, are means for states to take back control over interpretation, because these gap-filling strategies substitute for judicial gap-filling. In the process, however, gap-filling power shifts from tribunals as default gap-fillers to states, which helps to explain the emergent backlash by arbitrators. Contract theory also adds nuance to existing narratives. For example, it suggests that more policy space does not automatically lower the investment protection a treaty offers. That is because contractors are willing to accept more commitments ex ante when they can seize regret ex post. Treaties with more policy space can thus include additional rather fewer protection obligations. In short, contract theory provides an attractive and revealing meta-framework of the treaty design evolution of IIAs.

---

[33] On the differences, *see id.* Cohen argues that the two gap-filling strategies by states and tribunals are not perfect substitutes. In the context of the gap-filling of IIAs, however, they come close with, for example, states incorporating gap-filling strategies by tribunals in subsequent treaties. Admittedly, contract theory simplifies the complex relationship between states and adjudicators.

[34] *See* Chapter 7.

A. Quest for Optimal Design Rather Than
Policy Space

A key insight of contract theory is that contracts require commitments as well as flexibility. A contract that has too much commitment is suboptimal because it prohibits desirable behavior (regret). A contract that has too much flexibility is suboptimal because it permits undesirable behavior (opportunism). Contracts thus need to contain the right mix of commitment and flexibility. As Anne van Aaken has shown, this reasoning resonates well in the IIA context. States want to reap the benefits of foreign investment by offering credible commitments of protection, but they also do not want to trade off too much sovereignty and make domestic regulatory action too costly.[35] States thus strive for an optimal level of protection that curbs opportunism (preventing too little investment protection) and seizes regret (preventing too much investment protection). Optimal treaty design is therefore about balancing commitment and flexibility in investment treaties.[36] States do not want to either over- or underprotect foreign investors.[37] Nor do they want to provide too much flexibility (for fear of abuse) or too little flexibility (for fear of undue constraint).[38] Optimal treaty design is about getting the balance between commitment and flexibility right.[39]

This need for balancing investment protection with host state sovereignty also lies at the heart of "quest for policy space" literature.[40] Early investment treaties

[35] There is considerable debate on the trade-offs or costs and benefits involved in IIA. Historically, scholars focused on the time-inconsistency problem between states and investors first articulated by Andrew Guzman. *See* Andrew T. Guzman, *Why LDCs Sign Treaties That Hurt Them: Explaining the Popularity of Bilateral Investment Treaties*, 38 VA. J. INT'L L. 639, 662–663 (1997); JAN PETER SASSE, AN ECONOMIC ANALYSIS OF BILATERAL INVESTMENT TREATIES 17–21 (2011). Under that paradigm, sovereignty is traded off against foregone investment inflows. As Burke-White and von Staden put it, "states essentially pay for the right to invoke [an exception] clause through the higher costs of capital they will face in the financial markets." W. Burke-White & A. Von Staden, *Investment Protection in Extraordinary Times: The Interpretation and Application of Non-Precluded Measures Provisions in Bilateral Investment Treaties*, 48 VA. J. INT'L L. 307, 403 (2007). However, since IIAs are negotiated between states rather than between investors and host states and since capital exporting home states rather than capital importing host states are chiefly responsible for treaty design, the actual trade-offs between commitment and flexibility are different during a negotiation. Since investment treaties are chiefly designed by rich capital exporting states, the contracting challenge arguably consists of striking a balance between investment protection abroad and safeguarding policy space at home.

[36] Van Aaken, *supra* note 3, at 517.

[37] Jan Kleinheisterkamp, *Investment Treaty Law and the Fear for Sovereignty: Transnational Challenges and Solutions*, 78 MOD. L. REV. 793–825, 795 (2015).

[38] The perennial tension between commitment and flexibility underlies all treaty design, *see* PELC, *supra* note 16 ("If the agreement is too tight, it will be undone by events. If it is too flexible, it will be undone by abuse.").

[39] On optimal design of international law, *see generally* JOOST PAUWELYN, OPTIMAL PROTECTION OF INTERNATIONAL LAW: NAVIGATING BETWEEN EUROPEAN ABSOLUTISM AND AMERICAN VOLUNTARISM (2008).

[40] *See generally* Kenneth J. Vandevelde, *A Comparison of the 2004 and 1994 US Model BITs: Rebalancing Investor and Host Country Interests, in* YEARBOOK ON INTERNATIONAL INVESTMENT LAW AND POLICY 2008–9 (Karl P. Sauvant ed., 2009); S. A. Spears, *The Quest for Policy Space in a New Generation of International Investment Agreements*, 13 J. INT'L ECON. L. 1037–1075 (2010).

were highly protective of investors and failed to account for host state policy space.[41] Changes in recent agreements are efforts to rebalance commitments and flexibility by limiting protections and by enhancing flexibilities in IIAs. In the language of contract theory, early IIAs failed to seize regret by failing to allow for legitimate intracontractual nonperformance of investment obligations, for example, through escape clauses. Inserting more policy space into IIAs is thus about finding an optimal balance between commitment and flexibility.

Importantly, however, the "quest for policy space" view misses an important part of the picture. It tends to presume that more host state flexibility automatically means lower investment protection.[42] Investment treaty design becomes a sliding scale between full host state sovereignty and rigid investment protection where more flexibility is traded off for fewer protection commitments. Contract theory, on the other hand, suggests that the relationship between commitment and flexibility is more complex. According to contract theory, more flexibility ex post is a prerequisite to induce more commitments ex ante.

Counterintuitively, then, IIAs with more exceptions can achieve *more* rather than *less* investment protection. Differently put, the relationship between flexibility and commitment is not zero-sum in IIAs. Rather states often only agree to additional investment protection commitments where exceptions provide some policy space. As will be discussed in more detail in Chapter 3, flexibility and commitments thus complement each other. Balancing the two is then not only about finding a middle ground between the right flexibility to seize regret and the right commitment to curb opportunism. It is also about managing their interdependence. High commitments often require high flexibility. Conversely, low flexibility can be a reason for why a treaty has low commitments.

B. Precision as Comprehensive Gap-Filling over Time

Scholars have observed that IIAs have become more precise over time.[43] The trend toward greater precision in IIAs is anticipated by contract theory, since more detailed and comprehensive contracting is a key strategy to render

---

[41] José E. Alvarez, *The Evolving BIT*, Transnat'l Disp. Mgmt. (2010).

[42] Stephen M. Schwebel, *The United States 2004 Model Bilateral Investment Treaty: An Exercise in the Regressive Development of International Law, in* Justice in International Law (2011); José E. Alvarez, *The Return of the State*, 20 Minn. J. Int'l L. 223 (2011).

[43] N. Jansen Calamita, *The Making of Europe's International Investment Policy: Uncertain First Steps*, 39 Legal Issues of Econ. Integration 301–330, 328 (2012); Caroline Henckels, *Protecting Regulatory Autonomy through Greater Precision in Investment Treaties: The TPP, CETA, and TTIP*, 19 J. Int'l Econ. L. 27–50 (2016); Mark S. Manger & Clint Peinhardt, *Learning and the Precision of International Investment Agreements*, 43 Int'l Interactions 1–21 (2017).

contracts more complete. The extent to which contractors strive for more completeness, however, depends on whether it is cost efficient for them to do so.

Achieving a highly complete and precise agreement is costly. States must anticipate future contingencies and invest considerable resources at the drafting stage to write more complete treaties. Because of these costs, drafting sophisticated agreements may initially not be cost efficient. This helps explain why early BITs tended to be short and relatively vague. Especially when sovereignty costs fell exclusively on the rule-taking developing counterpart, there was little incentive on the part of rule-making home states to engage in more comprehensive contracting to carefully delineate obligations and carve out policy space.

This initial calculus, however, has changed over time. As Anne van Aaken writes: "Reactions by states due to learning effects are likely and they can already be diagnosed . . . One way of doing this is for states to write more complete contracts."[44] The surge of ISDS cases revealed the costs of incomplete contracting with adjudicators filling gaps through unanticipated or conflicting interpretations. Tribunals similarly confused intracontractual behavior to seize regret with extracontractual opportunism. Furthermore, the rise of bidirectional investment flows meant that the system's dominant rule-makers began facing ISDS claims themselves. As developed states bore more of the cost of incompleteness it became efficient to write more complete agreements.

At the same time, contracting states could not "reinvent the wheel" and fundamentally depart from prior practice even if an alternative treaty design was readily available. Countries had anchored themselves in a particular treaty language by concluding hundreds of IIAs that would have been costly to renegotiate.[45] Moreover, new treaty language that deviated from existing practice could undermine existing agreements.[46] States thus adjusted rather than revolutionized their practice by adding detail and clarifications to existing vague clauses.[47] Evolution rather than revolution was all the more efficient, because existing provisions had already been tested in investment arbitration. States could

---

[44] Van Aaken, *supra* note 3, at 531, 534.

[45] Furthermore, investment treaties originally sought to provide consistent state practice to reinforce the existence of a universal customary international law minimum standard for the protection for investments abroad. This custom would have been undermined through divergent practice. *See* KENNETH J. VANDEVELDE, U.S. INTERNATIONAL INVESTMENT AGREEMENTS 31 (2009).

[46] *Id.* at 110. Former US negotiator Kenneth Vandevelde points out that the United States was often unwilling to compromise on changing language in specific negotiations fearing that such concessions could be interpreted as clarifications of already concluded treaties, thereby not only changing the level of protection of the agreement at issue but also of all those before it.

[47] Behavioral economists would expect states to make incremental improvements to their treaties in response to changing circumstances as part of a decision-making process known as "anchoring and adjustment." As Thaler and Sustein explain, "[y]ou start with some anchor and adjust in the direction you think is appropriate." RICHARD H. THALER & CASS R. SUNSTEIN, NUDGE: IMPROVING DECISIONS ABOUT HEALTH, WEALTH, AND HAPPINESS 23 (rev. & expanded ed. 2009).

use their clarifications to contract in or out of these interpretations.[48] Finally, clarifications in new treaties could indirectly update the interpretation of similar language in older agreements.[49] Highly path-dependent adjustment to treaty design that produced greater precision was thus a perfectly rational and efficient gap-filling strategy to respond to a changing environment.

C. Taking Back Control by Rewriting Terms of Delegation

Finally, contract theory also helps understand the dynamics between states and investment tribunals accommodating the taking-back-control literature. Contract theory views judicial gap-filling and comprehensive contracting as two substitutable strategies to close contractual gaps. When contractors leave contractual gaps open, they delegate gap-filling powers to courts; when they go to the length of closing contractual gaps ex ante, they alleviate the need for judicial gap filling ex post.

Older incomplete IIAs delegated significant gap-filling power to investment arbitrators. As arbitrator Charles Brower put it, states draft "intentionally vague term[s], designed to give adjudicators a quasi-legislative authority."[50] Indeed, faced with incompleteness, adjudicators have little choice but to close contractual gaps in order to apply a vague treaty to specific facts. In contrast, more complete treaties close these gaps so as to limit the need for judicial lawmaking. As states conclude progressively more detailed agreement, they thus take power away from tribunals. Indeed, in some instances, state-driven gap-filling is used to explicitly overrule or exclude past judicial gap-filling.[51] Changes in contractual completeness are then also shifts in gap-filling power and alter how interpretive questions are decided and by whom.

This relative empowerment of contracting states and disempowerment of tribunals in more complete IIAs creates a tension in investment arbitration practice. Part II of this book will return to this tension in depth. The fact that new treaties are interpreted like old ones can in part be understood as pushback from

---

[48] Cree Jones & Weijia Rao, *Sticky BITs*, 61 HARV. INT'L L.J. 357–406 (2020); Wolfgang Alschner, *The Impact of Investment Arbitration on Investment Treaty Design: Myth Versus Reality*, 42 YALE J. INT'L L. (2017).

[49] As David Gantz points out, through legal argumentation and the use of precedent in investment arbitration newly concluded treaties can affect the interpretation of older agreements and vice versa. David A. Gantz, *The Evolution of FTA Investment Provisions: From NAFTA to the United States-Chile Free Trade Agreement*, 19 AM. U. INT'L L. REV. 679, 688–689, 766 (2003). Chapter 7 will engage with this reasoning in detail.

[50] Charles H. Brower II, *Investor-State Disputes under NAFTA: The Empire Strikes Back*, 40 COLUM. J. TRANSNAT'L L. 43, 78 (2001).

[51] For specific instances of states reacting to controversial awards, *see* Jones & Rao, *supra* note 48.

arbitrators who see the dominant gap-filling status they so long enjoyed threatened through state-driven gap-filling. By rolling back state-driven gap-filling in more complete IIAs, tribunals preserve the interpretive control they enjoyed under incomplete agreements. In short, contract theory provides a lens to understand the dynamics of control and backlash between states and tribunals.

In summary, contract theory provides an attractive meta-framework for understanding the changing design of investment treaties and accommodates partial narratives relating the quest for more policy space, precision, and state control over arbitrators. The remainder of this chapter revisits the empirical results derived in Chapter 1 and argues that the transformation of investment agreements over time has been a drive toward greater contractual completeness (Figure 2.1).

IV. Evolution toward More Complete IIAs

The design variation of IIAs, the y-axis of Figure 2.1, can be interpreted as variation of the treaties' contractual completeness. States may not be perfectly rational actors that consciously seek to develop optimal agreements. Indeed, IIAs are often the result of diverse and at times obscure internal decision-making processes and asymmetric international negotiations.[52] However, contract theory provides a fitting descriptive framework to map the design outcomes resulting from states' lawmaking: a progression toward more complete IIAs.

The evolution of IIA design is a story of progressive gap-filling. Contracting states have made use of the four gap-filling strategies introduced in section II to close gaps left open in highly incomplete IIAs. States differ in the extent to which they pursue each of those strategies. Furthermore, some countries prioritize one gap-filling strategy or another. Although treaties therefore differ in their degree of contractual completeness, the overall trajectory is shared. IIAs across the board have become more complete over time.

A. Mimicking the CCC Design—More Comprehensive and Detailed Contracting

The first strategy for filling gaps consists of more comprehensive and detailed drafting.[53] Contracting states have made increasing use of that strategy. One proxy for detailed drafting is treaty length. Average BIT length has increased from around 2,700 words in the 1990s to almost 10,000 words by the end of the

---

[52] *See generally* Lauge N. Skovgaard Poulsen, Bounded Rationality and Economic Diplomacy: The Politics of Investment Treaties in Developing Countries (2015).

[53] Schropp, *supra* note 1, at 84.

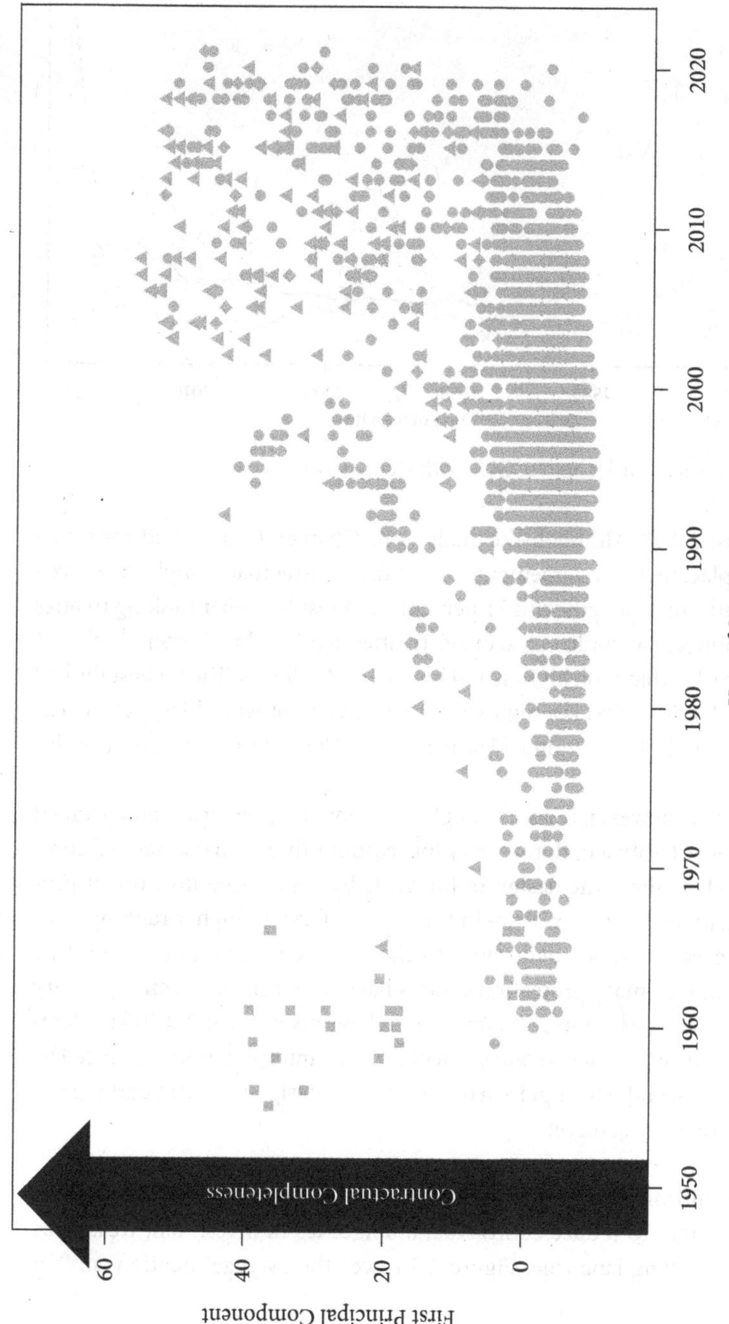

Figure 2.1 The major content variation of IIAs (y-axis) revealed through the principal component analysis is best understood as treaties' varying levels of contractual completeness with incomplete IIAs having low scores and more complete IIAs having high scores

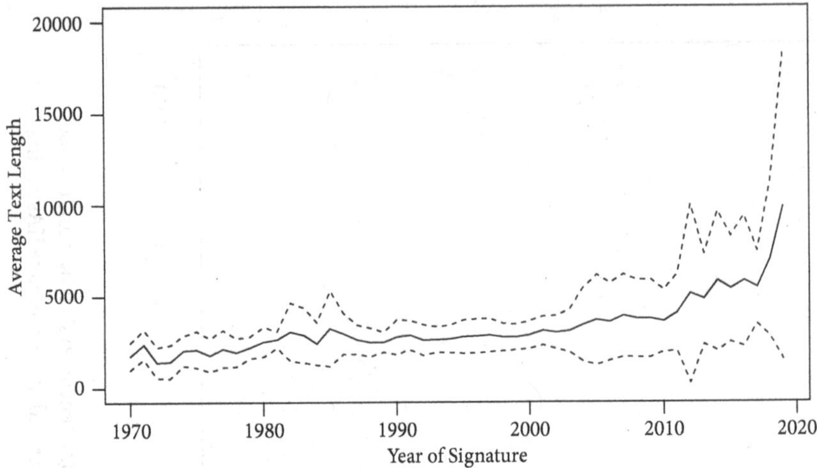

Figure 2.2 Average word length of BITs with standard deviation

2010s (Figure 2.2).[54] Although the analysis in Chapter 1 controlled for treaty length, the placement of agreements along the contractual completeness axis correlates with treaty length with 71 percent. As a result, higher ranking treaties tend to be longer, while lower scoring treaties tend to be shorter. Table 2.1 regroups the BITs that rank highest and lowest in PC1 terms. The highest ranked Rwanda–USA BIT (2008) is a highly detailed agreement with thirty-seven articles. In contrast, the lowest ranked Hungary–Viet Nam BIT (1994) is only twelve articles long.

Length per se, however, is only a rough proxy for comprehensive and detailed drafting because treaty length may vary for reasons other than contractual completeness. States mimic the design of the CCC by delineating investment protection obligations in greater detail in three ways. First, in higher ranking IIAs, states have inserted explicit definitions to clarify the content and scope of their treaties. Second, primary protection clauses have been clarified. Third, primary obligations that are ambiguous or superfluous have been discarded. These elements produce more complete treaties, reject extreme interpretations advanced by arbitral tribunals, and often opt for a moderation in design to square curbing opportunism with seizing regret.

1. More Definitional Language

States have sought to reduce contractual ambiguities in investment treaties by employing clarifying language. Figure 2.3 traces the average mentions of "for

---

[54] This comparison focuses on BITs to make text length comparable.

Table 2.1 Highest and lowest ranked BITs by PC1 score (descending)

Top 10 BITs by Principal Component Score Name and Text Length in Words		Bottom 10 BITs by Principal Component Score Name and Text Length in Words	
Rwanda–USA BIT (2008)	15,393	Hungary–Viet Nam BIT (1994)	2,552
Chile–Hong Kong BIT (2016)	17,627	Belarus–Czechia BIT (1996)	2,460
USA–Uruguay BIT (2005)	16,642	Hungary–Mongolia BIT (1994)	2,305
Australia–Hong Kong BIT (2019)	13,112	Czechia–Hungary BIT (1993)	2,428
Canada–Senegal BIT (2014)	12,833	Czechia–Estonia BIT (1994)	2,524
Canada–Serbia BIT (2014)	11,269	Hungary–Ukraine BIT (1994)	2,338
Canada–Ivory Coast BIT (2014)	15,210	Czechia–Latvia BIT (1994)	2,598
Canada–Guinea BIT (2015)	12,582	South Korea–Poland BIT (1989)	2,242
Canada–Kosovo BIT (2018)	13,166	Hungary–Moldova BIT (1995)	2,336
Burkina Faso–Canada BIT (2015)	13,040	Albania–Hungary BIT (1996)	2,839

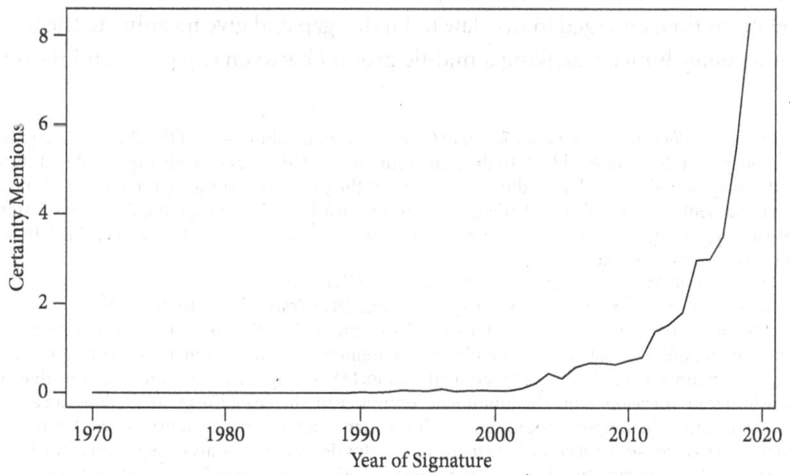

Figure 2.3 Average mentions of "for greater certainty" or "for the avoidance of doubt" per IIA over time

greater certainty" or "for the avoidance of doubt" in IIAs over time, which have increased drastically over time. The results correlated to 60 percent with the completeness scores. A broadened list of definitional words that includes "certainty," "clarity," "doubt," "include," "understood," "means," "nothing," "construed," and "example" results in the highest scoring USA–Rwanda BIT (2008) having 101 mentions of certainty words. The treaty also contains a total of twenty-four explanatory footnotes.

With three such mentions, NAFTA (1992) pioneered the systematic use of such clarifying language. One example is NAFTA Article 1110(8), which clarifies that "[f]or purposes of this Article and *for greater certainty*, a non-discriminatory measure of general application shall not be considered a measure tantamount to an expropriation of a debt security or loan covered by this Chapter solely on the ground that the measure imposes costs on the debtor that cause it to default on the debt" (emphasis added). In a later ISDS submission, the United States explained that such "for greater certainty" language is "not to create or limit a right or obligation but to reflect an understanding that the scope of a particular right or obligation is *already implied* in other provisions of the text."[55]

While some of the clarifications inserted into more complete IIAs aim to prospectively rule out an anticipated ambiguity (like the preceding NAFTA example), others react to (and correct) past (mis)interpretations by arbitral tribunals. The USA–Uruguay BIT (2005), for example, was the first agreement to define the crucial threshold concept of "investment" that delineates the scope of the treaty and the jurisdiction of tribunals. BITs with low principal component scores tend to leave the definition of the term unclear, vaguely stating that the concept entails "every type of asset."[56] Read literally, as Zachary Douglas points out, even a metro ticket could thus qualify as an investment.[57] Conflicting interpretations then emerged in case law to fill this gap and give meaning to the term and its outer limits.[58] Striking a middle ground between expansive and narrow

---

[55] *Pope & Talbot Inc. v. The Government of Canada*, Second Submission of the United States, May 25, 2000, para. 6 (emphasis added). In the same vein, the United States recently explained that these clarifications signal an "understanding [. . .] of what the provisions of the agreement would mean even if that sentence were absent." United States of America Third Non-Disputing Party Submission, *Omega Engineering LLC and Oscar Rivera v. Republic of Panama*, ICSID Case No. ARB/16/42, February 3, 2020, footnote 24.

[56] *See generally* SCOPE AND DEFINITION: A SEQUEL (UNCTAD ed., 2011).

[57] ZACHARY DOUGLAS, THE INTERNATIONAL LAW OF INVESTMENT CLAIMS 163 (2009).

[58] On one extreme, a line of cases followed *Fedex v. Venezuela* and *Salini v. Morocco* and stipulated that a transaction has to satisfy four cumulative requirements to qualify as an investment ("*Salini criteria*"): (1) commitment of capital, (2) certain duration, (3) assumption of risk, and (4) a contribution to the host state's development. The annulment committee in *Mitchell v. Congo* struck down an award for assuming jurisdiction when the underlying investment—an American law firm in the Democratic Republic of Congo—did not contribute to the host state's development thus failing to meet the *Salini* criteria. On the other extreme, the annulment committee in *Malaysian Salvors v. Malaysia* denied the existence of such investment criteria and annulled an award that had applied them concluding that the term investment excludes simple sale contracts, but does not have any intrinsic meaning absent

approaches in the case law, the BIT clarified that "an investment means every asset . . . that has the characteristics of an investment, including such characteristics as the commitment of capital or other resources, the expectation of gain or profit, or the assumption of risk."[59]

2. Clarifying Protective Obligations

States have also sought to clarify heavily litigated provisions such as fair and equitable treatment (FET) and expropriation.

Fair and equitable treatment. No clause epitomizes vagueness more than FET. As discussed in greater detail in Chapter 5, the clause was initially understood as a customary international law reference. The 1967 Organisation for Economic Co-operation and Development (OECD) Draft Convention on the Protection of Foreign Property, on which subsequent European BITs were modeled, explained in the commentary accompanying the Convention that FET was to be understood as grounded in the international law minimum standard.[60] But in subsequent case law a disagreement emerged whether FET denotes an autonomous standard of protection or is linked to the customary international law minimum standard.[61] Tribunals encountering an FET clause without an international law reference have generally interpreted it as setting forth a standard autonomous to customary international law.[62]

In response to these jurisprudential developments, contracting states have sought to reaffirm FET's grounding in the customary international law minimum standard. The USA–Uruguay BIT (2005), for instance, provides in Article 5(2) that "paragraph 1 [detailing the FET obligation] prescribes the customary international law minimum standard of treatment of aliens as the minimum standard of treatment to be afforded to covered investments." These and similar references have since proliferated in the IIA universe (see Figure 2.4).

a definition by the contracting or disputing parties. *See Fedax v. Venezuela*, ICSID Case No. ARB/ 96/3, Decision on Jurisdiction, July 11, 1997, para. 43; *Salini v. Morocco*, ICSID Case No. ARB/00/4, Decision on Jurisdiction, July 23, 2001, para. 56; *Patrick Mitchell v. Democratic Republic of the Congo*, ICSID Case No. ARB/99/7, Decision on the Application for Annulment of the Award, November 1, 2006, paras. 30–33, 48; *Malaysian Historical Salvors, SDN, BHD v. The Government of Malaysia*, ICSID Case No. ARB/05/10, Decision on the Application for Annulment, April 16, 2009.

[59] This formulation includes some of the *Salini* criteria, but, notably, does not mention the contribution to host state development. At the same time, it is more restrictive than what the *Malaysian Salvors* annulment committee deemed to be the ICSID default rule and thus occupies a middle ground between the extreme positions taken in case law.

[60] Notes to art. 1(a), OECD, *Draft Convention on the Protection of Foreign Property. Texts with Notes and Comments* (1967), available at http://www.oecd.org/investment/internationalinvestmen tagreements/39286571.pdf (last accessed July 20, 2017).

[61] Rudolf Dolzer & Christoph Schreuer, Principles of International Investment Law 134 (2d ed. 2012).

[62] Fair and Equitable Treatment, xiv (UNCTAD ed., 2012).

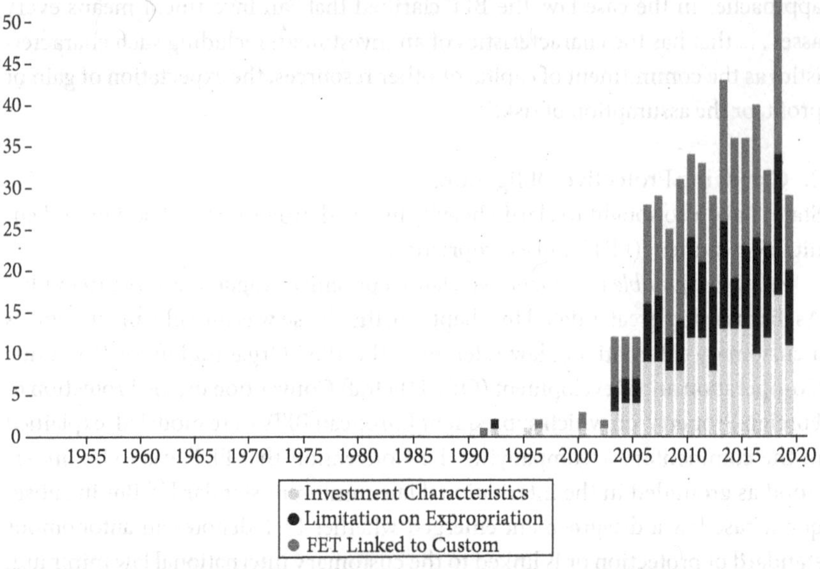

Figure 2.4 Clarifying scope of protective obligations (number of agreements with clause by year of signature 1970–2019; source: EDIT)

Indirect expropriation. Another heavily litigated clause in investment law is expropriation. Similar to FET, compensation for expropriation has historically been tied to customary international law. Several tribunals have held that the expropriation clause itself is a codification or incorporation by reference of the customary international law on expropriation.[63] Moreover, arbitral tribunals have widely recognized that customary international law distinguishes between expropriatory measures mandating compensation and general bona fide regulations not giving rise to compensation.[64]

---

[63] *AIG Capital Partners, Inc. and CJSC Tema Real Estate Company v. Republic of Kazakhstan*, ICSID Case No. ARB/01/6, Award, October 7, 2003, para. 10.3.1 ("Article III incorporates into the BIT international law standards for 'expropriation' and 'nationalisation'"). Similarly, *Generation Ukraine Inc. v. Ukraine*, ICSID Case No. ARB/00/9, Final Award, September 16, 2003, para. 11.3.

[64] *Methanex Corporation v. United States of America*, UNCITRAL, Final Award, August 3, 2005, pt. IV, ch. D, para. 7 ("as a matter of general international law, a non-discriminatory regulation for a public purpose, which is enacted in accordance with due process and, which affects, *inter alios*, a foreign investor or investment is not deemed expropriatory and compensable."). Similarly, the *Saluka v. Czech Republic* tribunal held that "[i]t is now established in international law that States are not liable to pay compensation to a foreign investor when, in the normal exercise of their regulatory powers, they adopt in a non-discriminatory manner bona fide regulations that are aimed at the general welfare." *Saluka Investments B.V. v. Czech Republic*, UNCITRAL, Partial Award, March 17, 2006, para. 255. *See also Glamis Gold, Ltd. v. The United States of America*, UNCITRAL, Final Award, June 8, 2009, para. 354. *El Paso Energy International Company v. Argentine Republic*, ICSID Case No. ARB/03/15, Award, October 31, 2011, paras. 236–240. *SAUR International S.A. v. Argentine Republic*, ICSID Case No. ARB/04/4, Decision on Jurisdiction and Liability, June 6, 2012, paras. 396–401.

Yet absent a clear textual link to customary international law, a risk remains that that an expropriation clause is not read in light of the underlying customary international rules. In response, contracting parties have begun to insert explanatory annexes into their IIAs. The first one to do so was again the USA–Uruguay BIT (2005) that explained in Annex B that the treaty's expropriation clause "is intended to reflect customary international law concerning the obligation of States with respect to expropriation" and that "[e]xcept in rare circumstances, non-discriminatory regulatory actions by a Party that are designed and applied to protect legitimate public welfare objectives, such as public health, safety, and the environment, do not constitute indirect expropriations." Again such clarifications have since proliferated widely (Figure 2.4).

As pointed out earlier, adding new language may close contractual gaps but can also open new ones. As Federico Ortino notes, even in its revised form, primary investment obligations such as FET or expropriation clauses remain standards rather than rules.[65] The main contribution of this clarifying language is, then, not to altogether close but to narrow contractual gaps, limiting the range of permissible interpretations and giving more guidance to future interpreters.

3. Abandoning Vague or Controversial Language

Surprisingly, given the trend toward greater contractual completeness, IIAs with high scores tend to also *omit* certain clauses that are prevalent in more incomplete IIAs. Three clauses are particularly prone to being omitted: (1) arbitrary or discriminatory measure prohibitions, (2) effective means clauses, and (3) umbrella clauses. Rather than lowering levels of contractual completeness these omissions can be understood as eliminating language that proved ambiguous or superfluous language creating costs of misinterpretation without yielding gains of additional investment protection.

Arbitrary or discriminatory measures. In its 2004 model BIT, the United States decided to omit a clause protecting investment from arbitrary or discriminatory measures that had hitherto featured in its BITs from the 1980s onward.[66] A clause prohibiting arbitrary or discriminatory measures appeared in Paragraph (a) of Article 1 of the 1967 OECD Draft Convention together with FET and language promising full protection and security.[67] The commentary to the Convention explained that "[i]t is a well-established general principle of international law

---

[65] Federico Ortino, *Refining the Content and Role of Investment "Rules" and "Standards": A New Approach to International Investment Treaty Making*, 28 ICSID Rev. 152–168 (2013).

[66] The decision attracted criticism for lowering the protective force of US treaties. Schwebel, *supra* note 42, at 157. Committee Report, *supra* note 78, at 10.

[67] "Each Party shall at all times ensure fair and equitable treatment to the property of the nationals of the other Parties. It shall accord within its territory the most constant protection and security to such property and shall not in any way impair the management, maintenance, use, enjoyment or disposal thereof by unreasonable or discriminatory measures."

that a State is bound to respect and protect the property of nationals of other States. From this basic principle flow the three roles [*sic*] contained in paragraph (a) of Article 1."[68] The commentary later refers to the prohibition of discriminatory measures as "a restatement of the law."[69] In the same vein, the letter of submission to the US Congress for ratification of the USA–Bolivia BIT (1998) explains that a similar tripartite paragraph in that treaty[70]

> sets out a minimum standard of treatment based on standards found in customary international law. The obligations to accord fair and equitable treatment and full protection and security are explicitly cited, as is each Party's obligation not to impair, through unreasonable and discriminatory means, the management, conduct, operation, and sale or other disposition of covered investments. The general reference to international law also implicitly incorporates other fundamental rules of customary international law regarding the treatment of foreign investment.

Even though the clause was thus conceived as a reference to customary international law, the absence of an explicit reference in the wording itself led arbitral tribunals to interpret it autonomously.[71] A literal interpretation, however, led to overlap and duplication between provisions. On one end, tribunals have found that "[a]ny measure that might involve arbitrariness or discrimination is in itself contrary to fair and equitable treatment."[72] On the other end, as stated by the *BG Group v Argentina* tribunal "a measure in breach of the national treatment or MFN standards . . . would unavoidably also be 'discriminatory' in the sense of [the arbitrary and discriminatory measure prohibition]."[73] Due to its overlap with FET on one side and with national and MFN treatment on the other side,

---

[68] *OECD Draft Convention Commentary*, *supra* note 60, at 8.

[69] *Id.* 11.

[70] Art. 2(3): "(a) Each Party shall at all times accord to covered investments fair and equitable treatment and full protection and security, and shall in no case accord treatment less favorable than that required by international law. (b) Neither Party shall in any way impair by unreasonable and discriminatory measures the management, conduct, operation, and sale or other disposition of covered investments."

[71] The Lauder tribunal, for instance, thus approached the standard based on its literal meaning: "The Treaty does not define an arbitrary measure. According to Black's Law Dictionary, arbitrary means '*depending on individual discretion; (...) founded on prejudice or preference rather than on reason or fact.*'" *Ronald S. Lauder v. Czech Republic*, UNCITRAL, Final Award, September 3, 2001, para. 221.

[72] *CMS Gas Transmission Company v. Republic of Argentina*, ICSID Case No. ARB/01/8, Award, May 12, 2005, para. 290. Similarly, *El Paso Energy International Company v. Argentine Republic*, ICSID Case No. ARB/03/15, Award, October 31, 2011, para. 290.

[73] *BG Group Plc. v. Republic of Argentina*, UNCITRAL, Award, December 24, 2007, para. 355. The 1967 *OECD Draft Convention*, in contrast, did not contain a National Treatment or MFN clause, making the nondiscrimination a useful addition.

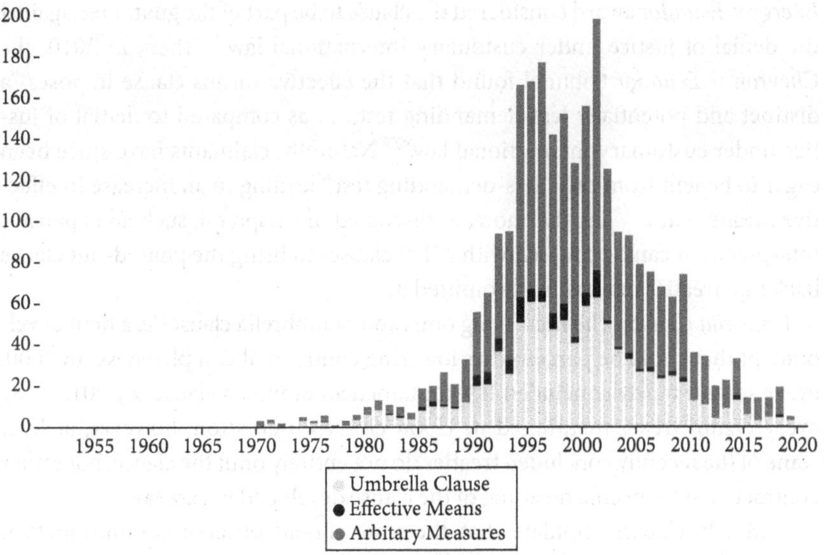

Figure 2.5 Phasing out unclear or redundant protective obligations (number of agreements with clause by year of signature 1970–2019; source: EDIT)

the arbitrary measures clause thus became largely redundant. Its exclusion in recent treaties with high completeness scores is part of an effort to remedy such redundancy. The clause is now being phased out around the globe (Figure 2.5). While in 2000 around 80 percent of newly concluded BITs contained the clause, this number had dropped to 30 percent by 2015.

Effective means. A similar fate has met the effective means clause. First introduced in the American treaty program in 1983 as a way to protect against denial of justice and to ensure access to local courts,[74] the clause became a sporadic but consistent feature of IIAs. At the height of its popularity in 2001, it was included in 7 percent of newly concluded agreements. It has since become extremely rare. Even its former champion, the United States has moved the clause from the treaty body into its preamble starting with the 2004 US model BIT. Commentators assert that the drafters made this revision, because they deemed customary international law and other treaty standards to provide sufficient protection, making the clause unnecessary and duplicative.[75]

Ironically, in parallel to its demise in treaty-making, effective means clauses have become popular in investment arbitration proceedings. The 2008 *Duke*

[74] Jessica Wirth, *"Effective Means" Means; The Legacy of Chevron v. Ecuador*, 52 COLUM. J. TRANSNAT'L L. 325, 331–332 (2013).
[75] VANDEVELDE, *supra* note 45, at 415; Wirth, *supra* note 74, at 333.

Energy v. Ecuador award considered the clause to be part of the guarantee against the denial of justice under customary international law.[76] Then, in 2010, the *Chevron v. Ecuador* tribunal found that the effective means clause imposes "a distinct and potentially less-demanding test . . . as compared to denial of justice under customary international law."[77] Naturally, claimants have since been eager to benefit from this "less-demanding test," leading to an increase in effective means claims.[78] Furthermore, as discussed in Chapter 4, such an expansive interpretation can be coupled with MFN clauses to bring the phased-out clause back into treaties that explicitly omitted it.

Umbrella clauses. The increasing omission of umbrella clauses is a final development that could be perceived as lowering contractual completeness. In 2000, every second newly concluded IIA contained an umbrella clause. By 2015, only every eighth treaty mentioned it. Upon closer observation, however, at least some of the recently concluded treaties do not entirely omit the clause, but rather contract on one specific meaning of the clause developed in case law.

Umbrella clauses stipulate that the state should observe commitments it entered into vis-à-vis the investor.[79] The clause has given rise to starkly divergent arbitral interpretations.[80] On one extreme, the tribunal in *Noble Venture v. Romania* found that an umbrella clause could transform contractual obligations under municipal law into treaty obligations, concomitantly turning contractual breaches into treaty breaches.[81] On the other extreme, the tribunal in *SGS v. Pakistan* rejected the claim that an umbrella clause could incorporate municipal obligations into the treaty, since it would render other substantive obligations in the BIT redundant and defeat any choice of forum clause agreed on in a contract.[82] It instead considered the umbrella clause to play a residual role in exceptional circumstances, for example, when the state fails to honor an arbitration clause previously agreed to in a contract.[83]

Occupying a middle ground, the tribunal in *SGS v. Philippines* held that an umbrella clause

---

[76] *Duke Energy Electroquil Partners and Electroquil S.A. v. Republic of Ecuador*, ICSID Case No. ARB/04/19, Award, August 18, 2008, para. 391.

[77] *Chevron Corporation (U.S.A.) and Texaco Petroleum Corporation (U.S.A.) v. Republic of Ecuador [I]*, PCA Case No. AA 277, Partial Award on the Merits, March 30, 2010, para. 244.

[78] *See generally* Wirth, *supra* note 74.

[79] *See generally* Anthony Sinclair, *The Origins of the Umbrella Clause in the International Law of Investment Protection*, 20 ARBITRATION INT'L 411–434 (2004).

[80] James Crawford, *Treaty and Contract in Investment Arbitration*, 24 ARB. INTERNATIONAL 351–374, 367–368 (2008).

[81] *Noble Ventures, Inc. v. Romania*, ICSID Case No. ARB/01/11, Award, October 12, 2005, paras. 53, 62.

[82] *SGS Société Générale de Surveillance S.A. v. Islamic Republic of Pakistan*, ICSID Case No. ARB/01/13, Award on Jurisdiction, August 6, 2003, paras. 167–168.

[83] *Id.* para. 172.

makes it a breach of the BIT for the host State to fail to observe binding commitments, including contractual commitments, which it has assumed with regard to specific investments. But it does not convert the issue of the extent or content of such obligations into an issue of international law.[84]

Under the latter view, as James Crawford explains, the umbrella clause provides an additional mechanism for the enforcement of contractual claims, without however altering the municipal law character of the underlying contractual obligation.[85] Hence, in that reading, the umbrella clause fulfills a jurisdictional rather than claim-transformational function. It is this latter interpretation of the umbrella clause, which is typically included in US treaties with higher scores.[86] Hence, just like new definitional language and more detailed obligations, these omissions do not reduce but clarify the scope of the contractual relationship closing gaps through more detailed contracting.

B. Seizing Regret—Adding Escape Clauses

In addition to mimicking the design of the CCC through more carefully tailored commitments, a second gap-filling strategy aims to replicate the CCC's effect through escape clauses. Escape clauses provide flexibility by allowing an intracontractual departure from an obligation where it is efficient to do so.[87] One type of flexibility clause is the contingency clause, which specifies outcomes ex ante that justify contractual nonperformance ex post.[88] In investment law, these clauses are better known as carveout or exceptions and come in two variants (1) public policy and security exceptions, and (2) coordinating exceptions.

1. Proliferating Public Policy and Security Exceptions
From its earliest days, BIT signatories were concerned that investment protection obligations could be interpreted as compromising the state's police powers, in particular when it comes to regulating health and public order.

---

[84] *SGS Société Générale de Surveillance S.A. v. Republic of the Philippines*, ICSID Case No. ARB/02/6, Decision on Jurisdiction, January 29, 2004, para. 128.

[85] Crawford, *supra* note 80, at 370.

[86] Article 24(1) of the USA–Uruguay BIT (2005), for example, sets out the scope of jurisdiction of an arbitral tribunal under the treaty as encompassing "a claim (i) that the respondent has breached (A) an obligation under Articles 3 through 10 [of the treaty], (B) an investment authorization, or (C) an investment agreement" with the latter two referring to contractual arrangements governed by municipal law. Hence, rather than abandoning the idea of umbrella clauses altogether, recent, more complete treaties retain it, albeit in its moderate, jurisdictional guise.

[87] SCHROPP, *supra* note 1, at 86.

[88] *Id.* at 86.

Already the Germany–Pakistan BIT (1959) specified in its Protocol that "[m]easures taken for reasons of public security and order, public health or morality shall not be deemed as discrimination." Yet as the field developed, these exceptions fell into increasing disuse. Only more recently have general public policy exceptions and national security exceptions become more widespread (Figure 2.6). By 2019, three out of four newly concluded treaties contained such exceptions.

Particularly noteworthy is a proliferation of public policy exceptions modeled on Article XX of the General Agreement on Tariffs and Trade (GATT). Those exceptions first emerged in Canadian agreements in the mid-1990s and are now also included in treaties of South American, African, Middle-Eastern, and Asian countries.[89] In contrast to security exceptions that often allow a respondent to auto-determine when the conditions of the exception are met, GATT XX–type clauses attach strict and verifiable condition to its invocation.[90] From a contract theoretical point of view, such tailored, tightly regulated policy exceptions are preferred since they allow contracting states and adjudicators to distinguish

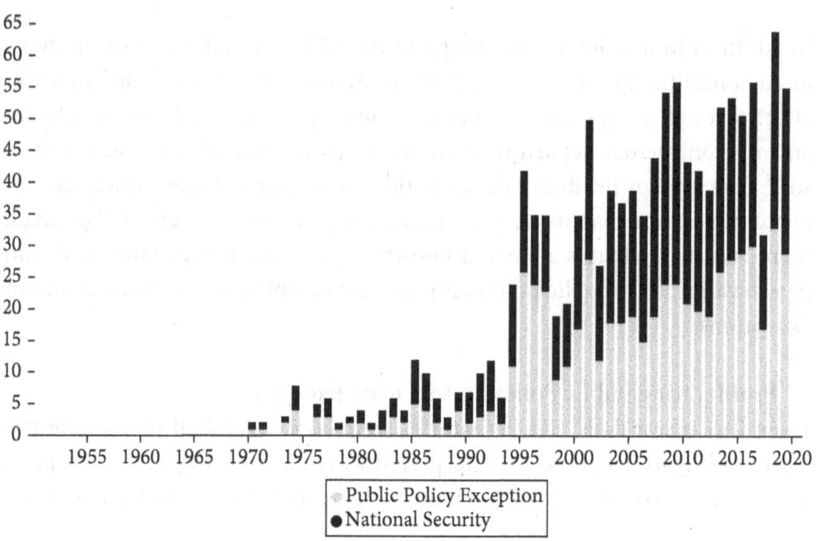

Figure 2.6 Proliferation of public policy and security exceptions (number of agreements with clause by year of signature 1970–2019; source: EDIT)

---

[89] *See, e.g.*, Sudan–Uganda BIT (2001), Singapore–Jordan BIT (2004), Saint Vincent and the Grenadines–Taiwan (2009), Japan–Columbia (2011), Turkey–Cameron (2012).

[90] These conditions are typically included in an introductory chapeau and often require a strong nexus ("necessary to") between the measure and the public policy objective. The Canada–Peru BIT (2006), for instance, reads:

> Subject to the requirement that such measures are not applied in a manner that would constitute arbitrary or unjustifiable discrimination between investments or between investors,

between seizing regret (using the exception) and opportunism (abusing the exception). These exceptions function as escape clauses. When their conditions are met, conduct otherwise inconsistent with the treaty becomes treaty-conforming, saving a respondent from liability.

2. Proliferating Economic Coordination Exceptions

Economic exceptions and exclusions—some applying to specific provisions, others to the treaty as a whole—form a second set of escape clauses. Contrary to public policy and national security exception, however, their primary purpose is not to provide policy space but to manage normative conflicts with overlapping international economic law regimes. As the contractual scope of IIAs expanded, it became increasingly important to ensure that IIAs do not prohibit welfare maximizing conduct that was specifically allowed or mandated by international tax, trade, intellectual property, or financial law (Figure 2.7).

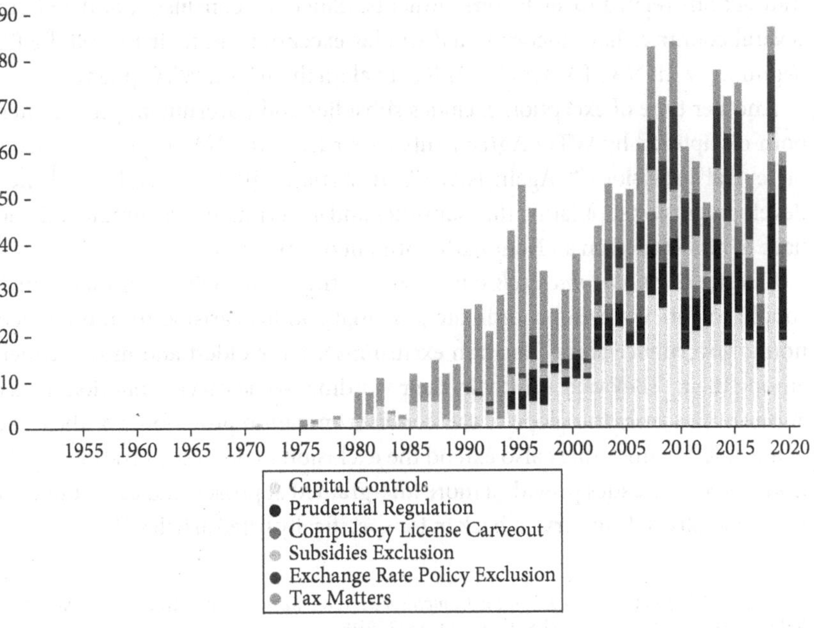

Figure 2.7 Rise of economic coordination exceptions and exclusions (number of agreements with clause by year of signature 1970–2019; source: EDIT)

or a disguised restriction on international trade or investment, nothing in this Agreement shall be construed to prevent a Party from adopting or enforcing measures necessary:

(a) to protect human, animal or plant life or health;
(b) to ensure compliance with laws and regulations that are not inconsistent with the provisions of this Agreement; or
(c) for the conservation of living or non-living exhaustible natural resources.

Clause-level exceptions. Possible inconsistencies between investment treaty obligations and other state commitments have arisen over time and risk to make IIAs overly constraining. First, with the conclusion of the WTO Agreements in 1994 potential conflicts emerged. Article 31 of the Agreement on Trade-Related Aspects of Intellectual Property Rights (TRIPS) allows countries to circumscribe the rights of patent holders by issuing compulsory licenses. Given that intellectual property rights also form part of the definition of investment in most IIAs, compulsory licenses could be conceptualized as expropriation.[91] In response, some WTO members have begun to carve them out from the scope of expropriation clauses in higher scoring IIAs to ensure that they are regulated exclusively by the TRIPS agreement.[92]

Similarly, Article XII of the General Agreement on Trade in Services (GATS) introduced a multilateral exception "in the event of serious balance-of-payments . . . [to] adopt or maintain restrictions on trade in services on which it has undertaken specific commitments, including on payments or transfers for transactions related to such commitments." Since the conclusion of the GATS, several countries have incorporated similar exceptions in their BITs and FTAs beginning with NAFTA Article 2014(1) to align them with WTO practice.[93]

Another type of exception excludes subsidies and government procurement both disciplined by WTO Agreements either from the IIA scope or the scope of several provisions.[94] Again NAFTA, in Article 1108(7), spearheaded these developments by stipulating that subsidies and government procurement do not have to be awarded on an National Treatment or MFN basis.

Treaty exceptions and exclusions. Contracting states have also increasingly sought to anticipate and coordinate potential conflicts arising from other economic governance areas. Taxation exclusions are the oldest and most frequent among them. They vary starkly in their wording, some carving out double taxation treaties from the scope of the nondiscrimination provision[95] or the treaty as a whole,[96] while others also extend the exclusion to domestic taxation regulation.[97] Recent treaties provide a more fine-grained approach and carve out taxation generally only to carve it back in for specifically listed articles .[98]

---

[91] Christopher Gibson, *A Look at the Compulsory License in Investment Arbitration: The Case of Indirect Expropriation*, 25 Am. U. Int'l L. Rev. 357 (2010).

[92] *See, e.g.,* Switzerland–Egypt BIT (2010), art. 6(6); Belgium–Colombia BIT (2009), art. IX(8); Canada–Panama BIT (1996), art. VI(1)b); USA–Uruguay BIT (2005), art. 6(5).

[93] These exceptions are particularly frequent in Japanese (e.g., Japan–Korea BIT (2002), art. 17(1)), Finnish (e.g., Finland–Zambia BIT (2005), art. 7(5)), Turkish (e.g., Turkey–Tanzania BIT (2011), art. 8(3)), and Mexican BITs (Mexico–Austria BIT (1998), art. 7(6).

[94] *See, e.g.,* USA–Uruguay BIT (2005), art. 14(5); Canada–BIT (1996), art. 6(2).

[95] United Arab Emirates–Pakistan BIT (1995), art. 3(4); Australia–Czech Republic BIT (1993), art. 4(b).

[96] Denmark–Russia BIT (1993), art. 11(3).

[97] Spain–Croatia BIT (1997), art. IV(4).

[98] Japan–Korea BIT (2002), art. 19(1) & (2). "Nothing in this Agreement shall apply to taxation measures except as expressly provided in paragraphs 2, 3 and 4 of this Article. Articles 1, 3, 7, 10, 22 and 23 shall apply to taxation measures."

Currency and prudential financial measure exceptions are a more recent addition. These exceptions strive to ensure that IIAs do not compromise a state's ability to regulate its financial system or to change its monetary policy. Both exceptions are first found in NAFTA Article 1410, which states in Paragraph 1 that "[n]othing in this Part [which includes Chapter 11] shall be construed to prevent a Party from adopting or maintaining reasonable measures for prudential reasons . . ." and in paragraph 2 that "[n]othing in this Part applies to non-discriminatory measures of general application taken by any public entity in pursuit of monetary and related credit policies or exchange rate policies." Similar clauses have been inserted into other high-scoring treaties, principally by the US, Canada, and Japan.[99]

In sum, treaties with higher contractual completeness scores tend to include more escape clauses to seize regret. These escape clauses regulate the interplay between states' regulatory prerogatives and investment protection (public policy and security exceptions), as well as other international economic regimes and IIAs (economic exceptions).

C. Relational Contracting

A third route to remedy contractual incompleteness disincentivizes opportunism through relationship-building. The more relational tissue holds the contract's provisions together, the less likely it will be that contractual gaps give rise to opportunism. Simon Schropp identifies two elements in this strategy, examples of which are increasingly found in high-scoring investment treaties: (1) diligent drafting and the use of preambular language, and (2) establishing an ongoing relationship between contractors.[100]

1. Diligent Drafting and Preambular Language

More complete treaties explicitly embed IIAs in wider concerns of the relationship between the contracting states both through more extensive preambles and new substantive clauses.

Preambles. Preambles are an important means to add contextual fabric to an IIA as they communicate a treaty's object and purpose and inform its interpretation. Preambles in low-scoring treaties tend to focus primarily on investment protection as overarching purpose. To provide a more nuanced picture of the multiple goals underlying IIAs, states have begun to insert more contextual language in their preambles including references to sustainable development and

---

[99] *See, e.g.,* USA–Uruguay BIT (2005), art. 20(1) and (2); Canada–Philippines BIT (1995), art. 11; Japan–Korea BIT (2002), arts. 17 & 18.

[100] SCHROPP, *supra* note 1, at 93.

human rights.[101] In the process, preambles have increased considerably in length from around one hundred words on average in the 1970s to over five hundred words on average in the 2010s.

Substantive clauses. In addition, states increasingly embed investment protection into the wider fabric of investment relations (Figure 2.8). Commitments not to weaken environmental or labor standards in order to attract investment first appeared in NAFTA Article 1114 and have since found their way growing number of high-scoring IIAs.[102] Similarly, corruption-related provisions have been included in more complete IIAs.[103] Some treaties also begin imposing obligations on investors, albeit in hortatory terms, through the use of corporate social responsibility (CSR). Such CSR clauses are increasingly inserted into IIAs.[104]

---

[101] Spears, *supra* note 40, at 1064–1069. A particularly extensive preamble constructing a nuanced contractual context can be found in the Austria–Nigeria BIT (2013):

> RECALLING that foreign direct investments are vital complements to national and international development efforts, as expressed at the United Nations International Conference on the Financing of Development held in Monterrey, Mexico, in March 2002 (the Monterrey Consensus), RECOGNISING that agreement upon the treatment to be accorded to investors and their investments will contribute to the efficient utilisation of economic resources, the creation of employment opportunities and the improvement of living standards, EMPHASISING that fair, transparent and predictable investment regimes based on the rule of law both complement and benefit the world trading system, DESIRING to strengthen their ties of friendship and to promote greater economic co-operation between them with respect to investment by nationals and enterprises of one Contracting Party in the territory of the other, REAFFIRMING the commitments under the 2006 Ministerial declaration of the UN Economic and Social Council of Full Employment and Decent Work, REFERING to the international obligations and commitments concerning respect for human rights, RECOGNISING that investment, as an engine of economic growth, can play a key role in ensuring that economic growth is sustainable, COMMITTED to achieving these objectives in a manner consistent with the protection of health, safety, and the environment, and the promotion of internationally recognised labour standards, EXPRESSING their belief that responsible corporate behaviour can contribute to mutual confidence between enterprises and host countries, EMPHASISING the necessity for all governments and civil actors alike to adhere to UN anti corruption efforts, most notably the UN Convention against Corruption (2003), TAKING NOTE OF the principles of the UN Global Compact, ACKNOWLEDGING that investment agreements and multilateral agreements on the protection of environment, human rights or labour rights are meant to foster global sustainable development and that any possible inconsistencies there should be resolved without relaxation of standards of protection, RECOGNIZING the existence of any Customs Union, Economic Union, Free Trade Area or Regional Economic Integration Agreement to which the Contracting Parties belong, and CONSIDERING that investment relations should be promoted and economic co-operation strengthened in accordance with the internationally accepted principles of mutual respect for sovereignty, equality, mutual benefit, non-discrimination and mutual confidence, HAVE AGREED AS FOLLOWS . . .

[102] *See, e.g.,* Japan–Iraq BIT (2012), art. 22; Switzerland–Mexico BIT (1995), Ad art. 3; Belgium–Sudan BIT (2005), art. 5(2).

[103] Guatamala–Trinidad and Tobago BIT (2013), art. 17(2): "In accordance with their respective laws and regulations, each Contracting Party shall endeavour to: . . . uphold anticorruption practices in accordance with the United Nations Convention Against Corruption, done at New York, October 31, 2003"; *see also* Japan–Iraq BIT (2012), art. 9.

[104] ALSCHNER & TUERK, *supra* note 35. One example that combines sustainable development considerations and investor responsibilities referencing the OECD Guidelines for Multinational Enterprises can be found in the Netherlands–United Arab Emirates BIT (2013):

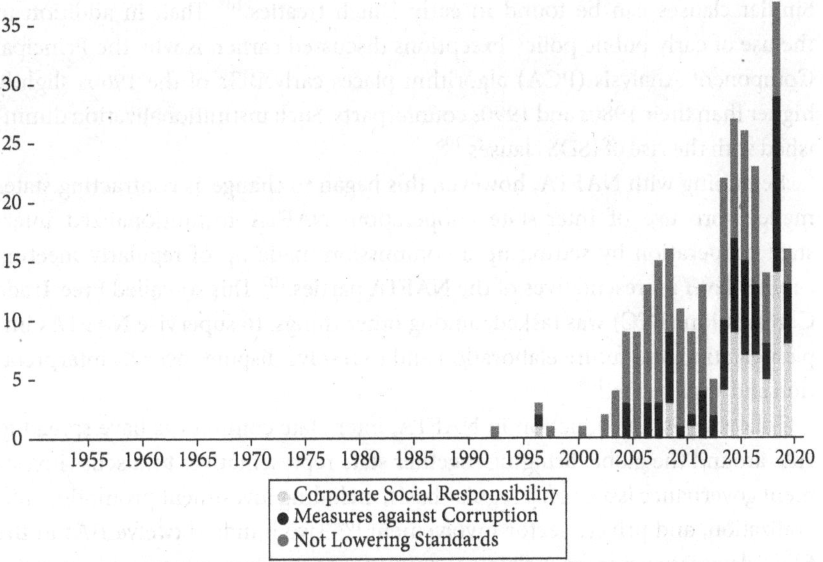

Figure 2.8 Provisions situating investment protection in broader fabric of investment relations (number of agreements with clause by year of signature 1970–2019; source: EDIT)

2. Relationship-Building between Contracting States

Higher scoring treaties also provide for structures that ensure ongoing dialogue and cooperation between states. In its early days, BITs often set up inter-state committees to build a relationship between the contracting states. The Switzerland–Niger BIT (1962), for instance, provides in Article 9 for the formation of a mixed commission at the request of one of the Contracting Parties to oversee the treaty's implementation:

> Une commission mixte se réunit à la demande de l'une ou l'autre des deux Parties Contractantes. Elle surveille l'application du présent accord et convient de toutes dispositions en vue d'améliorer les relations économiques entre les deux pays.

Article 2: 2. Both Contracting Parties recognize the right of each Contracting Party to establish its own level of domestic environmental protection and its own sustainable development policy and priorities, and to adopt or modify its environmental laws and regulations and shall strive as far as possible to continue to improve their laws and regulations.

3. Each Contracting Party shall promote as far as possible and in accordance with their domestic laws the application of the OECD Guidelines for Multinational Enterprises to the extent that is not contrary to their domestic laws.

Similar clauses can be found in early Dutch treaties.[105] That, in addition to the use of early public policy exceptions discussed earlier, is why the Principal Component Analysis (PCA) algorithm places early BITs of the 1960s slightly higher than their 1980s and 1990s counterparts. Such institutionalization diminished with the rise of ISDS clauses.[106]

Beginning with NAFTA, however, this began to change as contracting states made more use of inter-state cooperation. NAFTA institutionalized inter-state cooperation by setting up a commission made up of regularly meeting cabinet-level representatives of the NAFTA parties.[107] This so-called Free Trade Commission (FTC) was tasked, among other things, to supervise NAFTA's implementation and future elaboration and to resolve disputes over its interpretation and application.[108]

Following its introduction in NAFTA, inter-state committees have spread to IIAs around the globe, bringing together state representatives to discuss investment governance issues on a regular basis, including investment promotion, liberalization, and private sector involvement.[109] Two hundred twelve IIAs in the EDIT dataset provide for such joint commissions, up from only twenty-five prior to NAFTA. IIAs are thus increasingly conceived as an ongoing relationship that is not exclusively concerned with investment protection but extends to the governance of investment relations more generally.

Nowhere is this more apparent than in recent Brazilian BITs that are explicitly styled as "investment cooperation" rather than "investment protection" agreement and institutionalize an ongoing inter-state cooperation that

---

[105] Netherlands–Sudan BIT (1970), art. XIV:

> (1) The Contracting Parties agree to establish a Mixed Commission, composed of representatives appointed by them. 2) The Mixed Commission shall meet at the request of one of the Contracting Parties, to discuss any matters pertaining to the implementation of the present Agreement and to consider means of promoting their economic co-operation. 3) The Mixed Commission shall keep under review the development of the economic relations between the two countries, both in bilateral and multilateral contexts. It shall moreover make recommendations to the respective Governments in cases where the objectives of this Agreement might be furthered and a fuller measure of economic cooperation might be obtained.

See similarly Netherlands–Cameroon BIT (1965), art. 11.

[106] One objective of ISDS was to pacify international relations by "push[ing] the home State of the investor back to the sidelines." *Republic of Ecuador v. United States of America*, PCA Case No. 2012-5, Expert Opinion of Prof. Christian Tomuschat (August 24, 2012). According to Tomuschat (para. 32), the object and purpose of BITs was that "[i]nvestment disputes should be taken out from their political context, being instead entrusted to independent arbitrators, the pronouncements of which the contracting parties would respect," which he contrasts to a process where "controversial points would be settled by agreement between the parties concerned, through a political process."

[107] NAFTA art. 2001(1) & (5).

[108] NAFTA art. 2001(2)–(4).

[109] *See, e.g.*, Japan–Papua New Guinea BIT (2011), art. 21; Japan–Malaysia FTA (2005), art. 92.

seeks to identify investment promotion opportunities and prevent investment disputes.[110]

D. Managing Delegation—Curtailing Judicial Gap-Filling

The final strategy to address contractual incompleteness is delegating adjudicatory and interpretive authority to courts or tribunal to fill contractual gaps ex post. From the outset, IIAs have made use of this gap-filling strategy. Early treaties exclusively delegated dispute settlement to inter-state tribunals, but starting in the late 1960s, delegation to ISDS tribunals became gradually more widespread, which through its frequent use in practice has eclipsed the former in importance. What sets high completeness treaties apart from low-scoring IIAs, however, are the terms of delegation.

These terms of delegation are becoming more explicit, curbing disputing parties' autonomy and arbitral discretion on procedural matters. While delegation-related treaty clauses had long occupied only one or two articles in IIAs, they have begun to outnumber substantive clauses sometimes 2:1.[111] These new procedural provisions can be grouped in three buckets. First, the bulk of new clauses clarifies and streamlines ISDS proceedings regulating everything from requirements of standing to consolidation of claims to the types of remedies available. In the process, they take away discretion from tribunals and disputants to decide these matters ad hoc.

Second, new clauses have enhanced transparency and public participation in ISDS proceedings. This includes provisions that allow opening ISDS hearings to the public, that permit the acceptance of amicus curiae submissions, or that make the publication of awards nondiscretionary. Together, these innovations align investment arbitration more closely with public law litigation paradigms.[112]

Third, contracting states have begun delegating ex post gap-filling to institutions other than ISDS tribunals. Starting with NAFTA Chapter 11, the number of treaty-based institutions to which gap-filling power is being delegated

---

[110] Catherine Titi, *International Investment Law and the Protection of Foreign Investment in Brazil*, 13 Transnat'l Disp. Mgmt. 8–10 (2016).

[111] In the first investment treaty between Germany and Pakistan signed in 1959, only a single article (out of fourteen) dealt with dispute settlement (which was exclusively inter-state). Thirty-five years later in NAFTA, one can count over thirty articles that deal with state-to-state and investor-state arbitration outnumbering fourteen substantive investment protection clauses.

[112] J. Anthony VanDuzer, *Enhancing the Procedural Legitimacy of Investor-State Arbitration Through Transparency and Amicus Curiae Participation*, 52 McGill L.J. 685 (2007). Jack J. Coe Jr., *Transparency in the Resolution of Investor-State Disputes—Adoption, Adaptation, and NAFTA Leadership*, 54 U. Kan. L. Rev. 1339, 1364–1369 (2005).

has expanded beyond arbitral tribunals with a view to allowing for more state interventions ex post. High-scoring IIAs also delegate power to expert bodies on taxation or financial regulation as well as inter-state committees regrouping state representatives. As a result, ISDS is "embedded" in a wider array of state and non-state interventions.[113] This has concomitantly reduced the exclusivity of ISDS gap-filling authority.

Nondisputing party interventions. NAFTA was the first modern investment treaty to enshrine the direct participation of nondisputing state parties in ISDS.[114] NAFTA Articles 1127 and 1129 "make the participation of non-disputing NAFTA Parties in Chapter 11 arbitrations [an] inter-governmental business":[115] the responding party has to deliver copies of the notice of claims as well as the pleadings to the other state parties (Article 1127) and share evidentiary documents upon request (Article 1129).[116] Most importantly, a nondisputing party has the right to make submissions to the tribunal on a question of interpretation upon serving notice to the disputing parties (Article 1128).[117] Such involvement has become commonplace in recent high-scoring FTAs and BITs.[118]

Renvoi to expert bodies of the contracting states. Renvoi provisions delegate specific issues raised in an investment dispute to representatives of contracting states. Under Article 2103(6) of NAFTA, the investor has to refer a claim against an allegedly expropriatory taxation measure to the tax authorities of the NAFTA parties before it can proceed to arbitration. If the authorities determine that the measure does not amount to an expropriation, this will preclude the claim from going forward, otherwise it falls back to the arbitral tribunal to decide. Similarly, under NAFTA Article 1415, the question whether a financial regulation challenged before investor-state arbitration is maintained for prudential reasons must be submitted to the NAFTA Financial Service Committee, consisting of representatives from the three NAFTA states' financial authorities. If they agree that the prudential exception in Article 1410 applies, this will preclude liability, otherwise the tribunal will have to make a finding on the issue. Although such

---

[113] Wolfgang Alschner, *The Return of the Home State and the Rise of "Embedded" Investor-State Arbitration, in* THE ROLE OF THE STATE IN INVESTOR-STATE ARBITRATION 293–333 (2015).

[114] Strictly speaking, nondisputing party interventions are not new. Already the 1962 version of the OECD Draft Convention on the Protection of Foreign Property foresaw such a right. *See* Annex, para 6b]; *see* ANTONIO R. PARRA, THE HISTORY OF ICSID 16 (2012). Yet before NAFTA, nondisputing party submissions were not included in BITs.

[115] Martin Hunter & Alexei Barbuk, *Procedural Aspects of Non-Disputing Party Interventions in Chapter 11 Arbitrations,* 3 ASPER REV. INT'L BUS. & TRADE L. 151, 163 (2003).

[116] Alschner, *supra* note 113.

[117] MEG KINNEAR, ANDREA BJORKLUND, & JOHN F. G. HANNAFORD, INVESTMENT DISPUTES UNDER NAFTA. AN ANNOTATED GUIDE TO NAFTA CHAPTER 11 1128–1122 (2006).

[118] *See, e.g.,* COMESA Investment Agreement (2007), art. 7(2), available at http://vi.unctad.org/ files/wksp/iiawksp08/docs/wednesday/Exercise%20Materials/invagreecomesa.pdf (last accessed January 31, 2014).

renvoi risks reducing the credibility of IIAs if tax agencies are subject to regulatory capture from governments,[119] these expert bodies typically enjoy independence under domestic law and possess an in-depth understanding of tax and financial matters that ISDS tribunals may lack, which justify their role.[120]

Authoritative interpretations. Pursuant to NAFTA Article 1131(2), the contracting parties can issue a joint interpretation through the NAFTA FTC, consisting of cabinet-level representatives of the contracting states,[121] which are binding on an investor-state tribunal. Moreover, under Article 1132, a contracting state can request the FTC to issue an authoritative interpretation as to the scope of nonconforming measures listed in the treaty's annexes carving out country specific measures or sectors from the scope of investment protection. When the FTC is unable to reach an agreement, the issue falls back to the investor-state tribunal to determine whether a challenged measure benefits from the carveout or not. Following NAFTA, authoritative interpretation clauses have spread to BITs and FTA investment chapters. While some treaties follow NAFTA in setting up inter-state committees charged with the task to issue such interpretations, others leave it directly with the contracting states.[122]

Denial of benefits. Denial of benefits clauses were first introduced through the American BIT program and are frequently found in higher scoring treaties. These denial of benefit clauses allow contracting parties to either jointly or unilateral decide to withdraw treaty protection for investments that are owned and controlled by investors originating from third parties.[123] The clause is thus a means to preserve the bilateral nature of the treaty bargain preventing "free-riding," that is, indirect investment channeled through the contracting parties merely to gain protection under the treaty.[124]

Together, more precise substantive and procedural rules, increased means of intervention by states, and the co-delegation of interpretive authority to state bodies in more complete IIAs curtails the gap-filling authority of tribunals in favor of gap-filling by the contracting states.

---

[119] Van Aaken, *supra* note 28. William Park thus labeled NAFTA art. 2103(6) a "tax veto" enjoyed by the contracting states. William W. Park, *Arbitration and the Fisc: NAFTA's Tax Veto*, 2 Chi. J. Int'l L. 231, 239 (2001); Abba Kolo, *Tax Veto as a Special Jurisdictional and Substantive Issue in Investor-State Arbitration: Need for Reassessment*, 32 Suffolk Transnat'l L. Rev. 475, 476 (2008).

[120] On the different motivations for investment treaty delegation, *see generally* van Aaken, *supra* note 28, at 19–22.

[121] NAFTA art. 2001(1).

[122] *See, e.g.*, Canada–Czech Republic BIT (2009), art. X(6); Mexico–Netherlands BIT (1998), Schedule Article 8(2).

[123] To trigger the clause, the third-party investment typically must either not have substantial economic activities in the other contracting states whose investor it formally is and/or originate from a country with which the denying party does not maintain diplomatic relations or with which economic transactions are prohibited.

[124] Loukas A. Mistelis & Crina Michaela Baltag, *Denial of Benefits and Article 17 of the Energy Charter Treaty*, 113 Penn St. L. Rev. 1301, 1302–1309 (2008).

V. Conclusion

Investment agreements have evolved toward greater contractual completeness. States have made use of the four gap-filling strategies identified by contract theory—(1) more complete contracting, (2) escape clauses, (3) relational contracting, and (4) refined terms of delegation—to render IIAs more complete. This chapter has thereby shown that contract theory provides a convincing meta-framework for characterizing the treaty design change revealed in Chapter 1. The evolution of IIAs is thus a story of progressive gap-filling. Moreover, contract theory provides an umbrella theory for accommodating existing narratives of treaty design change that conceive it as a quest for policy space, precision, or taking back control from arbitrators. By highlighting their interaction and correcting their blind spots, contract theory provides useful analytical tools not only for conceptualizing treaty design change but also for understanding the interplay between contractors and adjudicators. Now that the y-axis in the map of treaty evolution is clear, it is time to turn to the x-axis and make sense of the changes observed over time.

3
Evolution as Americanization

I. Introduction

This chapter contextualizes and explains the transformation of investment agreements toward more contractual completeness. Along the x-axis, the map of investment treaty variation reveals different phases of treaty design innovation (see Figure 3.1) that are intimately connected with developments in North American treaty practice. These innovations subsequently spread around the globe. The evolution of IIAs is thus a gradual Americanization of treaty design.

The origins of investment treaties coincide with an initial decline of contractual completeness. In the late 1950s and early 1960s, two models of investment agreements coexisted. Whereas European states introduced the bilateral investment treaty (BIT)—a short and simple treaty that focused exclusively on investment protection (producing low completeness scores), the United States remained committed to preexisting Friendship, Commerce, and Navigation (FCN) treaties that embedded investment protection in a broader economic context (producing higher completeness scores). As FCN treaties proved difficult to negotiate, especially with developing countries, they fell into disuse and BITs became the model of choice to govern investment relations.

Three waves of treaty design innovation followed that emerged from North American treaty practice and that produced ever more complete agreements. First, when the United States joined the BIT movement in 1982, it combined FCN treaty elements with European BIT design and added new obligations and exceptions to further improve the resulting amalgamation. Ten years later, in 1992, a second wave of innovation occurred with NAFTA. Its Chapter 11 adapted the BIT model to govern investment relations between developed states and situated investment protection in a broader policy context. The final stage of American innovation (and the most modest of the three) reflected the experience of the United States and Canada as respondents in NAFTA investment arbitration and the increased domestic politicization of investment policymaking after 2004.

This North American innovation then diffused around the globe. In a changing policy environment marked by proliferating investment claims and bi-directional investment flows that made every state a potential respondent in investment arbitration, countries began to depart from the short and simple

Investment Arbitration and State-Driven Reform. Wolfgang Alschner, Oxford University Press. © Oxford University Press 2022. DOI: 10.1093/oso/9780197644386.003.0004

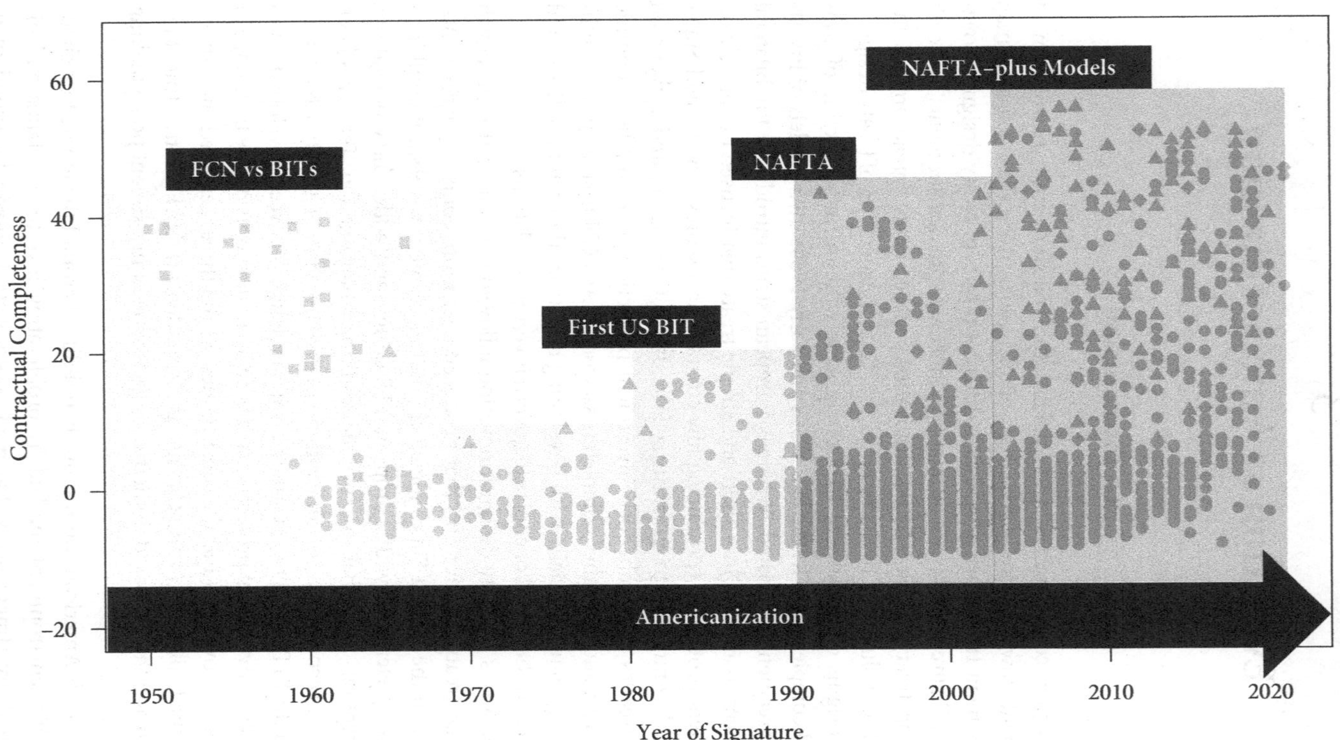

Figure 3.1 The evolution of IIAs

European model and turned toward the NAFTA model forged in reciprocal investment flows and tried and tested in arbitration. Global IIA design became Americanized and more complete in the process.

Finally, starting in the mid-2010s, the IIA universe has been growing increasingly diverse. While treaties with high completeness scores have become the rule, states increasingly disagree on the mix of appropriate gap-filling strategies. While some countries follow the American lead in drafting ever more detailed treaties, others, such as Brazil, prioritize relational contracting as preferred gap-filling strategy, and again others, led by the European Union, emphasize judicial gap filling, but through a standing tribunal, not ad hoc arbitration. IIA design is thus in flux.

The overall picture that emerges from this empirical review of seven decades of treaty-making is one of gradual state-driven change. Commentators often tend to portray the evolution of IIAs design as states reacting to ISDS cases. They miss, however, that the bulk of treaty design innovation predates the rise in investment claims. Yes, ISDS deepened preexistent trends toward more detailed and comprehensive contracting, hastened the diffusion of already existing American-style agreements, and, more recently, convinced states to make more far-reaching adjustments, like the European Union's shift to standing tribunals. In the aggregate, however, the evolution of treaty design is not about states reacting to ISDS. States have been proactive innovators all along anticipating future trends and continuously clarifying original intent.

This chapter is structured as follows. Section II discusses the origins of IIAs' evolution contrasting the BIT and FCN model. Section III explores the three waves of innovations emanating from North American practice that have changed the IIA universe. Section IV shows how these innovations spread globally, leading to an Americanization of IIA design and gradually more complete IIAs. Section V points to a recent, new phase as different design approaches for more complete agreements emerge that place emphasis on alternative gap-filling strategies.

II. Origins: FCN Treaties and BITs as Competing Models of Investment Protection Treaties

The first phase of IIA design evolution is marked by the shift from the more contractually complete FCN treaties to the less contractually complete BITs. FCN treaties were broad in scope and moderate in design, providing for both investment protection norms and host state flexibility mechanisms. BITs in contrast, were short and simple agreements focusing exclusively on investment protection. FCN treaties and BITs originated from separate governance traditions and came to represent two competing models of investment protection treaties.

A. FCN Treaties as Part of Symmetrical
North–North Relations

FCN treaties emerged from the context of symmetrical investment relations among developed countries. Following its independence, the United States began concluding so-called Friendship, Commerce, and Navigation treaties, first with France in 1778 and later with several other European and South American countries.[1] Originally, these treaties primarily dealt with commercial matters, guaranteeing most-favored-nation (MFN) treatment in trade, and covered consular relations, immigration, as well as religious and personal rights of citizens abroad.[2] The protection of alien property rights constituted a mere incidental feature of these early FCN treaties, but they already included some of the protective standards that would later become common in IIAs such as nondiscrimination, full protection and security, or the protection of property against expropriation.[3]

Over time, the investment dimension of FCN treaties became first more prominent and then dominant. Through World War I, the United States had turned from a capital importer to a capital exporter.[4] This change in economic orientation prompted an adjustment of American FCN treaty practice. Beginning with the 1923 USA–Germany FCN treaty, the United States began to systematically expand the treaties' scope, protecting the rights of companies abroad in addition to those of natural persons.[5] The treaties also began strengthening the protection of private property.[6] This trend continued after the Second World War. With international trade becoming subject to multilateral rules through the inception of

---

[1] Herman Walker, *Modern Treaties of Friendship, Commerce and Navigation*, 42 MINN. L. REV. 805 (1957); KENNETH J. VANDEVELDE, BILATERAL INVESTMENT TREATIES: HISTORY, POLICY, AND INTERPRETATION 19–26 (2010); Herman Walker, *Treaties for the Encouragement and Protection of Foreign Investment: Present United States Practice*, 5 AM. J. COMP. L. 229–247, 231 (1956).

[2] K. S. Gudgeon, *United States Bilateral Investment Treaties: Comments on Their Origin, Purposes, and General Treatment Standards*, 4 INT'L TAX & BUS. L. 105, 108 (1986); *see also* Nicholas DiMascio & Joost Pauwelyn, *Nondiscrimination in Trade and Investment Treaties: Worlds Apart or Two Sides of the Same Coin?*, 102 AM. J. INT'L L. 48–89 (2008) (commenting on the common origins of trade, investment, and human rights law).

[3] VANDEVELDE, *supra* note 1, at 21–26.

[4] Robert R. Wilson, *A Decade of New Commercial Treaties*, 50 AM. J. INT'L L. 927, 928 (1956).

[5] Herman Walker, *Provisions on Companies in United States Commercial Treaties*, 50 AM. J. INT'L L. 373–393 (1956); Wayne Sachs, *New U.S. Bilateral Investment Treaties*, 2 INT'L TAX & BUS. LAW. 192, 196 (1984).

[6] Robert R. Wilson, *Property-Protection Provisions in United States Commercial Treaties*, 45 AM. J. INT'L L. 83 (1951).

the GATT in 1947, FCN treaties increasingly turned their focus on the protection of investment abroad. In postwar FCN treaties, investment-related provisions then made up almost half of the treaty body.[7] FCN agreements had effectively become "Treaties for the Encouragement and Protection of Foreign Investment."[8] Kenneth Vandevelde thus rightfully calls them the "first bilateral investment treaties."[9]

Although FCN treaties did not contain a special mechanism enabling foreign investors to launch claims before international tribunals, treaty rights could be enforced through domestic courts. In the United States, FCN treaties were "self-executing," meaning that foreign investors could rely on them directly.[10] In particular, Japanese investors made use of FCN provisions to challenge discriminatory employment laws or compel the issuance of certificates of incorporation in the United States.[11] In reviewing the impact of FCN treaties, John Coyle thus finds that "FCN treaties served as an important check on the ability of the states and localities to enforce laws that imposed limitations on an alien's ability to work."[12] While constitutional guarantees subsequently developed by the US Supreme Court as well as new treaties or statutes have since limited the practical importance of the rights granted under FCN treaties, the domestic enforceability of FCN treaties has provided, and occasionally still provides, vital protection to foreign investors.[13]

The conclusion of new FCN treaties and, more generally, investment treaty-making between developed countries began to decline in the 1960s. Under the auspices of the OECD, member states agreed to adopt two capital liberalization codes in 1961.[14] Yet efforts to conclude a multilateral investment protection agreement under the OECD umbrella, which culminated in the 1967 OECD Draft Convention on the Protection of Foreign Property,[15] ultimately failed due to opposition from

---

[7] Walker, *supra* note 1, at 234.

[8] *Id.* at 229.

[9] Kenneth J. Vandevelde, The First Bilateral Investment Treaties: U.S. Postwar Friendship, Commerce and Navigation Treaties (2017).

[10] William S. Dodge, *Investor-State Dispute Settlement Between Developed Countries: Reflections on the Australia-United States Free Trade Agreement*, 39 Vand. J. Transnat'l L. 13 (2006).

[11] Judith Miller, *Title VII and the FCN Treaty: The Exemption of Japanese Branch Operations from Employment Discrimination Laws*, 7 B.C. Int'l & Comp. L. Rev. 67 (1984); Dodge, *supra* note 10, at 13.

[12] John F. Coyle, *The Treaty of Friendship, Commerce and Navigation in the Modern Era*, 51 Colum. J. Transnat'l L. 302–508, 320 (2013).

[13] *Id.* at 342–344.

[14] OECD Council, *Code of Liberalisation of Capital Movements and Code of Liberalisation of Current Invisible Operations* (adopted December 12, 1961). The codes have been amended several times since. For the current version of the codes, see http://www.oecd.org/investment/investment-policy/codes.htm (last accessed May 31, 2015).

[15] The text of the Convention can be access at http://acts.oecd.org/Instruments/ShowInstrumentView.aspx?InstrumentID=242&InstrumentPID=237&Lang=en&Book= (last accessed May 31, 2015).

Southern European OECD members.[16] Instead, the OECD Council adopted a resolution affirming the commitment of OECD members to the principles laid out in the Draft Convention and suggested that it should form the basis of future agreements.[17] European countries subsequently used the 1967 Draft Convention as a template to negotiate bilateral investment treaties with developing countries.[18] The failure to conclude the Convention, however, marked the preliminary end of investment law-making efforts between developed countries.

Three principal reasons had alleviated the need for setting strong investment protection rules between developed countries starting in the 1960s. First, the emergence of a Western community of rule-of-law-based democracies that shared a common notion of "embedded liberalism" lessened the need for positive norms that outlawed undesirable economic interventionism.[19] Second, investment flows increased considerably between OECD members even in the absence of investment protection diminishing the need for investment promoting agreements.[20] Third, and perhaps most importantly, attention had shifted to safeguarding investment opportunities in developing countries, where legal structures were less developed, investment flows below potential, and the risk of expropriation and other governmental interference higher. As the importance of investment law in governing symmetrical North–North relations faded, developed countries' efforts centered on providing investment protection in North–South relations.

B. BITs and Asymmetrical North–South Investment Relations

BITs emerged in the context of such North–South relations, which were governed by power asymmetries and unidirectional investment flows instead of symmetry and reciprocity.[21] Prior to BITs, European countries and the United States were

---

[16] Peter T. Muchlinski, *The Rise and Fall of the Multilateral Agreement on Investment: Where Now?*, INT'L LAW. 1033–1053, 1036 (2000).

[17] OECD Council, *Resolution on Draft Convention on the Protection of Foreign Property* (adopted October 12, 1967), available at http://www.oecd.org/daf/inv/internationalinvestmentagreements/39286571.pdf (last accessed May 31, 2015).

[18] STEPHAN W. SCHILL, THE MULTILATERALIZATION OF INTERNATIONAL INVESTMENT LAW 39–40 (2009).

[19] On the postwar economic order and "embedded liberalism," *see generally* John Gerard Ruggie, *International Regimes, Transactions, and Change: Embedded Liberalism in the Postwar Economic Order*, 36 INT'L ORG. 379–415 (1982).

[20] *See, e.g.*, S. Thomsen, *Investment Patterns in a Longer-Term Perspective*, OECD Working Paper Int. Invest. OECD Invest. Div., 8 (2000) ("OECD investors typically invest in the largest and richest markets, which are found for the most part within the OECD area itself. Since 1982, 75 per cent of OECD [investment] outflows have gone to other OECD countries").

[21] K. Miles, *International Investment Law: Origins, Imperialism and Conceptualizing the Environment*, 21 COLO. J. INT'L ENVTL. L. & POL'Y 1–557 (2010).

able to impose legal protection for their nationals in the Southern hemisphere during the nineteenth century through other means.[22] In territories under colonial rule or influence, this imposition occurred through formal annexation, concession agreements, consular arrangements carving out an extraterritorial jurisdiction, or colonial municipal law.[23] With respect to the newly independent states of South America, customary international law provided the legal basis for investment protection. If a host state injured a foreign national through conduct that fell below the international minimum standard of treatment, the home state could espouse the claim of its citizens against the host state under the law of diplomatic protection.[24]

The exercise of diplomatic protection claims in the late nineteenth and early twentieth centuries led to severe conflicts and served to justify military interventions by Northern countries in Latin America—it was the era of "gunboat diplomacy."[25] South American countries sought to mitigate the perceived harshness of customary international law most famously through the Calvo Doctrine that aimed at replacing an absolute minimum standard of treatment with a relative standard not to treat foreign investors any worse than their domestic counterparts.[26] Given the unidirectional flow of capital and the uneven bargaining power, however, industrialized countries had little incentive to abandon the minimum standard of treatment since its sovereignty costs fell exclusively on the states of the South.[27]

The enforcement of the minimum standard through diplomatic protection, however, attracted criticism also from the North. Early commentators, such as Lauterpacht and Brierly, were critical of the doctrine of diplomatic protection since it entangled home states in investment disputes risking political or even military inter-state confrontation.[28] In response, twentieth-century efforts focused on pacifying and privatizing investment disputes. In 1907, signatories to

[22] Jonathan Gimblett & O. Thomas Johnson, Jr., *From Gunboats to BITs: The Evolution of modern International Investment Law*, *in* Yearbook on International Investment Law & Policy Vol. 2010–2011 (Karl P. Sauvant ed., 2011); Miles, *supra* note 21, at 168; M. Sornarajah, The International Law on Foreign Investment 36–38 (3rd ed. 2010).

[23] Charles Lipson, Standing Guard: Protecting Foreign Capital in the Nineteenth and Twentieth Centuries 12–16 (1985); Gimblett & Johnson, Jr., *supra* note 22, at 650–651.

[24] Edwin Montefiore Borchard, The Diplomatic Protection of Citizens Abroad: Or, the Law of International Claims 349 (1915) ("Each state in the international community is presumed to extend complete protection to the life, liberty and property of all individuals within its jurisdiction. . . . If it fails in this duty towards an alien, responsibility is incurred to the state of which he is a citizen, and international law authorizes the national state to extract reparation for the injury sustained by its citizens.").

[25] Lipson, *supra* note 23, at 53–57; Vandevelde, *supra* note 1, at 29–30; Miles, *supra* note 21, at 7–8; Gimblett & Johnson, Jr., *supra* note 22, at 651–654.

[26] Santiago Montt, State Liability in Investment Treaty Arbitration: Global Constitutional and Administrative Law in the BIT Generation 1 (2009).

[27] Miles, *supra* note 21.

[28] *See* Dodge, *supra* note 10, at 8 (quoting the two scholars).

the Second Hague Peace Conference agreed to refrain from using force to recover debts, if claims were submitted to inter-state arbitration.[29] After World War I, bilateral arbitration treaties proliferated and contract-based investor-state arbitrations emerged.[30] A breakthrough occurred in 1965 through the International Centre for Settlement of Investment Disputes (ICSID) Convention, which set up an institutional architecture for the settlement of investor-state disputes. Through the ICSID Convention home states effectively promised not to pursue diplomatic protection claims; in return, the host states would agree (in a separate instrument) to settle disputes directly with the foreign investor through international arbitration.[31] This privatization of investment disputes effectively removed the home state from investment disputes and allowed "the true complainant [the investor] to face the true defendant [the host state]."[32] Hence, as stated by Jonathan Gimblett and Thomas Johnson, perhaps the greatest achievement of investment law of that period was the transition "from a world in which a foreign-investment dispute might be a *casus belli*, to one in which most such disputes are not even the subjects of diplomatic correspondence between the relevant governments."[33]

Although the development of arbitration diffused the antagonism between North and South with respect to the means of settling investment disputes, it did not alter the tension over the substance of investment protection rules. After World War II, Western states encountered stark resistance against their view of international investment law as communist countries rejected Western concepts of property rights and former empires dissolved into newly independent states critical of their colonial heritage.[34] As an alternative to the international investment law advocated by First World states, the Second and Third World promoted a new vision of international economic relations: the New International Economic Order.[35] In this new order, investor rights were to be subordinated to state-driven economic development and industrial policy; among others,

---

[29] Final Act of the Second Peace Conference, *Convention respecting Limitation of Employment of Force for Recovery of Contract Debts* (adopted October 18, 1907), art. 1, available at http://avalon.law.yale.edu/20th_century/hague072.asp (last accessed May 31, 2015).

[30] Gimblett & Johnson, Jr., *supra* note 22 ,at 654–661.

[31] Joost Pauwelyn, *At the Edge of Chaos: Foreign Investment Law as a Complex Adaptive System, How It Emerged and How It Can Be Reformed*, 29 ICSID Rev. 372–418, 403 (2014) ("Limits on unilateralism by home States were exchanged for limits on unilateralism by host States. It is this very bargain between home and host States that gradually shifted protection of foreign investment from the clan-type communal realm of power relations between States, toward an individualized arena of rules-based settlement").

[32] Jan Paulsson, *Arbitration Without Privity*, 10 ICSID Rev. 232–232, 256 (1995).

[33] Gimblett & Johnson, Jr., *supra* note 22, at 650.

[34] Kenneth J. Vandevelde, *Sustainable Liberalism and the International Investment Regime*, 19 Mich. J. Int'l L. 373 (1997) (revisiting the intellectual underpinnings of investment law and its periods of contestation).

[35] Gimblett & Johnson, Jr., *supra* note 22, at 669–681.

compensation for expropriation was to be appropriate (rather than full) and hortatory (rather than compulsory) and decided based on domestic rather than international law.[36] Several UN General Assembly Resolutions and Draft Conventions codified this alternative view of investment relations.[37]

At the same time, developing countries restricted access to foreign investors and terminated foreign ownership over natural resources or means of production in widespread nationalization programs.[38] Third World countries had also grown more reluctant to agree to arbitration.[39] And Second World countries had neither an interest nor a prior obligation to submit their nationalization programs to arbitral review.[40] It was in this setting that Northern states began to contemplate the conclusion of investment treaties also with developing countries to defend the customary international law minimum standard and to safeguard the protection of their investors abroad.[41] In that spirit, the German banker Hermann Abs and the English diplomat Hartley Shawcross proposed a Draft Convention in 1959 that consolidated "what are believed to be fundamental principles of international law regarding the treatment of the property, rights, and interests of aliens."[42] The so-called 1959 Abs–Shawcross Draft Convention inspired what would soon after become the bilateral investment treaty.

C. FCN vs. BITs

In their endeavor to codify investment protection with developing countries, Northern states therefore had a choice between two types of treaties.[43] On the

---

[36] UN General Assembly, *Charter of Economic Rights and Duties of States*, Res. 3281 (XXIX), UN Doc. A/RES/3281(XXIX) (adopted December 12, 1974), art. 2(2)c). Commentators diverge in their assessment of the impact of this contestation on investment law. VANDEVELDE, *supra* note 1, at 48 (arguing that this contestation had little impact on BITs); SORNARAJAH, *supra* note 22, at 67 S. P. SUBEDI, INTERNATIONAL INVESTMENT LAW: RECONCILING POLICY AND PRINCIPLE (2008) (arguing that the contestation had a lasting impact). For an in-depth analysis, *see* NICO SCHRIJVER, SOVEREIGNTY OVER NATURAL RESOURCES: BALANCING RIGHTS AND DUTIES (1997).

[37] *See* UN General Assembly, *Permanent Sovereignty over Natural Resources*, UN Doc. A/RES/1803 (XVII) (adopted December 14, 1962). UN General Assembly, *Declaration on the Establishment of a New International Economic Order*, UN Doc. A/RES/S-6/3201. UNCTAD, *Draft International Code of Conduct on the Transfer of Technology* (1985). Reprinted in UNCTAD, INTERNATIONAL INVESTMENT INSTRUMENTS: A COMPENDIUM, vol. I, no. 14 (1996).

[38] Kenneth J. Vandevelde, *A Brief History of International Investment Agreements*, 12 U.C. DAVIS J. INT'L L. & POL'Y 157, 166–171 (2005).

[39] MONTT, *supra* note 26, at 55.

[40] Gimblett & Johnson, Jr., *supra* note 22, at 671.

[41] VANDEVELDE, *supra* note 1, at 48–49, 56.

[42] Hermann Abs & Hartley Shawcross, *The Proposed Convention to Protect Private Foreign Investment—Introduction*, 9 J. PUB. L. 115, 119 (1960).

[43] Another type of investment agreement not considered here are state-backed investment insurance schemes that protect foreign investors against political risk abroad and subrogate ensuing claims so that the home state may recover compensation due to the investor. While some countries,

one hand, they could sign FCN treaties also with developing countries. This was the route primarily pursued by the United States, which started concluding FCN treaties with a number of ideologically friendly developing countries after World War II.[44] On the other hand, in late 1959, Germany signed the first treaty for the promotion and protection of investments with Pakistan modeled on the Abs–Shawcross Draft. The treaty marked the beginning of the European-style BIT that was tailored to the specific needs of Northern capital protection in the South and, in contrast to the more comprehensive FCN, focused only on investment protection. In the 1960s, it was far from clear whether European-style BITs or American-style FCN treaties would eventually carry the day in governing North–South investment relations.

In some respects, FCN treaties and BITs were markedly similar. Apart from minor differences in language, both treaty models shared very similar substantive investment protection clauses.[45] The USA–Pakistan FCN treaty, concluded in the same year (1959) as the first BIT between Germany and Pakistan, for instance, contained the same core investment protection standards, such as nondiscrimination, full protection and security, compensation for expropriation, and transfer of funds, as its BIT counterpart.[46] Also, neither of the two agreements provided for investor-state arbitration, since BITs began to include ISDS provisions, "what has turned out to be their primary—indeed, their only truly important—difference from modern FCN treaties"[47] in investment protection terms, only in the late 1960s. These similarities are not accidental, since BIT drafters built on earlier FCN treaty practice including wording such as "fair and equitable treatment" when devising the first BITs.[48]

At the same time, both models also displayed fundamental differences that help explain their starkly different completeness scores. First, the treaties differed in their approach to investment protection. Whereas BITs were short, simple, and focused only on investment protection, FCN treaties were comprehensive and complex agreements covering establishment rights, trade, navigation,

such as Germany, dealt with subrogation in BITs, the United States concluded bespoke International Investment Guarantee Agreements with developing countries. *See* Jon H. Moll, *Intergovernmental Agreements under the U.S. Investment Guaranty Programs*, 43 IND. L.J. 34 (1968). As noted by Taylor St. John, the postwar investment governance entailed three broader themes: substantive investment rules, arbitration, and insurance. TAYLOR ST. JOHN, THE RISE OF INVESTOR-STATE ARBITRATION: POLITICS, LAW, AND UNINTENDED CONSEQUENCES 70 (2018). I am grateful to Filip Batselé for pointing this out.

[44] Gimblett & Johnson, Jr., *supra* note 22, at 678.

[45] *See* Coyle, *supra* note 2, at 350–351.

[46] Gimblett & Johnson, Jr., *supra* note 22, at 678; JASON WEBB YACKEE, SACRIFICING SOVEREIGNTY: BILATERAL INVESTMENT TREATIES, INTERNATIONAL ARBITRATION, AND THE QUEST FOR CAPITAL 39 (2007).

[47] Gimblett & Johnson, Jr., *supra* note 22, at 679.

[48] Abs & Shawcross, *supra* note 42, at 119.

intellectual property, and even human rights, in addition to investment disciplines. Herman Walker explained the merit of a holistic approach to investment protection as follows:

> The building and operation of a motor factory by a big corporation clearly is "investment" in its major "economic development" connotation; but how can, and why should, treaty protection be written that does not cover also, at the other end of the business scale, the individual entrepreneur engaged in a sales activity? ... [The FCN treaty] regards and treats investment as a process inextricably woven into the fabric of human affairs generally; and its premise is that investment is inadequately dealt with unless set in the total "climate" in which it is to exist. A specialized "investment agreement" [i.e., a BIT] based on a narrower premise would be to that extent unrealistic and inadequate.[49]

The protection of property abroad was thus only one aspect of the wider protection accorded under FCN treaties. The advantage of regulating investment in its wider policy context, however, also became the major drawback of FCN treaties. As Mark Bergmann notes: "[T]he attempt to address very complex issues in the context of such a broad spectrum of relations detracted from the utility of the FCN as an investment protection device."[50] In particular, the breadth of issues involved, made negotiation of these treaties cumbersome and politicized.[51] The comparative advantage of BITs then lay in their "brevity and simplicity."[52] As a special-purpose vehicle, the BIT avoided politically contentious issue areas, speeding up negotiation, and allowed negotiators to focus on investment protection only.[53]

Second, FCN treaties emerged from the context of symmetrical North–North economic relations, while BITs were specifically designed to govern asymmetric North–South capital flows. This, in turn, had repercussions on treaty design. FCN treaties, as agreements among equals, were firmly embedded in the principle of reciprocity.[54] As Walker observed, "the limits of [an FCN-type] investment treaty are set by the degree to which the United States is willing to bind its own domestic policy."[55] Put in contract theoretical terms, reciprocity in law

---

[49] Walker, *supra* note 1, at 244.

[50] M. S. Bergman, *Bilateral Investment Protection Treaties: An Examination of the Evolution and Significance of the US Prototype Treaty*, 16 N.Y.U. J. INT'L L. & POL. 1, 7 (1983).

[51] Calvin A. Hamilton & Paula I. Rochwerger, *Trade and Investment: Foreign Direct Investment Through Bilateral and Multilateral Treaties*, 18 N.Y. INT'L L. REV. 44 (2005); Walker, *supra* note 1; Gudgeon, *supra* note 2, at 108.

[52] Gudgeon, *supra* note 2, at 110.

[53] *Id.* at 108. V. H. Ruttenberg, *The United States Bilateral Investment Treaty Program: Variations on the Model*, 9 U. PA. J. INT'L BUS. L. 121, 124–125 (1987).

[54] LIPSON, *supra* note 23, at 9.

[55] Walker, *supra* note 1, at 246; similarly, Walker, *supra* note 1, at 810.

and in fact created an incentive for developed countries to design more complete treaties that curbed opportunism while seizing regret, that is, balancing protective obligations with flexibility clauses to preserve the right to regulate in sensitive policy areas, since they did not know ex ante which party would be victim and which would be injurer.[56] Symmetrical economic relations thus rendered FCN treaties "essentially moderate in their content and purport."[57] These characteristics of FCN treaties did not change as treaties were concluded with developing countries.[58] For example, the 1959 US FCN treaty with Pakistan contains a range of carveouts and exceptions, including relating to public health and national security.[59]

BITs, in contrast, were developed in the context of asymmetrical investment relations. Formally, BITs provided reciprocal investment protection. Yet, as F.A. Mann put it, in the context of unidirectional investment flows from North to South, "reciprocity is to a large extent a matter of prestige rather than reality."[60] Former US negotiator José Alvarez is even more direct stating that early BITs' "references to 'reciprocal' investment flows was something of a fraud [...] [t]he regulatory burdens of th[ese] treat[ies] fell almost entirely on [the] (LDC) BIT partners."[61] In contract theoretical terms, it was thus clear which party would be injurer and which would be victim. Contrary to FCN treaties' complex trade-off of rights and obligations, early BITs were not about striking a balance between investment protection abroad and policy space at home.[62] Rather they sought to "*regulate* the [developing] FDI host state."[63] The result was a treaty design that focused exclusively on investment protection and did not comprehensively address host state flexibility.

The contractual incompleteness of early BITs is then not altogether surprising in contract theoretical terms. It was simply not efficient for developed countries as dominant rule-makers to design more complex and fine-tuned treaties that carefully seized regret since the burden of performance fell exclusively on the

---

[56] For examples of such investment-related flexibility clauses, *see, e.g.,* the USA–Pakistan FCN Treaty (1959), arts. II(3), VII(2), IX(3), XII(2), and XX.

[57] Walker, *supra* note 1, at 246.

[58] In part, this can be explained by the fact that FCN treaties, like later BITs, were based on model templates. *See* Wilson, *supra* note 4, at 928.

[59] *See, e.g.,* US–Pakistan FCN (1959), arts. II(3) and XX.

[60] F. A. Mann, *British Treaties for the Promotion and Protection of Investments*, 52 Brit. Y.B. Int'l L. 241–254, 241 (1982).

[61] José E. Alvarez, *The Evolving BIT*, Transnat'l Disp. Mgmt. 3 (2010).

[62] Jeswald W. Salacuse & Nicholas P. Sullivan, *Do BITs Really Work: An Evaluation of Bilateral Investment Treaties and Their Grand Bargain*, 46 Harv. Int'l L.J. 67, 77 (2005)("An investment treaty between two developed States, both of whose nationals expect to invest in the territory of the other, would be based on the notion of reciprocity and mutual protection. However, this bargain would not seem applicable in the context of a treaty between a developed, capital-exporting State and a poor, developing country whose nationals are unlikely to invest abroad").

[63] Alvarez, *supra* note 61, at 3.

developing country partner. The primary goal of developed countries was to curb opportunism of the host state. They thus preferred to err on the side of over- rather than underprotecting their investors.

Given the perceived one-sidedness, early commentators were skeptical that BITs would be widely adopted. Stanley Metzger commenting on the 1959 Abs–Shawcross Draft Convention noted that, as opposed to FCN treaties, the Convention lacked sufficiently broad exception clauses allowing legitimate derogation from investment protection obligations.[64] As a result, the Convention would "create a regime far more 'protective' of private foreign investment than that created by (a) existing international law; (b) existing domestic law of most countries, including the United States; or (c) existing bilateral [FCN] treaties."[65] He was convinced that "neither the United States nor any other country will be prepared to commit itself to observe its private contracts with a foreign national 'at all times.' Countries, developed or underdeveloped, are not going to forego regulating business and investments in the public interest."[66] Consequently, he was skeptical that countries would accept the Convention and "'bargain away' their power to regulate foreign-owned investment,"[67] especially since foreign investment was flowing into many of these countries even in the absence of such protection.[68]

Yet history proved him wrong. In the 1960s and 1970s, the competition of the two models was decided in favor of the short and simple BITs. Tensions between developed and developing states had started to subside in the late 1970s with more and more countries embracing liberal economic thought and policies in the 1980s and 1990s.[69] Among the factors responsible for this shift was the collapse of communism in Eastern Europe, a reconsideration of development strategies from import-substitution to export-led growth and the serious debt crisis experienced by many developing countries in the 1980s.[70] Foreign investment was not perceived anymore as a threat to national sovereignty or a means of foreign control but as an important source of finance for economic development. As a result, more and more developing countries accepted the one-sided European-style BITs "that hurt them" to reap expected development benefits arising from increased foreign investment inflows, in exchange for limiting their right to regulate and expropriate.[71]

---

[64] Stanley D. Metzger, *Multilateral Conventions for the Protection of Private Foreign Investment*, 9 J. Pub. L. 133, 135 (1960).

[65] *Id.* at 133–134.

[66] *Id.* at 138.

[67] *Id.* at 139.

[68] *Id.* at 137.

[69] Kenneth J. Vandevelde, *Of Politics and Markets: The Shifting Ideology of the BITs*, 11 Int'l Tax & Bus. Law. 159 (1993).

[70] Vandevelde, *supra* note 34, at 386–390; Vandevelde, *supra* note 1, at 59–64.

[71] Andrew T. Guzman, *Why LDCs Sign Treaties That Hurt Them: Explaining the Popularity of Bilateral Investment Treaties*, 38 Va. J. Int'l L. 639 (1997); Salacuse & Sullivan, *supra* note 62.

In hindsight, contractual incompleteness was a major reason for the success of BITs. Their specialization on investment protection avoided politically sensitive areas covered by the broader FCNs. The vagueness of BITs furthermore offered sufficient room for various readings making the treaties attractive for a wider audience. Similarly, the deceptive simplicity and brevity of their language convinced many developing states that they were signing onto statements of goodwill rather than binding legal commitments. Lauge Poulsen's empirical research on the diffusion of BITs suggests that developing countries systematically overestimated the benefits of BITs, including their potential to enhance investment inflows, and underestimated their costs in terms of legal liability.[72] BITs were mistaken as "photo opportunities,"[73] mere "ink on paper"[74] or purely "symbolic gestures."[75] It was thus not uncommon to sign treaties without engaging in any meaningful negotiations.[76] In short, contractual incompleteness may have fueled the initial success of BITs.

This contractual incompleteness grew over time. The 1960s and 1970s marked a period of experimentation in European BIT practice.[77] Early BITs still reflected part of the more symmetric and moderate FCN spirit and displayed higher completeness scores compared to later BITs. For example, as noted in Chapter 2, carveouts to protect public health were common in early BITs. Such exceptions then almost fully disappeared in European BITs of the 1980s and 1990s, and treaty design largely converged around short and simple treaties that focused exclusively on investment protection. Unsurprisingly then, the lowest scoring IIAs in the dataset are European BITs concluded in the 1990s when the model had been stripped bare of its more moderate FCN roots.

Once more and more developed countries started to accept BITs, their numbers skyrocketed. At the same time, the FCN treaty model met its demise. The United States concluded its last FCN treaty with Thailand in 1966.[78] A subsequent negotiation with the Philippines was abandoned in the early 1970s.[79] In 1982, the United States signed its first BIT with Panama. By that time, most

---

[72] Lauge Poulsen, Sacrificing Sovereignty by Chance: Investment Treaties, Developing Countries, and Bounded Rationality (2011); Lauge Poulsen, *Bounded Rationality and the Diffusion of Modern Investment Treaties*, Int'l Stud. Q. (2013); Lauge N. Skovgaard Poulsen, Bounded Rationality and Economic Diplomacy: The Politics of Investment Treaties in Developing Countries (2015).

[73] Poulsen, *supra* note 72, at 16.

[74] *Id.* at 239.

[75] *Id.* at 280.

[76] Lauge Poulsen, *The Politics of South-South Bilateral Investment Treaties, in* The Politics of International Economic Law 200 (T. Broude, M. L. Busch, & A. Porges eds., 2011).

[77] Wolfgang Alschner & Dmitriy Skougarevskiy, *Consistency and Legal Innovation in the BIT Universe*, Stanford Public Law Working Paper, 19–21 (2015).

[78] Ruttenberg, *supra* note 53, at 124.

[79] Gudgeon, *supra* note 2, at 108.

European countries had already launched their BIT programs.[80] By the late 1980s, all major OECD countries had embraced the concept of BITs.[81] Until the end of 1989, the BIT universe consisted of 385 treaties. This figure more than quadrupled to 1857 by the end of 1999.[82]

III. Three Waves of Innovation

Beginning in the 1980s, but only becoming more widespread in the 1990s and 2000s, a gradually changing economic, political, and legal landscape then turned the original virtues of BITs stemming from their contractual incompleteness—their specialization, brevity, and simplicity—into liabilities. As circumstances changed and investment relations became more reciprocal, it became increasingly efficient· for developed countries to draft more complete treaties. The resulting innovations emanated from North American practice in three consecutive waves.

A. Wave 1: 1982—The United States Joins the BIT Universe and Incorporates FCN Heritage

When the United States joined the BIT universe in 1982, it added two new dimensions to BITs. First, the United States did not abandon its FCN heritage, but integrated several FCN treaty design elements into its BIT program. Second, the United States used the policy shift to include novel design features into investment treaties. Contemporary commentators were thus of the opinion, that "the [1982 US] Model BIT is not only quite different from a standard FCN, but also quite different from the European BIT program."[83]

First, when the United States shifted from FCN treaties to BITs in the early 1980s, it included three FCN treaty elements into its BITs that offered additionally investment protection but had been largely absent in European agreements.

Pre-establishment provisions. European treaties traditionally focused on post-establishment protection leaving it to the host states to admit investment in accordance with its laws and regulations. American BITs, however, also contained pre-establishment commitments that had traditionally been found in FCN

---

[80] VANDEVELDE, *supra* note 1, at 54–55.

[81] The only OECD members without BITs at the end of the 1980s were Iceland and Ireland.

[82] UNCTAD, BILATERAL INVESTMENT TREATIES: 1959–1999 1 (2000), http://unctad.org/en/docs/poiteiiad2.en.pdf (last accessed June 2, 2015).

[83] Ruttenberg, *supra* note 53, at 125. Footnotes omitted.

treaties.[84] The typical American IIA also offered national treatment and MFN treatment to foreign investors for the phases of acquisition and establishment.

Entry of personnel. Operating a foreign direct investment sometimes requires managerial or technical skills unavailable in the host country. Traditionally, however, European BITs left the entry of workers or managers unregulated. In contrast, FCN treaties placed the investing individual center stage.[85] US BITs continued the long-standing FCN practice including provisions governing the entry and sojourn of personnel and senior management in their treaties.[86]

Transparency by publishing investment-related laws. Knowing the host country's domestic legal framework is crucial for deciding where to invest. Moreover, once the investment has been made, such knowledge ensures compliance with domestic rules and regulations. FCN treaties thus contained obligations to publish laws impacting trade and investment.[87] US BITs, in turn, continued this practice.[88]

Second, the drafters of the 1982 US model BIT not only integrated tried FCN elements but also sought to improve on the weakness of both BITs and FCN treaties. One perceived shortcoming of European BITs lay in the vagueness of their investment treaty provisions.[89] In a premonition of future concerns over unpredictable and inconsistent ISDS awards, K. Scott Gudgeon noted "that the European model lacked sufficient specific guidance in the enforcement context."[90] In response, the language of the 1982 US model became particularly (for some commentators even overly) detailed and complex and included novel treaty features.[91] The resulting American BITs were perceived as offering higher levels of investment protection than those of European states.[92]

---

[84] UNCTAD, *The role of international investment agreements in attracting foreign direct investment to developing countries* 20 (2009) ("looking from the perspective of developing countries, there are two BIT models: [a] 'protection only' BITs mostly with European countries and other developing countries; and [b] liberalizing BITs concluded mainly with the United States and Canada, and more recently, with Japan").

[85] Coyle, *supra* note 12, at 350, stating that "[t]he transition from the FCN treaty to the BIT, moreover, represents a transition from a treaty regime concerned with protecting individuals to one concerned with protecting investment."

[86] 1982 U.S. Model BIT, art. 5(b); NAFTA art. 1107; 2012 U.S. Model BIT, art. 9.

[87] *See* 1959 USA–Pakistan FCN Treaty, art. XV (the article's scope, however, was limited to trade matters).

[88] *See* 1984 U.S. Model BIT, arts. II(8) and IX.

[89] Bergman, *supra* note 50, at 8; Ruttenberg, *supra* note 53, at 125; P. M. K. Robin, *The Bit Won't Bite: The American Bilateral Investment Treaty Program*, 33 AM. U. L. REV. 931, 941 (1983); Sachs, *supra* note 5, at 204.

[90] Gudgeon, *supra* note 2, at 110.

[91] The language was simplified in subsequent US BITs, *see* Pamela B. Gann, *The U.S. Bilateral Investment Treaty Program*, 21 STAN. J. INT'L L. 373, 374 (1985); for criticism of the rigidity of the early US BIT model, *see* Ruttenberg, *supra* note 53.

[92] At the time of its conclusion, commentators were skeptical about the success of US BITs given the higher level of investment protection obligations it entailed. *See* Gann, *supra* note 91, at 439 ("The slow development of the BIT program is attributable to the high level of investment protection sought by U.S. negotiators").

Linking FET to international law. One element to enhance certainty consisted of a textual reference to international law in the fair and equitable (FET) and full protection and security clauses in Article II (4) of the 1982 US model BIT.[93] Such a direct textual reference was absent in many European BITs, although as discussed in Chapter 5, the link to custom was understood to be implied by the text.[94]

Effective means clause. US BITs mandated that the contracting parties "provide effective means of asserting claims and enforcing rights with respect to covered investments."[95] The clause sought to protect investors against denial of justice and to ensure access to local courts.[96]

Performance requirements. Host states have an incentive to require investors to source goods and services locally. While such performance requirements embed an investment more firmly into the economy of the host state and generate spillovers, they also lead to distortions as the investors cannot obtain the goods or services from the most efficient provider. By limiting the host state's ability to impose performance requirements, investment treaties protect the freedom of business and free trade. The US BIT program was the first to regulate performance requirements in investment treaties.[97]

Importantly, the US BIT program not only offered more protection than European BITs but also more host state flexibility. Aside from general exceptions on national security, US BITs included country-specific schedules of reservation, known as nonconforming measures, that had already been used in the more symmetrical context of FCN treaties to mitigate the harshness of protection clauses. FCN treaties typically included nonconforming measures to carve out sensitive policy areas from national treatment and MFN treatment. For example, the United States typically maintained restrictions regarding the foreign acquisition of businesses in the field of communications, air or water transport, and the exploitation of land or other natural resources in their FCN treaties.[98] The early US BITs continued this practice, but moved the listing of nonconforming measures to the annexes.[99] Nonconforming measures exclude specific sectors from

<hr>

[93] *See also* VANDEVELDE, *supra* note 1, at 76.

[94] Some European BITs, in particular those concluded by France, contain such a reference. The 1967 *OECD Draft Convention* on which most European BITs are modeled did not contain an explicit textual reference. Its commentary, however, links "fair and equitable treatment" and "constant protection and security" to the international law minimum standard. *See* Chapter 5.

[95] *See, e.g.*, USA–Senegal BIT (1996), art. 2(9).

[96] Jessica Wirth, *"Effective Means" Means; The Legacy of Chevron v. Ecuador*, 52 COLUM. J. TRANSNAT'L L. 325, 331–332 (2013).

[97] ANDREW NEWCOMBE & LLUÍS PARADELL, LAW AND PRACTICE OF INVESTMENT TREATIES: STANDARDS OF TREATMENT 422 (2009); Robin, *supra* note 89, at 949–950; Bergman, *supra* note 50, at 18; Ruttenberg, *supra* note 53, at 126.

[98] *See, e.g.*, USA–Germany FCN Treaty (1954), art. VII(2).

[99] *See, e.g.*, 1994 U.S. Model BIT, art. II(2)(a).

liberalization, but also limited the protective scope of performance requirements or sojourn of personnel clauses.[100]

This development of including *more* exceptions to achieve *more* protection is perfectly consistent with contract theory. As discussed in Chapter 2, the principle means for producing higher levels of cooperation ex ante is to provide more flexibility ex post. That is exactly what happened in the US BIT program: more commitments were made possible by concomitantly increasing the level of flexibilities. Indeed, there is an almost perfect positive correlation between the inclusion performance requirements and the occurrence of nonconforming measure reservations in the treaty data. In practice, that meant that countries only agreed to performance requirements, if they retained flexibility by carving out some measures or sectors from scope of the treaty.

In conclusion, the entry of the United States into the BIT universe marked an increase in contractual completeness. One part of this increase is due to investment protection clauses not found in European BITs. Another part is due to additional exceptions. The surprising contract theoretical insight is thus borne out: flexibility clauses are not necessarily a means to lower investment protection but can be a tool to expand it.

B. Wave 2: 1992—The NAFTA Moment

The conclusion of NAFTA marked a second wave of IIA design innovation. The importance of NAFTA for the evolution of IIAs toward greater contractual completeness cannot be overstated. Chapter 2 already provided a taste of NAFTA's many "firsts." Indeed, most reform features commonly associated with states' reaction to rising ISDS claims, from certainty language to exceptions, to state involvement in ISDS, predate the surge of ISDS cases and originated in NAFTA making the treaty the first new-generation IIA. Two circumstances surrounding NAFTA's conclusion are responsible for its unique design and secured its special status in the history of international investment law.

First, NAFTA is special because it was the first time that two major developed countries with significant mutual stock of foreign investment signed an investment agreement that contained consent to investment arbitration.[101] Four years

---

[100] Article 14(1) of the USA–Uruguay BIT (2005), for instance, states that "Articles 3 [National Treatment], 4 [MFN], 8 [Performance Requirements], and 9 [Senior Management and Boards of Directors] do not apply to" a list of scheduled nonconforming measures annexed to the treaty.

[101] J. Anthony VanDuzer, *Investor-State Dispute Settlement under NAFTA Chapter 11: The Shape of Things to Come*, 35 CAN. Y.B. INT'L L. 263, 266 (1997); Daniel M. Price, *An Overview of the NAFTA Investment Chapter: Substantive Rules and Investor-State Dispute Settlement*, 27 INT'L LAW. 727, 736 (1993); Mark Clodfelter, *US State Department Participation in International Economic Dispute Resolution*, 42 S. TEX. L. REV. 1273, 1283 (2001) ("The United States, and for that matter Canada

earlier, in 1988, Canada and the United States had already concluded an FTA with investment chapter. However, that treaty had only contained a rudimentary set of provisions and no ISDS following Canada's persistent objection to agree to more extensive investment protection.[102] In NAFTA, the United States was committed to concluding a more extensive investment chapter principally to protect US investment in Mexico.[103] Prior to signing NAFTA, Mexico had not concluded any investment treaties and instead had been a vocal opponent of Northern concepts of investment law and had a track record of expropriations without full compensation.[104]

As the negotiations proceeded, however, Canada, and not Mexico, became the country most resisting US efforts to include a strong investment chapter.[105] A Mexican negotiator recalls that on the issue of investment protection, "Mexico was closer to the US than Canada. We wanted more discipline than Canada. Canada based its position on the Canada–USA FTA, which for us had little substance. Canada was more afraid of foreign investment."[106] While Canada expressed readiness to be bound by investment rules vis-à-vis Mexico, it was determined to resist more extensive protection of American investment.[107] Among others, Canada was pushing for the inclusion of a GATT XX–type general exception into NAFTA Chapter 11, which eventually became a more toned-down environmental measures clause in NAFTA Article 1114.[108]

The ultimate text of NAFTA Chapter 11 was a compromise less extensive in protection than what the United States had initially intended.[109] Indeed, a text-as-data analysis of the NAFTA negotiations shows that the final text is roughly equidistant to the initial proposals tabled by the three states.[110] More symmetrical

and Mexico, took a very big step into the unknown when they signed on to Chapter 11 . . . Even though the United States has been party to a fair number of BITs, which have arrangements resembling Chapter 11, we have never done so with states that have so much investment in our territory").

---

[102] Jean Raby, *The Investment Provisions of the Canada–United States Free Trade Agreement: A Canadian Perspective*, 84 AM. J. INT'L L. 394, 395 (1990) ("Canada is the big winner on investment . . . Canada's ability to regulate and control American direct investment has not been drastically reduced by the FTA").

[103] Charles N. Brower & Lee A. Steven, *Who Then Should Judge: Developing the International Rule of Law under NAFTA Chapter 11*, 2 CHI. J. INT'L L. 193 (2001).

[104] *Id.* at 194. Jennifer A. Heindl, *Toward a History of NAFTA's Chapter Eleven*, 24 BERKELEY J. INT'L L. 672, 678 (2006); David A. Gantz, *Resolution of Investment Disputes under the North American Free Trade Agreement*, 10 ARIZ. J. INT'L & COMP. L. 335, 337–338 (1993).

[105] Heindl, *supra* note 104, at 681.

[106] MAXWELL A. CAMERON & BRIAN W. TOMLIN, THE MAKING OF NAFTA: HOW THE DEAL WAS DONE 101 (2002).

[107] *Id.* at 101.

[108] MEG KINNEAR, ANDREA BJORKLUND, & JOHN F. G. HANNAFORD, INVESTMENT DISPUTES UNDER NAFTA. AN ANNOTATED GUIDE TO NAFTA CHAPTER 11, at 1114–1111 (2006).

[109] Heindl, *supra* note 104, at 683–684.

[110] Alschner et al., *What Can the Negotiations of NAFTA 1.0 Teach Us about the Fate of NAFTA 2.0?*, Ottawa Faculty of Law Working Paper No. 2018-05.

economic relations and hard bargaining had thus led the negotiators toward compromise and moderation.

Second, NAFTA is special because it marked a further rapprochement between trade and investment governance introducing the coordination exceptions discussed in Chapter 2. Trade and investment rules have always been interconnected.[111] FCN treaties provided for trade and investment clauses under a single umbrella and the 1948 Havana Charter, founding document of the International Trade Organization, which never saw the light of day, contained both investment and trade rules.[112] Starting in the early 1980s, however, the nexus between the two began to become even tighter including but not limited to the new elements inserted in US investment treaties. In 1982, a GATT Panel was convened upon request of the United States to assess the conformity of Canada's Foreign Investment Review Act (FIRA) with GATT rules.[113] The FIRA made approval and operation of foreign investment projects contingent on the use of locally sourced goods and export performance.[114] By finding these trade-related investment measures (TRIMs) to be inconsistent with GATT's national treatment provision, the panel report formulated a prohibition of performance requirements that inspired later codification in the WTO TRIMs Agreement.[115]

While investment measures were thus beginning to intrude into the trade realm, the conclusion of the Uruguay Round in 1994 also brought trade rules to bear on investment matters. The GATS, the WTO's Agreement on services, governs the market access and, to a more limited extent, the operations of foreign investment in services (mode 3) as well as the entry and sojourn of individuals (mode 4).[116] Moreover, intellectual property rights were protected by the WTO TRIPS Agreement, but were also considered an "investment" under most BITs.[117] Given this overlap—and the fact that these WTO Agreements were negotiated at the same time as NAFTA—the encounter of trade and investment law in NAFTA provided an opportunity for cross-fertilization.

This cross-fertilization produced many of the coordination exceptions discussed in Chapter 2. A carveout for prudential financial regulations developed

---

[111] Tomer Broude, *Investment and Trade: The "Lottie and Lisa" of International Economic Law?*, 8 TRANSNAT'L DISP. MGMT. (2011); JÜRGEN KURTZ, THE WTO AND INTERNATIONAL INVESTMENT LAW: CONVERGING SYSTEMS (2016).

[112] Mary E. Footer, *On the Laws of Attraction: Examining the Relationship Between Foreign Investment and International Trade, in* PROSPECTS IN INTERNATIONAL INVESTMENT LAW AND POLICY: WORLD TRADE FORUM 105–138, 107–110 (Roberto Echandi & Pierre Sauve eds., 2013).

[113] Todd S. Shenkin, *Trade-Related Investment Measures in Bilateral Investment Treaties and the GATT: Moving Toward a Multilateral Investment Treaty*, 55 U. PITT. L. REV. 541, 560 (1993).

[114] *Id.* at 561–562.

[115] Footer, *supra* note 112, at 116; KURTZ, *supra* note 111, at 49–50.

[116] Footer, *supra* note 112, at 113–115. *See also* Rudolf Adlung, *Multilateral Investment Disciplines: Don't Forget the GATS!*, COLUMBIA FDI PERSPECTIVES, No. 117 (March 17, 2014).

[117] Peter B. Rutledge, *TRIPS and BITS: An Essay on Compulsory Licenses, Expropriation, and International Arbitration*, 13 N.C. J.L. & TECH. ON. 149–287 (2012).

in the GATS was integrated into NAFTA and applied to Chapter 11.[118] Moreover, NAFTA Article 1110(7) clarified that NAFTA's expropriation clause "does not apply to the issuance of compulsory licenses granted in relation to intellectual property rights," thereby ensuring compatibility of trade and investment rules.[119] Finally, NAFTA Chapter 21 introduced a list of general exceptions that applied both to goods and investment such as exceptions on national security (Article 2102), taxation (Article 2103), and balance of payments (Article 2104). Hence, the encounter of trade and investment rules in NAFTA raised new compatibility issues that were resolved through nuanced coordinating exception provisions.

As important as the original negotiation and design choices was NAFTA's effect on subsequent ISDS and IIA practice. Within a decade of its conclusion, NAFTA had given rise to an extensive volume of claims that challenged the contracting parties' ability not only to defend their respective cases but also to uphold their common understanding of the bargain struck. The innovative structure of NAFTA's arbitration provisions embedded investors' claims in a wider array of inter-state control mechanisms discussed in Chapter 2, enabling contracting parties to submit their reading of the treaty in disputes involving other NAFTA parties (Article 1128 nondisputing party submissions) and allowing them to issue joint interpretations among all three NAFTA parties that were binding on tribunals (Article 1131(2)).[120]

Initially, the unanticipated wave of claims, especially against Canada and the United States, came as an unwelcomed surprise.[121] As Brower and Steven note,

> some of the distress felt by Canada and the United States over NAFTA Chapter 11 has been caused by the novel and disconcerting fact of having to live up to the same substantive and procedural guarantees that they have required of their BIT partners.[122]

The NAFTA cases, however, also provided an opportunity to develop expertise in defending against claims and to flesh out the meaning of key provisions through

---

[118] *See* NAFTA, art. 1410.

[119] For the potential (in)compatibility, *see also* Christopher Gibson, *A Look at the Compulsory License in Investment Arbitration: The Case of Indirect Expropriation*, 25 AM. U. INT'L L. REV. 357 (2010); Rutledge, *supra* note 117.

[120] VanDuzer, *supra* note 101, at 282 ("This is an important distinction between the process under Chapter 11 and that under the Arbitral Rules governing disputes not subject to NAFTA. Each of the sets of Arbitral Rules is designed solely as a process to resolve disputes between parties. In contrast, the Chapter 11 dispute settlement involves the interpretation of a multilateral instrument—an issue in which all the NAFTA Parties have a stake").

[121] M. Kinnear & R. Hansen, *The Influence of NAFTA Chapter 11 in the BIT Landscape*, 12 U.C. DAVIS J. INT'L L. & POL'Y 101, 104 (2005) ("the volume or type of arbitration that was instituted under NAFTA Chapter 11 was not easily predictable. Nor could anyone have foreseen the number of cases between Canadian and American disputing parties").

[122] Brower & Steven, *supra* note 103, at 195.

litigation.[123] By defending their cases—often successfully—and by making use of NAFTA's novel procedural architecture, the contracting parties proved NAFTA to be a workable instrument that, albeit far from being perfect, provided a balance between investment protection and regulatory freedom.

In addition, NAFTA had profound effects on the subsequent BIT and FTA practices of the NAFTA parties.

Mexico. NAFTA was the first investment treaty signed by Mexico. Subsequently, the country became a frequent user of both BITs and FTAs. The initial impact of NAFTA on both types of agreements was uneven, however. Mexico used NAFTA Chapter 11 as a template for its FTA negotiations. Chapter XVII of the Colombia–Mexico FTA (1994) and Chapter 9 of the Chile–Mexico FTA (1998) closely mirror NAFTA Chapter 11 in language and design. While Mexico did not follow NAFTA-derived language in its BITs with the same consistency, it did incorporate several NAFTA features. Its BITs include procedural provisions borrowed from NAFTA, for example, that require loss to gain standing for arbitration or that permit authoritative interpretations by the contracting parties, but also substantive ones, such as the obligation not to lower environmental standards.[124] These provisions were absent in contractually incomplete European BITs. As a result, the treaties Mexico signed with European countries, for example, the 1995 BIT with Switzerland or the 1998 BITs with the Netherlands, Belgium, and Germany, became outliers within the otherwise quite coherent treaty networks of European states due to their relatively higher contractual completeness.[125]

Canada. The impact of NAFTA on Canadian treaties was even more profound. Not only did NAFTA Chapter 11 inspire investment chapters in subsequent FTAs. It also fundamentally changed the Canadian BIT program. In 1996, Canada signed an FTA with Chile. With 89 percent of text in common, its Chapter G closely tracks the language and structure of NAFTA Chapter 11.[126] NAFTA also marked a major shift in Canada's BIT program. When signing its first BIT in 1989 with Russia, Canada followed the OECD Draft Convention as a BIT template.[127] As a result, early Canadian BITs were highly contractually incomplete—they were short and simple agreements similar in design to European BITs.

---

[123] *Id.* at 201.

[124] *See, e.g.,* the Mexico–Switzerland BIT (1995) Schedule "Settlement of Disputes between a Party and an Investor of the Other Party" and the Protocol.

[125] *See* http://mappinginvestmenttreaties.com for further information.

[126] Wolfgang Alschner, Julia Seiermann, & Dmitriy Skougarevskiy, *Text of Trade Agreements (ToTA)—A Structured Corpus for the Text-as-Data Analysis of Preferential Trade Agreements,* 15 J. EMPIRICAL LEGAL STUD. 648–666 (2018).

[127] Kinnear & Hansen, *supra* note 121, at 103.

Following the conclusion of NAFTA in 1992, however, the length of Canadian BITs doubled as innovations from NAFTA's Investment Chapter 11 were introduced into its new BITs.[128] Canadian BITs from its 1993 treaty with Latvia onward contained (1) novel commitments on liberalization, performance requirements, and sojourn of personnel; (2) carveouts or exceptions for compulsory licenses, cultural industries (also found in NAFTA Article 2106), and prudential measures, as well as (3) procedural innovations such as binding interpretations. The perhaps most important innovation were GATT XX–type general exceptions, which Canada had unsuccessfully sought to integrate in NAFTA's investment chapter, and which marked the first time such exceptions were found in IIAs.[129] None of these elements are present in earlier Canadian BITs. This change is illustrated in Figure 3.2.

The drastic nature of this shift from the OECD to the NAFTA model is well illustrated in negotiations between South Africa and Canada a few years later, which were documented by Lauge Poulsen.[130] South Africa had built its post-apartheid BIT program around the contractually incomplete European treaties

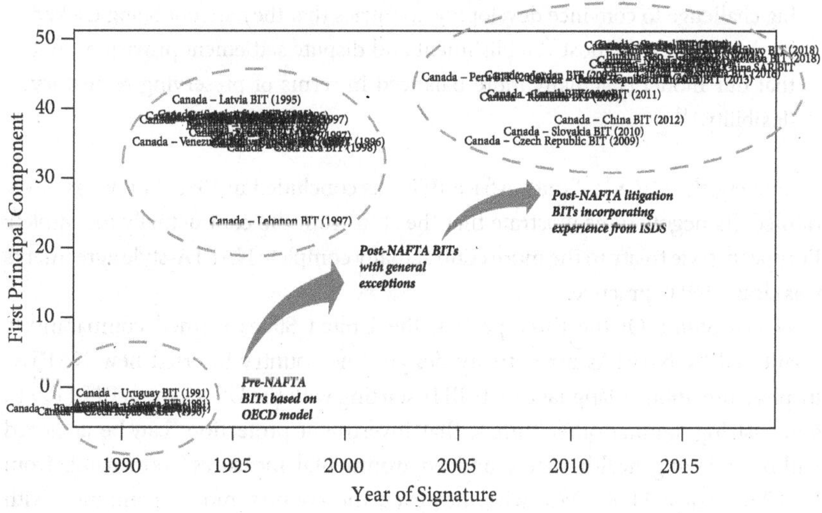

Figure 3.2 Evolution of Canadian BITs

---

[128] James McIlroy, *Canada's New Foreign Investment Protection and Promotion Agreement*, 5 J. WORLD INVESTMENT & TRADE 621–646, 623–629 (2004).

[129] General public policy not modeled on GATT were first included in the 1985 Singapore–China BIT, *see generally* Wolfgang Alschner & Kun Hui, *Missing in Action: General Public Policy Exceptions in Investment Treaties, in* YEARBOOK ON INTERNATIONAL INVESTMENT LAW AND POLICY 2018 (Lisa E. Sachs, Jesse Coleman, & Lise Johnson eds., 2019).

[130] Poulsen, *supra* note 76, at 279–282.

after having signed its first BIT with the United Kingdom in 1994.[131] When Canada then entered into negotiations with South Africa for a BIT based on the NAFTA template in the mid-1990s, this created profound confusion. The South African negotiator confessed:

> The Canadians were a nightmare. I think it was mostly an ego thing, but they took a very difficult stance. These were people who took BITs as real and serious legal instruments with teeth, rather than what they really are, namely pure signals. . . . The treaties are a symbolic gesture, so why be so pedantic and difficult in worrying so much about the legal details? It was very difficult.[132]

On the other side, the Canadian negotiator interviewed by Poulsen was equally exasperated:

> Even if we find interested developing countries, it is always a challenge to explain why our model actually provides more flexibility than European models. It takes a long time to explain to them why our model is better than what they've done in the past. The liberalization provisions are not that difficult, but it is a big challenge to convince developing countries that they are not being tricked by the detail of the post-establishment and dispute settlement provisions, but that our model is actually more balanced in terms of preserving regulatory flexibility.[133]

Ultimately, the Canada–South Africa BIT was concluded in 1995, but it was never ratified. Its negotiations illustrate that the shift from the contractually incomplete European-style treaty to the more contractually complete NAFTA-style agreements was clearly felt in practice.

United States. Of the three parties, the United States seemed comparatively unaffected by NAFTA's novel treaty design. The country inserted new NAFTA-inspired preambular language in its BITs starting with the US–Georgia BIT (1994), emphasizing, among other things, that investment protection "can be achieved without relaxing health, safety and environmental measures," borrowing from NAFTA Article 1114. Otherwise, however, the country mostly continued with its prior model BIT leading to a disconnect between its FTA and BIT practice.[134] US policymakers may have seen little reason to include the special safeguards inserted into NAFTA also in agreements with Estonia, Georgia, or Jamaica that

---

[131] *Id.* at 276.

[132] *Id.* at 280.

[133] POULSEN, *supra* note 72, at 280.

[134] Wolfgang Alschner, Julia Seiermann, & Dmitriy Skougarevskiy, *Text-as-Data Analysis of Preferential Trade Agreements: Mapping the PTA Landscape*, UNCTAD Research Paper, 23 (2017).

were characterized by more asymmetrical underlying investment flows that made claims from these countries' investors less likely. This perception only changed once the United States became a victim of investment claims in the late 1990s and early 2000s, prompting a realignment of its BIT and FTA practice from 2004 onward.

C. Wave 3: 2004—The Revised US and Canadian Model BITs

The final step in the staircase of North American legal innovation was the publication of the revised US and Canadian model BITs in 2004, which reflected the two countries' experience as respondents in investment arbitration. In 1997, the first investment arbitration claims were filed against Mexico and Canada under NAFTA; in 1998 the first claim was launched against the United States.[135] The rise of investment arbitration fundamentally altered the perception and political processes underlying investment treaties. At the same time, it had relatively little effect on investment treaty design leading to refinements of the NAFTA treaty model (NAFTA-plus) rather than a reinvention of treaty design.[136]

The events leading up to the 2004 revisions marked a change of mindset especially among US negotiators and policymakers. The NAFTA claims had debunked long-held beliefs that only states with poor rule of law records would become targets of investment claims and that sophisticated legal systems, like that of the United States, were immune to challenges pursuant to investment treaties.[137] Moreover, these investment claims turned investment treaties into a politically salient issue. Prior to the rise of investment arbitration, investment treaties passed below the political and public radar in North America as technical instruments to curb governmental abuse against vulnerable investors abroad. But when foreign investors challenged public health measures in Canada

---

[135] *Metalclad v. United Mexican States*, ICSID Case No. ARB(AF)/97/1, *Ethyl Corp v. Canada* (UNCITRAL), *The Loewen Group, Inc. & Raymond L. Loewen v. USA*, ICSID Case No. ARB(AF)/98/3.

[136] Wolfgang Alschner, *The Impact of Investment Arbitration on Investment Treaty Design: Myth Versus Reality*, 42 YALE J. INT'L L. (2017).

[137] Alvarez, *supra* note 61, at 3 ("The United States could afford to assume that its laws and practices were already consistent with the minimal standards contained in its BITs."); prior to the rise of investment claims against Canada and the United States, a widely held assumption was that investment claims would only be launched against developed countries, since developed countries already offered adequate protection to foreign investors. *See, e.g.,* Voss, stating that "[a]n active investment protection and promotion policy exists only in relations with Third World countries. In all the industrial countries there is a comparable and sufficiently stable protection framework so that investments flow freely to their optimal economic use." Jürgen Voss, *The Protection and Promotion of Foreign Direct Investment in Developing Countries: Interests, Interdependencies, Intricacies,* 31 INT'L & COMP. L.Q. 686–708, 688 (1982).

(*Ethyl v. Canada*, ultimately settled)[138] and the United States (*Methanex v. United States*, ultimately decided in favor of the United States),[139] they sparked a public debate on the potential of NAFTA Chapter 11 to undermine public interest measures.[140]

The hostile political environment against investment agreements prompted a hiatus in the Canadian and the US BIT programs in the late 1990s. Both countries used this period to take stock and to reach out to proponents and skeptics of investment protection in order to develop a new model agreement that would incorporate the lessons learnt from NAFTA.[141] The 2002 US Bipartisan Trade Promotion Authority Act (TPA) then contained a political concession toward investment law skeptics in setting out the negotiation objectives of investment treaties:

> [T]he principal negotiating objectives of the United States regarding foreign investment are to reduce or eliminate artificial or trade-distorting barriers to foreign investment, while ensuring that foreign investors in the United States are *not accorded greater substantive rights with respect to investment protections than United States investors in the United States*, and to secure for investors important rights comparable to those that would be available under United States legal principles and practice.[142]

It was thus the domestic political process that shifted the focus of the US BIT program from exclusively protecting investment abroad (curbing opportunism) to also preserving policy space at home (seizing regret). The 2002 TPA moderated the US position vis-à-vis investment protection.[143] In practice, that meant aligning the country's NAFTA and BIT practices.

---

[138] *Ethyl Corp v. Canada*, UNCITRAL. *See also* Weiler Todd, *The Ethyl Arbitration: First of Its Kind and a Harbinger of Things to Come*, 11 AM. J. INT'L L. ARB. 187 (2001).

[139] *Methanex Corp. v. United States*, UNCITRAL, Final Award of the Tribunal on Jurisdiction and Merits, August 3, 2005.

[140] *See, e.g.*, the public citizens leaflet on the case, available at http://www.citizen.org/trade/article_redirect.cfm?ID=6221 (last accessed May 3, 2015).

[141] Céline Lévesque, *Influences on the Canadian FIPA Model and the US Model BIT: NAFTA Chapter 11 and Beyond*, 44 CAN. Y.B. INT'L L. 249, 251–253 (2006). A summary of stakeholder input can be found in the *Report of the Subcommittee on Investment Regarding the Draft Model Bilateral Investment Treaty* presented to the State Department's Advisory Committee on International Economic Policy, January 30, 2004, available at http://www.ciel.org/Publications/BIT_Subcmte_Jan3004.pdf (last accessed May 3, 2015).

[142] 2002 Bipartisan Trade Promotion Authority Act (TPA), 19 U.S. Code Chapter 24, para. 3802(b)(3), available at https://www.law.cornell.edu/uscode/text/19/chapter-24. *See also* David A. Gantz, *The Evolution of FTA Investment Provisions: From NAFTA to the United States–Chile Free Trade Agreement*, 19 AM. U. INT'L L. REV. 679, 704–709 (2003).

[143] To some commentators, the 2002 TPA was even reminiscent of the Calvo Doctrine. O. M. Garibaldi, *Carlos Calvo Redivivus: The Rediscovery of the Calvo Doctrine in the Era of Investment Treaties*, 3 TRANSNAT'L DISP. MGMT. (2006).

The main innovation of the 2004 models consisted of incorporating the lessons learned from NAFTA litigation.[144] These were targeted refinements to NAFTA. In particular, the models codified earlier interpretations by the NAFTA Free Trade Commission with respect to the nature of FET being grounded in the customary international law minimum standard of treatment and concerning transparency in arbitral proceedings including open arbitral hearings and amicus curiae submissions.[145] The model BITs also reacted to several controversies that had emerged in case law, for example, over the meaning of "investment" or the distinction between indirect expropriation and nondiscriminatory public interest regulation.[146]

Proponents of the 2004 US model heralded its ability to strike a balance between investment protection and sovereignty concerns.[147] Opponents of the template, in contrast, argued that it drastically lowered the level of investment protection alleging that states try to escape their investment commitments in light of rising claims against them.[148] As Alvarez put it: "If the United States led the charge in favor of investor protections [with its 1982 model treaty], it now appears to be leading the drive in the opposite direction."[149] Similarly, Schwebel lamented the "perplexities and deficiencies" of the 2004 model BIT that result in a lowering of investment protection standards and called the model a "regressive development of international law."[150]

Substantively, however, the 2004 United States and Canadian model BITs are better understood as refined versions of NAFTA or "NAFTA-plus."[151] As Gilbert Gagné and Jean-Frédérique Morin put it, "the recent US FTAs and model BIT do not reveal a thorough policy reorientation but rather adjustments to the policy at the basis of NAFTA's investment chapter."[152] Similarly, Céline Lévesque

---

[144] G. Gagne & J. F. Morin, *The Evolving American Policy on Investment Protection: Evidence from Recent FTAs and the 2004 Model BIT*, 9 J. INT'L ECON. L. 357–382 (2006); Lévesque, *supra* note 141; Andrea J. Menaker, *Benefiting from Experience: Developments in the United States' Most Recent Investment Agreements*, 12 U.C. DAVIS J. INT'L L. & POL'Y 121–129 (2006).

[145] The NAFTA Free Trade Commission, Notes of *Interpretation* of Certain Chapter 11 Provisions, July 31, 2001, was integrated through Article 5 and its Annex of the 2004 U.S. Model BIT. The NAFTA Free Trade Commission, *Statement of the Free Trade Commission on non-disputing party participation*, October 7, 2003 was integrated through Articles 28 and 29 of the US model BIT.

[146] Alschner, *supra* note 136. The same lessons learnt were simultaneously integrated into the US FTA practice; for a detailed discussion, *see* Clodfelter, *supra* note 101.

[147] Kenneth J. Vandevelde, *A Comparison of the 2004 and 1994 US Model BITs: Rebalancing Investor and Host Country Interests, in* YEARBOOK ON INTERNATIONAL INVESTMENT LAW AND POLICY 2008–9 (Karl P. Sauvant ed., 2009).

[148] José E. Alvarez, *The Return of the State*, 20 MINN. J. INT'L L. 223, 234 (2011).

[149] *Id.* at 235.

[150] Stephen M. Schwebel, *The United States 2004 Model Bilateral Investment Treaty: An Exercise in the Regressive Development of International Law, in* JUSTICE IN INTERNATIONAL LAW (2011).

[151] Kinnear &and Hansen, *supra* note 121; Lévesque, *supra* note 141; Gagne &and Morin, *supra* note 144.

[152] Gagne & Morin, *supra* note 144, at 357.

described the Canadian and US 2004 BIT models as codifying NAFTA practice.[153] The 2004 US model BIT merely distilled NAFTA best practices into the BIT format. Crucially, then, the most radical and far-reaching design changes in North American IIA practice took place in 1992 (when completeness scores jumped by 20 points) and not in 2004 (when completeness scores increased by 10 points). North American design innovation is therefore an example of proactive state-driven change that mostly predates the rise of investment claims.

The NAFTA parties began swiftly integrating the refined models into their newly concluded agreements. The United States signed BITs with Uruguay (2005) and Rwanda (2008), closely based on the model,[154] which score among the most contractually complete IIAs given their detail and complexity.[155] In addition to the two BITs, the United States concluded FTAs with Singapore and Chile in 2003 and with Morocco and Central America (DR–CAFTA) in 2004 that closely mirrored the NAFTA-plus model.[156] Canada signed its first BIT following the new model with Peru in 2006, which is among the longest agreement in the BIT universe with fifty-one articles. Since then, Canada has signed over a dozen FTAs with investment chapters and BITs that follow the new design (see Figure 3.2). Mexico, too, benefited from the innovation among its neighbors and began concluding progressively more complete BITs that drew from the language of the two models (Figure 3.3).

IV. Global Diffusion of American Treaty Design

In the early 2000s, the NAFTA-plus model began to diffuse outside of North America, leading to a gradual global shift away from incomplete BITs mirrored on European practice and toward contractually more complete agreements

---

[153] Lévesque, *supra* note 141, at 249.

[154] Wolfgang Alschner & Dmitriy Skougarevskiy, *Mapping the Universe of International Investment Agreements*, 19 J. Int'l Econ. L., 572 (2016).

[155] The most recent 2012 US model BIT revision made only slight additions to its predecessor and has not yet been used in a BIT. On the elaboration process, *see* Peter Muchlinski, *Trends in International Investment Agreements: Calls for Reforms of Model Bilateral Investment Treaties in Norway, South Africa and the United States, in* Yearbook on International Investment Law and Policy 2009–10 (2010). For reactions to the model BIT, *see* Sarah Anderson et al., *The New U.S. Model Bilateral Investment Treaty: A Public Interest Critique*, Institute for Policy Studies, May 9, 2012, available at http://www.ips-dc.org/reports/the_new_us_model_bilateral_investment_treaty_a_p ublic_interest_critique. *See also* Bill Waren, *Old Trade Deal Wine in New Bottle*, Friends of the Earth, May 4, 2012, available at http://www.foe.org/news/blog/2012-05-old-trade-deal-wine-in-new-bot tle-us-model-for-trans; Mark Kantor, *The New U.S. Model BIT: If Both Sides Are Angry With You, You Must Be Doing Something Right*, 5 N.Y. Disp. Resol. Law., no. 2, 47–61 (2012).

[156] Clodfelter, *supra* note 101. In contrast, the USA–Bahrain FTA (2004) did not have an investment chapter and the USA–Australia FTA (2004) provided for investment protection clauses, but, following resistance from Australia, omitted enforcement through ISDS. *See* Dodge, *supra* note 10.

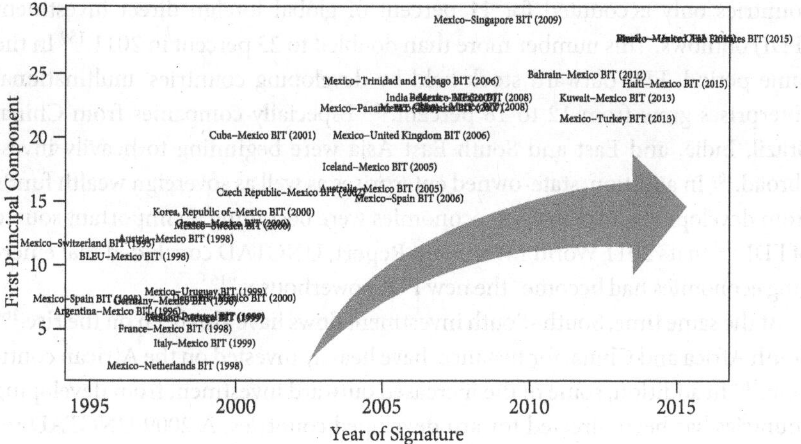

Figure 3.3 Evolution of Mexican BITs

inspired by North American practice. "[NAFTA] Chapter 11 is the most comprehensive investment accord to date. [...] The chapter ought to set a standard for further multilateral and bilateral investment accords in the hemisphere."[157] These words by Daniel Price written in 1993 shortly after the conclusion of NAFTA have proved accurate in the ensuing decades as North American practice began inspiring similarly contractually complete treaties around the world.

This "Americanization" of the IIA universe was driven by (1) a growing symmetry in investment relations through bidirectional investment flows as well as developments in investment arbitration and (2) increasing politicization of domestic investment relations. In combination, these factors incentivized countries to shift toward more complete IIAs copying from the tried-and-tested North American treaty practice as an alternative to the traditional European BIT.

A. New Symmetry in Investment Relations

Since the early 2000s, investment relations have become progressively more symmetrical as investment increasingly flows bidirectionally and developing countries turn from capital importer to capital exporters.[158] In 2001, developing

---

[157] Price, *supra* note 101, at 736; similarly Clodfelter, *supra* note 101, at 1283 ("[NAFTA] can serve as a model for investor-state dispute resolution provisions in other agreements").

[158] Axel Berger, *Recognising the Signs of the Times: Investment Protection in the 21st Century*, Current Column of Bonn: German Development Institute/Deutsches Institut für Entwicklungspolitik (DIE), October 22, 2012, https://www.die-gdi.de/en/the-current-column/article/recognising-the-signs-of-the-times-investment-protection-in-the-21st-century/ (last accessed May 3, 2015).

countries only accounted for 11 percent of global foreign direct investment (FDI) outflows. This number more than doubled to 23 percent in 2011.[159] In the same period, FDI outward stock held by developing countries' multinational enterprises grew from 12 to 18 percent.[160] Especially companies from China, Brazil, India, and East and South East Asia were beginning to heavily invest abroad.[161] In addition, state-owned enterprises as well as sovereign wealth funds from developing and transition economies were becoming an important source of FDI.[162] In its 2011 World Investment Report, UNCTAD concluded that emerging economies had become "the new FDI powerhouses."[163]

At the same time, South–South investment flows have also been on the rise.[164] South Africa and China, for instance, have heavily invested on the African continent.[165] In addition, some of the increased outward investment from developing countries has been directed toward developed countries. A 2009 UNCTAD report concluded that "[i]nvestment flows that were once a one-way street from developed countries to developing countries increasingly become busy two-lane roads."[166] The distinction between capital-exporting and capital-importing countries thus began to blur, as emerging economies became home to global investors and OECD countries host to some of that investment. Investment protection and market liberalization became key policy objectives for developing countries' IIA negotiators, while Northern IIA policymakers grew increasingly worried about preserving policy space.[167]

In addition, symmetry also became a more important factor as developed countries entered into investment treaties among themselves. After having stopped concluding investment agreements in the 1960s, the 2010s saw an unprecedented reversal of this trend as negotiations between major developed countries over trade agreements that contained investment chapters were concluded. The 2014 signing of the Comprehensive Economic and Trade Agreement (CETA) between Canada and the European Union and the 2017 conclusion of the Comprehensive and Progressive Agreement for Trans-Pacific Partnership (CPTPP) connecting Japan, Canada, Australia, and New Zealand in addition

---

[159] UNCTAD, WORLD INVESTMENT REPORT 2011: NON-EQUITY MODES OF INTERNATIONAL PRODUCTION AND DEVELOPMENT 9 (2011).

[160] *Id.* at 9.

[161] *Id.* at 6–7.

[162] *Id.* at 9. UNCTAD, WORLD INVESTMENT REPORT 2012. TOWARDS A NEW GENERATION OF INVESTMENT POLICIES 13 (2012).

[163] UNCTAD, *supra* note 159, at xii.

[164] *Id.* at 32.

[165] *Id.* at 32.

[166] UNCTAD, THE PROTECTION OF NATIONAL SECURITY IN IIAs 2 (2009).

[167] Southern investment in the North has given rise to new anxiety as companies in a "strategic sector" or "critical infrastructure" are threatened by takeovers from developing countries' investors. *See* Karl P. Sauvant, *FDI Protectionism Is on the Rise*, World Bank Policy Research Working Paper 5052 (2009).

to several other emerging economies are cases in point. The considerable mutual investment stock in these countries brought symmetry and reciprocity more heavily to bear on investment negotiations and moderated the content of investment protection provisions in line with North American practice and greater contractual completeness.[168]

Finally, developments in investment arbitration have made claims against states, including developed countries, more likely creating symmetry even in contexts where underlying investment flows remain highly unidirectional. Complex corporate structures today allow a company to quickly become a protected foreign "investor" under any IIA.[169] Furthermore, broad interpretations of the concept of "investor" and "investment" in ISDS cases, which include minority shareholding and their indirect claims for company losses, often make multiple investment treaties potentially applicable in a single investment project.[170] As Bart Legum succinctly put it: "The reality that foreign capital is highly fungible and the breadth of the definitions of investor and investment thus combine to effectively transform the facially bilateral obligations of the BIT into an obligation that the host State must consider potentially applicable to all investors."[171] Given that treaty protection provides an incentive for companies to become "foreign," claims were even launched by nationals against their home states through foreign vehicles.[172] In short, even in the absence of meaningful bidirectional investment flows, a state can become subject to investment claims.

Since no signatory to an IIA can today feel safe from investment claims a new symmetry began to pervade investment treaty-making. While in the past, the developing host country would bear the compliance burden under an investment treaty, negotiators today contract under a veil of ignorance not knowing which state party to the IIA may be "victim" and "injurer." Add to that the better understanding of IIAs and their potential dangers.[173] It thus became efficient for

---

[168] For a text-as-data analysis of these new treaties, *see* Wolfgang Alschner & Dmitriy Skougarevskiy, *The New Gold Standard? Empirically Situating the Trans-Pacific Partnership in the Investment Treaty Universe*, 17 J. WORLD INVESTMENT & TRADE (2016); Alschner I Skougarevskiy, *supra* note 154.

[169] SCHILL, *supra* note 18, at 221. Although states are beginning to curtail this practice through denial of benefits clauses.

[170] D. Gaukrodger, *Investment Treaties and Shareholder Claims for Reflective Loss: Insights from Advanced Systems of Corporate Law*, OECD Working Papers on International Investment, OECD Investment Division (2014); SCHILL, *supra* note 18.

[171] B. Legum, *Defining Investment and Investor—Who Is Entitled to Claim?*, 22 ARB. INT'L 521, 525 (2006).

[172] One of the most well known and ultimately dismissed cases resulted from a purposeful corporate restructuring of Philip Morris Australia into a Hong Kong incorporated company in order to challenge Australia's plain packaging legislation under the Hong Kong–Australia BIT.

[173] On the learning from ISDS claims both indirectly (claims against other states) and directly, *see* Poulsen, *supra* note 72; Lauge Poulsen & Emma Aisbett, *When the Claim Hits: Bilateral Investment Treaties and Bounded Rational Learning*, 65 WORLD POL. 273–313 (2013); Mark S. Manger & Clint

developed and developing countries alike to write more complete treaties, which spell out the rights and obligations of the contracting parties explicitly. As a result, countries have increasingly designed IIAs that not only curb opportunism of their BIT partners abroad but also preserve their own ability to seize regret at home.

B. Increasing Domestic Politicization of Investment Law

This symmetry alone may not have been enough to change established practices. In particular, when attendant bargaining and innovation costs are very real for the ministry administrating IIAs, yet benefits are more diffuse because they accrue to the country as a whole, bureaucratic inertia may weigh in favor for continuing with business as usual.[174] A second major force behind the broader transformation of IIAs was the domestic politicization of investment treaties, which prompted change in national investment policies.

Both in developed and in developing countries, IIA negotiations used to be technical matters that passed below the political radar. A Mexican official involved in BIT negotiations interviewed by Lauge Poulsen, for instance, stated that "[b]y contrast with FTA agreements, there was no legal review, control, or scrutiny to the content. . . . Often BIT negotiations have been done by a couple of guys; they sent it to parliament with no real discussion."[175] Similarly, a South African negotiator concurs that the treaties were "very under-politicized. One or two times we explained it all to the parliamentary committee, but even there it was acknowledged as a technical agreement."[176] Equally, in developed countries the level of domestic politicization of investment agreements was very low. In contrast to trade agreements, that produced political opposition from import-competing industries, there was little that could spark domestic controversy over IIAs, given that the burden of IIAs was thought to fall primarily on the developing country partner and effects in terms of dislocating production abroad were not proven.[177]

Peinhardt, *Learning and the Precision of International Investment Agreements*, 43 INT'L INTERACTIONS 1–21 (2017).

[174] Sergio Puig, *Does Bureaucratic Inertia Matter in Treaty Bargaining-Or, Toward a Greater Use of Qualitative Data in Empirical Legal Inquiries*, 12 SANTA CLARA J. INT'L L. 317 (2013); Alschner, *supra* note 136.

[175] POULSEN, *supra* note 72, at 247.

[176] *Id.* at 288.

[177] KENNETH J. VANDEVELDE, U.S. INTERNATIONAL INVESTMENT AGREEMENTS 31, 35, 45 (2009); Gudgeon, *supra* note 2, at 112–113 ("the framers of the Model BIT were unaware of any proven relationship between the existence of FCN treaties or European BITs and investment flows").

This gradually began to change because of two main processes. First, the integration of investment chapters into trade agreements brought the attention long devoted on the latter also to bear on investment policymaking.[178] When trade and investment met in NAFTA, investment rules suddenly became a controversial issue. Ross Perot, candidate in the 1992 US presidential elections, for instance, popularized NAFTA's potential to divert US investments to Mexico through a "giant sucking sound" as jobs, industry, and investment move south.[179] Second, investment arbitration claims also politicized investment policymaking. For example, investment claims sparked political debate and controversy in South Africa and India, prompting both states to reconsider their investment treaty programs.[180]

In other countries, ISDS claims did not develop a politicizing effect because their occurrence had remained secret.[181] Germany, for instance, had been hit by its first investment claim already in 2001, yet that fact remained unknown until 2008 when journalists revealed it.[182] Once investment claims against Germany became known, in particular, the well-publicized claim of the Swedish energy provider Vattenfall asking for compensation for the country's withdrawal from nuclear power, the issue entered the political discourse.[183] In Germany, this coincided with the launch of free trade negotiations with the United States over a Transatlantic Trade and Investment Partnership. The combination of claims with FTA negotiations turned investment rules from a technical issue only known to experts into a political controversy in just a few years. ISDS triggered strong

---

[178] On the political nature of trade agreements, *see* Robert D. Putnam, *Diplomacy and Domestic Politics: The Logic of Two-Level Games*, 42 INT'L ORG. 427–460 (1988).

[179] "We have got to stop sending jobs overseas. It's pretty simple: If you're paying $12, $13, $14 an hour for factory workers and you can move your factory South of the border, pay a dollar an hour for labor, . . . have no health care—that's the most expensive single element in making a car—have no environmental controls, no pollution controls and no retirement, and you don't care about anything but making money, there will be a giant sucking sound going south." *New York Times* transcript of the Clinton-Bush-Perot presidential debate on October 15, 1992, available at http://www.nytimes.com/1992/10/16/us/the-1992-campaign-transcript-of-2d-tv-debate-between-bush-clinton-and-perot.html (last accessed June 3, 2015).

[180] A claim against South Africa's Black Economic Empowerment Legislation in the mining sector led South Africa government to review its investment policy. *See* POULSEN, *supra* note 72, at 262ff; Muchlinski, *supra* note 155. In India, a wave of claims prompted the adaptation of a new model BIT. *See* https://mygov.in/group-issue/draft-indian-model-bilateral-investment-treaty-text/ (last accessed May 3, 2015).

[181] Alschner, *supra* note 136.

[182] *Ashok Sancheti v. Germany*; IA Reporter, *Court documents reveal that Indian investor filed treaty claim against UK government in 2006; Foreign Office views UNCITRAL-based disputes as confidential and declines to disclose their existence*, vol. 1, no. 18 (November 25, 2008), available at http://www.iareporter.com/downloads/20100107_13/download (last accessed June 3, 2015). The terms of the settlement remain unknown.

[183] *Vattenfall AB and others v. Federal Republic of Germany*, ICSID Case No. ARB/12/12. *See also Why Vattenfall Is Taking Germany to Court*, VATTENFALL NEWS, December 9, 2014, available at http://corporate.vattenfall.com/news-and-media/news/2014/why-vattenfall-is-taking-germany-to-court/ (last accessed June 3, 2015).

opposition from civil society groups and even sparked mass protests with the result that senior German politicians called for vetoing any treaty that included such a mechanism.[184]

C. Embracing American IIA Design

Faced with symmetrical investment flows, rising risks of investment claims, and a politicization of investment rules, policymakers outside of North America began reconsidering their earlier treaty design choices. The more complete NAFTA-plus template presented a readily available and attractive alternative to the traditional incomplete European BIT. Third states could freeride on the United States and Canada's experience as respondents in investment arbitration by copying from its practice.

The ensuing shift to more complete IIAs inspired by North American treaties has been global. In the case of South America, diffusion of North American design features took a direct path as states contracted with the NAFTA parties and then became norm diffusers of NAFTA-plus treaties with third states.[185] In contrast, in East Asian, the diffusion of American design elements occurred mostly indirectly as states, such as Japan, Taiwan, Singapore, or China, took independent inspiration from North American practice. Finally, the NAFTA-plus model also inspired the work of international organizations, such as UNCTAD and non-governmental institutions, such as IISD, in their reporting and technical assistance which further diffused NAFTA-plus elements to developing countries.[186] The 2006 IISD model agreement, for example, borrowed many NAFTA-plus plus elements, which, in turn, influenced the treaty practice of African states through technical assistance.[187] The following selection of examples illustrates the global trend of incorporating North American design elements.

Japan. Japan began its investment treaty practice in 1977 when it signed its first BIT with Egypt using the European-style, incomplete BIT model.[188] On the basis

---

[184] *Germany to Reject EU–Canada Trade Deal—Sueddeutsche Newspaper*, REUTERS, July 26, 2014, available at http://www.reuters.com/article/2014/07/26/germany-canada-trade-idUSL6N0Q10CS2 0140726?irpc=932&ref=browsi (last accessed June 3, 2015). *See also* Ralph Alexander Lorz, *Germany, the Transatlantic Trade and Investment Partnership and Investment-Dispute Settlement: Observations on a Paradox*, COLUM. FDI PERSP., no. 132, October 13, 2014.

[185] For a partial graphic illustration, *see* Alschner, Seiermann, & Skougarevskiy, *supra* note 134, at 21.

[186] UNCTAD, for example, routinely highlights treaty practice that originated in North America in its flagship publication, the World Investment Report. *See, e.g.*, UNCTAD, WORLD INVESTMENT REPORT 2005: TRANSNATIONAL CORPORATIONS AND THE INTERNATIONALIZATION OF R&D (INCLUDES CD-ROM) 26–28 (2006), https://www.un-ilibrary.org/content/books/9789211554991 (last accessed October 6, 2021).

[187] Wolfgang Alschner, Manfred Elsig, & Simon Wüthrich, *The Imprint on International Institutions on Bilateral Investment Treaties*, Working Paper (on file with the author).

[188] Shotaro Hamamoto & Luke Nottage, *Foreign Investment In and Out of Japan: Economic Backdrop, Domestic Law, and International Treaty-Based Investor-State Dispute Resolution*, Sydney Law School Legal Studies Research Paper No. 10/145 December 2010, at 4.

of that template, eight more agreements were concluded over the next twenty-five years. Then in 2002, Japan's treaty practice changed fundamentally, and the country started to conclude what Hamamoto and Nottage call a "new generation" of Japanese agreements.[189] Hamamoto and Nottage do not explain that change. However, it coincided with the conclusion of Japan's first FTA,[190] the Singapore–Japan FTA (2002), which contained an investment chapter modeled on NAFTA Chapter 11, including pre-establishment national and MFN treatment, a detailed arbitration mechanisms similar to NAFTA, a denial of benefits clause, and a prudential-measures carveout. The fusion of investment and trade concerns in Japan's FTA with Singapore seems to have spurred innovation also in its BIT practice, similarly to NAFTA's impact on Canadian investment treaties in the mid-1990s. North American treaty features absent in previous Japanese BITs, such as pre-establishment national and MFN treatment and the prohibition of performance requirements, were then included in the Japan–South Korea BIT (2002).[191] Today, Japanese IIAs rank as the most complex and comprehensive agreements alongside those of Canada and the United States and mirror many of their design choices.

China. Commentators have observed a "partial 'NAFTA-ization'" of the Chinese investment treaty program over time.[192] As Axel Berger writes, "[f]rom a policy-diffusion perspective, it is interesting to note that China has been willing to incorporate innovative NAFTA-inspired investment rules in individual agreements."[193] Chinese BITs were long influenced by strong hesitations about international arbitration and a conservative design that privileged host state rights over investor interests.[194] After 1998, China's growing outward investment progressively led to more protective BITs.[195] Yet it was only recently that China turned toward a treaty design modeled on US treaty practice seeking to balance inward and outward investment interests.[196] At the same time, as Berger explains, "China is pursuing a flexible approach that adapts to the BIT models preferred by the relevant partner country."[197] Its 2009 BIT with Switzerland is

---

[189] Hamamoto & Nottage, *supra* note 188.

[190] *Id.* at 9–10.

[191] *See* the comparative table at *id.* at 22–23.

[192] Axel Berger, *Investment Rules in Chinese PTIAs—A Partial "NAFTA-ization, in* Preferential Trade and Investment Agreements: From Recalibration to Reintegration (Rainer Hofmann, Stephan W. Schill, & Christian J. Tams eds., 2013).

[193] Axel Berger, *Investment Rules in Chinese PTIAs—A Partial "NAFTA-ization,"* 33 (2013), http://papers.ssrn.com/abstract=2171765 (last accessed August 4, 2013).

[194] Cai Congyan, *China–US BIT Negotiations and the Future of Investment Treaty Regime: A Grand Bilateral Bargain with Multilateral Implications,* 12 J. Int'l Econ. L. 457–506, 461–462 (2009); Berger, *supra* note 193, at 9.

[195] Axel Berger, *China's New Bilateral Investment Treaty Programme: Substance, Rational and Implications for International Investment Law Making, in* The Politics of International Economic Law: The Next Four Years, Washington, DC, November 2008, at 14–15 (2008). Stephan W. Schill, *Tearing Down the Great Wall: The New Generation Investment Treaties of the People's Republic of China,* 15 Cardozo J. Int'l & Comp. L. 73, 81–83 (2007).

[196] Congyan, *supra* note 194, at 486; Berger, *supra* note 192. This "Americanization," however, is only partial, as Chinese BITs do not include investment liberalization provisions normally found in American treaties. *See generally* Berger, *supra* note 195.

[197] Berger, *supra* note 193, at 14.

thus closer in design to traditional European treaty practice, while the Canada–China BIT from 2012 closely follows the Canadian model BIT.

ASEAN. Following its creation in 1967 by Indonesia, Malaysia, Philippines, Singapore, and Thailand, ASEAN developed a more pronounced orientation toward economic integration in the 1970s and in 1987, three years after Brunei had joined the organization, concluded the first regional investment treaty.[198] The treaty was short and simple closely following European-style BITs. Cambodia, Lao, Vietnam, and Myanmar joined the organization in the 1990s. At the same time ASEAN members began signing investment treaties among themselves, creating a spaghetti bowl of overlapping agreements.[199] In the 2000s, gradual Americanization took hold among the ASEAN members, culminating in the adoption of the ASEAN Comprehensive Investment Agreement in 2009. The agreement contains pre-establishment national and MFN treatment, performance requirements, sojourn of personnel and publication of laws clauses (i.e., first stage American elements); carveouts for compulsory licenses, transfer exceptions, prudential carveouts and a NAFTA-style arbitration mechanism that includes binding joint interpretations (i.e., second stage American elements); but also clarifies indirect expropriation and FET provisions and adds transparency in the arbitral proceedings (i.e., third-stage American elements).

CPTPP. Several of the ASEAN countries, along with Mexico, Canada, Japan, Australia, New Zealand, and the United States signed the Trans-Pacific Partnership (TPP) in 2016. The agreement is perhaps one of the most striking examples of Americanization: 81 percent of the text of its investment chapter was copied from the 2006 US–Colombia FTA.[200] As Todd Allee and Andrew Lugg write: "US treaty language is pre-eminent in the TPP, suggesting that the USA had heavy influence in writing this important new agreement."[201] Although the United States withdrew from the TPP after Donald Trump took office as US president in 2017, the remaining states retained the bulk of the TPP text, only amending or suspending two dozen of its articles, when they concluded the CPTPP in 2018.

South America. Several states in South America quickly embraced the NAFTA-plus model. Chile, for example, had initially been invited to join NAFTA but, when that failed, signed agreements with Canada (1996) and Mexico (1998) closely modeled on NAFTA. In 2003 Chile signed an FTA with the United States, internalizing the NAFTA-plus language. The country then became a promoter

---

[198] *Agreement among the Government of Brunei Darussalam, the Republic of Indonesia, Malaysia, the Republic of the Philippines, the Republic of Singapore and the Kingdom of Thailand for the Promotion and Protection of Investments,* Manila, December 15, 1987.

[199] Wolfgang Alschner, *Regionalism and Overlap in Investment Treaty Law: Towards Consolidation or Contradiction?,* 17 J. INT'L ECON. L. 271–298, 279–280 (2014).

[200] Alschner & Skougarevskiy, *supra* note 168.

[201] Todd Allee & Andrew Lugg, *Who Wrote the Rules for the Trans-Pacific Partnership?,* 3 RESEARCH & POLITICS 2053168016658919, 4 (2016).

of NAFTA-style IIAs itself, signing an FTA with South Korea the same year that closely trailed NAFTA's Chapter 11. Chile has signed corresponding agreements with a range of South America and East Asian states since.

Similarly, Colombia's first exposure to the NAFTA model occurred in 1994 when it signed an FTA with Mexico, which included an investment chapter modeled on NAFTA. Several NAFTA-type FTAs followed, including the Colombia–US FTA (2006). With respect to BITs, the agreements signed by Colombia until 2000 were firmly embedded in the European treaty model. After a five-year hiatus, this began to change with the Colombia–Spain BIT (2005) that included some NAFTA elements such as an exclusion of compulsory licenses or transfer exceptions.[202] In 2007, Colombia then introduced a new model BIT. As a Colombian representative later explained, the model was "drafted after careful consideration of [investor-state arbitration] awards from that time, interpretations from the NAFTA Free Trade Commission and consultations with UNCTAD officials."[203] The new model and subsequent Colombian BITs began to include many of the features of the 2004 US model BIT, such as clarifications of the notion of indirect expropriation or the linking of FET to customary law.[204] With the new model, Colombia then became a NAFTA-plus norm entrepreneur. The BIT with Peru, signed in December 2007, included further NAFTA features including, but not limited to, interpretative interventions by the contracting parties and prudential measure carveouts. Colombia even carried some of NAFTA's features, like a provision on investment and the environment, into British IIA practice where such language was absent, through their 2010 BIT.

COMESA. Shifting to the African continent, the Americanization of the IIA universe there has been closely associated with regional integration efforts. The largest regional investment treaty in Africa is the Common Market for Eastern and Southern Africa (COMESA) Common Investment Area signed in 2007 and spanning all the way from Egypt to Swaziland along the East African coast, comprising nineteen member countries. The Investment Area "reflects certain new developments taken in US and Canadian Model BITs."[205] Among others, it integrates language linking FET to customary international law, differentiating indirect expropriation and bona fide regulation, carving out compulsory licenses and including arbitration innovations such as limitation periods, standing requirements, and open hearings from NAFTA and the 2004 US model BIT.

---

[202] *See* arts. 4(7), 6(3-4), and 10(5). *See similarly* Colombia–Switzerland BIT (2006).

[203] Statement of Colombia, United Nations Conference on Trade and Development (UNCTAD) World Investment Forum, Geneva, October 14, 2014, available at https://worldinvestmentforum.unc tad.org/wp-content/uploads/2014/10/Vargas-Saldarriaga.pdf.

[204] The model BIT can be accessed at http://www.italaw.com/documents/inv_model_bit_colom bia.pdf (last accessed May 3, 2015).

[205] Muchlinski, *supra* note 155, at 33.

European Union. The arguably most significant development for the Americanization of the IIA universe has occurred in Europe. In December 2009, the Lisbon Treaty entered into force, endowing the European Union with new competence to conclude investment agreements as part of its common commercial policy.[206] At that point the European Union had to decide whether it should continue signing investment treaties using the traditional European "gold standard"—agreements marked by their simplicity and brevity—or shift to a American-style treaties.[207] The first agreements signed by the European Union, the CETA with Canada in September 2014, pointed to an Americanization. Its investment chapter contains many of the features found in earlier Canadian agreements—but not European ones—including an investment liberalization component, the prohibition of performance requirements, entry of senior management (i.e., first stage American elements), new public policy flexibilities and coordinating exceptions (i.e., second stage American elements), and clarifications, for example, on indirect expropriations (i.e., third-stage American elements). By 2014, commentators thus spoke of EU practice "converging towards NAFTA."[208]

This review of changing investment practices is illustrative of a global trend. As Nikos Lavranos put it, the "NAFTA-model is de facto rapidly becoming the new standard investment model treaty for the whole world."[209] Similarly, Jansen Calamita writes: "Clearer and more specific expression of the meaning of treaty is not simply a North American fetish. Rather it is by now well on its way to becoming international best practice."[210]

This gradual Americanization does not mean that states around the world started concluding agreements that are identical to NAFTA or the United States' model agreement. In practice, states often selectively mixed and matched elements from the North American practice with language and elements of their own design.[211] The partial nature of this NAFTA-ization explains why in Figure 3.1 many recent treaties score higher than older BITs, but not quite as high as recent US or Canadian treaties. The trend, however, was clear. States looked to and replicated North American treaty design, which resulted in a wave of medium- to high-scoring IIAs over the last two decades that differ markedly from the highly incomplete IIAs inspired by early European BITs.

---

[206] *See* art. 188C(1) of the Treaty of Lisbon (Article 207(1) Treaty on the Functioning of the European Union (TFEU)).

[207] Nikos Lavranos, *The New EU Investment Treaties: Convergence towards the NAFTA Model as the New Plurilateral Model BIT Text?* (2013), http://papers.ssrn.com/abstract=2241455 (last accessed August 4, 2013).

[208] Filippo Fontanelli & Giuseppe Bianco, *Converging Towards NAFTA: An Analysis of FTA Investment Chapters in the European Union and the United States,* 50 Stan. J Int'l L. 211–359 (2014); Lavranos, *supra* note 207.

[209] Lavranos, *supra* note 207, at 3.

[210] N. Jansen Calamita, *The Making of Europe's International Investment Policy: Uncertain First Steps,* 39 Legal Issues of Econ. Integration 301–330, 328 (2012).

[211] Wolfgang Alschner & Dmitriy Skougarevskiy, *Convergence and Divergence in the Investment Treaty Universe—Scoping the Potential for Multilateral Consolidation,* 8 Trade, L. & Dev. (2016).

V. A New Diversity

Early signs suggest that the IIA regime has recently moved into a new phase of its development. Previous decades were marked by relative homogeneity, disrupted, at times, through spurs of innovation that created opposing treaty models (FCN versus BITs, European versus American IIAs). For long periods, however, a specific treaty design dominated. Highly incomplete BITs dominated much of the 1960s to 1990s. The mid-2000s through the mid-2010s then saw countries adopt the gap-filling strategies pioneered by North America to respond to more symmetrical investment relations, international arbitration, the encounter between trade and investment rules, and a more vibrant domestic policy debate.

The latest phase in the evolution of IIA's development, starting around 2015, now points to a new phase of greater diversity. Not only are states selectively copying from North American practice. They are starting to disagree more fundamentally on the mechanisms by which gaps should be filled.

Although North American treaties make use of all four gap-filling strategies, Canadian and US IIAs place most emphasis on the first and second gap-filling strategy: contractors' ability to write more comprehensive agreements and finely crafted escape clauses. North American IIAs are long, detailed, and highly complex, replete with footnotes and clarificatory annexes. They epitomize the attempt to approximate the complete contingent contract ideal that closes all gaps and foresees all future contingencies. Recent shifts in treaty practice now propose alternative treaty designs.

Brazil. Brazil re-entered the IIA universe with a new treaty model in 2015. The so-called Cooperation and Facilitation Investment Agreements try to solve the deficiencies of contractual incompleteness through the third gap-filling strategy: relational contracting. As the name suggests, the treaty model places emphasis on cooperation and investment facilitation.[212] Domestically, the focus lies on establishing a host-state–investor dialogue by replacing ISDS with mechanisms to mediate and prevent investment disputes, including through a new ombudsman institution. Internationally, the agreements aim to foster inter-state cooperation over investment matters, including through inter-state dispute settlement, joint institutions, and investment promotion efforts.

European Union. The position of the European Union has evolved post the 2014 CETA as well. In response to public demands for more transparency and participation, the EU Commission initiated a public consultation on investor-state arbitration in 2015.[213] It then proposed a novel mechanism to replace

---

[212] Catherine Titi, *International Investment Law and the Protection of Foreign Investment in Brazil,* 13 Transnat'l Disp. Mgmt. (2016); Vivian Gabriel, *The New Brazilian Cooperation and Facilitation Investment Agreement: An Analysis of the Conflict Resolution Mechanism in Light of the Theory of the Shadow of the Law,* 34 Conflict Resol. Q. 141–161 (2016).

[213] European Commission, *Fact Sheet, Report on the online consultation on investment protection and investor-to-state dispute settlement in the Transatlantic Trade and Investment Partnership*

existing ISDS with a bilateral standing tribunal and appellate instance, which should eventually be consolidated into a multilateral investment court. During the legal scrubbing phase of CETA, a standing tribunal with appeal review replaced the previous ISDS mechanism effectively amounting to a renegotiation of the CETA investment chapter.[214] Other EU treaties with Singapore and Vietnam similarly include the standing tribunal and appellate instance. Seen in contract theoretical terms, the European Union thereby places new emphasis on the fourth strategy: judicial gap-filling—albeit with a different type of adjudication as compared to traditional ISDS.

Although each of these strategies produce more complete IIAs, they differ in principle. Drafting more detailed agreements is about empowering the original state parties and taking gap-filling authority away from tribunals. European IIAs, in contrast, enhance delegation and empower adjudicators by further institutionalizing ex post judicial gap-filling. Similarly, more complete drafting ex ante is supposed to substitute for the management of relations ex post prioritized by Brazilian treaties. These different visions of how to render IIAs more complete currently play out both in the negotiation of new IIAs and in multilateral negotiations. In the short term, these different approaches produce greater diversity and, in part, break with the path-dependent evolution that characterized the Americanization of IIA design. In the longer term, they may produce an alternative design that replaces the currently dominant American-style IIA.

VI. Conclusion

The evolution of IIAs is a history of gradual state-driven change toward more contractual completeness. States have been the protagonists all along, proactively changing their agreements to close gaps left open in earlier contracting. Much of this innovation predates the rise of investment claims, originated in North American practice and then spread around the globe. More complete IIAs that differ starkly from incomplete earlier BITs have thus become the dominant design model in recent treaties. The remainder of this book will focus on the impact of this state-driven treaty design change. How do American-style, more complete IIAs fare in practice? And what prevents new treaties from producing new outcomes in ISDS? Part II will assess this question.

Agreement, Strasbourg, January 13, 2015, available at http://europa.eu/rapid/press-release_MEMO-15-3202_en.htm (last accessed May 3, 2015).

[214] Alschner & Skougarevskiy, *supra* note 154.

PART II
NEW TREATIES, OLD OUTCOMES

4
Reversing Innovation through MFN

I. Introduction

Inspired by North American innovations, states have concluded ever more complete investment agreements. This state-driven change of the law in the books, however, has thus far failed to translate into a change of the law in action. The first-wave ISDS awards rendered under more complete IIAs instead suggests that new treaties are being read like old ones.

Part II of this book explores the dynamics behind this recent set of awards. It focuses on the three normative devices chiefly responsible for why new, more complete, American-style treaties produce interpretive outcomes that mirror those of old, incomplete, European-style IIAs: most-favored-nation (MFN) clauses (Chapter 4), customary international law (Chapter 5), and precedent (Chapter 6). MFN, custom, and precedent each create a direct link between the interpretation of old- and new-generation IIAs. Tribunals have made use of these devices to roll back clarifications and exceptions and to contest the replacement of hitherto dominant judicial gap-filling with state-driven gap-filling.

Writing new treaties to produce new outcomes is tough because the meaning of investment treaty provisions is only partially crafted at the drafting stage. Much of it only emerges through practice. Nowhere is this more apparent than when it comes to MFN clauses. A few early ISDS awards—*AAPL*, *Maffezini*, *MTD*—coined the idea that these clauses could directly incorporate treaty provisions from third IIAs concluded by the respondent state. This triggered a frenzy of investor claims seeking to expand the jurisdiction of tribunals, to modify the conditions for access to arbitration, and to import more favorable substantive clauses.[1] As a result, MFN today threatens to undermine more complete IIAs and to reverse treaty design innovation.

---

[1] *See generally* Yas Banifatemi, *The Emerging Jurisprudence on the Most-Favoured-Nation Treatment in Investment Arbitration, in* INVESTMENT TREATY LAW: CURRENT ISSUES. REMEDIES IN INTERNATIONAL INVESTMENT LAW EMERGING JURISPRUDENCE OF INTERNATIONAL INVESTMENT LAW. VOL. III 241–273 (Andrea K. Bjorklund, Ian A. Laird, & Sergey Ripinsky eds., 2009); Yannick Radi, *The Application of the Most-Favoured-Nation Clause to the Dispute Settlement Provisions of Bilateral Investment Treaties: Domesticating the "Trojan Horse,"* 18 EUR. J. INT'L L. 757–774 (2007); Facundo Pérez-Aznar, *The Use of Most-Favoured-Nation Clauses to Import Substantive Treaty Provisions in International Investment Agreements,* 20 J. INT'L ECON. L. 777–805 (2017).

Investment Arbitration and State-Driven Reform. Wolfgang Alschner, Oxford University Press. © Oxford University Press 2022. DOI: 10.1093/oso/9780197644386.003.0005

MFN clauses have been around for centuries. They prevent nationality-based discrimination, level the playing field among foreign nationals, and ensure that bargains are updated dynamically by extending more favorable concessions given elsewhere.[2] In international trade law, MFN is seen as a "cornerstone" of the multilateral WTO regime.[3] It would be violated if a state discriminated between its trading partners by charging a duty of 10 percent on wine from state B, but of 20 percent on wine from state C. So what makes MFN clauses so controversial in ISDS?

In practice, investors rarely claim that the host state breached MFN by discriminating between two foreign investments.[4] Rather, most claimants use MFN as a gateway to import more favorable treaty terms from third IIAs into the treaty that is being litigated (the base treaty). These imported provisions are then directly applied. Instead of paying compensation for violating MFN (as is the norm for all other standard of treatment breaches in ISDS) or having the option to eliminate the advantage by violating (or renegotiating) the third IIA, states have to comply with a clause from another treaty directly and immediately. MFN thus acts as placeholder for a de facto rewriting of treaties.

This reading of MFN has far-reaching consequences for state-driven treaty design change. Since vague terms in older, incomplete IIAs have been interpreted as offering more protection than their more precise counterparts in newer, more complete IIAs, MFN risks rolling back state-driven innovation by reading old clauses into new treaties. Innovation of decades could thereby become meaningless, with states locked into past practice. If an extreme interpretation of MFN is accepted, MFN clauses could altogether override treaty design difference and "harmonize investment protection at the most elevated level [of investment protection] available."[5] Instead of the map of diverse treaties developed in Chapter 1, investment treaty design would be reduced to a single spot where treatment is most favorable to investors. And that spot would not even have to correspond to an actual treaty. Some commentators and tribunals agree that MFN can selectively incorporate third-treaty benefits without concurrently importing attending limitations.[6] MFN would thus allow investors to manufacture a custom-made agreement offering more protection than any actual treaty in existence.[7]

---

[2] *See, e.g.*, Stephan W. Schill, *Mulitilateralizing Investment Treaties through Most-Favored-Nation Clauses*, 27 BERKELEY J. INT'L L. 496–569, 507 (2009). Jürgen Kurtz, *The MFN Standard and Foreign Investment: An Uneasy Fit?*, 5 J. WORLD INVESTMENT & TRADE 861–886, 861 (2004).

[3] Appellate Body Report, Canada—Autos, WT/DS139/AB/R, WT/DS142/AB/, May 31, 2000, para. 69.

[4] UNCTAD, MOST-FAVOURED-NATION TREATMENT 5 (2010).

[5] Schill, *supra* note 2, at 521.

[6] STEPHAN W. SCHILL, THE MULTILATERALIZATION OF INTERNATIONAL INVESTMENT LAW 159 (2009).

[7] Some tribunals have rejected this idea of selective interpretation; *see, e.g.*, *Garanti Koza LLP v. Turkmenistan*, ICSID Case No. ARB/11/20, Award, December 19, 2016, para. 375 (the "MFN claim

This chapter takes a closer look at MFN clauses and the practice surrounding them to gauge just how much of the diversity and innovation identified in Part I of this book risks being reversed through MFN. The chapter starts by showing that MFN has been used to roll back stated-driven change. It then discusses how we got here. A series of early ISDS decisions amplified through academic commentary popularized the notion of MFN as overriding or even multilateralizing treaty design differences to a point where tribunals accepted the incorporation of more favorable substantive provisions without question or analysis. While a growing pool of commentators and tribunals has since sought to correct this practice by rebutting unwarranted presumptions and aligning the operation of MFN in ISDS with other fields of international law, the idea that MFN overrides treaty design differences in significant ways continues to be widely held.

The final part of this chapter shows that an expansive view of MFN's ability to override treaty design differences is mistaken. Even if a generous interpretation of the clause is adopted, the impact of MFN is much more modest than what is generally assumed. In fact, MFN, if correctly applied, preserves most treaty design differences identified in Chapter 1 and upholds state-driven innovation. In particular, MFN clauses generally do not override language introduced to clarify jurisdictional or substantive provisions, preserve the procedural innovations relating to the conduct of arbitration, prevent the importation of entirely new obligations, and leave exceptions untouched. In short, MFN upholds rather than overrides treaty differences and respects design innovation.

II. Rolling Back Treaty Innovation through MFN

The risk that MFN overrides investment treaty design and reverses innovation in practice is real. This section systematically reviews awards that have considered the importation of substantive standards via MFN. That investigation reveals that ISDS tribunals have accepted arguments that (1) reverse clarifications of vague investment protective standards, (2) reintroduce extra protection that are concurrently phased out in treaty practice, and (3) bypass policy exceptions included in IIAs to safeguard regulatory space. MFN clauses thus have the potential to cancel out treaty reform, ratchet up the protection of investors, and upset the delicate balance between protecting investment (curbing opportunism) and safeguarding states' policy space (seizing regret) struck in more complete IIAs.

---

presents two significant difficulties: First, Garanti Koza appears to seek to mix provisions of different treaties to create a custom-made treaty provision that does not appear in any treaty entered into by the Respondent.").

A. MFN Is Frequently Used to Import
More Favorable Substantive Clauses

A substantial number of ISDS awards have imported substantive clauses from third IIAs to alter the design of the base treaty under which the ISDS proceeding was brought.[8] Out of fifty-six cases where investors sought to use MFN to import a substantive provision from a third IIA, they succeeded fully or partially on nineteen occasions. Every third MFN claim relating to substantive importation has therefore been successful. The remaining awards either declined to decide the issue, for example, because it was not necessary for the resolution of the dispute, or rejected the investor's argument on factual or normative grounds (thirty-seven awards).

As Table 4.1 shows, the bulk of these fifty-six awards was initiated under base treaties with low levels of contractual completeness scores and targets low-completeness treaties. Since most litigation has occurred under low- or medium-scoring IIAs, the dominance of low-low relations is to be expected. Furthermore, all nineteen accepted importations of substantive standards via MFN were based on low-scoring IIAs. Out of the nine awards launched under high-scoring treaties, all MFN claims failed.[9]

It would be misleading, however, to conclude that MFN preserves treaty design innovation in high-scoring IIAs. First, none of these awards under high-scoring treaties refused the application of MFN to import more favorable treatment in principle. They rather rejected the argument on jurisdictional grounds,[10] based on factual

Table 4.1 IIAs connected through the fifty-six awards with MFN claims that sought to import substantive treatment and their success and rejection frequency

		Third IIA Completeness Score			Outcome of MFN claim	
		High	Medium	Low	Rejected	Accepted
Base IIA Completeness Score	High	3	2	4	9	
	Medium			1	1	
	Low		4	42	27	19

[8] I am grateful to Bin Cheng for his assistance with this analysis.

[9] NAFTA accounts for five cases, followed by the Canada–Venezuela BIT (2), the Canada–Costa Rica BIT (1), and the United States–Uruguay BIT (1).

[10] *Nova Scotia Power Incorporated v. Bolivarian Republic of Venezuela*, ICSID Case No. ARB(AF)/11/1, Award, April 30, 2014, para. 150; *Italba Corporation v. Oriental Republic of Uruguay*, ICSID Case No. ARB/16/9, Award, March 22, 2019, para. 128.

circumstances,[11] because the investor did not meet its burden of proof,[12] because the measure fell under NAFTA's government procurement carveout,[13] or because it was not necessary for the case outcome to decide the MFN claim.[14]

Second, only few more complete IIAs explicitly prohibit the importation of substantive provisions from third IIAs. Some IIAs restrict MFN's application to future treaties, preventing the incorporation of clauses from old IIAs through MFN.[15] Others stipulate that clauses from third treaties cannot by themselves constitute "more favorable treatment."[16] However, most MFN restrictions in more complete IIAs only prohibit the incorporation of arbitration-related clauses, leaving intact the possibility to import substantive standards.[17]

Finally, more complete IIAs seem particularly vulnerable to MFN-based arguments. Table 4.2 lists the clauses that have been successfully imported via MFN. Most awards where MFN claims succeeded concerned the incorporation of fair and equitable treatment (FET) clauses. In many of these disputes, the base IIA already contained an FET clause and MFN was used to access a more

Table 4.2 Clauses that have been successfully imported via MFN[*]

Imported Provision	Awards That Accepted Importation
Fair and Equitable Treatment	12
Full Protection and Security	7
Umbrella Clause	4
Arbitrary or Discriminatory Treatment	2
Effective Means	2
Standard of Compensation	1

[*]Since several awards involved successful MFN claims on multiple clauses, the sum of these claims is higher than the nineteen awards with successful claims.

---

[11] *Infinito Gold Ltd. v. Costa Rica*, ICSID Case No. ARB/14/5, Award, June 3, 2021, paras. 745–754; *Chemtura Corporation v. Government of Canada*, UNCITRAL (formerly Crompton Corporation v. Government of Canada), Award, August 1, 2010, para. 235. *Apotex Holdings Inc. and Apotex Inc. v. United States of America*, ICSID Case No. ARB(AF)/12/1, Award, August 27, 2014, para. 9.71.

[12] *United Parcel Service of America Inc. v. Government of Canada*, ICSID Case No. UNCT/02/1, Award, May 24, 2007, para. 184.

[13] *ADF Group Inc. v. United States of America*, ICSID Case No. ARB (AF)/00/1, Award, January 9, 2003, para. 197; *Mesa Power Group, LLC v. Government of Canada*, UNCITRAL, PCA Case No. 2012-17, Award, March 24, 2016, para. 507.

[14] *Gold Reserve Inc. v. Bolivarian Republic of Venezuela*, ICSID Case No. ARB(AF)/09/1, Award, September 22, 2014, para. 624.

[15] *See, e.g.,* Canada–Burkina Faso BIT (2015), Annex III.1.

[16] *See, e.g.,* CETA (2016) art. 8.7(4).

[17] *See, e.g.,* Japan–United Arab Emirates BIT (2018), art. 4(6); TPP art. 9.5.

favorable version of the clause. In addition, around a quarter of awards brought back protective provisions that have been phased out in modern treaty practice, such as umbrella clauses, arbitrary or discriminatory treatment, and effective means clauses. Finally, although thus far unsuccessful, MFN could be used to water down policy exceptions. That bodes ill for more complete IIAs that could see clarifications reversed, outdated clauses reintroduced, and exceptions watered down.

B. Rolling Back Clarifications of Protective Standards

Chapter 2 identified more detailed contracting through the clarification of hitherto vague and open-textured standards, such as FET or expropriation, as a major hallmark of the transition from incomplete to more complete IIAs. As discussed then, this development is best understood not as a lowering of investment protection levels but as their specification: a range of permissible interpretations of a clause is narrowed often by opting for a middle ground between state or investor-friendly readings. Nevertheless, some tribunals and scholars have viewed older, vague, and open-textured standards as offering more protection to investment than their more clearly defined recent equivalents and have suggested that such "more favourable" treatment could be incorporated using MFN.

In relation to FET, for example, Patrick Dumberry argues that "a stand-alone FET clause provides (at least in theory) 'better' legal protection to a foreign investor than an FET clause linked to 'international law' or the [minimum standard of treatment] MST under custom."[18] A broadly worded MFN clause would thus allow investors "to benefit from a better standalone FET clause contained in an older BIT . . . [and to] bypass the type of restrictive FET clauses increasingly found in most recent BITs."[19] The NAFTA tribunal in *Pope and Talbot v. Canada* similarly asserted that if NAFTA's FET clause were less protective than a stand-alone FET provision in a third BIT concluded by NAFTA states, investors "would simply turn to Articles 1102 [National Treatment] and 1103 [MFN Treatment] for relief."[20] In the same vein, the tribunal *Paushok v. Mongolia* constituted under the Mongolia–Russia BIT (1995) found that "[i]f there exists any other BIT between Mongolia and another state which provides for a more generous provision

---

[18] Patrick Dumberry, *Shopping for a Better Deal: The Use of MFN Clauses to Get "Better" Fair and Equitable Treatment Protection*, 33 ARB. INT'L 1–16, 6 (2017).

[19] *Id.* at 11.

[20] *Pope and Talbot Inc. v. Canada*, Award on the Merits of Phase II, April 10, 2001, UNCITRAL, para. 117.

relating to fair and equitable treatment, an investor under the Treaty is entitled to invoke it."[21]

If investors can convince ISDS tribunals that vague FET provisions (or, for that matter, vague expropriation, full protection and security clauses, etc.) in earlier, incomplete BITs offer more protection than their more detailed contemporary counterparts, decades of treaty drafting could be reversed. The consequences of this would be dramatic. Consider the Canadian treaty network. All but one of Canada's treaties explicitly links FET to customary international law.[22] That one agreement, the Canada–Hungary BIT of 1991, which predates most Canadian BITs and broadly provides in Article 3 that investments "shall at all times be accorded fair and equitable treatment," could, through the MFN clause in all subsequent Canadian treaties, override thirty years of concluding more detailed FET clauses.[23] In short, if more detailed language is equated with less protection, MFN is poised to be a powerful tool for reading new treaties in light of old ones.

C. Bringing Back Phased-Out Protective Standards

A second major development highlighted in Chapter 2 concerned the gradual phasing out of several protective standards that were considered overly vague or duplicative. Language providing "effective means of asserting claims" prevalent in early US agreements has been omitted from the treaty body and/or moved to the preamble in recent treaties, based on the understanding that the remaining substantive and procedural provisions provide equivalent effects. Umbrella clauses, popular in early BITs, have similarly fallen into disuse or have been replaced (in US treaties) by a separate arbitration route for contractual claims. Yet, as noted in Chapter 2, the declining use of these clauses in treaty practice has been accompanied by an expansive interpretation of the same provisions in ISDS practice. Against that backdrop, investors have sought to use MFN to bring back these provisions and to reinforce their controversial reading as providing more favorable treatment.

In *White Industries v. India*, for example, the claimant was able to import an "effective means" clause from the India–Kuwait BIT (2001) into the Australia–India BIT (1999).[24] Basing its analysis on the earlier *Chevron v. Ecuador* award,

---

[21] *Sergei Paushok, CJSC Golden East Company, CJSC Vostokneftegaz Company v. Mongolia*, Award, April 28, 2011, UNCITRAL, para. 570.

[22] Patrick Dumberry, *The Importation of "Better" Fair and Equitable Treatment Standard Protection Through MFN Clauses: An Analysis of NAFTA Article 1103*, 14 TRANSNAT'L DISP. MGMT. (2017).

[23] Note that once CETA, the agreement between Canada and the European Union, comes into force, it will replace the Canada–Hungary BIT.

[24] *White Industries Australia Limited v. The Republic of India*, UNCITRAL, Final Award, November 30, 2011, paras. 11.2.1–11.2-9.

the arbitrators found "that the 'effective means' standard is *lex specialis* and is a distinct and potentially less demanding test, in comparison to denial of justice in customary international law."[25] Whether a state provided such effective means has to be "measured against an objective, international standard" and requires "the host State [to] establish a proper system of laws and institutions and that those systems work effectively in any given case."[26] Undue delays or systemic problems of the court system may indicate a breach of the standard.[27] Hence, in complete contrast to the perceived redundancy that motivated states to phase out the "effective means" language from treaties, the tribunal used prior case law to construe the "effective means" clause as a distinct standard that provides far-reaching protections to investors, which MFN could import as more favorable treatment.

In *EDF v. Argentina*, claimants successfully relied on MFN to import an umbrella clause from the Luxembourg–Argentina BIT (1990) into the France–Argentina BIT (1991).[28] The tribunal then adopted an expansive interpretation of the umbrella clause, concluding that serious breaches of contractual commitments are lifted to the level of a treaty breach by an umbrella clause and found that Argentina had indeed breached the contract and thus the treaty.[29] The tribunal thereby accepted a double extension that significantly enlarged the scope of the France–Argentina BIT: first, MFN imported an umbrella clause absent in the original BIT, and then that umbrella clause, in turn, imported contractual commitments undertaken between the host state and claiming investor. While recent treaty practice has sought to reinforce the separation between treaty and contract claims, MFN risks perpetuating their conflation.

Investors thus use MFN to bring back provisions that states have purposefully discarded.[30] Tribunals that accept such argumentation are rolling back state-driven change. Furthermore, they are often also reinforcing a particularly controversial arbitral interpretation that appear far removed from the meaning of a clause that states intended. Last but not least, this problem is likely to get worse rather than better as states are beginning to phase out additional obligations

---

[25] *Id.*, para. 11.3.2.

[26] *Id.*

[27] *Id.*

[28] *EDF International S.A., SAUR International S.A. and León Participaciones Argentinas S.A. v. Argentine Republic*, ICSID Case No. ARB/03/23, Final Award, June 11, 2012, paras. 930–936. *See also Mr. Franck Charles Arif v. Republic of Moldova*, ICSID Case No. ARB/11/23, Award, April 8, 2013, para. 395, and *Consutel Group S.p.A. in liquidazione v. People's Democratic Republic of Algeria*, PCA No. 2017-33, Award, February 3, 2020, paras. 357–359 (finding that umbrella clauses constitute substantive rather than procedural treatment and can hence be incorporated into base treaty via MFN).

[29] *EDF v. Argentina*, Final Award, paras. 940, 970.

[30] Other claims relate to the import of "protection against unreasonable or arbitrary measures" equally phased out in recent BITs. *See, e.g., Garanti Koza LLP v. Turkmenistan*, ICSID Case No. ARB/11/20, Award, paras. 276, 393.

deemed controversial, such as, in some cases, FET[31] or indirect expropriation,[32] which could then be brought back using earlier BITs via MFN. MFN's potential to thwart state-driven change is thus likely to grow.

D. Bypassing Exceptions

Another development discussed in Chapter 2 concerned the inclusion of additional exceptions into more complete IIAs as escape clauses. This came in two variants. First, starting with the US BIT program, additional protections were introduced—preestablishment liberalization, sojourn of personnel, and performance requirements—which were accompanied by new specific exceptions, so-called nonconforming measures. This confirmed the more general contract-theoretical insight that more commitments ex ante require and are enabled through more flexibility ex post. Second, more complete IIAs have included new general exceptions to protect public policy concerns, including public health, the environment, and national security. MFN risks rolling back these developments by cherry-picking more favorable provisions from third treaties without incorporating related exceptions and by bypassing exceptions in the base treaties with reference to third agreements where such exceptions are absent or narrower.

In *Siemens v. Argentina*, for example, the investor was allowed to cherry-pick only the more favorable pre-arbitration waiting period without having to accept the less favorable fork-in-the-road provision of the third treaty. The tribunal accepted that "since a treaty has been negotiated as a package, for other parties to benefit from it, they also should be subject to its disadvantages. The disadvantages may have been a trade-off for the claimed advantages."[33] But it went on to find that an MFN clause, based on its plain wording, exclusively incorporates the more favorable treatment.[34] This practice, which Stephan Schill labels "[m]ultilateralizing benefits without extending disadvantage,"[35] allows investors to reconstruct treaties along their preferences—taking from third

---

[31] The Indian model BIT does not explicitly provide for an FET clause. *See* Prabhash Ranjan & Pushkar Anand, *The 2016 Model Indian Bilateral Investment Treaty: A Critical Deconstruction*, 38 Nw. J. Int'l L. & Bus. 28 (2017).

[32] Brazilian Cooperation and Facilitation Investment Agreements, aside from other innovations, explicitly exclude indirect expropriation from the scope of the treaty. *See* Martin Dietrich Brauch, *The Best of Two Worlds? The Brazil–India Investment Cooperation and Facilitation Treaty*, Investment Treaty News, March 20, 2020, available at https://www.iisd.org/itn/en/2020/03/10/the-best-of-two-worlds-the-brazil-india-investment-cooperation-and-facilitation-treaty-martin-dietrich-brauch/.

[33] *Siemens A.G. v. The Argentine Republic*, ICSID Case No. ARB/02/8, Decision on Jurisdiction, August 3, 2004, para. 120.

[34] *Id.*

[35] Schill, *supra* note 2, at 533.

treaties only what advantages them while eschewing the strings normally attached to these benefits. Such use of MFN unravels the careful balance struck between commitments and flexibilities that enable the more comprehensive contracting in more complete IIAs.

Turning to general exceptions, the investor in *CMS v. Argentina* sought to bypass an essential security clause in the US–Argentina BIT (1991) by pointing to third IIAs that lacked such an exception and thus ostensibly offered more favorable treatment.[36] While the tribunal ultimately rejected this assertion, finding that the mere absence of an exception does not render a third treaty more favorable, it did indicate that if a third IIA had contained a more favorable exception, the outcome might have been different.[37] Hence, even if exceptions might not be bypassed altogether, escape clauses could potentially be rendered more investor-friendly through MFN. As a result, MFN risks circumventing exceptions or may render them less potent by incorporating more lenient exceptions. One of the main treaty design devices used by states to balance investment protection with states' regulatory space may thus become undone through MFN.

In conclusion, the potential of MFN to override treaty design differences and to roll back treaty innovation is significant. New treaties risk producing old outcomes. How did we get here? For some commentators, states simply made poor treaty design choices and now "have to live with the consequences of bad drafting."[38] More likely, however, tribunals' expansive interpretation of MFN took states by surprise.

III. From Nondiscrimination to Multilateralization

Whereas the idea that MFN prevents discrimination is uncontroversial, the notion that MFN overrides treaty design differences is not. In fact, the concept of MFN clauses as automatically importing terms from third treaties only emerged in early ISDS awards, was amplified by scholarship, and subsequently became entrenched as a largely unquestioned practice. As tribunals accepted that overriding differences between agreements was "exactly the result which the parties intended by the incorporation in the BIT of an MFN clause,"[39] they paid little attention to the wording and limitations of MFN clauses. MFN turned from

---

[36] *CMS Gas Transmission Company v. The Republic of Argentina*, Award, May 12, 2005, ICSID Case No. ARB/01/8, para. 343.

[37] *Id.*, para. 377.

[38] Dumberry, *supra* note 19, at 9.

[39] *White Industries Australia Limited v. The Republic of India*, UNCITRAL, Final Award, November 30, 2011, paras. 11.2.3–4.

protection-against-discrimination to multilateralization-by-design. A recent trend in case law and academic commentary has sought to correct this practice.

A. The Dual Nature of MFN in ISDS

MFN clauses protect against nationality-based discrimination between foreign investments. They are found in the vast majority of IIAs. A typical MFN clause in an investment treaty reads:

> Each Contracting Party shall accord to investments made in its territory by investors of the other Contracting Party treatment not less favourable than that accorded to investments by its own investors or by investors of any third State, whichever is the more favourable.[40]

MFN clauses in investment treaties have been interpreted in two very different ways by arbitral tribunals depending on the type of discrimination at issue.[41] On the one hand, when applied to discriminatory domestic conduct, MFN has been conceived as an ordinary standard of treatment that can be breached by a host state. The claimant, in order to prove a violation of MFN, has to show that, first, there are two or more comparable foreign investments, and second, that they received differential treatment in law or in fact on the ground of nationality. If an ISDS tribunal finds a discrimination against the claiming investor, it will assert that a breach of the MFN obligation occurred and will award damages to the foreign investor. MFN operates here like its sister nondiscrimination obligation, national treatment, with which it often co-occurs in treaty language, and which protects against nationality-based discrimination between national and foreign investments.

Standard-of-treatment disputes involving MFN are rare and highly fact-intensive. For example, in *Parkerings v. Lithuania*, a construction company consortium led by the Norwegian investor Parkerings asserted that it had been treated less favorably than a Dutch construction company over the building of car parks in the city of Vilnius.[42] In its assessment, the tribunal drew heavily from its own national treatment findings as well as prior national treatment case law on the grounds that

---

[40] Denmark–Mexico BIT (2000), art. 3(2).

[41] Simon Batifort & J. Benton Heath, *The New Debate on the Interpretation of MFN Clauses in Investment Treaties: Putting the Brakes on Multilateralization*, 111 Am. J. Int'l L. 873–913, 880–881 (2017); Facundo Pérez-Aznar, *The Fictions and Realities of MFN Clauses in International Investment Agreements*, 112 AJIL Unbound 55–59 (2018).

[42] *Parkerings-Compagniet AS v. Republic of Lithuania*, ICSID Case No. ARB/05/8, Award, September 11, 2007.

> *Most-favoured-nation* (MFN) clauses are by essence very similar to *"National Treatment"* clauses. They have similar conditions of application and basically afford indirect advantages to their beneficiaries, namely a treatment no less favourable than the one granted to third parties.[43]

The tribunal ultimately rejected Parkerings' allegations on the grounds that the two investments were not comparable, since they had a very different impact on the UNESCO-protected old town of Vilnius.

On the other hand, if the discrimination takes place not under national law but under another international treaty, ISDS tribunals have interpreted MFN as allowing a foreign investor to directly access the more favorable substantive or procedural treatment conferred to investors in a third treaty. Most investment cases involving MFN are such incorporation-by-reference claims. In these cases, tribunals have generally not required claimants to point to an existing comparable third investment or to prove any actual losses resulting from the discrimination, nor is a formal violation of the MFN standard of treatment found or damages awarded. Instead, MFN functions as a gateway: once the claimant has identified a more favorable provision in another IIA concluded by the host state, that provision is immediately and directly incorporated into the base treaty. It is then the imported clause, and not the MFN clause, which is being applied and against which compliance is assessed and, if a violation is found, on which basis damages are calculated.

While this difference in operation of MFN clauses depending on the source of discrimination is mostly tacit, some tribunals have acknowledged it explicitly. As the *Renta 4 v. Russia* tribunal put it in an incorporation-by-reference claim to enlarge the jurisdiction of the tribunal:

> To be clear: the Claimants are not seeking to establish that Russia breached [the MFN] obligation under the basic treaty (the Spanish BIT) by failing explicitly to grant to Spanish investors the same access to international arbitration as the access the Claimants say is enjoyed by Danish investors. The question is instead simply whether Article 5(2) [the MFN clause] of the Spanish BIT evidences Russia's consent that this Tribunal's jurisdiction should have an ambit beyond that of Article 10 [the dispute settlement clause].[44]

---

[43] *Id.* para. 366.

[44] *Renta 4 S.V.S.A, Ahorro Corporación Emergentes F.I., Ahorro Corporación Eurofondo F.I., Rovime Inversiones SICAV S.A., Quasar de Valors SICAV S.A., Orgor de Valores SICAV S.A., GBI 9000 SICAV S.A. v. The Russian Federation*, SCC No. 24/2007, Award on Preliminary Objections, March 20, 2009, para. 83 (original emphasis omitted, new emphasis added).

Similarly, the tribunal in *EURAM v. Slovakia* rejected the respondent's argument that the claimant had failed to show a discriminatory treatment in violation of the MFN clause and explained that

> the Claimant in the present case is not making a claim for relief for an alleged breach of the MFN clause but is arguing that the effect of that clause is that it is entitled to the benefit of higher standards of protection provided for in other treaties. Accordingly, it is not a matter of comparison with the actual treatment accorded to a specific third State investor, but of comparison between the standard of treatment guaranteed to a group of investors by one treaty and the standard of treatment guaranteed to another group of investors by another treaty.[45]

An MFN clause, as interpreted by these arbitral tribunals, therefore operates in two very different ways: when addressing a situation of discrimination in *domestic* law or conduct, it functions as a standard of treatment akin to national treatment; when it concerns a situation of discrimination in *international* law, it operates as an importer of third-treaty obligations.

B. Emergence through Case Law, Amplified through Scholarship, Entrenched through Practice

In principle, there is nothing unusual or controversial about MFN's application to discrimination stemming from other international treaties rather than domestic conduct. In international law, it is well established that MFN can apply to more favorable treatment assumed by the respondent state in third treaties. Several decisions by the International Court of Justice (ICJ) as well as the work of the International Law Commission (ILC), including through its 1978 MFN Draft Articles, affirm this.[46] In fact, states have long inserted MFN clauses into trade agreements precisely to benefit from concessions made by treaty partners in future negotiations with third states.[47]

Crucially, however, as Facundo Perez-Anzar has pointed out, outside the ISDS realm, international law has treated such claims as concerning breaches of MFN

---

[45] *European American Investment Bank AG (EURAM) v. Slovak Republic*, UNCITRAL, Award on Jurisdiction, August 22, 2012, para. 435.

[46] *See, e.g.*, *Rights of Nationals of the United States of America in Morocco* (France v. United States of America), Judgment, August 27, 1952, 190-1; Anglo-Iranian Oil Co. (United Kingdom v. Iran) (Judgment, Jurisdiction, July 22, 1952) 1952 ICJ Rep. 93, 109. ILC, *Draft Articles on Most-Favoured-Nation Clauses with Commentaries*, YEARBOOK OF THE INTERNATIONAL LAW COMMISSION, vol. II, pt. Two (1978).

[47] Kurtz, *supra* note 2, at 836.

rather than as a matter of automatically importing and applying provisions from third treaties.[48] For example, in the 1956 *Ambatielos* case, the question before the Commission of Arbitration was not whether the clauses on "full protection and security" and protection from "denial of justice" absent in the base treaty should be incorporated into the agreement at issue between Greece and the United Kingdom and applied, but whether their presence in third treaties indicated a violation of the MFN clause of the base agreement.[49] Similarly, in the *Anglo-Iranian Oil Company* case, the ICJ stated that MFN clauses operate within in the confines of the doctrine of *res inter alios acta*—the third treaty does not alter the terms of base treaty.[50] And in *Rights of Nationals of the United States of America in Morocco*, the ICJ rejected the argument by the United States that MFN "should be regarded as a form of drafting by reference rather than as a method for the establishment and maintenance of equality of treatment without discrimination amongst the various countries concerned."[51] In that case, Morocco's refusal to treat American nationals as favorably as other nationals would not have resulted in a breach of a third-treaty clause incorporated by reference, but would have produced a discrimination and violation of MFN.[52] Finally, disputes before the WTO routinely deal with MFN claims that have their origins in discriminatory international agreements, such trade agreements that provide preferential market access to some but not other countries. Yet the analysis of WTO panels and the Appellate Body focuses on determining whether a breach of MFN has occurred and not on the automatic incorporation of the said advantage.[53] Outside of ISDS, MFN claims are thus about determining whether an MFN clause has been violated and not about automatically importing external treaty clauses.

The ISDS-specific idea of MFN directly incorporating and applying third-treaty clauses was developed incrementally through the creative arguments of investors that were endorsed by tribunals. Already in the first BIT case, *AAPL v. Sri Lanka*, the investor invoked the MFN clause to circumvent the civil disturbance exception in the Sri Lanka–United Kingdom BIT (1980) with references

[48] Pérez-Aznar, *supra* note 1. *But also see* Michael Waibel, *Putting the MFN Genie Back in the Bottle*, 112 AJIL UNBOUND 60–63 (2018). He suggests that the debate over MFN in ISDS reflects a deeper disagreement over the default meaning of MFN clauses in general international law.

[49] Pérez-Aznar, *supra* note 1, at 794–795.

[50] Schill, *supra* note 2, at 507; Tony Cole, *The Boundaries of Most Favoured Nation Treatment in International Investment Law*, 33 MICH. J. INT'L L. 537, 560–563 (2012).

[51] *Rights of Nationals of the United States of America in Morocco* (France v. United States of America), Judgment, August 27, 1952, 190-1; Cole, *supra* note 51, at 563–564.

[52] Pérez-Aznar, *supra* note 1, at 793.

[53] For example, cases have dealt with preferential import quotas for bananas granted by the EC to former colonies as part of a trade agreement (EC–Bananas, WT/DS27) or, preferential access for American cars to the Canadian market based on an Auto Pact between the two states (Canada–Autos, WT/DS139, WT/DS142).

to the Switzerland–Sri Lanka BIT (1981) where such language was absent.[54] While the tribunal ultimately found that the claimant had not proven that the provisions of the BIT with Switzerland were more favorable,[55] it accepted, without providing deeper explanations, that MFN could be "invoked to increase the host State's liability in case a higher standard of international protection becomes granted to investments."[56]

This conclusion was taken a step further by the subsequent *Maffezini v. Spain* award rendered in 2000, when the tribunal allowed an investor to bypass the mandatory eighteen-month pre-arbitration waiting period in the Argentina–Spain BIT (1991) by incorporating a shorter waiting period from the Chile–Spain BIT (1991).[57] Against the objections of Spain that third treaties are *res inter alios acta*,[58] the tribunal concluded that "if a third-party treaty contains provisions for the settlement of disputes that are more favorable to the protection of the investor's rights and interests than those in the basic treaty, such provisions may be extended to the beneficiary of the most favored nation clause."[59]

Finally, in a 2004 award, the tribunal in *MTD v. Chile* accepted that the investor could use the MFN clause of the Malaysia–Chile BIT (1992) to make claims on the basis of the more favorable protections Chile had included in BITs with Croatia (1994) and Denmark (1993).[60] Chile did not object to the incorporation-by-reference and only argued that, if these clauses applied, Chile had acted consistently with them.[61] The tribunal ultimately found no violation of the Chile–Croatia and Chile–Denmark BITs.[62] Hence, in a string of early cases, creative argumentation by investors, sometimes coupled with the respondent state's tacit acceptance, was endorsed by tribunals. These cases laid the seeds for the idea that MFN could operate as a gateway to third treaties.

Scholarship amplified the impact of *AAPL*, *Maffezini*, and *MTD* and further developed the incorporation-by-reference concept. Stephan Schill published an influential book in 2009 in which he built on the argument that investors could directly import more favorable treatment from third treaties.[63] He explained that no finding of breach of MFN or any additional act of transformation was

---

[54] *Asian Agricultural Products Ltd. v. Sri Lanka*, ICSID Case No. ARB/87/3, Final Award, June 27, 1990, para. 26(D).

[55] *Id.*, para. 54.

[56] *Id.*, para. 43.

[57] *Emilio Agustín Maffezini v. The Kingdom of Spain*, ICSID Case No. ARB/97/7, Decision of the Tribunal on Objections to Jurisdiction, January 25, 2000.

[58] *Id.*, para. 42.

[59] *Id.*, para. 56.

[60] *MTD Equity Sdn. Bhd. and MTD Chile S.A. v. Republic of Chile*, ICSID Case No. ARB/01/7, Award, para. 105.

[61] *Id.*, para. 100.

[62] *Id.*, paras. 106, 187–188, 204–206.

[63] SCHILL, *supra* note 6, at 126.

required.[64] Instead, "MFN clauses allow an investor to immediately rely on any more favorable benefits granted to investors under the host State's third-country BITs."[65] Taking this reasoning a step further, Schill asserted that, in fact, states had purposefully designed MFN clauses to "multilateralize the bilateral inter-State treaty relationships and harmonize the protection of foreign investments in a specific host State."[66]

Conceiving MFN as a multilateralizer of treaty obligation had important practical consequences, as Schill explained. First, it forestalls any backsliding of investment protection in later agreements. According to Schill, "MFN treatment has a constitutional function, because it locks States into a multilateral framework and makes abandoning standards of protection adopted previously more difficult."[67] Second, MFN clauses override dissimilar treaty designs and "level the differences in the standard of protection offered by varying investment treaties."[68]

This intellectual reconceptualization of MFN's effect from protection-against-discrimination to incorporation-by-reference, and finally, to multilateralization-by-design was instrumental for entrenching the idea that the very purpose of MFN was to override treaty design differences. As the *White Industries* tribunal put it before quoting Schill's work, the investor is "availing itself of the right to rely on more favourable substantive provisions in the third-party treaty [. . . which] is exactly the result which the parties intended by the incorporation in the BIT of an MFN clause."[69] In the same vein, the *Berschader* tribunal asserted that "[i]t is *universally agreed* that the very essence of an MFN provision in a BIT is to afford to investors all material protection provided by subsequent treaties."[70] The *EDF* tribunal considered itself bound to accept the incorporation-by-reference argument by the claimant since "[t]o interpret the BIT otherwise would effectively read the MFN language out of the treaty."[71] The idea that MFN could import treaty clauses and override design differences had become entrenched as the "very essence" of MFN clauses.

---

[64] Schill's grounds his reasoning in the ILC MFN Draft Article 9 (1), which provides that "[u]nder a most-favoured-nation clause the beneficiary State *acquires* . . . those rights which fall within the limits of the subject matter of the clause." *Id.* at 123, 127. Schill, *supra* note 2, at 507. Yet, as Facundo Pérez-Aznar points out, the ILC used the same "acquire" language when discussing the operation of National Treatment. Pérez-Aznar, *supra* note 1, at 793.

[65] Stephan W. Schill, *Allocating Adjudicatory Authority: Most-Favoured-Nation Clauses as a Basis of Jurisdiction—A Reply to Zachary Douglas*, 2 J. INT'L DISP. SETTLEMENT 353–371, 365 (2011).

[66] Schill, *supra* note 2, at 504; SCHILL, *supra* note 6, at 123, 195.

[67] Schill, *supra* note 2, at 509.

[68] SCHILL, *supra* note 6, at 123.

[69] *White Industries Australia Limited v. The Republic of India*, UNCITRAL, Final Award, November 30, 2011, paras. 11.2.3–4.

[70] *Vladimir Berschader and Moïse Berschader v. The Russian Federation*, SCC Case No. 080/2004, Award, April 21, 2006, para. 179 (emphasis added).

[71] *EDF v. Argentina*, para. 932.

This entrenchment had two consequences. First, as Simon Batifort and Benton Heath point out, once a presumption had widely taken hold that MFN clauses are designed to directly import third-party terms, tribunals rarely reassessed that claim against the specific language of the MFN clauses at issue.[72] Third-party standards were mechanically imported without deeper analysis and potential limitations in the wording of MFN clauses were left unexplored. Second, the focus of analysis shifted from the MFN clause to its target as litigants, tribunals, and scholars probed just how far incorporation-by-reference could go and debates raged on whether MFN could import procedural benefits improving access to arbitration or, even more controversially, consent to arbitration from third treaties.[73] Meanwhile, the underlying notion of incorporation-by-reference, especially insofar as it related to more favorable substantive provisions in third treaties, and of MFN's dual nature became widely accepted.

C. Putting the Genie Back in the Bottle

This entrenchment of a controversial interpretation of MFN took states by surprise. The practice of dealing with MFN as a matter of breach in other areas of international law had little prepared states for the dual-nature argument in ISDS. It is furthermore implausible that countries had engaged in far-reaching treaty differentiation and innovation while simultaneously purposefully including MFN clauses to undermine these very same efforts.[74] Moreover, as Part I of this book has shown, states have not sought to craft treaty standards that achieve *maximum* levels of investment protection, as Schill implies—rather, they have pursed *optimal* levels of protection, balancing protection with flexibility. In the same vein, contracting states never behaved as if they felt locked into previously adopted standards of protection through MFN as quasi-constitutional restraint on their contractual freedom. Instead, they have refined and, at times, departed from existing practice to innovate their treaty design through state-driven change.

---

[72] Batifort & Heath, *supra* note 42.

[73] Crudely simplified, one camp adamantly rejects the alteration of the arbitration arrangement set out in the base treaty citing the contracting states' *ratione voluntatis*, which cannot be expanded through MFN. *See, e.g., Impregilo S.p.A. v. Argentine Republic,* ICSID Case No. ARB/07/17, Concurring and Dissenting Opinion of Professor Brigitte Stern, June 21, 2011, paras. 44–56. The other camp considers dispute settlement clauses as simply another, albeit very important, standard of treatment subject to MFN. *See, e.g., National Grid P.L.C. v. Argentine Republic,* UNCITRAL, Decision on Jurisdiction, June 20, 2006, paras. 84–93; *RosInvestCo UK Ltd. v. Russian Federation,* SCC Case No. Abr. V 079/2005, Award on Jurisdiction, October 5, 2007, paras. 132–135.

[74] Cole, *supra* note 51, at 576. (calling it a "the sheer implausibility that States A and B negotiated treaty language that would have absolutely no effect."). Tomoko Ishikawa, *4 Keeping Interpretation in Investment Treaty Arbitration "on Track": The Role of State Parties,* RESHAPING THE INVESTOR-STATE DISPUTE SETTLEMENT SYSTEM 115–149, 131–132 (2015) (highlighting that treaty design differences can indicate a deliberate choice that would be overridden through MFN) .

Patrick Dumberry, with the benefit of hindsight, points out that states could have excluded or explicitly limited the scope of MFN clauses in subsequent treaties to avoid having MFN override treaty design differences.[75] Understood this way, broadly worded MFN clauses are just the result of poor drafting choices that states now have to live with. Yet the fact that states did insert such explicit MFN limitations but only *after* the incorporation-by-reference interpretation of MFN in ISDS became widespread, instead suggests that the dual-nature jurisprudence was unanticipated.[76] The interpretation of MFN clauses as multilaterlization-by-design simply took states by surprise. And as this jurisprudence became more widespread, states indeed sought to "put the MFN genie back in the bottle"[77] by adding new limitations to MFN in the majority of IIAs concluded in the 2010s.

Aside from states, more recent tribunals and academic commentators have also sought to challenge the idea of an automatic incorporation by reference with a view to reconciling the operation of MFN in ISDS and in international law. In a thoughtful article on MFN, Tony Cole, for example, argued that incorporation-by-reference should be viewed as a "right to claim" whereby a third-treaty clause is only incorporated once the investor requests equivalent treatment, rather than as an "instantaneous obligation."[78] The incorporation of treatment would thus necessitate a positive act by a tribunal in order to make the treatment available and only override treaty differences for those disputants who exercise their right to claim.[79] That would mirror the operation of MFN under international law whereby more favorable treatment is a consequence of a claim and breach of MFN rather than an "instantaneous obligation" incorporated by reference.

In a similar vein, Zachary Douglas considered the idea of automatically importing a provision from another treaty through MFN to be a mere "fiction."[80] Instead, according to him, an investor must first demonstrate that there is a breach of MFN, that is, showing that there has been less favorable treatment between comparable investments; only once a breach of the primary rule of MFN is established, a tribunal can proceed to the secondary rule of granting the remedy to declare that the investor is entitled to the more favorable treatment.[81] Douglas thus attempted to make sense of incorporation-by-reference through MFN as a function of secondary international norms, while, for Schill, incorporation is

---

[75] Dumberry, *supra* note 19, at 7–9.

[76] Wolfgang Alschner, *The Impact of Investment Arbitration on Investment Treaty Design: Myth Versus Reality*, 42 YALE J. INT'L L. 58 (2017).

[77] Waibel, *supra* note 49.

[78] Cole, *supra* note 51, at 569.

[79] *Id.* at 570.

[80] Zachary Douglas, *The MFN Clause in Investment Arbitration: Treaty Interpretation off the Rails*, 2 J INT. DISP. SETTLEMENT 97–113, 106 (2011).

[81] *Id.* at 107.

part of the primary rule and does not require finding a breach of MFN.[82] Finally, Batifort and Heath's 2017 *American Journal of International Law* article and Facundo Perez-Aznar's work, which challenge incorporation-by-reference as being at odds with the plain language of many MFN clauses and international law practice, have given further impetus for a scholarly reassessment of the role of MFN in ISDS.[83]

Tribunals have similarly revisited MFN's dual-nature idea, in part to pay closer attention to the wording of MFN clauses and, in part, to align ISDS jurisprudence with international law practice. In the 2016 *İçkale v. Turkmenistan* award, for example, the tribunal rejected the incorporation of an FET clause from a third BIT into the base treaty. It noted that the MFN clause in the base treaty required a comparison of foreign investors in "a similar situation" and reasoned that this limitation "cannot be read, in good faith, to refer to standards of investment protection included in other investment treaties between a State party and a third State."[84]

In the same year, two awards found that tribunals should assess MFN clauses like standards of treatment rather than as a gateway to incorporate third clauses or consent. The tribunal in *Menzies v. Senegal* reasoned that even if MFN imposes an obligation to offer consent to arbitration, states, by virtue of their sovereignty, remain free to breach that obligation.[85] In the same vein, international law professor and frequent counsel before the ICJ, Marcelo Kohen, explained in his dissenting opinion in *Venezuela US v. Venezuela* that "MFN clauses do not possess the power to express consent, even though they would be able to impose the obligation to consent to international arbitration if their content allows so" and, as a result, they can be breached but not import a tribunal's jurisdiction.[86]

In short, the tide may be beginning to turn. The dual-nature theory of MFN has become more controversial and tribunals and commentators have sought to align the interpretation of MFN with that of international law around the notion of breach rather than instantaneous incorporation. If this trend were to continue, tribunals would likely increasingly follow the same methodology when assessing discrimination in domestic or international law and thus preserve treaty design differences and state-driven change to a greater extent.

---

[82] Schill, *supra* note 66, at 364.

[83] Pérez-Aznar, *supra* note 1; Batifort & Heath, *supra* note 42.

[84] *İçkale İnşaat Limited Şirketi v. Turkmenistan*, ICSID Case No. ARB/10/24, ICSID Case No ARB/10/24, Award, March 8, 2016, para. 329.

[85] *Menzies Middle East and Africa SA and Aviation Handling Services International Ltd. v. Senegal*, ICSID Case No ARB/15/21, Award, August 5, 2016.

[86] *Venezuela US, S.R.L. (Barbados) v. Bolivarian Republic of Venezuela*, PCA Case No. 2013-34, Dissenting Opinion of Professor Marcelo G. Kohen, July 26, 2016, para. 32.

IV. The Limits of MFN

Irrespective of the disagreement over whether more favorable terms in third treaties trigger an MFN breach or an automatic incorporation by references, commentators across camps agree that the specific wording of an MFN clause and its treaty context ultimately determines (and constrains) the reach of MFN.[87] Schill, for example, explains that "[l]imitations on the operation of MFN clauses either flow from explicit restrictions of the clause itself or are implied from limitations in the application of the basic treaty containing the clause."[88] At the same time, ISDS tribunals have not always accorded the necessary attention to the wording of MFN clauses. According to Batifort and Heath, tribunals have generally followed a top-down approach accepting incorporation-by-reference as a matter of principle rather than a bottom-up approach that considers the effect of each MFN clause on its own merit.[89] This tendency has resulted in "an unduly uniform approach to the function of MFN provisions."[90] Other empirical studies have similarly shown that divergent interpretations of MFN clauses by arbitral tribunals are generally driven by varying interpretive approaches rather than textual differences.[91]

That is unfortunate, because a careful consideration of the explicit and implicit limitations placed on MFN clauses can dispel many myths about their practical impact. While some scholars continue to argue that MFN can unravel treaty design differences at a large scale,[92] this final section shows that—even assuming that MFN works so as to automatically incorporate third-treaty clauses—the limitations placed on most MFN clauses significantly reduce the treaty design differences that MFN can override. Due to these limitations of the clause or the base treaty, even tribunals that take an expansive view of the effect of MFN clauses should in most cases find that MFN only imports more favorable treaty terms in rare circumstances. MFN therefore preserves most treaty design differences identified in Part I and accommodates state-driven treaty innovation.

---

[87] Kurtz, *supra* note 2, at 872. *See, e.g., Salini Costruttori S.p.A. and Italstrade S.p.A. v. Hashemite Kingdom of Jordan*, ICSID Case No. ARB/02/13, Decision on Jurisdiction, November 29, 2004, paras. 116–118; *Wintershall Aktiengesellschaft v. Argentine Republic*, ICSID Case No. ARB/04/14, Award, December 8, 2008, paras. 61, 166–167, 172.

[88] SCHILL, *supra* note 6, at 142.

[89] Batifort & Heath, *supra* note 42.

[90] *Id.* at 874.

[91] J. A. Maupin, *MFN-based Jurisdiction in Investor-State Arbitration: Is There Any Hope for a Consistent Approach?*, 14 J. INT'L ECON. L. 157–190 (2011).

[92] *See, e.g.,* Julien Chaisse & Jamieson Kirkwood, *Chinese Puzzle: Anatomy of the (Invisible) Belt and Road Investment Treaty*, 23 J. INT'L ECON. L. 245–269 (2020).

A. Limitations Based on the Scope of the Base Treaty

First, MFN clauses are constrained by the scope of the treaty in which they are placed. This encompasses jurisdictional limitations as well as exceptions and exclusions applying to the treaty.

1. No Circumvention of the Jurisdictional Scope of the Base Treaty

According to Schill, "a treaty's scope of application, as regards its subject matter (*ratione materiae*), its temporal dimension (*ratione temporis*) and its personal applicability (*ratione personae*), can delimit the scope of application of an MFN clause contained in that treaty."[93] In *Tecmed v. Mexico*, as well as *MCI v. Ecuador*, for instance, the claimants tried to rely on an MFN clause to bring host state measures within the scope of the treaty that occurred prior to its adoption. In each case, the tribunal rejected the importation of a more favorable temporal scope as this would amount to a retroactive application of the base treaty.[94] The same logic applies to all other jurisdictional matters. With regard to *ratione materiae* considerations, the tribunal in *Société Générale v. Dominican Republic* held that the MFN clause "applies only to the treatment accorded to such defined investment, but not to the definition of 'investment' itself."[95] Hence, even if another treaty contains a more expansive definition of investment (or definition of investor), MFN cannot be used to alter it.

This reasoning has important implications for treaty design innovation. MFN does not reverse reforms in recent more complete IIAs that refine the definitional scope of the agreement. For example, MFN preserves treaty innovation that narrows the definition of investment or investors, for example, by imposing characteristics that investments need to meet to qualify as investments. Similarly, MFN cannot be used to roll back exclusions that carve out sovereign debt or portfolio investment from the definitions of investment by reference to agreements that lack such exclusions. The jurisdictional terms of an IIA cannot be altered by MFN.

---

[93] Schill, *supra* note 2, at 523.

[94] *Tecnicas Mediambientales Tecmed S.A. v. the United Mexican States*, ICSID Case No. ARB (AF)/00/02, Award, May 29, 2003, para. 69. *M.C.I. Power Group L.C. and New Urbine, Inc. v. Republic of Ecuador*, ICSID Case No. ARB/03/6, Award, July 31, 2007, paras. 118–128.

[95] *Société Générale v. The Dominican Republic*, LCAI Case No. UN 7927, Award on Preliminary Objections to Jurisdiction, September 19, 2008, para. 41. Similarly, *Rafat Ali Rizvi v. Republic of Indonesia*, ICSID Case No. ARB/11/13, Award on Jurisdiction, July 16, 2013, para. 220; *Metal-Tech Ltd. v. Republic of Uzbekistan*, ICSID Case No. ARB/10/3, Award, October 4, 2013, paras. 145–163. *Vannessa Ventures Ltd. v. Bolivarian Republic of Venezuela*, ICSID Case No. ARB(AF)/04/6, Award, January 16, 2013, para. 133.

2. No Circumvention of General Exceptions or Exclusions

MFN also cannot be used to bypass general exceptions and exclusions in the base treaties as these clauses limit the scope of application of the base treaty's substantive obligations including MFN.[96] In *Mesa v. Canada,* for example, the claimant sought to circumvent NAFTA's exclusion of government procurement measures in NAFTA Article 1108(7)a) by pointing to other Canadian agreements that lacked such a carveout. The tribunal rejected the attempt and explained that "[f]or an MFN clause in a base treaty to allow the importation of a more favorable standard of protection from a third party treaty, the applicability of the MFN clause in the base treaty must first be established."[97] Since the exclusion prevented the application of MFN, it could not be invoked to attract more favorable treatment.[98] Similarly, the tribunal in *CMS v. Argentina* found that MFN could not be used to circumvent the necessity clause in the Argentina–US BIT with reference to third BITs by Argentina that did not contain such a clause.[99] Other frequently encountered exclusions carving out taxation matters from the treaty's scope will similarly restrict the operation of the clause.[100]

By the same logic, MFN clauses also cannot attract a more favorable exception in a third treaty. Since exclusions and exceptions limit the application of MFN, the question simply does not arise whether another exception would be more favorable, because MFN does not apply in the first place once the conditions of the base treaty's exception are met. In conclusion, investors cannot use the absence or the more favorable wording of an exclusion or exception in another BIT to bypass an exception enshrined in the base treaty. Flexibility mechanisms and escape clauses are thereby insulated from MFN's operation, which then preserves a major component of IIA design evolution toward more contractual completeness.

B. Limitations Based on the Scope of the MFN Clause

MFN clauses, like any other treaty provision, have to be interpreted in light of the Vienna Convention on the Law of Treaties (VCLT). The clauses' text and context thus matter in determining the scope and effect of MFN.[101]

---

[96] Schill, *supra* note 2, at 522.

[97] *Mesa Power Group, LLC v. Government of Canada,* UNCITRAL, PCA Case No. 2012-17, Award, March 24, 2016, para. 401.

[98] *Id.* 402–403.

[99] *CMS v. Argentina,* Final Award, para. 377.

[100] Kurtz, *supra* note 2, at 876; Cole, *supra* note 51, at 741.

[101] Radi, *supra* note 1, at 760.

1. MFN-Based Exception

Explicit textual limitations are the most obvious way in which MFN clauses can be circumscribed. From early on, most European treaties have carved out regional economic integration organizations (REIOs) from the scope of the MFN obligation in order to prevent benefits granted as part of European economic integration efforts from being extended to third IIA parties.[102] Sometimes double taxation treaties are also excluded from the scope of MFN.[103] Agreements following NAFTA have attached specific reservations to the MFN obligation that, for example, carve out subsidies from the scope of MFN and allow each contracting party to specify sectors and measures in their schedules that are exempted from the MFN clause. MFN-based exceptions also include, of course, explicit limitations or clarifications that seek to correct developments in ISDS. In CETA, for example, the European Union and Canada stipulated in Article 10.7(4), that "[s]ubstantive obligations in other international investment treaties and other trade agreements do not in themselves constitute 'treatment', and thus cannot give rise to a breach of this Article, absent measures adopted or maintained by a Party pursuant to those obligations." Such explicit limitations limit the scope of application of MFN.

2. *Ejusdem generis* and the Notion of "Treatment"

Even absent a specific limitation, MFN clauses "can only attract matters belonging to the same category of subject as that to which the clause itself relates."[104] For example, an MFN clause contained in a commercial treaty cannot be used to incorporate by reference more favorable treatment on diplomatic immunity from a third treaty.[105] This so-called *ejusdem generis* principle of the interpretation of MFN enunciated in the *Ambatielos* case has since been affirmed by the ILC MFN draft articles[106] and is widely used in investment arbitration jurisprudence.[107] Beyond the obvious example just given, however, it is often difficult to apply in practice.[108]

What exactly are the outer limits of the "subject matter" of an MFN clause? Answering this question crucially depends on the wording of the clause itself. Some treaties explicitly specify the scope of an MFN clause. The Barbados–Venezuela BIT (1994), for instance, specifies in Article 3(3) that the MFN

---

[102] UNCTAD, THE REIO EXCEPTION IN MFN TREATMENT CLAUSES (2004).

[103] UNCTAD, *supra* note 4, at 47.

[104] *The Ambatielos Case*, 1953 ICJ Rep. 10, Judgment, May 19, 1953, reprinted in the ILC, *Commentaries to the MFN Draft Articles*, *supra* note 717, at 28.

[105] UNCTAD, *supra* note 4, at 24.

[106] ILC, *Commentaries to the MFN Draft Articles*, *supra* note 717, at 28.

[107] *See, e.g., Daimler Financial Services AG v. Argentine Republic*, ICSID Case No. ARB/05/1, Award, August 22, 2012, para. 211.

[108] Schill, *supra* note 2, at 515.

obligation "shall apply to the provisions of Articles 1 to 11 of this Agreement." Yet, as Marcelo Kohen points out, this seemingly explicit language is itself subject to conditions of "material and/or logical possibility" since applying MFN to some articles ostensibly covered would lead to "ridiculous results," including the application of MFN to itself (Article 3) or its exceptions (Article 7).[109]

Contracting states can also specify that the MFN clause covers subject matters not explicitly dealt with elsewhere in the treaty. The Canada–China BIT (2012), for instance, does not contain any investment liberalization commitments, but spells out that "each Contracting Party shall accord [MFN treatment] with respect to the *establishment, acquisition* . . . of investments in its territory." This specification was supposedly inserted to ensure that if China subsequently signed an investment treaty with the United States or the European Union containing a liberalization dimension, the ensuing benefits must be extended to Canada.[110]

Applying the *ejusdem generis* principle is most challenging when the MFN clause generically mandates "no less favourable treatment"[111] than that accorded to other foreign investors. It is then a question of interpretation how far the notion of "treatment" extends. To begin with, most of the procedural innovations introduced in more complete IIAs such as the filing of nondisputing state party submissions or clauses regulating the conduct of arbitration are not "treatment" of investors and thus arguably fall outside of the ambit of an MFN clause that is limited to "treatment." Investors can thus not point to MFN to roll back the transparency and participation elements of ISDS procedures in more recent treaties. Whether other procedural elements defining access to (rather than conduct of) arbitration are subsumed under "treatment" is a more controversial issue, on which tribunals and commentators disagree.[112]

It is equally challenging to determine the confines of "treatment" when it comes to substantive clauses. On the one hand, tribunals have universally accepted that a more favourable version of a clause already present in the base treaty or referenced in the preamble is covered by the *ejusdem generis* principle.[113] On the other hand, the extension of "treatment" to include the incorporation of obligations not found in the base treaty has been more controversial. As discussed earlier, some tribunals have accepted that effective means or umbrella

---

[109] *Venezuela US, S.R.L. (Barbados) v. Bolivarian Republic of Venezuela*, PCA Case No. 2013-34, Dissenting Opinion of Professor Marcelo G. Kohen, July 26, 2016, para. 11.

[110] *China, U.S. To Start Negative List BIT Negotiations*, Xinhua, July 9, 2014, http://news.xinhua net.com/english/china/2014-07/10/c_133472362.htm (last accessed September 5, 2014).

[111] Italy–Jamaica BIT (1993), art. 3(1).

[112] A line of cases following *Maffezini v. Spain* has considered procedural elements governing the investor's access to arbitration, such as waiting periods prior to the filing of investment claims, as "treatment" subject to MFN.

[113] *Sergei Paushok, CJSC Golden East Company and CJSC Vostokneftegaz Company v. Government of Mongolia*, Award on Jurisdiction and Liability, April 28, 2011, para. 570. In part, this result was driven by the specific formulation of the MFN clause.

clauses could be added to treaties that lacked them.[114] In contrast, the tribunal in *Hochtief v. Argentina* stated that "the MFN clause stipulates how investors must be treated when they are exercising the rights given to them under the BIT but does not purport to give them any further rights in addition to those given to them under the BIT."[115] Hence, according to the tribunal, the MFN clause could not "create wholly new rights where none otherwise existed under the [base treaty]."[116] This conclusion echoes the work of the ILC, which cautioned that "[u]nless this [MFN] process is strictly confined to cases where there is a substantial identity between the subject-matter of the two sets of clauses concerned, the result in a number of cases may be to impose upon the granting State obligations it never contemplated."[117]

The four corners of the treaty therefore delineate the scope of the subject matter covered by the MFN clause if the clause itself does not specify the breadth of treatment. The principle of *ejusdem generis* then limits "treatment" to the type of protective obligations granted in the base treaty.[118] Differently put, MFN cannot be used to broaden the subject matter jurisdiction of a tribunal. As Facundo Perez-Anzar points out, "the inclusion of a new obligation into the base treaty and an attendant determination of whether there has been a breach of the imported provision, ultimately, . . . is a broadening of the tribunal's jurisdiction."[119] The *ejusdem generis* principle is a check against such an extension of jurisdiction and ensures, in the words of the ILC, that states are not "bound beyond the obligations they have undertaken."[120]

A final argument against the inclusion of investment protection obligations not found in the base treaty concerns the intentions of the parties. The ILC makes clear that an "[MFN] clause can only operate in regard to the subject-matter which the two States had in mind when they inserted the clause in their treaty."[121] As shown in Chapter 2, states are purposefully excluding some protective clauses from recent agreements. It would defeat their intent if these same obligations

---

[114] *White Industries Australia Limited v. The Republic of India*, UNCITRAL, Final Award, November 30, 2011, paras. 11.2.1–11.2-9. *EDF v. Argentina, supra* note 703, paras. 930–936.

[115] *Hochtief Aktiengesellschaft v. Argentine Republic*, ICSID Case No. ARB/07/31, Decision on Jurisdiction, October 24, 2011, para. 79.

[116] *Id.*, para. 81.

[117] ILC, *Commentaries to the MFN Draft Articles, supra* note 717, at 30.

[118] Tarcisio Gazzinia & Attila Tanzib, *Handle with Care: Umbrella Clauses and MFN Treatment in Investment Arbitration* 17, 984. ("The ejusdem generis principle requires that both international treaties—that including a MFN clause and that invoked by the applicant—contain a provision dealing with the same subject-matter.") It should be noted, however, that the *MTD* tribunal considered the obligation to provide FET in the base treaty to encompass a wider range of other treatment provisions, including umbrella clauses. *See MTD Equity Sdn. Bhd. and MTD Chile S.A. v. Republic of Chile*, ICSID Case No. ARB/01/7, Award, para. 104.

[119] Pérez-Aznar, *supra* note 1, at 799; Ishikawa, *supra* note 75, at 116 (arguing similarly that this is an instance of "broadening the scope of a treaty through an MFN clause").

[120] LC, *Commentaries to the MFN Draft Articles, supra* note 717, at 30.

[121] *Id.* 27.

would be reinserted in the same treaty through the backdoor of MFN clauses. Therefore, *EDF* and *White Industries* were wrongly decided. A proper reading of the *ejusdem generis* principle, barring clear language in the MFN clause to the contrary, obliges tribunals to reject the importation of entirely new obligations into the base treaty and preserves treaty innovation of phasing out outdated or duplicative protective standards.[122]

In sum, *ejusdem generis* limits the subject matter of the MFN clause to a type of protection already granted within the four corners of the treaty. It can thus be used, for example, to enhance the standard of compensation for expropriation.[123] In contrast, MFN clauses cannot go beyond the subject matter of the clause as informed by its treaty context preventing the incorporation of phased out protections, but also additional liberalizations commitments, sojourn of personnel clauses, contractual commitments, or other subject matters not explicitly mentioned in the clause or covered in the base treaty.

3. Treatment Must Be "More Favorable"

The treatment granted in the third treaty will only be subject to MFN if it is more favorable than that of the base treaty. The burden rests on the claimants to prove this assertion. Much of the legal innovation described in Chapter 2 is directed toward reducing ambiguity in treaty language through more detailed drafting. Since more ambiguous clauses are not necessarily more favorable clauses, investors have found it difficult to circumvent certainty-oriented language through MFN.

In *ADF v. United States*, the claimant failed to prove that the FET standard contained in the US BITs with Estonia and Albania actually affords higher protection than that granted by NAFTA Article 1105.[124] The tribunal in *Chemtura v. Canada* rejected the same MFN claim based on Canadian treaty practice on similar grounds.[125] Thus far, NAFTA's minimum standard of treatment clause has thus proven immune to circumvention through MFN. Attempts to reinsert protective clauses, such as the prohibition against arbitrary and discriminatory treatment that were discarded as redundant or moved to the preamble starting with the 2004 US model BIT, should fail on the same grounds. Since their content is already encompassed by other obligations, notably FET, their exclusion would not result in less favorable treatment.

On procedural matters, claimants had more success in demonstrating "less favourable treatment" when, as in the *Maffezini v. Spain* case, waiting periods

---

[122] For a similar argument, *see* Gazzinia & Tanzib, *supra* note 119, at 985.

[123] *CME Czech Republic B.V. v. Czech Republic*, UNCITRAL, Final Award, March 14, 2003, para. 500. *But see* dissenting opinion: *CME Czech Republic B.V. v. The Czech Republic*, UNCITRAL, Separate Opinion of Ian Brownlie, March 14, 2003, paras. 11–12.

[124] *ADF Group Inc. v. United States of America*, ICSID Case No. ARB(AF)/00/1, Award, January 9, 2003, paras. 193–194.

[125] *Crompton (Chemtura) Corp. v. Government of Canada*, Award, August 2, 2010, paras. 235–236.

are imposed in the base treaty but are absent in the third treaty. Even then, however, it remains controversial what the "most favorable treatment" comparison entails. As Cole points out, two questions in particular remain unresolved.[126] First, is it the subjective perception of more favorable treatment advanced by the claimant that counts, or is "more favorable" understood as relating to the class of investors as a whole? Second, does the comparison entail a provision-by-provision analysis, or does it require a more holistic assessment of treatment, which also considers the interrelatedness of provisions and their respective benefits and the burdens?

Current case law largely follows a claimant-centered, provision-by-provision comparison. At its extreme, as done in *Siemens v. Argentina*, the investor is allowed to cherry-pick only the more favorable waiting period without having to accept the less favorable fork-in-the-road provision of the third treaty. Cole advances a more convincing conceptualization of the less favorable treatment comparison. First, if MFN operates as an "instantaneous obligation" rather than a "right to claim," "less favorable treatment" has to be assessed with respect to covered investors as a class rather than on an individual basis.[127] That makes sense given that, under today's dominant view, the more favorable treatment will be automatically incorporated well before and independently of the particular position of any individually claiming investor. The only way favorability can then be assessed is by considering it as relating to covered investors as a class.

Second, treaty obligations must be conceived as an interrelated package. As highlighted in Chapters 2 and 3, commitments are enabled through flexibility—an equilibrium that would be upset if cherry-picking would be allowed. In that vein, Cole suggests that whenever evidence of such a trade-off is available, the provision should be considered as a package rather than individually, which then alters considerations of what is more favorable.[128] Chapter 3 illustrated, for instance, that liberalization commitments or performance requirements first inserted in American BITs strongly correlate with the insertion of reservation and nonconforming measure schedules. As a result, investors could only access the package—the obligation and the reservation—rather than cherry-pick exclusively the former.

An example helps illustrate why this matters. As mentioned earlier, the Canada–China BIT (2012) extends MFN to the investment's pre-establishment phase so that Canadian investors can claim any liberalization benefits granted by China in a future treaty, for example, with the United States. But if Canadian

---

[126] Cole, *supra* note 51, at 178–185.

[127] *Id.* at 582–584. While favorable to the class as a whole, this could potentially hurt an individual investor and be used as defense by states to deny the application of the treatment enshrined in the base treaty, which is more favorable to the claiming investor, but less favorable to the class, *see* Cole, *supra* note 51, at 585.

[128] *Id.* at 578–581.

investors were able to cherry-pick, that is, receive market access without having to accept the nonconforming measures China reserves in its schedule vis-à-vis the United States, Canadian investors would effectively be better placed than American investors through MFN. In short, less favorable treatment requires a holistic assessment of both benefits and limitations.

Collectively, the findings of this final section suggest that MFN clauses, even if interpreted expansively, do not generally reverse or override the treaty design innovation identified in Part I of this book. Table 4.3 summarizes the limitations of

Table 4.3 Assuming that MFN can incorporate by reference third-treaty provisions, its operation leaves most of the state-driven treaty design innovations of Part I intact

Limitation	Explanation	Innovation
Limitations of treaty scope		
1. Jurisdictional scope of the treaty 2. Exceptions and exclusions	MFN cannot be used to alter the *ratione materiae, ratione temporis,* or *ratione personae* scope of the base treaty. MFN cannot be used to circumvent exclusions and exceptions that limit the scope of application of the base treaty by pointing to the absence of such exceptions in the third treaty.	Protects narrower IIA scope or definition of investment (e.g., exclude portfolio investment) from MFN. Protects new carveout or general exceptions from being overridden or hollowed out by MFN.
Limitations within the MFN clause		
1. MFN-based reservations and exceptions 2. *Ejusdem generis* and the notion of "treatment" 3. "…not less favorable"	MFN cannot attract matters that are explicitly or implicitly carved out from the scope of the base treaty's MFN clause. MFN can only attract matters that form part of the subject matter of the clause. Textual limitations (e.g., enumerations of the benefits covered) or contextual limitations (e.g., "treatment" as circumscribed by the treaty) define the subject matter of the clause. Non-treatment treaty provisions are not covered by the clause absent language to this effect. MFN only attracts explicitly more favorable language. Less ambiguous treaty language is neither more nor less favorable. Moreover, favorability must be assessed by comparing (1) investors as a class (rather than individual claimants) and (2) treaty obligations as interrelated packages (rather than cherry-picking individual benefits while ignoring a concomitant burden).	Matters carved out from MFN, such as procedural obligations, cannot be imported through MFN. Phased-out obligations such as umbrella clauses cannot be reintroduced via MFN. Procedural innovations, e.g., transparency norms in arbitration, are not "treatment" and cannot be rolled back via MFN. Clarifications of protective standards (e.g., linking FET to customary international law) are not more favorable and cannot be overridden via MFN. More favorable obligations need to be incorporated as a package with the exceptions that accompany them.

MFN and how they protect treaty design innovation. Therefore, although some tribunals have misconstrued MFN clauses and created risks that innovation is rolled back, and new treaties are read like old ones, a more balanced interpretation of MFN would severely limit the clause's effect to override treaty design differences and preserve state-driven change.

V. Conclusion

MFN risks treating new treaties like old ones. Treaty provisions phased out in recent practice have been brought back, and clarifications of protective standards risk being reversed through MFN. Furthermore, tribunals have allowed cherry-picking of only more favorable terms and mused about MFN attracting more investment-friendly exclusions and exceptions. Such an interpretation of MFN risks rolling back state-driven change as outdated, and ostensibly more favorable clauses from old IIAs are read into new agreements. Yet, as this chapter has shown, the effect of MFN on treaty design differences is much more limited than the findings of some tribunals or the writing of some scholars would suggest. Even if MFN is conceptualized as an instantaneous obligation that directly and immediately imports third-treaty standards into a base treaty, most if not all of the innovations of IIA's evolution toward more complete treaties described in Chapter 2 will be shielded from its operation. That is because the MFN clause and the treaty that surround it place explicit and implicit limitations on its operation. MFN, if interpreted correctly, therefore accommodates treaty design differences.

5

Overriding Differences through Custom

I. Introduction

Customary international law represents a second means for rolling back innovation and overriding treaty design differences. Investment treaties exist against the backdrop of preexisting customary law principles.[1] These customary norms delineate commitments owed to foreign investors, such as providing a minimum standard of treatment.[2] They also enshrine flexibilities enjoyed by states, such as the freedom to exercise their regulatory police powers in a nondiscriminatory way without incurring an obligation to compensate for ensuing losses.[3] Customary law commitments and flexibilities thereby provide a baseline, allowing contracting parties to agree on more ambitious obligations or more far-reaching exceptions in their treaties.

On the one hand, custom has emerged as a vital tool for states to write more contractually complete and balanced IIAs.[4] As discussed in Chapter 2, states

---

[1] ANDREW NEWCOMBE & LLUÍS PARADELL, LAW AND PRACTICE OF INVESTMENT TREATIES: STANDARDS OF TREATMENT 2, 12 (2009). As discussed in Part I, these customary law principles were controversial and contested and the purpose of BITs was to reinforce them. At the same time, as will be discussed in this chapter, at least among Western capital exporters there was wide agreement in the mid-twentieth century that principles of customary law predating BITs existed.

[2] Edwin Borchard, *The "Minimum Standard" of the Treatment of Aliens*, 33 PROCEEDINGS OF THE AMERICAN SOCIETY OF INTERNATIONAL LAW AT ITS ANNUAL MEETING (1921–1969) 51–74, 60 (1939) ("It is thus apparent that both in its substantive and procedural aspects international law, as evidenced by diplomatic practice and arbitral decision, has established the existence of an international minimum standard to which all civilized states are required to conform under penalty of responsibility.").

[3] According to the OECD, "[i]t is an accepted principle of customary international law that where economic injury results from a bona fide non-discriminatory regulation within the police powers of the State, compensation is not required." *See* OECD (2004), *"Indirect Expropriation" and the "Right to Regulate" in International Investment Law,"* OECD WORKING PAPERS ON INTERNATIONAL INVESTMENT, 2004/04, at 5. While some authors have questioned the nature of the police powers doctrine as a rule of customary international law, given that it seems to originate from American legal practice, there is agreement among commentators that certain acts are so fundamental to the exercise of governmental authority that they do not attract compensation even if they infringe on property rights. *See, e.g.,* M. SORNARAJAH, THE INTERNATIONAL LAW ON FOREIGN INVESTMENT 283 (1994).

[4] It should be noted that customary law can also become relevant even if the treaty does not explicitly refer to custom, e.g., via interpretation (Article 31(3)c)) or as part of the applicable law. *See generally* Jorge E. Vinuales, *Customary Law in Investment Regulation Symposium: International Investment Regulation: Trends and Challenges*, 23 ITALIAN Y.B. INT'L L. 23–48 (2013).

Investment Arbitration and State-Driven Reform. Wolfgang Alschner, Oxford University Press. © Oxford University Press 2022. DOI: 10.1093/oso/9780197644386.003.0006

have explicitly contracted on custom to fill interpretive gaps in otherwise vague clauses or to recall the flexibility norms that custom provides, such as the police powers doctrine.[5] Compared to an autonomous treaty standard additive to custom, this embedding of treaty language in custom moderates a treaty's effect and rejects extreme state or investor-friendly interpretations.[6] Custom thus helps advance state-driven reforms toward optimally balanced and contractually complete IIAs.

On the other hand, custom can also upset state-driven change and override intentional design differences. First, tribunals struggle to tell when states contract on custom and when they contract out of it. As a result, tribunals have confused states' effort to go beyond custom, for example, through general exceptions, as codifications of custom and thereby rolled back innovations. Second, the increased reliance on custom has fueled debates on where exactly the customary baseline lies, with investors vigorously arguing that custom has evolved over time toward increased investment protection. The shift of litigation away from the design of the applicable treaty to custom empowers tribunals at the expense of the contracting states since custom is primarily revealed through litigation and arbitral awards boosting the importance of precedent and judicial gap-filling.

This chapter seeks to put custom in its place. The key for upholding contractual choices in ISDS practice lies in recognizing when states contract on custom and when they go beyond it in more complete IIAs. Section II shows that tribunals systematically confuse the two or use the idea of an evolving custom to undermine custom's moderating effect. As a result, they roll back innovation, override treaty design differences, and read new treaties like old ones. Section III traces the historical interaction between treaties and custom to better understand when states meant to contract on or go beyond custom. It shows that there is considerable evidence that states crafted their more complete treaties so as to use custom as a *floor* for granting flexibilities and a *ceiling* for providing certain investment protections. Section IV offers guidance on how tribunals can support state-driven treaty design choices by recognizing when states meant to contract on custom and when not.

---

[5] *Id.* (arguing that customary international law is the main expression of sovereignty in investment law and does not require explicit treaty references in order to apply).

[6] Considering an FET clause as linked to the customary international law minimum standard, for example, has been interpreted as moderating the investment protection it offers; similarly, interpreting a general exception as codifying customary law police powers tends to lower the policy space it provides. *See* NEWCOMBE & PARADELL, *supra* note 1, at 263–264. Wolfgang Alschner & Kun Hui, *Missing in Action: General Public Policy Exceptions in Investment Treaties, in* YEARBOOK ON INTERNATIONAL INVESTMENT LAW AND POLICY 2018 (Lisa E. Sachs, Jesse Coleman, & Lise Johnson eds., 2019).

II. Rolling Back Innovation through Custom

In ISDS practice, customary international law has been used in two ways to override treaty design differences, to roll back recent design innovation, and to read more complete IIAs like incomplete ones. First, arbitral tribunals have accepted the argument advanced by investors that the customary minimum standard of treatment has evolved through the conclusion of thousands of BITs and is now converging with the higher standard of protection offered under IIAs that do not explicit link the treatment of investors to custom. Second, arbitral tribunals have interpreted the insertion of general exceptions in recent, more complete IIAs as codifying existing customary international law flexibilities rather than as providing new, autonomous escape clauses.

Both lines of interpretation share a common core. In each case, the reference to custom is used to move the focus away from the specific language of the applicable IIA and to ground the analysis instead in sources that ostensibly crystallize the state of custom, such as earlier arbitral awards. This shift in perspectives disempowers the contracting states and undermines the impact of new treaty language. At the same time, it enhances the importance of early ISDS awards dealing with custom and reinforces the role of tribunals as gatekeepers of legal evolution.

A. Increasing Commitments through Custom

Chapter 2 showed that states have crafted more complete agreements by clarifying previously vague and open textured standards. In part, this has been done by explicitly linking protections to customary international law. More complete IIAs often root FET as well as full protection and security in the customary internal law minimum standard. When arbitral tribunals encounter such novel treaty language that explicitly mentions the customary international law minimum standard, their analysis typically follows a two-tier pattern.

The assessment usually starts with the widely cited *Neer* decision rendered by the US–Mexico Claims Commission in 1926, which sought to delineate the content of the customary minimum standard of treatment.[7] According to the Commission, to violate international law the treatment of aliens has to amount to an "outrage, bad faith, or a willful neglect of duty" or it has to arise from an "insufficiency of governmental action so far short of international standards that

---

[7] RUDOLF DOLZER & CHRISTOPH SCHREUER, PRINCIPLES OF INTERNATIONAL INVESTMENT LAW 139–141 (2nd ed. 2012). NAFTA respondent states have consistently argued that *Neer* represents the minimum standard of treatment and thereby made the case the starting point of arbitral analyses.

every reasonable and impartial man would readily recognize its insufficiency".[8] The *Neer* standard thereby imposes a high liability threshold. In contrast, the majority of ISDS tribunals interpreting clauses that lack explicit references to custom, so-called "autonomous" or "unqualified" FET provisions, have not required evidence of "bad faith" or "outrageous" conduct to establish a treaty violation.[9] The *Neer* standard is thus seen as offering less protection than an FET provision without link to the minimum standard.[10]

Investors under treaties such as NAFTA that root FET in the minimum standard have sought to benefit from higher protection by arguing that the minimum standard has evolved since *Neer* though the conclusion of thousands of BITs.[11] The second question ISDS tribunals thus face is whether the minimum standard to which these treaties refer is different from the minimum standard in the 1920s.[12] To adduce evidence of an evolving custom, investors routinely point to the decisions of international tribunals,[13] as well as to the thousands of investment treaties with "autonomous" FET clauses.[14] Swayed by this evidence, the *Pope & Talbot v. Canada* tribunal was the first ISDS tribunal to assert in 2002 that "applying the ordinary rules for determining the content of custom in international law, one must conclude that the practice of states is now represented by those [investment] treaties."[15] A few months later, the *Mondev v. USA* tribunal equally found that

---

[8] *L. F. H. Neer and Pauline Neer (U.S.A.) v. United Mexican States*, October 15, 1926, at 61–62.

[9] DOLZER & SCHREUER, *supra* note 7, at 140.

[10] *See, e.g.,* STEPHAN W. SCHILL, THE MULTILATERALIZATION OF INTERNATIONAL INVESTMENT LAW 269 (2009).

[11] On the question of whether treaties are proof of custom, *see* Céline Braumann, *Taxes and Custom: Tax Treaties as Evidence for Customary International Law*, 23 J. INT'L ECON. L. 747–769 (2020).

[12] *See, e.g., ADF Group Inc. v. United States*, Award, January 9, 2003, para. 179.

[13] For example, investors routinely cite the *ELSI* case before the ICJ, which dealt with an FCN treaty prohibiting "arbitrary" state conduct. The ICJ found that it prohibits a "wilful disregard of due process of law, an act which shocks, or at least surprises, a sense of judicial propriety," which has been interpreted as imposing a lower threshold than *Neer*. *See Elettronica Sicula S.p.A. (ELSI)* (United States of America v. Italy), para. 128.

[14] The argument is based on the assertion that highly uniform bilateral treaties can give rise to custom in "rather exceptional circumstances"; *see* Tarcissio Gazzani, *The Role of Customary International Law in the Field of Foreign Investment*, 8 J. WORLD INVESTMENT & TRADE 691–716, 701 (2007). According to Stephen Schwebel, "Customary international law governing the treatment of foreign investment has been reshaped to embody the principles of law found in more than two thousand concordant bilateral investment treaties." Stephen M. Schwebel, *The Influence of Bilateral Investment Treaties on Customary International Law*, 98 PROCEEDINGS OF THE ANNUAL MEETING (AMERICAN SOCIETY OF INTERNATIONAL LAW) 27–30, 27 (2004). For a review of the academic debate whether FET has become a standard of customary law, *see* Patrick Dumberry, *Has the Fair and Equitable Treatment Standard Become a Rule of Customary International Law?*, 8 J. INT'L DISP. SETTLEMENT 155–178 (2017).

[15] *Pope & Talbot Inc. v. The Government of Canada*, UNCITRAL, Award in Respect of Damages, May 31, 2002, para. 62.

such a body of concordant [BIT] practice will necessarily have influenced the content of rules governing the treatment of foreign investment in current international law. It would be surprising if this practice and the vast number of provisions it reflects were to be interpreted as meaning no more than the *Neer* Tribunal (in a very different context) meant in 1927.[16]

The *Merrill v. Canada* tribunal concurred that "today's minimum standard is broader than that defined in the *Neer* case."[17] The 2015 *Bilcon v. Canada* award shows that this line of cases, while not universally embraced by NAFTA tribunals, continues to guide some arbitrators. After considering the previously cited awards, the *Bilcon* tribunal concluded that "the international minimum standard has evolved over the years towards greater protection for investors."[18]

A number of tribunals beyond NAFTA have echoed the view that the evolution of custom has led to its convergence with an autonomously interpreted FET clause.[19] The *CMS v. Argentina* tribunal found that "the Treaty standard of fair and equitable treatment [. . .] is not different from the international law minimum standard and its evolution under customary law."[20] Similarly, the *Rumeli v. Kazakhstan* tribunal concluded that the "treaty standard of fair and equitable treatment is not materially different from the minimum standard of treatment in customary international law."[21] This line of ISDS cases has given rise to what Patrick Dumberry termed the "convergence theory," according to which "custom had evolved so rapidly that it now had the same content as an autonomous FET clause."[22]

The construct of a rapidly evolving custom that converges with autonomous FET clauses rolls back state-driven change in three ways. First, it undercuts the intended moderating effect of linking protections to custom and instead increases the international baseline for investment protection. Indeed, investors have begun to use customary international law arguments and MFN

---

[16] *Mondev International Ltd. v. United States of America*, ICSID Case No. ARB(AF) 99/2, Award, October 11, 2002, para. 117.

[17] *Merrill and Ring Forestry L.P. v. Canada*, ICSID Case No. UNCT/07/1, Award, March 31, 2010, para. 213.

[18] *Bilcon of Delaware et al. v. Government of Canada*, PCA Case No. 2009-04, Award on Jurisdiction and Liability, March 17, 2015, para. 435.

[19] *Biwater Gauff (Tanzania) Limited v. United Republic of Tanzania*, ICSID Case No. ARB/05/22, Award, July 24, 2008, para. 592 ("the actual content of the treaty standard of fair and equitable treatment is not materially different from the content of the minimum standard of treatment in customary international law."); *Occidental v. Ecuador*, Award of July 1, 2004, para. 190.

[20] *CMS Gas Transmission Company v. The Republic of Argentina*, ICSID Case No. ARB/01/8, Award, May 12, 2005, para. 284.

[21] *Rumeli Telekom A.S. and Telsim Mobil Telekomunikasyon Hizmetleri A.S. v. Republic of Kazakhstan*, ICSID Case No. ARB/05/16, Award, July 29, 2008, para. 611.

[22] Patrick Dumberry, The Fair and Equitable Treatment Standard: A Guide to NAFTA Case Law on Article 1105 113 (2013).

interchangeably to enhance the investment protection offered by the base treaty. In *İçkale v. Turkmenistan*, for example, the investor first claimed that the MFN clause allowed it to rely on more favorable protective clauses from other BITs and, in the alternative, argued that it could invoke the same clauses because they had become "an international customary norm for Turkmenistan" by virtue of being included in many of Turkmenistan's treaties.[23] While the tribunal correctly rejected that claim, the example underscores that the idea of an evolving custom has become a tool for increasing the baseline of investment protection akin to MFN.

Second, the idea of an evolving custom allows tribunals to read new treaties in light of old ones. While "autonomous" FET clauses tend to be found in older, incomplete agreements, FET clauses explicitly rooted in custom tend to be included in recent, more complete IIAs. When the content of "autonomous" clauses is reintroduced through the backdoor of an evolving custom, new treaties are interpreted like old ones.[24] Ironically, vague "autonomous" FET language in incomplete treaties motivated the treaty design reform to clarify and moderate the content of FET through customary law references in the first place. Yet that same outdated "autonomous" FET practice is subsequently used to undermine that correction, taking contracting parties back to square one.

Third, the idea of a rapidly evolving custom empowers tribunals at the expense of states. As Schill put it, "attempts to relink the content of investment treaties to customary international law cannot be viewed only as an effort to establish the meaning of fair and equitable treatment, they are also part of the struggle to determine whether tribunals or States have the ultimate power of interpreting investment treaties and the principles they contain."[25]

In theory, establishing custom requires evidence of state practice and *opinio juris*.[26] Some recent treaties explicitly restate this general international law axiom. Well-reasoned judicial decisions may crystalize custom.[27] Yet they cannot by themselves create custom.[28] In practice, however, empirical research has shown that tribunals tend not to conduct an independent assessment of the existence of treaty practice or *opinio juris*; instead they tend to pay lip service to custom's requirements and then use earlier judicial decisions as evidence of the

---

[23] *İçkale Insaat Limited Sirketi v. Turkmenistan*, ICSID Case No. ARB/10/24, Award, March 8, 2016, paras. 314, 338.

[24] SCHILL, *supra* note 10, at 273.

[25] *Id.* at 269–270.

[26] As the ICJ put it, to be evidence of custom "[n]ot only must the acts concerned amount to a settled practice [state practice], but they must also be such, or be carried out in such a way, as to be evidence of a belief that this practice is rendered obligatory by the existence of a rule of law requiring it [opinio juris]." *North Sea Continental Shelf*, Judgment, ICJ Rep. 1969, at 3, 45, para. 77.

[27] Patrick Dumberry, *The Role and Relevance of Awards in the Formation, Identification and Evolution of Customary Rules in International Investment Law*, 33 J. INT'L ARB. 274 (2016).

[28] *Id.* at 270–271.

state of custom and its evolution toward greater protection.[29] As a result, Schill's conclusion, drawn a decade ago, still rings true today: states' efforts to "domesticate" tribunals by linking FET to custom have largely been unsuccessful.[30]

B. Lowering Flexibilities through Custom

Another hallmark of the shift from incomplete to more complete agreements discussed in Chapter 2 consists of the inclusion of new flexibility language to seize regret. On the one hand, states have sought to achieve more policy space by explicitly contracting into customary international law flexibilities. According to the general international law police powers doctrine, a nondiscriminatory public purpose regulation is generally not compensable unless a state had made specific commitments to the investor.[31] States have explicitly incorporated this principle in the form of clarifications to their expropriation provisions in recent treaties.[32] In addition, states have included new escape clauses, such as general security and public policy exceptions, into their agreements to exempt governmental conduct from liability that would otherwise violate the treaty.[33]

These innovations have been challenged by two generations of ISDS awards that conflated the role of customary international law flexibilities and autonomous exceptions. First, a series of awards against Argentina confused an essential security exception with the customary international law excuse of necessity. Second, a more recent line of cases adopted interpretations that fused customary international law flexibilities, such as the right to exercise police powers, with general public policy exceptions. In both cases, equating general treaty exceptions

[29] *Id.* at 281–284. Ole Kristian Fauchald, *The Legal Reasoning of ICSID Tribunals—An Empirical Analysis*, 19 EUR. J. INT'L L. 301–364 (2008). To some extent, this practice may be a natural "translation" as state-driven and judicial lawmaking interact. Harlan Cohen, *International Law's Erie Moment*, 34 MICH. J. INT'L L. 249–308, 270 (2013) ("The development of 'custom' via adjudication is not merely a continuation of that rule's development, but its transformation into something new.").

[30] SCHILL, *supra* note 10, at 275 (making that point in relation to NAFTA case law).

[31] American Law Institute, vol. 1, 1987, sec. 712, cmt. g ("[a] state is not responsible for loss of property or for other economic disadvantage resulting from bona fide general taxation, regulation, forfeiture for crime, or other action of the kind that is commonly accepted as within the police power of states, if it is not discriminatory."). The doctrine has been widely affirmed in ISDS practice, *see, e.g., Methanex v. USA*, pt. IV, ch. D, para. 7; *AWG Group Ltd. v. Argentine Republic*, UNCITRAL, Decision on Liability, July 30, 2010, para. 139; *Tza Yap Shum v. Republic of Peru*, ICSID Case No. ARB/07/6, Award, July 7, 2011, paras. 145–146. *See generally* Catharine Titi, *Police Powers Doctrine and International Investment Law, in* GENERAL PRINCIPLES OF LAW AND INTERNATIONAL INVESTMENT ARBITRATION 323–343, 325–327 (Filippo Fontanelli, Attila Tanzi, & Andrea Gattini eds., 2018).

[32] Annex B, United States–Uruguay BIT (2005). For a review, *see id.* at 338–339.

[33] W. Burke-White & A. Von Staden, *Investment Protection in Extraordinary Times: The Interpretation and Application of Non-Precluded Measures Provisions in Bilateral Investment Treaties*, 48 VA. J. INT'L L. 307 (2007); Amelia Keene, *The Incorporation and Interpretation of WTO-Style Environmental Exceptions in International Investment Agreements*, 18 J. WORLD INVESTMENT & TRADE 62–99 (2017).

with custom collapses distinct lines of defense in litigation and lowers the policy space these exceptions offer.

The first generation of awards that lowered the flexibility provided by treaty-based exceptions involved a series of ICSID cases launched by investors in the gas distribution sector under the Argentina–United States BIT (1991) in the wake of Argentina's 2001 economic crisis.[34] As part of its measures to alleviate the crisis, Argentina had converted gas distribution tariffs from dollars to pesos, causing losses to foreign-owned gas distributors as the Argentinian currency collapsed. Argentina justified its acts as emergency measures permitted both under the state of necessity defense in customary international law and under Article XI of the Argentina–United States BIT, which explicitly permits "measures necessary for the maintenance of public order, the fulfillment of its obligations with respect to the maintenance or restoration of international peace or security, or the Protection of its own essential security interests."

The *CMS*, *Enron*, and *Sempra* tribunals adopted an interpretation that conflated both grounds of defense.[35] Customary international law as codified in Article 25 of the Articles on State Responsibility precludes wrongfulness for what would otherwise be an internationally wrongful act, but based on strict conditions: the measure has to constitute the only way for a state to safeguard an essential interest when faced with a situation of necessity to which it had not itself contributed.[36] The three tribunals read these conditions into the treaty exception to define what "necessary" meant in the context of the Article XI.[37] In doing so, the tribunals introduced new, stricter requirements into the essential security

---

[34] Anne van Aaken & Jürgen Kurtz, *Prudence or Discrimination? Emergency Measures, the Global Financial Crisis and International Economic Law*, 12 J. INT'L ECON. L. 859–894 (2009).

[35] For an academic commentary on these cases, *see* Jürgen Kurtz, *Adjudging the Exceptional at International Law: Security, Public Order and Financial Crisis*, 59 INT'L & COMP. L.Q. 325–371 (2010); DIANE A. DESIERTO, NECESSITY AND NATIONAL EMERGENCY CLAUSES: SOVEREIGNTY IN MODERN TREATY INTERPRETATION (2012); Alan O. Sykes, *Economic "Necessity" in International Law*, 109 AM. J. INT'L L. 296 (2015).

[36] ILC, *Draft Articles on Responsibility of States for Internationally Wrongful Acts With Commentaries*, YEARBOOK OF THE INTERNATIONAL LAW COMMISSION, vol. II, pt. Two (2001), Article 25.

[37] The *CMS v. Argentina* award dealt with the issue only implicitly, partly because the arguments by the parties centred around the question whether the Article XI of the US–Argentina BIT was self-judging or not. *See CMS Gas Transmission Company v. The Republic of Argentina*, ICSID Case No. ARB/01/8, Award, May 12, 2005, para. 374 ("a substantive review that must examine whether the state of necessity or emergency meets the conditions laid down by customary international law and the treaty provisions."); *Sempra Energy International v. The Argentine Republic*, ICSID Case No. ARB/02/16, Award, September 28, 2007, para. 376 ("the Treaty provision [Article XI] is inseparable from the customary law standard insofar as the definition of necessity and the conditions for its operation are concerned."); Similarly, *Enron Corporation and Ponderosa Assets, L.P. v. Argentine Republic*, ICSID Case No. ARB/01/3, Award, May 22, 2007, para. 333 ("Treaty does not define what is to be understood by essential security interest . . . This is what makes necessary to rely on the requirements of state of necessity under customary international law, as outlined above in connection with their expression in Article 25 of the Articles on State Responsibility, so as to evaluate whether such requirements have been met in this case.").

exception and reduced the policy space offered by the provision. Unsurprisingly, the tribunals applying that more onerous standard, then went on to find that Argentina's conduct could not be justified under the treaty, because Argentina had contributed to the crisis and its emergency measures were not "the only way" to react to it.[38]

Argentina requested annulment in all three cases on the grounds that the tribunals' confusion of treaty exceptions with customary law resulted in a manifest excess of power—one of the grounds for annulment under Article 52 of the ICSID Convention. The *CMS* annulment committee concluded that conflating the scope and requirements of the two distinct legal norms amounted to a manifest error of law.[39] In the annulment committee's view, the tribunal had not examined whether the conditions of Article XI were met.[40] Yet it deemed its hands tied by the limited mandate for annulment committees under the ICSID Convention given that the tribunal had applied the law—however "cryptically or defectively."[41] The committee added, however, that if it were a court of appeal, it would have modified award.[42]

The *Sempra* annulment committee was less cautious and decided to annul the award. The committee stressed that the customary international law on necessity and the national security exception in Article XI of the BIT were distinct legal norms and dealt with very different circumstances.[43] The committee asserted that by not investigating Article XI of the BIT independently, the tribunal had not merely applied it incorrectly, but had, in fact, not applied it all, which amounted to a manifest excess of power.[44] The *Enron* annulment committee equally decided to annul the award, but on different grounds. It found that the tribunal engaged in a manifest excess of power by not conducting its own legal assessment of whether Argentina's measures constituted the "only way" to respond to the economic crisis and instead applied an expert opinion.[45] The committee did not take issue with the tribunal's conflation of treaty and custom.[46]

Together, the two annulments and the strong rebuke of the *CMS* committee discouraged subsequent tribunals from making the same mistake. A decade later, the tribunal in *CC/Devas v. India*, for example, rejected the investor's argument

---

[38] *CMS v. Argentina*, paras. 323 & 329; *Sempra v. Argentina*, paras. 350 & 354; *Enron v. Argentina*, paras. 308 & 312.

[39] *CMS v. Argentina*, Decision on Annulment, para. 130.

[40] *Id.*, para. 135.

[41] *Id.*, para. 135.

[42] *Id.* paras. 135f.

[43] *Sempra v. Argentina*, Decision on Annulment, paras. 197–204.

[44] *Id.*, paras. 216–219.

[45] *Enron v. Argentina*, Decision on Annulment, paras. 364–377 & 405. The expert report was among the evidence produced by the claimant that stated that the measures adopted by Argentina were not the only way to respond to the crisis.

[46] *Id.*, para. 405.

that the conditions of the customary law necessity defense should be read into the security exception of the India–Mauritius BIT (1998).[47] Citing the *CMS* annulment committee, the tribunal concluded that the treaty-based exception "has nothing to do with the 'state of necessity' defence."[48] The tribunal in *Deutsche Telekom v. India* similarly rejected an attempt by the claimant in relation to the security exception in the Germany–India BIT (1995).[49] The tribunal explained that the treaty exception was distinct from and imposed less onerous requirements than the customary international law defense of the state of necessity.[50] When it comes to security exceptions, the case law thus seems well settled in recognizing the distinction between treaty and customary law and in upholding the explicit choices of states to expand policy space through their treaties beyond what is offered under custom.

The same cannot be said for a more recent generation of awards that have conflated general public policy exceptions with customary law. The tribunal in *Bear Creek v. Peru* had to review an indirect expropriation claim in relation to the revocation of a mining license under the Canada–Peru FTA (2009).[51] Peru argued that the measure was a legitimate exercise of the state's police powers and was justified in any case under the treaty's general exception in Article 2201.1(3).[52] The tribunal ultimately found that the conditions of the exception had not been met and that an indirect expropriation had taken place. In its analysis, the tribunal asserted that the existence of a general exception displaced other exceptions from general international law.[53] There was thus "no need to enter into the discussion [. . .] regarding the jurisprudence concerning any police power exception."[54] By treating general exceptions as displacement of customary law flexibilities, the tribunal not only failed to recognize police powers as a customary law safeguard protecting policy space.[55] It also ignored the treaty's interpretative Annex 812.1

---

[47] *CC/Devas (Mauritius) Ltd., Devas Employees Mauritius Private Limited and Telecom Devas Mauritius Limited v. India*, PCA Case No. 2013-09, Award on Jurisdiction and Merits, July 25, 2016.

[48] *Id.*, para. 254.

[49] *Deutsche Telekom v. India*, PCA Case No. 2014-10, Interim Award, December 13, 2017.

[50] *Id.*, para. 228–229.

[51] *Bear Creek Mining Corporation v. Republic of Peru*, ICSID Case No. ARB/14/21, Award, November 30, 2017, para. 124.

[52] *Id.*, paras. 337, 459–470.

[53] *Id.*, para. 472.

[54] *Id.*, para. 473.

[55] Philip Sands offered a partial dissent in the case. Paradoxically, he agreed with the majority that the general exception displaces the customary police powers exception but, in a nod to the first generation of awards confusing treaties and custom, also stressed that the exception did not preclude customary law on necessity. *See* Partial Dissent Philippe Sands, *Bear Creek Mining Corporation v. Republic of Peru*, ICSID Case No. ARB/14/21, Award, November 30, 2017, para. 41. A more consistent position would be to treat both situations equally insofar as treaty-based exceptions should not be presumed to displace custom unless they explicitly codify or exclude it.

on expropriation that explicitly codified the police powers doctrine and that had been flagged as highly pertinent in Canada's nondisputing party submission.[56]

The tribunal in *Copper Mesa v. Ecuador* fared little better.[57] It also dealt with the revocation of a mining concession, this time under the Canada–Ecuador BIT (1996), which contained a similar general public policy exception in Article XVII(3). The tribunal began by acknowledging that the legitimate exercise of police powers provides a separate defense under international law that exists in addition to the general exception in the treaty.[58] It nevertheless concluded that they could be dealt with jointly as they "turn on the same factors."[59] The tribunal then found that the concession was revoked in an arbitrary manner and without due process and thus failed the conditions of both the police powers exception and the requirements of the treaty exception's chapeau.[60] Conflating the analysis of both flexibility mechanisms is problematic. Police powers carve out certain measures from the scope of expropriation, whereas an exception saves a measure that was previously found to violate a treaty provision.[61] They thus operate differently and come into play at different points of the legal analysis. Hence, even if they were to "turn on the same factors," they would have to be investigated separately and at different stages of the proceeding.

The most egregious conflation of flexibilities in treaty and custom occurred in the 2021 *Eco Oro Minerals v. Colombia* award.[62] Litigated under the Canada–Colombia FTA (2008), it similarly dealt with an environmental measure that had curtailed the mining concession of a Canadian investor. After finding a breach of FET, the tribunal majority went on to consider Colombia's defense under the FTA's general exception clause in Article 2201(3). Both the respondent and the host state, Canada, via its nondisputing party submission, argued that the exception, provided its conditions were met, would shield a measure from liability and

---

[56] *Bear Creek Mining Corporation v. Republic of Peru*, ICSID Case No. ARB/14/21, Submission of Canada Pursuant to Article 832 of the Canada–Peru Free Trade Agreement, June 9, 2016, paras. 4–6. For academic commentary on this omission, *see* Joshua Paine, *Bear Creek Mining Corporation v Republic of Peru: Judging the Social License of Foreign Investments and Applying New Style Investment Treaties*, 33 ICSID Rev. 340–348 (2018).

[57] *Copper Mesa Mining Corporation v. Republic of Ecuador*, PCA No. 2012-2, Award, March 15, 2016.

[58] *Id.*, para. 6.58.

[59] *Id.*

[60] *Id.*, paras. 660–668.

[61] On the distinction between flexibility offered under primary obligations versus exceptions, *see, e.g.*, Jorge E. Viñuales, *Seven Ways of Escaping a Rule: Of Exceptions and Their Avatars in International Law*, *in* EXCEPTIONS AND DEFENCES IN INTERNATIONAL LAW (Lorand Bartels & Federica Paddeu eds., 2019); Caroline Henckels, *Scope Limitation or Affirmative Defence? The Purpose and Role of Investment Treaty Exception Clauses*, *in* EXCEPTIONS AND DEFENCES IN INTERNATIONAL LAW (Lorand Bartels & Federica Paddeu eds., 2018).

[62] *Eco Oro Minerals Corp. v. Republic of Colombia*, ICSID Case No. ARB/16/41, Decision on Jurisdiction, Liability and Directions on Quantum, September 9, 2021.

from the payment of compensation for a violation of an investment protection clause.[63]

The tribunal disagreed. It denied the explicit hierarchy introduced by the exception whereby environmental concerns trump investment protection concerns under strict conditions and stated instead that "neither environmental protection nor investment protection is subservient to the other."[64] It then characterized the exception clause in Article 2201(3), which was modeled on GATT XX, as a *permission* that allows adopting environmental measure but still requires the payment of compensation in case a treaty obligation is violated.[65] Echoing the Argentina cases, the tribunal justified its reasoning with reference to the customary law conditions precluding wrongfulness whereby even if a conduct is excused, the state must still compensate.[66] Furthermore, it reasoned that had it been the intentions of the states to exclude liability to pay compensation through the exceptions, they would have made it explicit as done in the police powers carveout of the treaty in Annex 811(2) b), which, except in rare circumstances excludes nondiscriminatory general public policy measures from the scope of indirect expropriation.[67]

The reasoning of the *Eco Oro* awards is troubling on four fronts. First, the award's interpretation deprived the exception of practical effect since a state would still need to compensate even if the exception's conditions were met. Second, it conflated the distinct legal concepts of customary law on conditions precluding wrongfulness with a treaty-based exception. It thereby repeated the mistakes of the *CMS, Sempra,* and *Enron* tribunals in failing to recognize treaty-based exceptions as a distinct defense. Third, by contrasting the police powers carveout as a valid exclusion of liability to the exception that still required the payment of compensation the tribunal played treaty flexibilities off against each other rather than construing them as complementary ways to defend a measure—as Canada had suggested in its nondisputing party submission.[68] Fourth, and most troublingly for the fate of state-driven change generally, the tribunal explicitly rejected the concordant submissions of the treaty drafters, Colombia and Canada, which had construed the exception as an escape from liability modeled on WTO law and instead superimposed its own reading of the clause that deprived it of practical effect.[69] The award is therefore a cogent

---

[63] *Id.*, paras. 364, 373–373, 378.

[64] *Id.*, para. 828.

[65] *Id.*, para. 829.

[66] *Id.*, para. 835.

[67] *Id.*

[68] Non-Disputing Party Submission of Canada, *Eco Oro Minerals Corp. v. Republic of Colombia,* ICSID Case No. ARB/16/41, February 27, 2020, para. 9. *See also* Viñuales, *supra* note 61; Henckels, *supra* note 61.

[69] Canada, as the nondisputing party, issued a detailed submission on the interpretation of the exception. Colombia fully endorsed that submission and urged the tribunal to follow Canada's interpretation. The tribunal rejected Canada's characterization. *Eco Oro Minerals Corp. v. Republic*

illustration of the interpretive "firewall" that can be erected by arbitrators against state-driven change.

In the aggregate, this second generation of awards undermines states' strategy of stacking complementary lines of defenses in more complete agreements. Under international law, states can safeguard policy space through a myriad of design choices: from exclusions that limit the scope of the treaty, to carveouts that narrow the scope of an obligation, to exceptions justifying noncompliance with an obligation, all the way to excuses suspending the wrongfulness of an otherwise illegal act.[70] Moreover, states can contract on custom or draft complementary treaty-based flexibilities. States like Canada seek to secure a maximum of regulatory flexibilities in their treaties by stacking or layering these different mechanisms. They incorporate references to police powers as well as complementary general exceptions.[71] As Canada explained in its nondisputing party submission in *Eco Oro*:

> Many of the investment provisions contain their own internal flexibilities that determine whether regulatory action is legitimate or if it amounts to a breach of an obligation. […] As a result, legitimate regulatory actions will rarely need to be justified on the basis of the general exception in Article 2201(3) because they will not constitute breaches of the investment obligations in the first place. In this sense, the general exceptions are an additional tool or a final "safety net" to protect the State's exercise of regulatory powers in pursuit of the specific legitimate objectives identified in the exceptions.[72]

Recent arbitral awards, however, have poked holes into that "safety net" by conflating references to custom to clarify primary obligations with general exceptions. As noted by Jorge Viñuales, there is a trend that tribunals "assume that treaties displace the customary concepts expressing sovereignty."[73] In addition, vice versa, tribunals like in *Bear Creek* or *Eco Oro* see custom displacing treaty concepts expressing sovereignty. Either way, instead of understanding more complete IIAs as offering layers of flexibility, in practice they are interpreted

---

of Colombia, ICSID Case No. ARB/16/41, Decision on Jurisdiction, Liability and Directions on Quantum, paras. 378, 836.

[70] Joost Pauwelyn, *Defenses and the Burden of Proof in International Law, in* EXCEPTIONS AND DEFENCES IN INTERNATIONAL LAW (Lorand Bartels & Federica Paddeu eds., 2019); Viñuales, *supra* note 61.

[71] It should be noted that the most recent 2021 Canada model BIT omits a general public policy exception.

[72] Non-Disputing Party Submission of Canada, *Eco Oro Minerals Corp. v. Republic of Colombia*, ICSID Case No. ARB/16/41, February 27, 2020, para. 9.

[73] Jorge E. Viñuales, *Too Many Butterflies? The Micro-Drivers of the International Investment Law System*, 9 J. INT'L DISP. SETTLEMENT 628–653, 650 (2018).

as providing only one line of defense under treaty and custom. When tribunals conflate general exceptions with customary law defenses, they thus lower policy space afforded by more complete agreements and roll back innovation.

III.   Treaties and Custom: A History of Linking and Delinking

In more complete IIAs, states have explicitly sought to link investment treaties to custom but have also used treaties to go beyond custom. The challenge lies in identifying which of these two categories a treaty norm belongs to. That is where the awards that have rolled back innovation went off track. They, in effect, confused protective provisions meant to codify a customary baseline as going beyond it (such as FET) and they mistook exceptions meant to add to custom as flexibilities codifying it. This section seeks to set that record straight. A historical review of how states linked treaties and custom helps understand how early investment treaties were rooted in custom and how later agreements created exceptions that sought to add to custom.

A.   Phase I: Codifying Custom

In large part, the investment treaty programs of Western industrialized states were efforts to codify customary rules of investment protection at a time when colonial empires were collapsing and newly independent states began challenging Western concepts of foreign property protection. Predating the first BITs, the United States and the United Kingdom had routinely used Friendship, Commerce, and Navigation (FCN) treaties to reinforce the customary international minimum standard of protection of alien property and full compensation in case of an expropriation.[74] Building on this trend, Hermann Abs and Hartley Shawcross published the Draft Convention on Investments Abroad in April 1959 to "restate" existing international law on the protection of foreign property abroad.[75] This restatement was meant to shore up customary law principles,

---

[74] Georg Schwarzenberger, *The Abs-Shawcross Draft Convention on Investments Abroad: A Critical Commentary*, 9 J. Pub. L. 147, 147 (1960); Herman Walker, *Treaties for the Encouragement and Protection of Foreign Investment: Present United States Practice*, 5 Am. J. Comp. L. 229–247, 232 (1956) (under FCN treaties, protected investors "shall receive not only equal protection, but also a certain minimum degree of protection, as under international law, regardless of a Government's possible lapses with respect to its own citizens.").

[75] Hermann Abs & Hartley Shawcross, *The Proposed Convention to Protect Private Foreign Investment—Introduction*, 9 J. Pub. L. 115, 119 (1960).

which had been disregarded by "some countries."[76] The language relating to FET and full protection and security in Article I reproduced the preexisting FCN wording.[77] The clause on expropriation in Article III sought to "to restate the minimum standards."[78] The Draft Convention also created novel rules.[79] Yet its core absolute standards of protection were thus framed as restating existing custom.

The pattern of restating custom continued in the 1960s through the work of the OECD to create a multilateral investment protection convention. The 1967 OECD Draft Convention on the Protection of Foreign Property, which itself was closely modeled on the earlier Abs-Shawcross text, explained in the commentary to the convention that the FET standard in Article I of the Convention "conforms in effect to the 'minimum standard' which forms part of customary law." It furthermore noted that Article III on expropriation "restates . . . recognized rules of international law." While the Draft Convention never became hard law, the OECD Council recommended it as a template for the bilateral treaties of its members. The Draft Convention "represented the collective view and dominant trend of OECD countries on investment issues and influenced the pattern of deliberations on foreign investment in that period."[80] The United Kingdom, which only started concluding BITs in the 1970s, used the language of the OECD Draft particularly extensively, often word for word, in its subsequent treaties.[81]

Early BIT practice of Western states inspired by the Abs-Shawcross Draft Convention and developed in parallel to the OECD talks attests to the same link between treaty protections and custom. Starting in the early 1960s, Switzerland, Belgium, France, and the Netherlands explicitly rooted their expropriation clauses in customary international law.[82] France and Switzerland furthermore

---

[76] *Id.* at 119 ("during the last few decades in some countries there has been a tendency to disregard them; and arguments have been sought and advanced to justify actions which are incompatible with the obligations which membership of the international community imposes upon states. However, international trade and commerce cannot thrive and prosper in an atmosphere of doubt and uncertainty. The need, therefore, arises of restating rules of mutual conduct of states in a convention.").

[77] *Id.* at 119; Schwarzenberger, *supra* note 74, at 152 ("Article I presents an imaginative attempt to combine the minimum standard with the standard of equitable treatment.").

[78] Abs & Shawcross, *supra* note 75, at 121.

[79] The more favorable treatment clause in Article VI and the arbitration mechanism in Article VII created novel rules.

[80] OECD, *Fair and Equitable Treatment Standard in International Investment Law*, OECD Working Papers on International Investment, 2004/03, at 4–5.

[81] Wolfgang Alschner, *Locked in Language: Historical Sociology and the Path Dependency of Investment Treaty Design, in* RESEARCH HANDBOOK ON THE SOCIOLOGY OF INTERNATIONAL LAW 347–368 (Moshe Hirsch & Andrew Lang eds., 2018); Wolfgang Alschner, Manfred Elsig, & Rodrigo Polanco, *Introducing the Electronic Database of Investment Treaties (EDIT): The Genesis of a New Database and Its Use,* 20 WORLD TRADE REV. 73–94 (2021).

[82] Switzerland–Tunisia BIT (1961), art. 3, Netherlands–Tunisia BIT (1963), art. 3, France–Tunisia BIT (1963), art. 4, BLEU–Tunisia BIT (1964), art. 3. On the consistent practice among capital exporting states on expropriation, *see* K. Scott Gudgeon, *Valuation of Nationalized Property under United States and Other Bilateral Investment Treaties Contemporary United States Practice: Chapter

explicitly linked FET to treatment under international law.[83] The Swiss Foreign Office wrote in 1979 that by using the words "fair and equitable treatment," Swiss treaties "refer to the classic principle of the law of nations according to which States must provide foreigners in their territory and their property with the benefit of the 'international minimum standard', i.e. granting them a minimum of personal, procedural and economic rights."[84]

The United States, which joined the BIT universe in 1982, and Canada, which concluded its first BIT in 1989, contained similar language in their treaties, which both countries understood to reference the customary international law minimum standard of treatment.[85] In a 1984 survey of the IIA practice among its member countries, the OECD reported that "[a]ccording to all Member countries which have commented on the point, fair and equitable treatment introduced a substantive legal standard referring to general principles of international law even if this is not explicitly stated."[86] In short, in the early days of the BIT regime, there appears to have been a broad understanding among Western capital exporting countries that their treaties in part codified custom.[87]

Importantly, however, neither the OECD Draft Convention nor the UK treaties closely modeled on it, made this link between treaty norms and their customary law root explicit in the treaty text. At least for the OECD Draft Convention, this choice may have been made on purpose to avoid mentions of custom that, at the time of the New International Economic Order debate, was a contested and

III, 4 THE VALUATION OF NATIONALIZED PROPERTY IN INTERNATIONAL LAW 101–132 (Richard B. Lillich ed., 1987).

[83] For Switzerland, *see* Switzerland–United Republic of Tanzania BIT (1965), art. 1; OECD, *Fair and Equitable Treatment Standard in International Investment Law*, OECD Working Papers on International Investment, 2004/03, at 10. For France, France–Syrian Arab Republic BIT (1977), art. 3.

[84] Author's translation (Original: "On se réfère ainsi au principe classique du droit des gens selon lequelles États doivent mettre les étrangers se trouvant sur leur territoire et leurs biens au bénéfice du 'standard minimum' international c'est-à-dire leur accorder un minimum de droits personnels, procéduraux et économiques.") Cited in F. A. Mann, *British Treaties for the Promotion and Protection of Investments*, 52 BRIT. Y.B. INT'L L. 241–254, 244 (1982).

[85] Patrick Dumberry, *The Importation of "Better" Fair and Equitable Treatment Standard Protection Through MFN Clauses: An Analysis of NAFTA Article 1103*, 14 TRANSNAT'L DISP. MGMT. 11–13 (2017).

[86] OECD, Committee on international investment and multinational enterprises, intergovernmental agreements relating to investment in developing countries, Doc. No 84/14 (May 27, 1984), at 12, para. 34, reprinted in Fourth Submission of the United States of America, November 1, 2000, *Pope & Talbot Inc. v. The Government of Canada*, UNCITRAL, para. 5.

[87] At the same time, the future importance of FET in ISDS practice was largely unanticipated and the clause itself was often believed to be a mere guiding principle. Archival research is bound to shed more light on the origins of early BIT practice in the coming years. *See* Mona Pinchis, *The Devil Is in the Details: Using Historical Methodology to Investigate "Fair" and "Equitable Treatment" Clauses in Post-War United States' Commercial Treaties*, in INTERNATIONAL INVESTMENT LAW AND HISTORY (Rainer Hoffmann, Stephan W. Schill, & Christian J. Tams eds., 2018).

controversial concept.[88] This omission, however, proved highly consequential. In the 1990s and 2000s, UK BITs served as models for a wide range of countries from Israel and India to former Eastern bloc countries, such as Hungary and the Czech Republic.[89] As a result, treaties without an explicit link between protective obligations and custom proliferated widely. Interpreters without knowledge of the origins of these clauses and their path-dependent development from earlier draft texts lost crucial context for how Western states wanted language such as "fair and equitable treatment" understood.

B. Phase II: Rise of Arbitration and the Delinking of Custom

1. FET—The Invention of the Autonomous Standard

The trouble started in 1982 when the renowned international lawyer F.A. Mann published an article on UK BITs, in which he made two controversial assertions.[90] First, he stated that " 'fair and equitable treatment' envisage[s] conduct which goes far beyond the minimum standard."[91] Although he conceded in a footnote that the OECD may have intended to limit FET to the customary international minimum standard, the plain wording of the clause betrays these intentions, and its "terms are to be understood and applied independently and autonomously."[92] Second, he concluded that it is up to the tribunal "to decide whether in all the circumstances the conduct in issue is fair and equitable or unfair and inequitable."[93] Not only did Mann question the link to custom but he framed FET as an obligation that bestows large discretion on tribunals to determine what is "fair" or "equitable."

Other early commentators reinforced these views. Rudolf Dolzer and Margrete Stevens in their 1995 book on *Bilateral Investment Treaties* argued that the absence of a textual link between FET and custom in many BITs "is probably evidence of a self-contained standard."[94] And Peter Muchlinski asserted in his 1995 treatise on *Multinational Enterprises and the Law* that FET "offers a general

---

[88] David Gaukrodger, Addressing the Balance of Interests in Investment Treaties: The Limitation of Fair and Equitable Treatment Provisions to the Minimum Standard of Treatment Under Customary International Law 11 (2017).

[89] Alschner, Elsig, & Polanco, *supra* note 81, at 83.

[90] It is noteworthy that Mann contradicted himself in a second publication published the same year stating the FET essentially codified "duty imposed by customary international law." F. A. Mann, The Legal Aspect of Money 510 (4th ed. 1982).

[91] Mann, *supra* note 84, at 244.

[92] *Id.* at 244 & footnote 1.

[93] *Id.* at 244.

[94] Rudolf Dolzer & Margrete Stevens, Bilateral Investment Treaties 60 (1995).

point of departure in formulating an argument that the foreign investor has not been well treated by reason of discriminatory or other unfair measures being taken against its interest. It is therefore a concept that depends on the interpretation of specific facts for its content."[95]

Early ISDS tribunals seized on this early scholarship as evidence that FET was delinked from custom and that it provided tribunals with considerable discretion. The *SD Myers* tribunal drew on Mann's article to characterize FET as an umbrella obligation that could encompass other NAFTA protections such as national treatment.[96] The *Pope & Talbot* tribunal relied on Mann to downplay the explicit link to custom in NAFTA's FET clause, arguing that "compliance with the fairness elements [in FET] must be ascertained free of any threshold that might be applicable to the evaluation of measures under the minimum standard of international law."[97]

Outside of NAFTA, the absence of a textual link between custom and FET in many treaties provided particularly fruitful ground for the development of an autonomous reading of FET. The 2004 *MTD v. Chile* award noted that "there is no reference to customary international law in the BIT in relation to fair and equitable treatment."[98] It thus proceeded to use dictionary definitions to give meaning to the unqualified FET clause in the BIT and concluded that FET "should be understood to be treatment in an even-handed and just manner, conducive to fostering the promotion of foreign investment."[99] An autonomous reading of FET had taken hold and gained prominence in later awards.[100] The *Rumeli v. Kazakhstan* tribunal, for example, used Mann's article to justify the assertion that the minimum standard and the fair and equitable standard had converged and that "the precise scope of the standard is . . . left to the determination of the Tribunal."[101] This expansive notion of FET as an autonomous standard, which gives wide discretion to tribunals, was well encapsulated by Charles Brower, who characterized the standard in 2003 as "exemplification of an intentionally vague term, designed to give adjudicators a quasi-legislative authority to articulate a variety of rules necessary to achieve the treaty's object and purpose in particular disputes."[102]

---

[95] P. MUCHLINSKI, MULTINATIONAL ENTERPRISES AND THE LAW 625 (1995).

[96] S.D. Myers, Inc. v. Government of Canada, UNCITRAL, Partial Award, November 13, 2000, paras. 265–266.

[97] *Pope & Talbot Inc. v. Government of Canada*, UNCITRAL, Award on the Merits of Phase 2, April 10, 2001, para. 111.

[98] *MTD Equity Sdn. Bhd. and MTD Chile S.A. v. Republic of Chile*, ICSID Case No. ARB/01/7, Award, May 25, 2004, para. 111.

[99] *Id.*, para. 113.

[100] Gaukrodger, *supra* note 88.

[101] *Rumeli Telekom A.S. and Telsim Mobil Telekomunikasyon Hizmetleri A.S. v. Republic of Kazakhstan*, ICSID Case No. ARB/05/16, Award, July 29, 2008, paras. 610–611.

[102] Charles H. Brower, *Structure, Legitimacy, and NAFTA's Investment Chapter*, 36 VAND. J. TRANSNAT'L L. 37, 66 (FN 163) (2003).

In summary, early ISDS awards buttressed by early academic commentary decoupled treaty and custom. The link between FET and the minimum standard so present in the OECD Draft Convention and early BITs had been lost. At the same time, scholarship had provided authority for an expansive view of tribunals' role in shaping the FET standard. This combination allowed an FET interpretation "autonomous" from custom to emerge in the first place and thereby provided material for the later argument that a widespread practice of concluding "autonomous" FET clauses had led to an evolution of custom toward that higher, autonomous standard.

2. Indirect Expropriation—The Sole Effects Doctrine

In parallel to the delinking of FET from its customary roots, early ISDS tribunals also began to debate whether IIAs added to custom by offering investors greater protection from indirect expropriation. Indirect expropriations do not involve a formal taking of property, but instead deprive investors of the possibility to make effective use of their asset.[103] The withdrawal of a permit to operate, for example, can neutralize the value of an investor's property without thereby affecting her ownership rights. While customary international law recognizes that an expropriation can occur indirectly, it draws a (blurry) line between state acts with expropriatory effect that give rise to an obligation to compensate and the nondiscriminatory, public purpose exercise of a state's police powers that may deprive investors of the enjoyment of their assets, but without thereby triggering an obligation to compensate.[104]

A majority of investment treaties define indirect expropriation as "measures having [an] *effect* equivalent to nationalisation or expropriation."[105] Several early tribunals have read this literally. According to them, under IIAs it is the effect of a measure and not its design or intent that determines whether an act amounts to an indirect expropriation.[106] As Ben Mostafa put it, "should the effect of a measure reach a certain threshold, a finding of expropriation is unavoidable."[107] This so-called "sole effects doctrine" enlarges the scope of potentially compensable governmental acts since it ostensibly encompasses general, nondiscriminatory regulatory measures otherwise falling into the customary police powers exception.

---

[103] DOLZER & SCHREUER, *supra* note 7, at 101.

[104] Admittedly, the boundary between measures allowed under the police powers doctrine and those qualifying as an indirect expropriation is hard to draw; *see* Ben Mostafa, *The Sole Effects Doctrine, Police Powers and Indirect Expropriation under International Law*, 15 AUSTL. INT'L L.J. 267–296 (2008); Prabhash Ranjan, *Police Powers, Indirect Expropriation in International Investment Law, and Article 31(3)(c) of the VCLT: A Critique of Philip Morris v. Uruguay*, 9 ASIAN J. INT'L L. 98–124 (2019).

[105] *See, e.g.*, art. 5 of the UK–Egypt BIT (1975) (emphasis added)

[106] Mostafa, *supra* note 104; Titi, *supra* note 31, at 329–333.

[107] Mostafa, *supra* note 104, at 279.

For example, in *Metalclad v. Mexico*, the first NAFTA tribunal to deal with an indirect expropriation concluded that the motivation or intent behind the governmental measure was not relevant; what mattered was that its measure's effects were tantamount to expropriation.[108] In the same vein, the tribunal in *Siemens v. Argentina* found that the Germany–Argentina BIT (1991) "refers to measures that have the effect of an expropriation; it does not refer to the intent of the State to expropriate."[109] Similarly, the *Tecmed v. Mexico* tribunal, while acknowledging the customary international law police power's exception, pointed to the effect-oriented language of the BIT and concluded that "the form of the deprivation measure is less important than its actual effects."[110] On the basis of this line of case law, the *Saipem v. Bangladesh* tribunal called the sole effects doctrine the "most significant criterion to determine whether the disputed actions amount to indirect expropriation or are tantamount to expropriation."[111]

While it is uncontroversial that a measure's effect plays a crucial role in determining whether an indirect expropriation has taken place, conceiving it as the exclusive or decisive criterion ignores the flexibility the police powers doctrine confers on states for regulatory interventions of a general nature that have incidental effects on individual private property rights. Like the "autonomous" reading of FET, a sole effects interpretation of indirect expropriation based on the treaty text alone therefore separates the concept from its customary law roots and imposes a more onerous reading of investment protection obligations on states.

C. Phase III: Arbitral Self-Correction and the Return of Custom

The interpretations of FET and indirect expropriation by early tribunals triggered a first legitimacy crisis of ISDS, particularly under NAFTA. From the outset, there was broad agreement among the three NAFTA contracting parties

---

[108] *Metalclad Corporation v. United Mexican States*, ICSID Case No. ARB(AF)/97/1, Award, August 30, 2000, para. 111. Other NAFTA tribunals reached a similar conclusion, *see Fireman's Fund Insurance Company v. United Mexican States*, ICSID Case No. ARB(AF)/02/01, Award, July 17, 2006, para. 176(f) ("the effects of the host State's measures are dispositive, not the underlying intent.").

[109] *Siemens v. Argentina*, Award, February 6, 2007, para. 270. *See also AWG Group Ltd. v. Argentine Republic*, UNCITRAL, Decision on Liability, July 30, 2010, para. 133 ("Each of the BIT articles [under consideration] specifically refers to the 'effects' of an expropriation measure and thus affirms the importance of evaluating the effects of a measure on the investment in determining whether an expropriation has taken place.").

[110] *Tecmed v. Mexico*, Award, May 29, 2003, para. 115–116.

[111] *Saipem S.p.A. v. People's Republic of Bangladesh*, ICSID Case No. ARB/05/07, Award, June 30, 2009, para. 133.

on the customary law roots of FET. In 2000, the United States intervened in *Pope & Talbot v. Canada* to clarify that "from its first use in investment agreements, 'fair and equitable treatment' was no more than a shorthand reference to elements of the developed body of customary international law."[112] In the same case, Mexico submitted that FET in NAFTA is limited to the minimum standard as expressed in the *Neer* case,[113] while Canada, as respondent, concurred and dedicated almost an entire submission to arguing why F.A. Mann's 1982 article did not constitute a valid authority for interpreting NAFTA's FET provision.[114] After the *Pope & Talbot* tribunal, unconvinced by these state interventions adopted a reading of FET as "additive to the requirements of international law,"[115] the three NAFTA parties issued an authoritative interpretation of NAFTA Article 1105 on July 31, 2001, through the NAFTA Free Trade Commission, clarifying that FET does not require treatment beyond the customary international minimum standard of treatment.[116]

This clarification oriented subsequent tribunals. On the one hand, it had the unintended effect described previously of prompting some NAFTA tribunals to contemplate an evolution of custom to observe the letter of the authoritative interpretation while circumventing its spirit and to introduce a more protective standard through the back door.[117] On the other hand, it also pushed tribunals to take the link between NAFTA's FET clause and the international minimum standard more seriously. The *Glamis v. US* tribunal embodies the latter approach. The tribunal stated that Article 1105 roots FET in the customary law minimum standard and emphasized that it was up the claimant to prove that the standard had evolved beyond *Neer* by pointing to relevant state practice and *opinio juris*.[118] The tribunal was not satisfied that the claimant's identification of language in other BITs and prior ISDS awards constituted sufficient proof for an evolution of custom.[119]

A similar corrective occurred on the issue of indirect expropriation. A 2002 PBS documentary "Trading Democracy" critically reviewed early NAFTA cases

---

[112] Fourth Submission of the United States of America, *Pope & Talbot Inc. v. The Government of Canada*, UNCITRAL, November 1, 2000, para.5.

[113] Mexico's Submission on the Interpretation of Article 1105 of the NAFTA, *Pope & Talbot Inc. v. The Government of Canada*, November 5, 2000, UNCITRAL.

[114] Canada's Response to Phase Two Post-Hearing Submissions of Mexico and United States, *Pope & Talbot Inc. v. The Government of Canada*, December 15, 2000, UNCITRAL, paras. 12–20.

[115] *Pope & Talbot Inc. v. Government of Canada*, UNCITRAL, Award on the Merits of Phase 2, April 10, 2001, para. 110.

[116] Notes of Interpretation of Certain Chapter 11 Provisions (NAFTA Free Trade Commission, July 31, 2001)

[117] SCHILL, *supra* note 10, at 275.

[118] *Glamis Gold, Ltd. v. The United States of America*, UNCITRAL, June 8, 2009, paras. 599–602.

[119] *Id.*, paras. 614–616.

centering, in part, on the indirect expropriation definition of the treaty.[120] As one environmental lawyer interviewed in the documentary put it:

> Generally, it's been understood that governments can do what they need to protect their people and their environment without having to pay if they diminish the value of property. But these corporations are using NAFTA Chapter Eleven to expand that and say governments do have to pay for every amount by which the value of their property is reduced. And one of the bases on which they've made that claim is the fact that NAFTA's Chapter Eleven uses this phrase "tantamount to expropriation." Not only do governments have to compensate when they expropriate or take away property, but they have to do so whenever they do something that is "tantamount to expropriation."[121]

The NAFTA parties subsequently sought to reinforce the role of customary international law and police powers in disputes involving NAFTA Article 1110 on expropriation in order to reject the sole effects theory. The United States first intervened in July 1999 in *Metalclad v. Mexico* through a nondisputing parties submission to clarify that NAFTA Article 1110 on expropriation was not meant to go beyond customary law.[122] In its 2003 submission in the *Methanex v. US* dispute, the United States then declared that "it is well-settled in international law that an allegation that an investment's profitability has been negatively impacted as a result of regulation is insufficient to support a finding of expropriation."[123] Moreover, the United States asserted the "principle of customary international law that, where economic injury results from a bona fide regulation within the police powers of a State, compensation is not required."[124]

Canada concurred in its nondisputing submission in the same case, highlighting that "[a] key aspect of the international law of expropriation is the exclusion of a state's regulatory or 'police power' from the scope of expropriation"[125] and pointed to NAFTA Article 1131(1), which makes customary international law part of the applicable law of NAFTA.[126] Mexico agreed that "States

---

[120] *Politics and Economy: Trading Democracy*, PBS DOCUMENTARY, February 1, 2002, transcript available at https://nsarchive2.gwu.edu/NSAEBB/NSAEBB65/transcript.html (last accessed October 15, 2021).

[121] *Id.*

[122] Submission of the United States of America, *Metalclad Corporation v. United Mexican States*, July 28, 1999, para. 14. The position was restated in *Metalclad Corporation v. United Mexican States*, ICSID Case No. ARB(AF)/97/1, Award, August 30, 2000, para. 27.

[123] U.S. Amended Statement of Defense, *Methanex Corporation v. United States of America*, December 5, 2003, para. 397

[124] *Id.*, para. 410.

[125] Canada's Fourth Submission per Article 1128, *Methanex Corporation v. United States of America*, UNCITRAL, January 30, 2004, para. 14.

[126] *Id.*, para. 16.

generally are not liable to compensate aliens for economic loss resulting from non-discriminatory regulatory measures taken to protect the public interest."[127] Ultimately, the *Methanex* tribunal rejected that the investor's loss of market share amounted to an expropriation, declaring instead that "as a matter of general international law, a non-discriminatory regulation for a public purpose, which is enacted in accordance with due process and, which affects, inter alios, a foreign investor or investment is not deemed expropriatory and compensable unless specific commitments had been given."[128]

The *Methanex* decision marked a shift away from the sole effects doctrine and (re-)drew the lines between compensable and noncompensable governmental interventions. Other tribunals outside of the NAFTA context followed suit. The *Saluka v. Czech Republic* tribunal applying the Czech Republic–Netherlands BIT (1991), for example, found that even though the treaty's expropriation clause "is drafted very broadly and does not contain any exception for the exercise of regulatory power," its use of the concept of deprivation "imports into the Treaty the customary international law notion that a deprivation can be justified if it results from the exercise of regulatory actions aimed at the maintenance of public order."[129] It went on to affirm that "[i]t is now established in international law that States are not liable to pay compensation to a foreign investor when, in the normal exercise of their regulatory powers, they adopt in a non-discriminatory manner bona fide regulations that are aimed at the general welfare."[130]

In short, customary international law was back. NAFTA tribunals began to increasingly accept the link between FET and the minimum standard of treatment. Similarly, the notion of police powers as carveout from what would otherwise constitute an indirect expropriation gained a foothold in ISDS practice.

D. Phase IV: Codifying Custom More Explicitly

A major lesson for states from early ISDS awards was the importance of making implicit customary law links explicit. As discussed in Chapters 2 and 3, starting with the US and Canadian model BITs of 2004, states began to insert references to custom into IIAs around the globe. These references are usually framed as clarifications ("for greater certainty") and often placed in footnotes and annexes. This is meant to convey a consistency in treaty practice and inform the reading

---

[127] Canada's Fourth Submission per Article 1128, *Methanex Corporation v. United States of America*, UNCITRAL, January 30, 2004, para. 13.

[128] *Methanex v. United States*, Award, August 3, 2005, pt. IV, ch. D, at 4, para. 7.

[129] *Saluka v. Czech Republic*, Partial Award, March 17, 2006, para. 262. *See also Continental Casualty v. Argentina*, Award, September 5, 2008, para. 275.

[130] *Id.*, para. 276.

of earlier treaties. For most OECD states, rooting FET in the customary minimum standards and limiting the scope of expropriation through police powers are not innovations or revisions. Indeed, given the prevalent understanding of FET in the 1950s to 1980s, the many references to custom in recent IIAs would have likely struck early BIT negotiators as an unnecessary redundancy. These references rather correct a misunderstanding arising from early ISDS awards and reaffirmed original intent that predated ISDS practice.

E. Phase V: Custom Confused

This brings us to the present, where, as discussed in the preceding section, custom fails to play the role states assigned to it. Clarifications in recent, more complete treaties have failed to correct past jurisprudential trends as new treaties have produced old outcomes. Worse, custom has emerged as a tool for rolling back innovation, whereby protection is ratcheted up via an evolving custom, and flexibilities are hollowed out by equating new exceptions with existing custom. Ensuring that innovation in the books translates into change in practice therefore requires more than precise drafting. It crucially depends on tribunals recognizing and acting on when states contract on custom and when they go beyond it.

IV. Recognizing When IIAs Contract on Custom
or Go Beyond It

If tribunals succeed in deciphering and accepting when states mean to contract on custom and when not, they can support state-driven design choices in two ways. First, they can lift up older, incomplete IIAs to higher levels of completeness by using custom to fill contractual gaps. Second, they can avoid lowering contractual completeness of newer agreements by respecting exceptions as complements rather than substitutes to customary international law. Instead of rolling back state-driven change, tribunals can thus use custom to achieve higher levels of contractual completeness altogether.

A. Contracting on Custom: When to Lift Up
Incomplete Agreements

Recent, more complete agreements have made explicit what earlier, incomplete agreements often left implicit. Tribunals should take these explicit references to custom seriously. When tribunals encounter language that links FET to the minimum standard or that includes a police power carveout in an indirect ex-propriation clause, arbitrators need to respect that choice and root their inter-pretations in custom, that is, state practice and *opinio juris*. Arbitral awards are by themselves not evidence of state practice or *opinio juris* or proof of an evolution of customary international law. If tribunals followed such guidance, awards like *Bilcon* would be avoided.

But tribunals can go a step further. The previous section has shown that there is ample evidence that OECD states used the terms "fair and equitable treatment" and "expropriation" as a shorthand for contracting on custom from the earliest days of the IIA regime. Such use of shorthand is common in treaty drafting. For example, IIAs routinely provide that states are to provide "prompt, adequate and effective" compensation in case of an expropriation. Investment lawyers will immediately recognize the so-called "Hull Formula" dating back to the 1938 US secretary of state's description of what compensation international law requires for nationalized foreign property.[131] As the OECD writes, "the Hull formula and its variations are often used and accepted and considered as part of customary international law."[132] Hence, although the words "prompt, adequate and effective" lack a textual reference to custom, they are widely understood as an embodiment of custom. K. Scott Gudgeon notes that "[r]eliance on such formulations . . . is unmistakably a conscious act by the parties to select and incorporate by reference a standard of international law elaborated by precedents and practice external to the treaty."[133] In short, states can reference custom without including the word "custom."

Tribunals ought to treat such implicit references to custom just like explicit ones. In the 1996 Oil Platforms ICJ judgment, Judge Higgens referred to FET as a "legal term[] of art well known in the field of overseas investment protection."[134] If FET is a legal term of art, tribunals need not start with dictionary definitions of "fair" or "equitable." Similar to their understanding of "prompt, adequate and effective," tribunals should root their interpretation of the words "fair and equitable treatment" in custom instead.

Moreover, given the historical context and the path dependency of treaty language, the absence of an expressed reference to custom cannot be taken as evidence of states' intent to create "autonomous" standards delinked from custom.

---

[131] Available at https://history.state.gov/historicaldocuments/frus1938v05/d665 ("The Government of the United States merely adverts to a self-evident fact when it notes that the applicable precedents and recognized authorities on international law support its declaration that, under every rule of law and equity, no government is entitled to expropriate private property, for whatever purpose, without provision for prompt, adequate, and effective payment therefor.").

[132] OECD, *"Indirect Expropriation" and the "Right to Regulate" in International Investment Law*, OECD Working Papers on International Investment, 2004/04, at 2.

[133] Gudgeon, *supra* note 82, at 104.

[134] *Oil Platforms*, Separate Opinion Judge Higgens [1996] ICJ Rep. 847, para. 39 (emphasis added).

Instead, as Martins Paperinskis concludes after an extensive review of primary legal materials, "customary standard has to play a decisive role in the interpretation of fair and equitable treatment."[135] Nor, given that historical evidence, should tribunals, as in the recent *Global Telecom Holding v. Canada* award, draw a distinction between a reference to "international law" and a reference to the "minimum standard of treatment."[136] As discussed in the previous section, these terms were used interchangeable in past practice.

Of course, that does not mean that states cannot deviate from past practice and break with path dependency to add to custom or to craft an autonomous treaty standard, including around the language of FET. Yet such a departure from an existing term of art with set meaning should not be lightly presumed and instead would require positive language, for example, by offering definitions of FET different from or additive to custom. The mere absence of an explicit textual link to custom, however, does not meet that threshold. Viewed in this light, recent treaties merely elucidate the link with custom and make explicit what states meant all along.

Recognizing a priori vague language as having acquired meaning rooted in custom creates opportunities. Not only does it mean that archival work or subsequent reaffirmation of original intent can shed light on old concepts. It also enables custom to fill contractual gaps in older agreements. Incomplete treaties with implicit links to custom can then be read like recent agreements that make this link explicit. In summary, because FET and expropriation are customary international law standards, they ought to be interpreted as such regardless of whether the treaty mentions the "minimum standard" or "police powers."

B. Going beyond Custom: How to Avoid Rolling Back Innovation in More Complete Agreements

As important as recognizing when states contract on custom are instances when states do not and instead use their treaties to go beyond custom. That is the case with general public policy exceptions, which have been confused by the *Bear Creek* tribunal as a codification of customary law police powers or misconstrued by the *Eco Oro* tribunal as operating like circumstances precluding wrongfulness. As Canada recently clarified in its nondisputing submission in *Eco Oro*,

---

[135] MARTINS PAPARINSKIS, THE INTERNATIONAL MINIMUM STANDARD AND FAIR AND EQUITABLE TREATMENT 169 (2013).

[136] *Global Telecom Holding S.A.E. v. Canada*, ICSID Case No. ARB/16/16, Award, March 27, 2020, para. 485. ("This Tribunal finds no support for Canada's endeavour to override the terms of the BIT and to draft into Article II(2)(b) a reference to the minimum standard that would limit the potential application of a wider range of international law principles than the minimum standard alone.").

general public policy exceptions should be understood as a "final safety net." They are *additive* to any flexibility states already enjoy under primary investment treaty obligations or customary international law. But the *Bear Creek* and *Eco Oro* tribunals are not alone in their failure to recognize the additive role of exceptions. From scholars to respondent states to arbitral tribunals, general public policy exceptions are still clouded in confusion and, as a result, are largely "missing in action."[137]

Scholars have struggled to situate general exceptions in the traditional investment law landscape. In fact, only a few academics share Canada's view that general exceptions provide an extra safety net that complements other flexibilities offered.[138] Commentators have instead expressed fear that the insertion of exceptions crowds out flexibilities states already enjoy under IIAs. They worry that balancing of investment protection and a state's regulatory freedom shifts completely from the primary obligations and custom to the exceptions.[139] According to these scholars, exceptions risk lowering policy space given that they tend to contain a closed list of policy grounds coupled with stricter conditions, whereas flexibilities read into primary obligations tend to be open-ended and more accommodating.[140] Some scholars have viewed exceptions as unnecessarily duplicative, because they would add little to existing flexibilities under primary norms or primarily codify customary international law on police power.[141] For others, dedicated flexibilities such as explanatory annexes that reserve the states' police powers in relation to indirect expropriation serve as a kind of *lex specialis* that preclude the application of general exceptions.[142] Hence,

---

[137] Alschner & Hui, *supra* note 6.

[138] Keene, *supra* note 33; JÜRGEN KURTZ, THE WTO AND INTERNATIONAL INVESTMENT LAW: CONVERGING SYSTEMS 180–183 (2016).

[139] Bradly J. Condon, *Treaty Structure and Public Interest Regulation in International Economic Law*, 17 J. INT'L ECON. L. 333–353, 342–343 (2014). According to him, "the presence of general exceptions that explicitly address public interest regulation makes it inappropriate to address public interest regulation in general scope provisions or specific limitations on the scope of specific obligations, since it would diminish the effect of general exceptions and risk making them redundant, at least to some extent."

[140] Mitchell, Munro, & Voon, *supra* note 14. Caroline Henckels, *Should Investment Treaties Contain Public Policy Exceptions?*, 59 B.C. L. REV. 2825, 2836–2837 (2018). Nicholas DiMascio & Joost Pauwelyn, *Nondiscrimination in Trade and Investment Treaties: Worlds Apart or Two Sides of the Same Coin?*, 102 AM. J. INT'L L. 48–89, 76 (2008).

[141] B. Legum & Ioana Petculescu, *GATT Article XX and International Investment Law*, in PROSPECTS IN INTERNATIONAL INVESTMENT LAW AND POLICY: WORLD TRADE FORUM 340–362, 362 (Roberto Echandi & Pierre Sauve eds., 2013). Andrew Newcombe, *General Exceptions in International Investment Agreements* 12, Draft Discussion Paper Prepared for BIICL Eighth Annual WTO Conference 13th and 14th May 2008, London, available at https://www.biicl.org/files/3866_andrew_newcombe.pdf.

[142] Céline Lévesque, *The Inclusion of GATT Article XX Exceptions in IIAs: A Potentially Risky Policy*, in PROSPECTS IN INTERNATIONAL INVESTMENT LAW AND POLICY: WORLD TRADE FORUM 368 (Roberto Echandi & Pierre Sauve eds., 2013).

investment law scholars have been reluctant to embrace general exceptions as an additional line of defense.

Respondent states have similarly struggled to recognize and utilize this additional safety net. Venezuela sought to justify the revocation of mining licenses on environmental grounds in three consecutive cases under the Canada–Venezuela BIT (1996) *Gold Reserve*, *Crystallex* and *Rusoro*—but failed to even invoke the general exception under the treaty. In another case involving a revoked mining permit, *Infinito Gold v. Costa Rica* under the Canada–Costa Rica BIT (1998), Costa Rica sought to justify its measure as protective of the environment, but confusingly invoked the treaty's right to regulate clause, which only allows environmental measures *otherwise consistent* with the treaty but not the general exception clause in its defense.[143]

In short, neither among respondent states nor in scholarship has the role of general exceptions as providing flexibilities additional to what is otherwise offered in custom or under primary obligations fully sunk in. Perhaps Canada's submission in *Eco Oro*, if endorsed more widely, will help clarify their role and ensure that they are given an effective interpretation. Aside from portraying general exceptions as an additional safety net, Canada's submission makes clear that their inclusion "cannot be used to broaden the scope of the primary obligation," alleviating fears in academia.[144] Furthermore, Canada explained that "[i]f the general exception applies, then there is no violation of the Agreement and no State liability. Payment of compensation would therefore not be required."[145] This corrects a misunderstanding by the *Bear Creek* and *Eco Oro* tribunals that the exception does not exempt a state from paying compensation, rendering the exception more potent.

If Canada's views are endorsed by future tribunals, exceptions will play a more meaningful role in ISDS practice. Reinforcing state-driven innovation in more complete agreements thus depends on recognizing public policy exceptions as novel, additive flexibilities rather than as codification of existing customary law safeguards.

V. Conclusion

References to custom are vital tools for states to moderate their commitments and flexibilities by linking them to a universal baseline. Tribunals, however, have

---

[143] *Infinito Gold Ltd. v. Republic of Costa Rica*, ICSID Case No. ARB/14/5, Decision on Jurisdiction, December 4, 2017.

[144] Non-Disputing Party Submission of Canada, *Eco Oro Minerals Corp. v. Republic of Colombia*, ICSID Case No. ARB/16/41, February 27, 2020, para. 23.

[145] *Id.*, para. 16.

struggled to recognize when states contract on custom and when they go beyond it. As a result of this confusion, some tribunals have increased investment protection based on the notion of a rapidly evolving customary international law driven by the conclusion of more demanding IIAs. Others have mistaken general exception as codifying custom and decreased the flexibility states enjoy under more complete agreements. Both trends risk lowering policy space and undermine innovation introduced in recent more complete IIAs. This chapter has sketched out how tribunals can uphold state-driven change by recognizing when states meant to contract on custom and when they meant to move beyond it in their treaties. Historical evidence and recent state submissions suggest that states intended to use custom as a *ceiling* on the interpretation of certain protective commitments and as a *floor* for enshrining flexibilities, which states can supplement with more extensive exceptions.

6
Perpetuating Mistakes through Precedent

I. Introduction

The decisions of previous arbitral tribunals provide the final means for rolling back innovation in recent, more complete agreements. In investment law, to borrow from Thomas Schelling, "precedent seems to exercise an influence that greatly exceeds its logical importance or legal force."[1] Technically, awards are only binding on the disputing parties, but not on subsequent tribunals.[2] In practice, however, litigants and tribunals routinely rely on prior arbitral awards to support their reasoning.[3] While tribunals differ in the degree to which they are guided by precedent, and some awards have more impact than others, early awards generally exert an influence over later ones.

In a system characterized by state-driven change, this prominent role of precedent limits the impact of treaty design innovation. Most existing cases have been litigated under older agreements, which roots precedent in outdated, incomplete treaty design.[4] Moreover, many recent treaty design innovations are conscious efforts, on the part of contracting states, to reject, correct, or recast previous arbitral (mis)interpretations.[5] When tribunals rely on precedent rendered under incomplete IIAs or on early arbitral interpretations at odds with current practice,

---

[1] 10 Thomas C. Schelling, The Strategy of Conflict 67 (1980) (Schelling is referring to precedent as a focal point generally, but the quote aptly captures the role of precedent in investment law).

[2] *See, e.g., Wintershall Aktiengesellschaft v. Argentine Republic*, ICSID Case No. ARB/04/14, Award, December 8, 2008, para. 194 ("*stare decisis* has no application to decisions of ICSID tribunals [. . .] The award of such tribunal is binding only on the parties to the dispute (Article 53 of the Convention)—not even binding on the State of which the investor is a national. Decisions and Awards of ad hoc ICSID tribunals have no binding precedential effect on successive tribunals, also appointed ad hoc between different parties."); *Methanex v. United States of America*, UNCITRAL, Partial Award, August 7, 2002, para. 141 ("[Prior awards] are not sources of law; and neither can be regarded as authority legally binding upon this Tribunal.").

[3] Ole Kristian Fauchald, *The Legal Reasoning of ICSID Tribunals—An Empirical Analysis*, 19 Eur. J. Int'l L. 301–364, 335 (2008) ("Case law was used as an interpretive argument in 92 out of 98 [examined ICSID] decisions.").

[4] UNCTAD, *Phase 2 of IIA Reform: Modernizing the Existing Stock of Old-Generation Treaties*, IIA Issues Note, June 2017, Issue 2, at 5.

[5] Wolfgang Alschner, *The Impact of Investment Arbitration on Investment Treaty Design: Myth Versus Reality*, 42 Yale J. Int'l L. (2017).

Investment Arbitration and State-Driven Reform. Wolfgang Alschner, Oxford University Press. © Oxford University Press 2022. DOI: 10.1093/oso/9780197644386.003.0007

there is a risk that past interpretive mistakes are perpetuated, new treaties are read in light of old case law, and innovation is rolled back.

The two previous chapters on MFN and custom have already exemplified the crucial role precedent plays in framing interpretive debates. The ISDS controversy on the role of MFN as multilateralizer of treaty design discussed in Chapter 4 would not have emerged so prominently but for the early *Maffezini v. Spain* award. Similarly, the early *Pope & Talbot v. Canada* decision discussed in Chapter 5 was instrumental in setting the stage for NAFTA's lasting controversy on the relationship between fair and equitable treatment (FET) and customary law. These decisions do not derive their outsized impact from internal characteristics. They are not particularly well-reasoned nor do they feature especially prominent arbitrators. Instead, these awards matter because they came early. In a system where previous cases affect later ones, early awards play an outsized role in shaping interpretation. *Maffezini* and *Pope & Talbot* gave specific meaning to hitherto vague clauses, which turned them into focal points for subsequent interpreters. Early awards thus set path-dependent developments in motion that frame subsequent interpretive debates.[6]

This path dependency of arbitral interpretations is bad news for state-driven change. States cannot go back in time to rewrite early arbitral decisions and re-base the interpretive path. They have to engage with interpretive questions on the terms set by earlier awards. As a result, states, in spite of their proactive law-making, are constantly forced to react and correct rather act and direct. That puts states at a disadvantage. States can at best assert a competing interpretive approach but find it difficult to fully displace existing lines of arbitral interpretations. In consequence, arbitral misinterpretations "stick" in spite of corrective measures. Precedent thereby creates continuity in a system where states seek change.

This chapter confronts this stickiness of precedent. It first shows that reliance on old case law is a systemic challenge because new, more complete treaties are being read like old, incomplete ones through precedent. In addition, precedent dulls the effect of corrective state interventions, including authoritative interpretations, annulment, and set-aside proceedings as well as targeted revisions of treaty language perpetuating past mistakes. The chapter then explores why precedent is sticky. It points to tribunals' preference for following prior cases, institutional incentives that favor citing past awards, ineffective controls, and the self-reinforcement of case law. The chapter concludes with a discussion of how states can force an "interpretive reset" by policing the use of precedent more effectively to ensure that new treaties are not read in light of old case law.

---

[6] Harlan Cohen, *International Law's Erie Moment*, 34 MICH. J. INT'L L. 249–308, 267 (2013).

II. Rolling Back Innovation through Precedent

Of the three practices discussed in Part II of this book, the reliance on precedent presents the most profound threat to state-driven change and treaty design innovation. First, new treaties risk being read like old ones when the reasoning of an award rendered under an incomplete treaty is applied to a more complete agreement. Second, when tribunals ground today's interpretations in old reasoning, they risk disregarding the numerous corrective interventions by states that occurred over the past twenty years. In both cases, when tribunals apply old precedent rather than new treaties, they risk sidestepping decades of normative evolution and rolling back state-driven change.

A. Interpreting More Complete Treaties Like Incomplete Ones

Two characteristics of ISDS make it particularly likely that new treaties are interpreted like old ones through precedent. First, the pool of precedent is skewed toward older, incomplete agreements. In 2017, UNCTAD reported that 90 percent of ISDS cases have been launched under IIAs concluded prior to 2000.[7] In contrast, most more complete IIAs have been signed post-2000 and are just beginning to be litigated. As a result, the universe of available precedent is dominated by awards rendered under older, incomplete agreements. Second, earlier research has shown that tribunals commonly cite cases rendered under agreements with dissimilar treaty design.[8] Out of 4,531 citations between ISDS cases, 75 percent connect IIAs that are relatively dissimilar, that is, that have less than 50 percent of words in common.[9] There is thus ample reason to be concerned that tribunals use precedent rendered under older incomplete agreement to interpret newer, more complete ones.

So how pervasively is precedent being used to interpret new treaties like old ones? Table 6.1 describes the large convenience sample of 4,531 citation connections between treaties based their treaty design differences along the contractual completeness axis developed in Part I. NAFTA (1992), for example, is a high completeness treaty, whereas the Czech Republic–Netherlands BIT (1991) is a low completeness treaty. If one NAFTA award cites another NAFTA case, this

---

[7] UNCTAD, *supra* note 3, at 5.

[8] Data based on Wolfgang Alschner, *Ensuring Correctness or Promoting Consistency? Tracking Policy Priorities in Investment Arbitration through Large-Scale Citation Analysis, in* THE LEGITIMACY OF INVESTMENT ARBITRATION EMPIRICAL PERSPECTIVES (Ole Kristian Fauchald, Daniel Behn, & Malcolm Langford eds., 2021).

[9] *Id.*

Table 6.1 Share of 4,531 citation connections between ISDS awards by IIAs' level of contractual completeness ("High" = principal component score of 30 or more; "Medium" = principal component score between 10 and 30, "Low" = principal component score below 10)

		Target		
		High %	Medium %	Low %
Source	High	11	4	5
	Medium	4	10	8
	Low	11	17	31

is counted as a citation between a high completeness source and a high completeness target. If a NAFTA case cites an award rendered under the Czech Republic–Netherlands BIT, it is counted as citation between a high completeness source and a low completeness target treaty.

Most citations connect low completeness treaties with other low completeness treaties (31%). But a non-negligible number of awards based on high completeness treaties cite awards rendered under low completeness treaties (5%). These are the potentially problematic instances where a more complete agreement is interpreted like a highly incomplete agreement. As of the time of this writing, these problematic high-to-low citations are primarily a phenomenon for high completeness BITs rather than FTAs with investment chapters. As shown in Table 6.2, almost three-fourths of all NAFTA citations go to other high completeness treaties—in fact, they all go to NAFTA. In contrast, for the two high completeness BITs in the sample only 15 and 22 percent of citations, respectively, go to other high completeness treaties, and most go to low completeness treaties. The data suggests that, in the minds of interpreters of high completeness treaties, the distinction between treaty design is much less pronounced than the distinction between treaty type (BIT vs. FTAs).[10]

To be sure, not all of these asymmetric high-to-low citations are problematic. There are valid reasons why a tribunal constituted under a more complete agreement may cite case law rendered under an incomplete treaty. For example, a tribunal may seek guidance from an earlier award on issues not explicitly regulated in either treaty, such as the calculation of damages or the allocation costs.[11]

---

[10] For a more in-depth discussion of the data, *see id.*

[11] For example, the early *Metalclad* and *Maffezini* awards are sometimes cited for their decision to award compound interests during the damages calculation. *See, e.g., Masdar Solar & Wind Cooperatief U.A. v. Kingdom of Spain*, ICSID Case No. ARB/14/1, Award, May 18, 2018, para. 665.

Table 6.2 Outward citations by litigated treaties with highest principle component scores in the dataset ("High" = principal component score of 30 or more; "Medium" = principal component score between 10 and 30, "Low" = principal component score below 10)

		Target		
		High %	Medium %	Low %
Source	NAFTA (1992)	73	12	15
	DR–CAFTA (2004)	48	21	32
	Canada–Ecuador (1996)	22	31	47
	Canada–Venezuela (1996)	15	21	64

In addition, even generally dissimilar treaties may have specific language in common, which can make reliance on a particular precedent highly appropriate. Moreover, a citation is not the same as following precedent. A tribunal may, for instance, simply restate the cases cited by the litigants without endorsing them. All these are valid reasons why dissimilar treaties may be connected through citations in an award. Unfortunately, however, not all asymmetric citations are benign, and some reflect a pattern of using precedent to read new treaties like old ones and to roll back innovation, as the following case studies help to illustrate.

Recall that one of most important differences between incomplete and more complete treaties identified in Chapter 2 and discussed in Chapter 5 consists of how treaties balance investment protection with non-economic values. Most more complete IIAs contain *explicit* exceptions that allow states to deviate from investment protection commitments in particular circumstances to protect non-investment public policy values.[12] Incomplete IIAs, in contrast, tend not to contain general exceptions. Absent specific balancing language, tribunals constituted under incomplete treaties have instead tended to read *implicit* limitations into primary investment protection provisions to afford states a degree of regulatory space.[13] Such explicit and implicit approaches to balancing investment

---

[12] *See* Amelia Keene, *The Incorporation and Interpretation of WTO-Style Environmental Exceptions in International Investment Agreements*, 18 J. WORLD INVESTMENT & TRADE 62–99 (2017).

[13] Bradly J. Condon, *Treaty Structure and Public Interest Regulation in International Economic Law*, 17 J. INT'L ECON. L. 333–353 (2014). Depending on the provision at issue, tribunals have imported such a balancing mandate by relying on customary law, like the police powers doctrine discussed in Chapter 5 (especially when dealing with indirect expropriation and FET claims), or by reading innocuous language (e.g., "in like circumstances" in national treatment clauses) as mandating a consideration of alternative policy justifications.

protection with non-economic concerns, however, differ conceptually in two crucial respects.[14]

First, more complete agreements provide for a clear hierarchy of policy objectives whereas tribunals under incomplete IIAs assume an a priori equality of competing values. Tribunals dealing with incomplete treaties tend to place investment protection and non-investment concerns on an equal footing and seek to harmoniously resolve their tension on a case-by-case basis so as to protect both sets of values. The *Electrabel v. Hungary* award, summarizing earlier ISDS decisions, for example, stated that the "host State is not required to elevate unconditionally the interests of the foreign investor above all other considerations in every circumstance";[15] instead, the state needs to balance the interests of investors with other legitimate policy concerns.[16] Similarly, the *Urbaser v. Argentina* tribunal noted that "[t]he BIT has to be construed in harmony with other rules of international law of which it forms part, including those relating to human rights."[17] The ideal outcome then is one where a host state observes both its obligations vis-à-vis investors *and* meets other public goals, such as the protection of human rights or of the environment. In contrast, more complete agreements tend to contain an explicit hierarchy of policy objectives.[18] When the conditions of an exception are met, a measure is exempted from liability.[19] The protection of human life or of the environment then *trumps* the obligation to protect investment under specific circumstances.

Second, incomplete and more complete IIAs differ in when and how balancing takes place. Balancing under incomplete treaties occurs exclusively under primary obligations as implicit limitations are read into protective obligations

---

[14] For a more in-depth discussion, *see* Wolfgang Alschner & Kun Hui, *Missing in Action: General Public Policy Exceptions in Investment Treaties*, in YEARBOOK ON INTERNATIONAL INVESTMENT LAW AND POLICY 2018, at 372–379 (Lisa E. Sachs, Jesse Coleman, & Lise Johnson eds., 2019).

[15] *Electrabel S.A. v. Republic of Hungary*, ICSID Case No. ARB/07/19, Award, November 25, 2015, para. 615.

[16] *Id.*

[17] *Urbaser S.A. and Consorcio de Aguas Bilbao Bizkaia, Bilbao Biskaia Ur Partzuergoa v. The Argentine Republic*, ICSID Case No. ARB/07/26, Award, December 8, 2016, para. 1200. *See also Tulip Real Estate and Development Netherlands B.V. v. Republic of Turkey*, ICSID Case No. ARB/11/28, Decision on Annulment, December 30, 2015, paras. 86–90 (noting the importance of systemic integration as a principle to harmonize divergent international norms).

[18] The *Aven v. Costa Rica* tribunal, for example, considered that the right-to-regulate clause in DR–CAFTA (2004) "essentially subordinate[s] the rights to investors [under the treaty] to the right of Costa Rica." *David R. Aven, Samuel D. Aven, Giacomo A. Buscemi and others v. Republic of Costa Rica*, ICSID Case No. UNCT/15/3, Award, September 18, 2018, para. 412.

[19] On the operation of a general exception contrasted to other flexibility mechanisms, *see* Jorge E. Viñuales, *Seven Ways of Escaping a Rule: Of Exceptions and Their Avatars in International law*, in EXCEPTIONS AND DEFENCES IN INTERNATIONAL LAW (Lorand Bartels & Federica Paddeu eds., 2019); Joost Pauwelyn, *Defenses and the Burden of Proof in International Law*, in EXCEPTIONS AND DEFENSES IN INTERNATIONAL LAW (Lorand Bartels & Federica Paddeu eds., 2019).

and, if a measure falls under their scope, no violation is found in the first place.[20] Tribunals enjoy considerable discretion in the justifications they consider and how they weigh public policy obligations against investment protection commitments.[21] At the same time, their interpretation of the scope of investment obligations will ultimately decide how much regulatory deference to afford to the host state.[22] As the tribunal in *Unglaube v. Costa Rica*, for example, put it in relation to the protective scope of FET, "[e]ven if such measures are taken for an important public purpose, governments are required to use due diligence in the protection of foreigners and will not be excused from liability if their action has been arbitrary or discriminatory."[23] Under more complete agreements, in contrast, the focus of the analysis shifts to the general exceptions, which adds an additional step in the analysis: after a violation of a primary obligations is found, a tribunal needs to assess whether an exception can justify that violation.[24] As part of that investigation, tribunals enjoy less discretion as compared to a balancing under primary obligations in vague, incomplete IIAs. They are instead limited to considering the specific conditions listed in the exceptions, they typically need to determine whether a measure is "necessary," and they usually also have to assess whether the conditions of a qualifying chapeau are met.[25]

As a result of the differences between incomplete and more complete agreements, case law rendered under older treaties lacking exceptions cannot simply, or at least not exclusively, be applied to inform balancing under newer treaties with exceptions. This does not mean that case law from incomplete agreements has to be discarded completely.[26] But the inclusion of general

---

[20] Condon, *supra* note 15, at 349 ("IIA tribunals have addressed public interest measures by limiting the scope of specific obligations, particularly those regarding non-discrimination, fair and equitable treatment and expropriation.").

[21] According to some scholars, this discretion creates uncertainty, which the inclusion of general exceptions can remedy, *see* JÜRGEN KURTZ, THE WTO AND INTERNATIONAL INVESTMENT LAW: CONVERGING SYSTEMS 180–183 (2016); Keene, *supra* note 14, at 189.

[22] *Antaris Solar GmbH and Dr. Michael Göde v. Czech Republic*, PCA Case No. 2014-01, Award, May 2, 2018, para. 360; *PV Investors v. Kingdom of Spain*, PCA Case No. 2012-14, Final Award, February 28, 2020, para. 583; *Electrabel S.A. v. Republic of Hungary*, ICSID Case No. ARB/07/19, Award, November 25, 2015, para. 181.

[23] *Marion Unglaube v. Republic of Costa Rica*, ICSID Case No. ARB/08/1, Award, May 16, 2012, para. 247.

[24] This presupposes that general exceptions are read as affirmative defenses rather than jurisdictional limitations. On the distinction, *see* Caroline Henckels, *Should Investment Treaties Contain Public Policy Exceptions Essays: Substantive and Procedural Reforms*, 59 B.C. L. REV. 2825–2844 (2018); *id.*

[25] Nicholas DiMascio & Joost Pauwelyn, *Nondiscrimination in Trade and Investment Treaties: Worlds Apart or Two Sides of the Same Coin?*, 102 AM. J. INT'L L. 48–89, 83 (2008).

[26] For example, case law may still inform the interpretation of primary obligations. Note, however, that some scholars have argued that the inclusion of general exceptions displaces any balancing under primary obligations, *see* Henckels, *supra* note 26, at 2835. However, this is not necessarily the case. The Canadian government, for example, maintains that exceptions provide a complementary safety net and do not substitute for balancing under primary obligations. *See* Non-Disputing Party Submission of Canada, *Eco Oro Minerals Corp. v. Republic of Colombia*, ICSID Case No. ARB/16/41, February 27, 2020, paras. 19–20.

exceptions changes how investment protection and other public policy values are being evaluated under more complete agreements. Unfortunately, in practice, several tribunals have simply substituted a bespoke investigating of exceptions under more complete agreements with the reasoning of past tribunals constituted under incomplete treaties that lack exceptions.

In two awards against Venezuela, tribunals applied old precedent rather than new treaties. In *Gold Reserve v. Venezuela*, a Canadian company Gold Reserve brought an investment claim against Venezuela alleging that the revocation of two of its exploration and mining permits violated several provisions of the Canada–Venezuela BIT (1997). Venezuela argued that it had canceled Gold Reserve's permits on environmental grounds.[27] In a 2014 award, the tribunal found that Venezuela had violated the BIT's FET obligation and awarded $713 million in damages.

Annex 10b) of the Canada–Venezuela BIT contains a general public policy exception that allows measures necessary to protect animal or plant life or relating to the conservation of living or nonliving exhaustible natural resources, provided that such measures are not applied in an arbitrary or unjustifiable manner, or do not constitute a disguised restriction on international trade or investment. But instead of applying the exception to balance investment and environmental protection, the tribunal exclusively focused on balancing under primary obligations, here FET, and applied precedent rendered under incomplete IIAs.

The tribunal grounded its analysis in "a few cases whose factual circumstances appear to be closer to the facts of the present case."[28] It started its analysis with the *Saluka v. Czech Republic* award rendered under the Netherlands–Czech Republic BIT (1991), which contains no general exception and ranks among the least contractually complete IIAs—at the opposite end of the contractual completeness axis as compared to the Canada–Venezuela BIT (1997). The tribunal then situated its reasoning in the previously described balancing jurisprudence under incomplete IIAs:

> The Tribunal acknowledges that a State has a responsibility to preserve the environment and protect local populations living in the area where mining activities are conducted. However, this responsibility does not exempt a State from complying with its commitments to international investors by searching ways and means to satisfy in a balanced way both conditions.[29]

---

[27] *Gold Reserve Inc. v. Bolivarian Republic of Venezuela*, ICSID Case No. ARB(AF)/09/1, Award, September 22, 2014, para. 590.

[28] *Id.*, para. 568.

[29] *Id.*, para. 595.

Contrary to the tribunal's assertion, however, Annex 10 would have exempted Venezuela "from complying with its commitments to international investors" for environmental reasons, provided that the chapeau and necessity test of the exception had been satisfied. While Venezuela's acts might not have met these conditions, the balancing between environmental protection and investment protection should arguably have been done under the Annex rather than exclusively as part of the FET analysis. Admittedly, Venezuela seemed not to have explicitly raised the exception. But given that it defended its acts as an environmental protection measure, the tribunal should have considered the exception even if only as interpretive context. By grounding its reasoning in precedent instead, the tribunal effectively read a new, more complete treaty like an old incomplete one. It ignored the existence of a general exception and the explicit policy flexibility it provided.

The tribunal in *Crystallex v. Venezuela* fared no better.[30] Again, the case concerned a mining license refused ostensibly on environmental grounds, and the case was litigated under the same Canada–Venezuela BIT (1997). The tribunal ultimately found that Venezuela's measures violated the treaty's FET obligation and constituted an expropriation.[31] Like the *Gold Reserve* decision, the *Crystallex* award did not mention the BIT's general exception and instead grounded its analysis in precedent. The tribunal referred to the previously cited *Unglaube v. Costa Rica*[32] award rendered under the Germany–Costa Rica BIT (1994), which lacks an equivalent exception, to proclaim that states enjoy deference over regulatory measures, but that such deference was not without its limits.[33] In particular, in the tribunal's eyes, serious procedural flaws in the state's dealing with the investor weighed against according deference.[34] The tribunal concluded that the refusal of the permit was arbitrary and nontransparent and thus violated the BIT's FET clause.[35] While the measure may have fallen foul of the chapeau requirements of the BIT's general exception for the same reasons, the tribunal ought to have proceeded to investigate Venezuela's environmental defense under the exception, given that the treaty explicitly provided how to balance competing values in its Annex 10. By failing to do so, the tribunal applied precedent rather than the applicable treaty and read a new, more complete IIA as if it were an older, incomplete one, rolling back treaty design innovation.

[30] *Crystallex International Corporation v. Bolivarian Republic of Venezuela*, ICSID Case No. ARB(AF)/11/2, Award, April 4, 2016.

[31] *Id.*, paras. 575, 623, 718.

[32] *Marion & Reinhard Unglaube v. The Republic of Costa Rica*, ICSID Case Nos. ARB/08/1 and ARB/09/20, Award, May 16, 2012.

[33] *Crystallex v. Venezuela*, Award, paras. 581–584.

[34] *Id.*, para. 585.

[35] *Id.*, paras. 591, 614.

Ignoring explicit balancing introduced through general exceptions and instead applying precedent rendered under incomplete agreements that lacked exceptions constitutes just one of the ways precedent may be used to roll back innovation. As discussed in Chapter 2, recent, more complete IIAs have introduced other important changes that set incomplete treaties apart from more complete ones, including detailed preambles, refined primary obligations, as well as procedural improvements, all of which arguably warrant novel interpretive approaches and raise new considerations.[36] As these more complete IIAs are beginning to be litigated, they will be confronted with a pool of precedent skewed toward incomplete agreements. There is thus ample risk that future tribunals will rely too much on precedent, in effect substituting new treaty language with old reasoning.

B. Circumventing Corrective State Interventions through Precedent

Even when precedent connects agreements of similar design, its use can be problematic. Precedent has a shelf life. The older a precedent, the likelier it reflects an outdated state of the law. This is particular true in ISDS where the past two decades have seen a series of state interventions aimed at correcting arbitral case law ranging from (1) authoritative interpretations followed up by consistent submissions in litigation, (2) annulments and set-aside proceedings, and (3) subtle clarifications in new treaties. But rather than consistently heeding the corrective feedback received from states, tribunals tend to perpetuate mistakes by continuing to root their analysis in awards that have been corrected by subsequent state interventions.

The average age of cited precedent—that is the time between a rendered award and the decision it cites—is growing in ISDS. Tribunals are increasingly grounding their analogical reasoning in decisions from a different era. In 2010, the average age of a cited award was just shy of four years. In 2016, the average age of precedent was eight years (Figure 6.1). In a field as dynamic as ISDS, where state-driven interventions actively seek to change interpretive trajectories, the growing age of cited case law makes it exceedingly likely that precedents predate corrective state interventions. Three concise case studies help illustrate this trend.

First, outdated precedent has been used to circumvent contracting states' corrective authoritative interpretations and nondisputing interventions. As discussed in Chapter 5, the 2001 *Pope & Talbot v. Canada* interim award offered

---

[36] S. A. Spears, *The Quest for Policy Space in a New Generation of International Investment Agreements*, 13 J. INT'L ECON. L. 1037–1075 (2010).

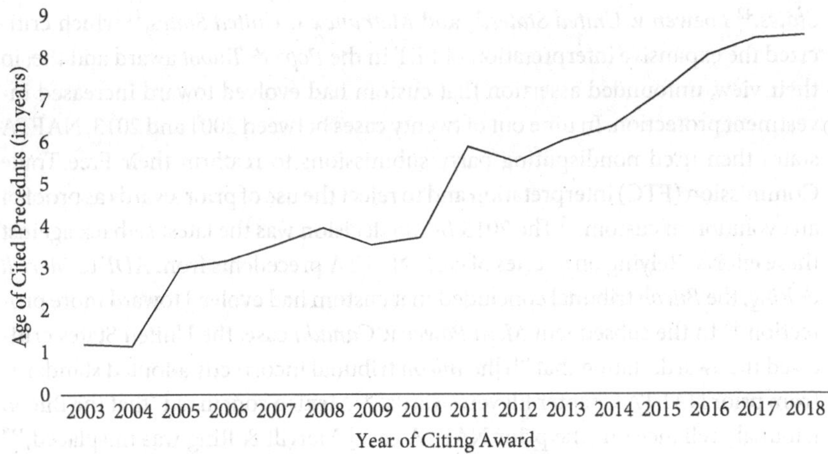

Figure 6.1 Average age of cited precedent (in years)

an expansive interpretation of FET in NAFTA Article 1105 as additive to the customary international law minimum standard. In response, the NAFTA contracting parties sought to correct what they perceived as a misinterpretation and issued an authoritative interpretation in July 2001 under NAFTA Article 1131 "to clarify and reaffirm" that FET under NAFTA does not "not require treatment in addition to or beyond" the customary minimum standard.[37] Rather than welcoming the interpretation as an affirmation of original intent,[38] the *Pope & Talbot* tribunal categorized the intervention as an attempt to amend the treaty, delegitimizing the corrective effort.[39] It also continued to adhere to an expansive interpretation of FET but, as discussed in Chapter 5, framed it under the guise of a custom rapidly evolving toward more investment protection.[40]

Ever since then, NAFTA states have struggled to correct and prevent what they perceived to be overly expansive interpretations of NAFTA Article 1105. In 2002, for example, the NAFTA parties filed concordant submissions in *Mondev v. United States*,[41] *ADF v. United*

[37] NAFTA Free Trade Commission, *Notes of Interpretation of Certain Chapter 11 Provisions*, sec. B (2), July 31, 2001, available at http://www.international.gc.ca/trade-agreements-accords-commerci aux/topics-domaines/disp-diff/NAFTA-Interpr.aspx?lang=eng (last accessed May 3, 2014).

[38] The *Methanex* tribunal later compared the authoritative interpretation as akin to the legislative branch of government legitimately overturning an interpretation of the judiciary, *see Methanex v. USA* at pt. IV, ch. C, at 10, para. 22.

[39] *Pope & Talbot Inc. v. The Government of Canada*, UNCITRAL, Award in Respect of Damages, May 31, 2002, paras. 24–47.

[40] *Id.*, paras. 58–65.

[41] *Mondev International Ltd. v. United States of America*, ICSID Case No. ARB(AF)/99/2, Award, October 11, 2002, paras. 106–109.

States,[42] *Loewen v. United States*,[43] and *Methanex v. United States*,[44] which criticized the expansive interpretation of FET in the *Pope & Talbot* award and the, in their view, unfounded assertion that custom had evolved toward increased investment protection. In nine out of twenty cases between 2001 and 2013, NAFTA states then used nondisputing party submissions to reaffirm their Free Trade Commission (FTC) interpretation and to reject the use of prior awards as proof of an evolution of custom.[45] The 2015 *Bilcon* decision was the latest setback against these efforts. Relying on a series of early NAFTA precedents from *ADF* to *Merrill & Ring*, the *Bilcon* tribunal concluded that custom had evolved toward more protection.[46] In the subsequent *Mesa Power v. Canada* case, the United States criticized the award, stating that "[t]he *Bilcon* tribunal incorrectly adopted standards from prior NAFTA Chapter Eleven awards."[47] Mexico concurred "that the Bilcon tribunal's reliance on [the prior NAFTA case] Merrill & Ring was misplaced,"[48] and Canada noted that the "Bilcon Award should be given limited weight in light of the fundamental errors made by the Tribunal . . . [which included] ignor[ing] the standard that the NAFTA Parties have mandated it to apply."[49] In short, precedent trumped more than a decade of corrective interventions by NAFTA states in *Bilcon*.

States have not been more successful with a second tool to correct arbitral misinterpretations: set-aside proceedings and annulments. ISDS does not provide for an appeal mechanism, but both the ICISD Convention and the New York Convention allow to void awards tainted by procedural improprieties (e.g., corruption) or an abuse of power on the part of the tribunal.[50] The grounds for review are narrow and exclude substantive errors of law.[51] Nevertheless,

---

[42] *ADF Group Inc. v. United States of America*, ICSID Case No. ARB(AF)/00/1, Award, January 9, 2003, paras. 119–126. As the United States explained in *ADF v. USA*, the *Pope & Talbot* tribunal "made no attempt to analyze either the consistency of State practice in investment treaties or whether any such State practice evidenced the opinio juris necessary to establish customary international law." Post-Hearing Submission of Respondent United States of America on Article 1105(1) and Pope & Talbot, June 27, 2002, *ADF Group Inc. v. United States of America*, ICSID Case No. ARB (AF)/00/1.

[43] Canada Second 1128 Submission (June 27, 2002), and Mexico Third 1128 Submission (July 2, 2002), *Loewen Group, Inc. and Raymond L. Loewen v. United States of America*, ICSID Case No. ARB(AF)/98/3.

[44] *Methanex v. USA*, Final Award, pt. II, ch. B, para. 21.

[45] Wolfgang Alschner, *The Return of the Home State and the Rise of "Embedded" Investor-State Arbitration, in* THE ROLE OF THE STATE IN INVESTOR-STATE ARBITRATION 293–333, 329 (2015).

[46] *Bilcon of Delaware et al. v. Government of Canada*, PCA Case No. 2009-04, Award on Jurisdiction and Liability, March 17, 2015, para. 435.

[47] Second Submission of the United States of America, *Mesa Power LLC v. Canada*, PCA Case No. 2012-17, June 12, 2015, para. 8.

[48] Second Submission of Mexico Pursuant to NAFTA Article 1128, *Mesa Power LLC v. Canada*, PCA Case No. 2012-17, June 12, 2015, para. 10.

[49] Canada's Observations on the Bilcon Award, *Mesa Power LLC v. Canada*, PCA Case No. 2012-17, May 14, 2015, paras. 1, 17.

[50] ICSID art. 52, New York Convention art. V.

[51] David D. Caron, *Reputation and Reality in the ICSID Annulment Process: Understanding the Distinction Between Annulment and Appeal*, 7 ICSID REV. 21–56 (1992).

annulment and set-aside proceedings provide states with a control lever over an award.[52] They also offer a potent remedy: an annulled or set-aside is voided—it ceases to exist, and litigants have to start proceedings anew.

But even such a potent control has not proved capable of policing precedent. The *Metalclad v. Mexico* award is a case in point. The *Metalclad* tribunal had concluded that the FET obligation in Article 1105 of NAFTA required that a state provide a transparent and predictable business framework.[53] Mexico sought to set aside the award in Canadian courts (the seat of arbitration) on the grounds that the tribunal had exceeded its jurisdiction. The Supreme Court of British Colombia agreed with Mexico. It found that the "principle of transparency is implemented through the provisions of [NAFTA] Chapter 18, not Chapter 11"[54] and set aside that portion of the award. This rendered part of the reasoning of the *Metalclad* award null and void. However, while the set-aside decision erased that passage in relation to the parties, the decision survived as precedent: the voided passage has since been cited at least nineteen times, and most references cite the paragraph approvingly and do not mention that the portion was set aside (Table 6.3).

The previously discussed *Gold Reserve v. Venezuela* is one of the cases applying the voided award as a quasi-zombie precedent. The tribunal noted, without caveat and without mentioning the set-aside proceedings, that "[t]he reasons given by the tribunal in the *Metalclad v Mexico* case for concluding that a breach of the FET provision had occurred can also be applied to the present case . . ." and went on to cite the very passage that was set aside.[55] The tribunal thus literally "applied" old, inadmissible precedent rather than the applicable law. Even a voided award can thus continue to haunt states as a zombie precedent.

A third way states have sought to correct precedent has been through the insertion of subtle clarifications in recent treaties. A major concern among the NAFTA contracting states has been that tribunals generally have not embarked on an independent assessment to establish the content of custom when investigating the minimum standard of treatment in NAFTA Article 1105. As Ole Kristian Fauchald concluded after an exhaustive content analysis of almost one hundred ICSID cases, "[n]o tribunal made its own assessment of whether a rule of customary international law existed, and only exceptionally did tribunals

---

[52] Anne van Aaken, *Control Mechanisms in International Investment Law, in* THE FOUNDATIONS OF INTERNATIONAL INVESTMENT LAW: BRINGING THEORY INTO PRACTICE 409–435 (Zachary Douglas, Joost Pauwelyn, & Jorge E. Viñuales eds., 2014).

[53] *Metalclad Corporation v. The United Mexican States*, ICSID Case No. ARB(AF)/97/1, Award, August 30, 2000, paras. 76, 88, & 99–101.

[54] Supreme Court of British Colombia, *The United Mexican States v. Metalclad Corporation*, 2001 BCSC 664, para. 71.

[55] *Gold Reserve Inc. v. Bolivarian Republic of Venezuela*, ICSID Case No. ARB(AF)/09/1, Award, September 22, 2014, para. 609.

Table 6.3 Treatment of voided passages of the *Metalclad* award in subsequent decisions until 2019

Affirmation of Voided Passage	Rejection of Voided Passage	Noting that Passage was Voided
1. *Daimler Financial Services AG v. Argentine Republic*, ICSID Case No. ARB/05/1, Dissenting Opinion of Judge Charles N. Brower, August 22, 2012 at para. 20 fn. 59; 2. *Ioan Micula and others v. Romania I*, ICSID Case No. ARB/05/20, Award, December 11, 2013 at paras. 531 & 866; 3. *Jan Oostergetel and Theodora Laurentius v. Slovak Republic*, UNCITRAL, Final Award, April 23, 2012 at para. 221; 4. *Mohammad Ammar Al-Bahloul v. Republic of Tajikistan*, SCC Case No. V064/2008, Partial Award on Jurisdiction and Liability, September 2, 2009 at para. 183; 5. *Bayindir Insaat Turizm Ticaret Ve Sanayi A.S. v. Islamic Republic of Pakistan*, ICSID Case No. ARB/03/29, Award, August 27, 2009 at para. 178; 6. *Occidental Exploration and Production Company v. Republic of Ecuador*, LCIA Case No. UN3467, Final Award, July 1, 2004 at para. 185; 7. *Gold Reserve Inc. v. Bolivarian Republic of Venezuela*, ICSID Case No. ARB(AF)/09/1, Award, September 22, 2014 at para. 609; 8. *LG&E Energy Corp., LG&E Capital Corp. and LG&E International Inc. v. Argentine Republic*, ICSID Case No. ARB/02/1, Decision on Liability, October 3, 2006 at para. 125 fn. 31.	1. *Casinos Austria International GmbH and Casinos Austria Aktiengesellschaft v. Argentine Republic*, ICSID Case No. ARB/14/32, Decision on Jurisdiction, June 29, 2018 at para. 242; 2. *Marvin Roy Feldman Karpa v. United Mexican States*, ICSID Case No. ARB(AF)/99/1, Award, December 16, 2002 at fn. 29; 3. *Mamidoil Jetoil Greek Petroleum Products Societe Anonyme S.A. v. Republic of Albania*, ICSID Case No. ARB/11/24, Dissenting Opinion of Steven A. Hammond, March 30, 2015 at para. 122; 4. *Cargill, Incorporated v. Republic of Poland*, ICSID Case No. ARB(AF)/04/2, Award, March 5, 2008 at para. 456; 5. *Eastern Sugar B.V. v. Czech Republic*, SCC No. 088/2004, Partial Dissenting Opinion, March 27, 2007 at para. 30; 6. *CMS Gas Transmission Company v. Republic of Argentina*, ICSID Case No. ARB/01/8, Award, May 12, 2005 at para. 278.	1. *Accession Mezzanine Capital L.P. and Danubius Kereskedohaz Vagyonkezelo v. Hungary*, ICSID Case No. ARB/12/3, Award, April 17, 2015 at paras. 174 & 177; 2. *Mobil Investments Canada Inc. and Murphy Oil Corporation v. Government of Canada*, ICSID Case No. ARB(AF)/07/4, Decision on Liability and on Principles of Quantum, May 22, 2012 at para. 140; 3. *Merrill & Ring Forestry L.P. v. Government of Canada*, ICSID Case No. UNCT/07/1, ICSID Administrated, Award, March 31, 2010 at para. 189; 4. *Marvin Roy Feldman Karpa v. United Mexican States*, ICSID Case No. ARB(AF)/99/1, Award, December 16, 2002 at para. 146 fn. 29 & para. 147; 5. *Pope & Talbot Inc. v. Government of Canada*, UNCITRAL, Award in Respect of Damages, May 31, 2002 at para. 25 fn. 8.

explicitly address questions concerning *opinio juris*."[56] Instead, NAFTA tribunals relied exclusively on prior awards to describe the state of custom.[57]

To prevent early NAFTA cases from influencing the jurisprudence under new agreements as ostensible descriptions of the state of customary law, states began to explicitly instruct tribunals to rely on states' practice and *opinio juris* to establish custom in new treaties. DR–CAFTA (2004), connecting the United States and Central American states, was the first IIA to conclude the novel language. While DR–CAFTA Article 10.5 largely reproduced NAFTA Article 1105 in linking FET to the customary international law minimum standard of treatment, it also provided in Annex 10-B that "[t]he Parties confirm their shared understanding that 'customary international law' generally and as specifically referenced in Articles 10.5, 10.6, and Annex 10-C results from a general and consistent practice of States that they follow from a sense of legal obligation." DR–CAFTA tribunals were thus clearly mandated to investigate states' practice and *opinio juris* when they assessed FET claims.

The first DR–CAFTA dispute on FET, *Railroad Development Corporation v. Guatemala*, provided a test case for whether that language succeeded in directing tribunals to independently investigate custom rather than applying precedent. The dispute concerned an order of the government of Guatemala to cancel a railroad operation concession previously awarded to an American investor.[58] The investor argued that the cancellation order violated DR–CAFTA's national treatment, expropriation, and the minimum standard of treatment clause in DR–CAFTA Article 10.5. The tribunal dismissed the former two claims for lack of merit but upheld the latter one.[59] In the process, the tribunal had to establish the content of the customary minimum standard of treatment. In its nondisputing party submission, the United States explained that Article 10.5 read in conjunction with Annex 10-B "express[es] an intent to guide the interpretation of that Article by the Parties' understanding of customary international law, *i.e.*, the law that develops from the practice and *opinio juris* of States themselves, rather than by interpretations [by arbitral tribunals] of similar but differently worded treaty provisions."[60]

The tribunal, however, disregarded the direction given in the explanatory Annex and the nondisputing party submission. It instead reviewed NAFTA

---

[56] Fauchald, *supra* note 3, at 311.

[57] Patrick Dumberry, *The Role and Relevance of Awards in the Formation, Identification and Evolution of Customary Rules in International Investment Law*, 33 J. Int'l Arb. 282–283 (2016).

[58] *Railroad Development Corporation v. Republic of Guatemala*, ICSID Case No. ARB/07/23, Award, June 29, 2012.

[59] On the case, *see generally* Omar E. García-Bolívar, *Railroad Development Corporation v Republic of Guatemala the First CAFTA Award on the Merits*, 28 ICSID Rev. 27–32 (2013).

[60] *Railroad Development Corporation v. Republic of Guatemala*, ICSID Case No. ARB/07/23, Submission of the United States of America, January 31, 2012, para. 3.

Article 1105 awards and found that customary international law is in a constant process of development.[61] It then concluded that "[the NAFTA Article 1105 case] *Waste Management II* persuasively integrates the accumulated analysis of prior NAFTA Tribunals and reflects a balanced description of the minimum standard of treatment."[62] On that basis, the tribunal "adopt[ed] the *Waste Management II* articulation of the minimum standard for purposes of this case."[63] In other words, the tribunal did not investigate the "general and consistent practice of States that they follow from a sense of legal obligation" as mandated by the Annex to elucidate the content of custom; it instead applied precedent. As Matthew Porterfield notes in his commentary of the decision, the tribunals "accept[ed], without any evidence of state practice or opinio juris, the pronouncements of previous tribunals as definitive evidence of the standard under CIL."[64] This was exactly what the treaty annex and the submission of the United States had urged the tribunal *not* to do. Yet the tribunal chose to substitute the findings by a different tribunal under a different treaty for its own analysis.

In summary, the reliance on precedent especially under newer agreements risks undermining the transition from incomplete to more complete agreements and blunts the impact of corrective state interventions that seek to right prior arbitral misinterpretations. When tribunals apply outdated precedent rather than new treaty language and fail to heed the direction provided by contracting states and review instances, they risk rolling back innovation and root cases under new treaties in old case law.

III. The Stickiness of Precedent

In ISDS, precedent "sticks" in spite of proactive and corrective state-driven change. Arbitral awards survive the updating of treaty design as well as corrective interventions and continue to exert influence over new cases. Once an arbitral award is rendered, it is surprisingly hard for states to prevent or discourage its future use as precedent. Why is precedent so resilient to changing treaties and corrective efforts? Precedent in ISDS sticks for at least four main reasons: (1) tribunals consider following precedent to be normatively desirable, (2) tribunals have an institutional incentive for following precedent, (3) ISDS lacks mechanisms to effectively police the use of precedent, and (4) precedents

---

[61] *RDC v. Guatemala*, Award, paras. 216–219.

[62] *Id.*, para. 219.

[63] *Id.*, para. 219.

[64] Matthew Porterfield, *A Distinction Without a Difference? The Interpretation of Fair and Equitable Treatment Under Customary International Law by Investment Tribunals*, IISD INVESTMENT TREATY NEWS (2012).

benefit from self-reinforcing tendencies that increase their normative pull over time and entrench them progressively deeper. As a result, states face an uphill battle in their efforts to achieve normative change.

A. Normative Preference for Following Precedent

Domestic and international law adjudicators, whether or not they are subject to a stare decisis rule, routinely draw from the reasoning of prior decisions. In the words of Dolores Bentolila, creating and following precedents, "whether formal or informal, binding or persuasive, seem[] to be an essential element and result of the adjudication process itself."[65] Following precedent, in a sense, is a natural part of adjudication.

Adjudicators' innate preference for following precedent stems at least in part from the perception that precedent promotes a set of core normative virtues. Reliance on precedent presents an efficient way to solve disputes, because decision makers can rely on existing solutions to address recurring legal problems.[66] Moreover, treating like cases alike prevents arbitrariness and ensures equality before the law.[67] Following precedent also promotes consistency as lines of similar cases produce similar outcomes.[68] Consistency, in turn, creates legal certainty, stability, and predictability and thereby generates reliable expectations of conduct, helps monitor compliance, and facilitates the amicable settlement of disputes in the shadow of the law.[69] In short, following precedent is normatively good—it is associated with core values of modern rule-of-law systems, such as efficiency, equality, predictability, and consistency.

This normative case for following precedent is echoed in investment arbitration. To Jan Paulsson, reliance on precedent cures some of ISDS rule-of-law shortcomings: "attention to prior decisions may be viewed as a type of anti-arbitrariness vaccine."[70] According to frequent arbitrator Gabriel Kaufmann-Kohler, investment tribunals may not have a legal obligation to abide by the

---

[65] DOLORES BENTOLILA, ARBITRATORS AS LAWMAKERS 2 (2017).

[66] As the well-known Justice Cardozo of the US Supreme Court put it, "the labor of judges would be increased almost to the breaking point if every past decision could be reopened in every case, and one could not lay one's own course of bricks on the secure foundation of the courses laid by others who had gone before him." Reprinted in Earl Maltz, *The Nature of Precedent*, 66 N.C. L. REV. 367–394, 370 (1987).

[67] *Id.* at 369, 371.

[68] Irene M. Ten Cate, *The Costs of Consistency: Precedent in Investment Treaty Arbitration*, 51 COLUM. J. TRANSNAT'L L. 418 (2013).

[69] C. H. Schreuer, *Diversity and Harmonization of Treaty Interpretation in Investment Arbitration*, 3 TRANSNAT'L DISP. MGMT. 10 (2006).

[70] Jan Paulsson, *The Role of Precedent in Investment Treaty Arbitration, in* ARBITRATION UNDER INTERNATIONAL INVESTMENT AGREEMENTS: A GUIDE TO THE KEY ISSUES 4.17 (Katia Yannaca-Small ed., 2nd ed. 2018).

reasoning of earlier tribunals, "but it seems well settled that they have a *moral obligation to follow precedents.*"[71] In doing so, investment tribunals are said to contribute to predictability and consistency in international investment law.[72] A similar view was expressed by the tribunal in *Planet Mining v. Indonesia*:

> The Tribunal considers that it is not bound by previous decisions. At the same time, it is of the opinion that it must pay due consideration to earlier decisions of international tribunals. Specifically, it deems that, subject to compelling contrary grounds, it has a duty to adopt solutions established in a series of consistent cases. It further deems that, subject to the specific provisions of a given treaty and of the circumstances of the actual case, it has a duty to contribute to the harmonious development of investment law, with a view to meeting the legitimate expectations of the community of States and investors towards certainty of the rule of law.[73]

Of course, there are also normative arguments that weigh *against* following precedent. To frequent arbitrator Brigitte Stern, case-specific correctness is more important than a desire to be consistent. According to her, tribunals have a "duty to decide each case on its own merits, independently of any apparent jurisprudential trend."[74] The quoted passage from *Planet Mining* similarly subjects reliance on precedent to the "specific provisions of a given treaty." Investment scholars have also pointed to the varying language and provisions of the investment treaty universe, which suggest that reasoning under one treaty may not automatically inform reasoning under a different treaty.[75] Otherwise, following precedent may produce lines of cases that risk being consistently wrong.[76] As one of the first tribunals toying with the idea of consistency in investment law jurisprudence

---

[71] Gabrielle Kaufmann-Kohler, *Arbitral Precedent Dream, Necessity or Excuse?*, 23 ARB. INT'L 357, 374 (2007) (emphasis in the original).

[72] Gabrielle Kaufmann-Kohler, *Is Consistency a Myth?*, in PRECEDENT IN INTERNATIONAL ARBITRATION 137 (Emmanuel Gaillard & Yas Banifatemi eds., 2008); *but see also* Thomas Schultz, *Against Consistency in Investment Arbitration*, in THE FOUNDATIONS OF INTERNATIONAL INVESTMENT LAW: BRINGING THEORY INTO PRACTICE 297–316 (Zachary Douglas, Joost Pauwelyn, & Jorge E. Viñuales eds., 2014).

[73] *Planet Mining Pty Ltd. v. Republic of Indonesia*, ICSID Case Nos. ARB/12/14 and 12/40, Decision on Jurisdiction, February 24, 2014, para. 85 (footnote omitted). *See similarly ADC Affiliate Limited and ADC & ADMC Management Limited v. Republic of Hungary*, ICSID Case ARB/03/16, Award, October 2, 2006, para. 293 ("cautious reliance on certain principles developed in [prior investment arbitration] cases, as persuasive authority, may advance the body of law, which in turn may serve predictability in the interest of both investors and host States.").

[74] *Burlington Resources Inc. v. Republic of Ecuador*, ICSID Case No. ARB/08/5, Decision on Jurisdiction, June 2, 2010, para. 100.

[75] Rudolf Dolzer, *Perspectives for Investment Arbitration: Consistency as a Policy Goal?*, in NEW DIRECTIONS AND EMERGING CHALLENGES IN INTERNATIONAL INVESTMENT LAW AND POLICY (Pierre Sauvé & Roberto Echandi eds., 2012) (arguing that consistency is elusive because of the fragmentation and diversity of IIAs).

[76] Schultz, *supra* note 75.

emphasized, "although different tribunals constituted under the ICSID system should in general seek to act consistently with each other, in the end it must be for each tribunal to exercise its competence in accordance with the applicable law, which will by definition be different for each BIT."[77] The question, then, is what normative consideration exerts the greater pull when tribunals assess the value of prior decisions—promoting systemic consistency or ensuring treaty-specific correctness?

If the citation behavior of tribunals is any guide as to their latent preferences, then the majority of tribunals favor promoting systemic consistency over ensuring treaty-specific correctness. Only 25 percent of citations between awards connect the same or highly similar agreements.[78] Tribunals that restrict the pool of relevant precedent to IIAs highly similar or identical to the IIA at issue and that thus seem to care more about treaty-specific correctness are in the minority.[79] Most tribunals, in contrast, cite prior decisions liberally including under very differently worded agreements. In conclusion, adjudicators, in general, and investment arbitrators, in particular, have a normative preference for following prior decisions in order to advance systemic rule-of-law goals, which, for the latter, in the aggregate trumps countervailing treaty-specific correctness considerations.

B. Institutional Incentives for Following Precedent

Scholars have also identified a set of institutional incentives that make investment tribunals more inclined to rely on precedent for strategic purposes. First, tribunals have an incentive to use precedent to enlarge and to legitimize their decision-making authority. According to Grisel and Stone Sweet, the delegation of adjudicatory power by the IIA parties to investment tribunals can be understood through the prism of principal-agent theory.[80] Tribunals are the agents of the contracting states, but they also have their own interests and will use their delegated power to assert greater autonomy and independence over time.[81] Precedent is one of the tools at their disposal. Tribunals can entrench interpretation that give more discretion to tribunals through precedent and can legitimize their own lawmaking by relying on the lawmaking of previous tribunals.[82] Grisel

---

[77] *SGS Société Générale de Surveillance S.A. v. Republic of the Philippines,* ICSID Case No. ARB/02/6, Decision on Jurisdiction, January 29, 2004, para. 97.

[78] Alschner, *supra* note 8.

[79] *Id.*

[80] Florian Grisel & Alec Stone Sweet, *Transnational Investment Arbitration: From Delegation to Constitutionalization?, in* Human Rights in International Investment Law and Arbitration (Pierre-Marie Dupuy, Ernst-Ulrich Petersmann, & Francesco Francioni eds., 2009).

[81] *Id.* at 120–122.

[82] *Id.* at 128.

and Stone Sweet note that this gradual empowerment of tribunals through, among others, a strong reliance on precedent, leads to a "judicialization" of investment arbitration, whereby tribunals define their role increasingly as agents of an investment arbitration community rather than of the contracting states.[83] This, in turn, may help explain the finding that tribunals, in the aggregate, have developed a preference for systemic consistency (which benefits a larger ISDS community) over case-specific correctness (which benefits the contracting parties to the specific treaty).

Second, individual adjudicators have an incentive to use precedent for strategical ends. At the International Court of Justice, for example, individual judges are known to use citations strategically in order to promote their own academic writings or prior decisions.[84] This tendency is likely more pronounced in ISDS given the unique features of the system. Sergio Puig has shown that the network of repeat arbitrators is tightly knit—a small number of arbitrators sit on a large number of ISDS cases.[85] Malcolm Langford, Daniel Behn, and Runar Lie have furthermore demonstrated that at least some of these arbitrators occupy multiple roles—acting as counsel in one arbitration and as arbitrator in another one.[86] The small-world nature of ISDS arbitrators coupled with their occasional "double hatting" creates incentives for strategic uses of precedent. An arbitrator may cite a case strategically to buttress an interpretive favorable to a case he or she is involved in as counsel. Other arbitrators may seek to brand themselves as being "pro-state" or "pro-investor" on the reappointment market by citing cases that are particularly favorable to investors and states strategically in order to signal their normative priors.

C. Lack of Effective Controls to Police Precedent

The liberal attitude among tribunals toward accepting precedent and the strategic use of precedent by arbitrators and tribunals is compounded by the fact that states lack effective control mechanisms to police the use of precedent. In their delegation of adjudicatory and interpretive authority to ISDS tribunals, contracting states have reserved legal and sociolegal controls—yet none of them was designed for policing precedent.[87]

---

[83] *Id.* at 124–126.

[84] Damien Charlotin, "Authorities" in International Dispute Settlement: A Data Analysis, PhD Thesis (June 2020), at 188 (on file with the author).

[85] Sergio Puig, *Social Capital in the Arbitration Market*, 25 EUR. J. INT'L L. (2014) 387–424.

[86] Malcolm Langford, Daniel Behn, & Runar Hilleren Lie, *The Revolving Door in International Investment Arbitration*, 20 J. INT'L ECON. L. 301–332 (2017).

[87] *See generally* Aaken, *supra* note 55.

Start with annulment and set-aside proceedings, which are the most potent control mechanisms under the ICSID and New York Conventions. They allow the parties to the arbitration to apply either to an ad hoc committee (under ICSID) or to domestic courts (under the New York Convention) to have an arbitral award voided. However, annulment and set-aside proceedings are designed to preserve the integrity of the arbitration process vis-à-vis the parties, not to police the future use of a decision by unrelated litigants. As a result, the voiding of awards has not prevented subsequent parties and tribunals from citing them as zombie precedents.

Precedents are also impervious to forms of sociolegal control. Not only do awards that are heavily criticized by the contracting parties, like the previously discussed *Pope & Talbot*, continue to be widely cited and followed. But precedent is also resilient in the face of criticism from other ISDS tribunals. Hopes that interpretive disagreements could be resolved organically through a converging jurisprudence have been largely disappointed thus far.[88] Jan Paulsson's prediction that "good awards will chase the bad, and set standards which will contribute to a higher level of consistent quality" has not materialized.[89]

Instead, case law on controversial substantive issues is becoming more balkanized with competing lines of reasoning coexisting with equal force. Take the opposing approaches to the reading of umbrella clauses enunciated in *SGS v. Philippines* and *SGS v. Pakistan*, for example. While the former tribunal held that the clause provides jurisdiction for the enforcement of contractual claims,[90] the latter envisaged a narrower role of the clause as a fail-safe, for example, being triggered only when the state fails to honor an arbitration clause previously agreed to in a contract, and rejected the notion that the clause could generally incorporate contractual claims into the treaty.[91] Both decisions are cited with roughly equal frequency in later awards (Figure 6.2). And that is despite of the fact that Switzerland, the investor's home state, complained about to *SGS v. Pakistan* tribunal's overly narrow interpretation of the treaty's umbrella clause to the ICSID Secretariat as being at odds with the intention of the parties.[92]

---

[88] Doak Bishop, *The Case for an Appellate Panel and its Scope of Review*, 2 Transnat'l Disp. Mgmt., no. 8, 9 (2005).

[89] Jan Paulsson, *International Arbitration and the Generation of Legal Norms: Treaty Arbitration and International Law, in* ICCA Congress Series No. 13, International Arbitration 2006: Back To Basics? 889 (A.J. van den Berg ed., 2007) ("There have indeed been some questionable decisions in investment arbitrations [. . .] but this comment must be seen in perspective; the Permanent Court of International Justice and the International Court of Justice themselves have authored some discredited judgments, and the normative influence of those judgments simply dissipate over time. We are in an early phase of dramatic extension of investment arbitration.").

[90] *SGS Société Générale de Surveillance S.A. v. Republic of the Philippines*, ICSID Case No. ARB/02/6, Decision on Jurisdiction, January 29, 2004, para. 128.

[91] *SGS Société Générale de Surveillance S.A. v. Islamic Republic of Pakistan*, ICSID Case No. ARB/01/13, Award on Jurisdiction, August 6, 2003, paras. 167–172.

[92] Note on the Interpretation of Article 11 of the Bilateral Investment Treaty Between Switzerland and Pakistan, attached to the Letter of the Swiss Secretariat for Economic Affairs to

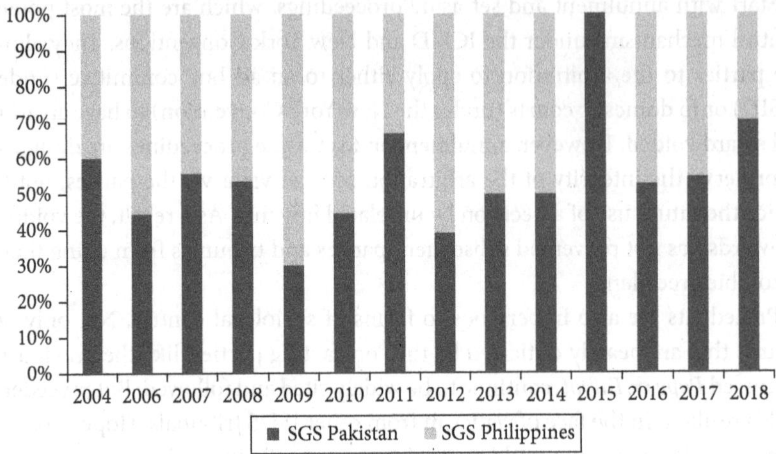

Figure 6.2 Share of unique citations from ISDS awards to SGS Pakistan and SGS Philippines per year

Moreover, although some controversial interpretations have fallen into disuse, such as the necessity cases discussed in Chapter 5, they are the exception rather than the rule. Instead, even awards heavily criticized by subsequent tribunals often continue to enjoy widespread popularity in some corners. For example, the interpretation of FET in the *Tecmed* award has been ridiculed in another award as "a programme of good governance that no State in the world is capable of guaranteeing at all times,"[93] and rejected by a string of tribunals.[94] And yet that very same *Tecmed* passage still enjoys widespread influence as precedent. Up to 2019, thirty-one awards have cited and endorsed it.[95] Hence, neither legal control mechanisms (like annulment) nor social ones (like criticism from states

the ICSID Deputy-Secretary General (October 1, 2003), reprinted in MEALEY's INT'L ARB. REP. (February 2004).

[93] *El Paso Energy International Company v. Argentina*, ICSID Case No. ARB/03/15, Award, October 31, 2011, at para. 342.

[94] *See, e.g., White Industries Australia Limited v. Republic of India*, UNCITRAL, Final Award, November 30, 2011, paras. 10.3.5–10.3.6; *OKO Pankki Oyj and others v. Republic of Estonia*, ICSID Case No. ARB/04/6, Award, November 19, 2007, paras. 242, 245; *Suez, Sociedad General de Aguas de Barcelona S.A. and Interagua Servicios Integrales de Agua S.A. v. Argentine Republic*, ICSID Case No. ARB/03/17, Decision on Liability, July 30, 2010, para. 205.

[95] *Casinos Austria International GmbH and Casinos Austria Aktiengesellschaft v. Argentine Republic*, ICSID Case No. ARB/14/32, Decision on Jurisdiction, June 29, 2018; *Parkerings-Compagniet AS v. Republic of Lithuania*, ICSID Case No. ARB/05/8, Award, September 11, 2007; *CC/Devas (Mauritius) Ltd., Devas Employees Mauritius Private Limited and Telcom Devas Mauritius Limited v. Republic of India*, PCA Case No. 2013-09, Award on Jurisdiction and Merits, July 25, 2016; *Murphy Exploration and Production Company International v. Republic of Ecuador II*, PCA Case No. 2012-16 (formerly AA 434), Partial Final Award, May 6, 2016; *Jan Oostergetel and Theodora Laurentius v. Slovak Republic*, UNCITRAL, Final Award, April 23, 2012; *Frontier Petroleum Services Ltd. v. Czech Republic*, UNCITRAL, Final Award, November 12, 2010; *BG Group Plc. v. Republic of*

and subsequent tribunals) are reliable means to police and limit an award's use as precedent.

The reasons even controversial awards survive as precedent are manifold. First, there are no institutional mechanisms specifically designed to police precedent. Second, litigants typically have no interest in letting extreme interpretations of past awards fade into the night. On the off chance that a tribunal may be swayed by a precedent, claimants and respondents vigorously cite cases that favor their respective positions. Tribunals, in turn, may feel compelled to engage with these authorities as part of their due process obligations vis-à-vis the parties.[96] Third, as mentioned earlier, tribunals have a self-interest in strategically following precedents that enlarge their zone of gap-filling discretion, and individual arbitrators have an interest in citing extreme cases to profile themselves as pro-state or pro-investor. Fourth, particularly controversial cases often serve as benchmark decisions in jurisprudential debates. *Metalclad*, for example, is associated with FET protecting a transparent and predictable business framework—irrespective of whether it was subsequently voided for that very

Argentina, UNCITRAL, Award, December 24, 2007; *Enron Creditors Recovery Corporation (formerly Enron Corporation) and Ponderosa Assets, L.P. v. Argentine Republic*, ICSID Case No. ARB/01/3, Award, May 22, 2007; *LG&E Energy Corp., LG&E Capital Corp. and LG&E International Inc. v. Argentine Republic*, ICSID Case No. ARB/02/1, Decision on Liability, October 3, 2006; *Greentech Energy Systems A/S and others v. Kingdom of Spain*, SCC Case No. V2015/150, Final Award, November 14, 2018; *Gavrilovic and Gavrilovic d.o.o. v. Republic of Croatia*, ICSID Case No. ARB/12/39, Award, July 26, 2018; *Luigiterzo Bosca v. Republic of Lithuania*, PCA Case No. 2011-04, Award, February 19, 2016; *Ioan Micula and others v. Romania I*, ICSID Case No. ARB/05/20, Award, December 11, 2013; *Reinhard Hans Unglaube v. Republic of Costa Rica*, ICSID Case No. ARB/09/20, Award, May 16, 2012; *Spyridon Roussalis v. Romania*, ICSID Case No. ARB/06/1, Award, December 1, 2011; *Rupert Binder v. Czech Republic*, UNCITRAL, Final Award (Redacted), July 15, 2011; *Alpha Projektholding GmbH v. Ukraine*, ICSID Case No. ARB/07/16, Award, November 8, 2010; *AES Summit Generation Limited and AES-Tisza Erömü Kft. v. Republic of Hungary*, ICSID Case No. ARB/07/22, Award, September 23, 2010; *Ioannis Kardassopoulos v. Georgia*, ICSID Case No. ARB/05/18, Award, March 3, 2010; *Joseph C. Lemire v. Ukraine II*, ICSID Case No. ARB/06/18, Decision on Jurisdiction and Liability, January 14, 2010; *Mohammad Ammar Al-Bahloul v. Republic of Tajikistan*, SCC Case No. V064/2008, Partial Award on Jurisdiction and Liability, September 2, 2009; *Bayindir Insaat Turizm Ticaret Ve Sanayi A.S. v. Islamic Republic of Pakistan*, ICSID Case No. ARB/03/29, Award, 27 August 2009; *Plama Consortium Limited v. Republic of Bulgaria*, ICSID Case No. ARB/03/24, Award, August 27, 2008; *Duke Energy Electroquil Partners and Electroquil S.A. v. Republic of Ecuador*, ICSID Case No. ARB/04/19, Award, August 18, 2008; *Cargill, Incorporated v. Republic of Poland*, ICSID Case No. ARB(AF)/04/2, Award, March 5, 2008; *Sempra Energy International v. Argentine Republic*, ICSID Case No. ARB/02/16, Award, September 28, 2007; *Eureko B.V. v. Republic of Poland*, Ad Hoc, Partial Award and Dissenting Opinion, August 19, 2005; *CMS Gas Transmission Company v. Republic of Argentina*, ICSID Case No. ARB/01/8, Award, May 12, 2005; *Occidental Exploration and Production Company v. Republic of Ecuador*, LCIA Case No. UN3467, Final Award, July 1, 2004; *MTD Equity Sdn. Bhd. and MTD Chile S.A. v. Republic of Chile*, ICSID Case No. ARB/01/7, Award, May 25, 2004; *Mamidoil Jetoil Greek Petroleum Products Societe Anonyme S.A. v. Republic of Albania*, ICSID Case No. ARB/11/24, Award, March 30, 2015; *Eastern Sugar B.V. v. Czech Republic*, SCC No. 088/2004, Partial Dissenting Opinion, March 27, 2007.

[96] Paulsson, *supra* note 73, at 4.10 ("to the extent that any party's case places central reliance on a proposition derived from previously decided cases, arbitrators are required to give consideration to them and to express their assessment of the persuasiveness of that reliance.").

reason—and subsequent awards agreeing with that interpretive statement cite *Metalclad* for the idea it coined.

Finally, tribunals may inadvertently cite "bad" precedent. Given the absence of binding precedent, each prior case carries a priori the same value. It is then for a tribunal to distinguish, reject, or follow the cases cited by litigants and, if it so desires, to invoke precedents of its own. In navigating the ensuing maze of case law, a tribunal may simply not pay sufficient attention to treaty design differences. Or it may overlook that a cited case has been voided or may not be aware of the criticism it attracted. In its nondisputing submission in the *Loewen v. US* case, Mexico, for example, complained "that the CME [v. Czech Republic] award cites Metalclad Corporation v. United Mexican States with approval at paragraph 606, apparently unaware of the fact that the Tribunal's findings regarding Article 1105 were set aside by the Supreme Court of British Columbia."[97] The CME tribunal may simply not have known better. Even in domestic law like the United States, where the Supreme Court sends strong signals when it reverses previous lines of interpretation, citation analysis has shown that it often takes years before a new authoritative precedent completely replaces an old one in practice.[98] Given the flat hierarchies, fragmented nature, and high activity rates of ISDS, the signal-to-noise ratio makes it considerably more difficult for ISDS tribunals to vet precedent candidates in depth. The absence of controls and the lack of information about a precedent's treatment make it challenging to control the use of precedent.

D. Self-Reinforcement of Precedent

The resilience of precedent to control mechanisms explains why precedents rarely disappear. The law of self-reinforcement helps to understand why precedent can exert even more normative pull than state interventions and innovations of treaty design. A branch of economic thought, known as historical institutionalism, has long investigated why certain institutional designs survive and thrive—even in the face of contestation and superior alternatives.[99] Their key insight is that "*when* things happen within a sequence affects *how* they happen."[100] Because they came early, arbitral awards like *Maffezini* have served as "focal points" that scholars and tribunals refer to and they continue to frame

---

[97] Second Submission Mexico in *Loewen Group, Inc. and Raymond L. Loewen v. United States of America*, ICSID Case No. ARB(AF)/98/3, November 9, 2001, at 4.

[98] James H. Fowler & Sangick Jeon, *The Authority of Supreme Court Precedent*, 30 SOC. NETWORKS 16–30, 26 (2008).

[99] Douglass Cecil North, *Institutions*, 5 J. ECON. PERSP. 97–112 (1991).

[100] James Mahoney, *Path Dependence in Historical Sociology*, 29 THEORY & SOC'Y 507–548, 511 (2000).

current investment law debates.[101] States seeking to change the interpretation of IIA provisions thus face an uphill battle: they have to displace not only awards but also the entrenched meaning these precedents embody.

Historical institutionalists study why institutions, once entrenched, are so difficult to displace even when ostensibly superior alternatives are available.[102] The classic example is the "QWERTY" keyboard.[103] It emerged in the 1870s as one of several possible technical solutions to the jamming of typewriters' typebars. By the 1890s it had become an industry benchmark. Other keyboard designs, however, allow for much faster typing. Yet QWERTY still dominates today's keyboards even though its technical justifications have long disappeared and alternative superior designs are available.

Historical institutionalists point to four self-reinforcing dynamics to explain how inefficient designs like QWERTY remain entrenched and outcompete later efficient alternatives, which provide important insights into why precedent sticks in ISDS.[104] First, sunk costs, such as irretrievable investment in a particular design (e.g., machinery producing QWERTY typewriters) make it costly to switch from one design to another. Second, learning effects make the use of a particular design more efficient over time (as more typists were trained on QWERTY, the design became more valuable). Third, coordination effects further entrench a design through standardization producing economies of scale (e.g., the typewriter industry aligned training and production with QWERTY). Fourth, adaptive expectations lead to further concentration as actors recast their beliefs around a design (e.g., QWERTY is how keyboards "are supposed to be" laid out). In combination, these factors create a self-reinforcing dynamic that further entrenches a design and makes it progressively more costly to switch—even if alternatives are otherwise available and more efficient.

Historical institutionalists thus argue, in essence, that today's actions are constraint by yesterday's events. The self-reinforcing forces that "lock in" an initial design produce path dependency.[105] For example, because of events in the 1870s, these pages are being laboriously typed on a QWERTY keyboard. As a result of path dependency, the initial conditions and, more broadly, timing matters. Since self-reinforcing dynamics operate irrespective of intrinsic design qualities, being "early" becomes more important than being "better." But initial conditions

---

[101] BENTOLILA, *supra* note 68, at 234–235. Bentolila refers to those focal points as *topoi* that guide legal. The term focal point was coined by SCHELLING, *supra* note 1.

[102] Paul Pierson & Theda Skocpol, *Historical Institutionalism in Contemporary Political Science, in* POLITICAL SCIENCE: STATE OF THE DISCIPLINE 693–721 (I. Katznelson & H. V. Milner eds., 2002).

[103] Paul A. David, *Clio and the Economics of QWERTY*, 75 AM. ECON. REV. 332–337 (1985).

[104] Based on Brian W. Arthur, *Self-reinforcing Mechanisms in Economics, in* THE ECONOMY AS AN EVOLVING COMPLEX SYSTEM (Philip W. Anderson ed., 1988).

[105] Mahoney, *supra* note 103, at 511.

often emerge by accident.[106] For example, a lucky mix of trial and error, support by venture capitalists, a partnership with the gun manufacturer Remington, and the timely, parallel development of "touch typing" propelled QWERTY into the pole position.[107] Path dependency fueled by self-reinforcement kept it there. In short, historical institutionalists show how a path-dependent process of accidental emergence and subsequent, self-reinforcing entrenchment can make a particular institutional design choice "stick."

This insight holds important lessons for understanding the power of precedent. When ISDS awards began to emerge, states had already concluded thousands of IIAs. The large stock of treaties, which could not be easily amended, terminated, or renegotiated, constituted a sunk cost for states, which favored incremental reforms over the redrafting of new rules from scratch.[108] Moreover, IIAs were themselves a product of path dependency: they were rooted in language first put together by a German banker and an English diplomat, had proliferated through multilateral coordination via the OECD, and had been shaped by adaptation and copying.[109] This large body of treaties with common roots justified in principle that awards rendered under one IIA could inform the interpretation of other IIAs.

Against this institutional backdrop, early awards became influential precedents through a self-reinforcing dynamic. First, awards such as *Metalclad* or *Pope & Talbot* provided an essential coordination function by filling contractual gaps. They created interpretive focal points specifying what vague concepts such as FET could mean and thereby helped shape expectations about the normative content of core investment obligations. Moreover, even subsequent criticism (or partial set-aside in the case of *Metalclad*) further entrenched the coordination function of early awards as these cases become emblematic of a particular interpretive gap-filling approach.[110] That is why, twenty years after *Maffezini v. Spain*, each case or academic article on MFN—whether or not it agrees with the decision—necessarily features a discussion of that early award. In fact, the more an award is contested, the more important becomes its role as a coordinating interpretive focal point. Already in 1956, John Henry Merryman observed that each citation breeds new citations, creating a self-reinforcing logic

---

[106] Paul Pierson, *Increasing Returns, Path Dependence, and the Study of Politics*, 94 AM. POL. SCI. REV. 251, 264 (2000).

[107] David, *supra* note 106.

[108] Wolfgang Alschner, *Locked in Language: Historical Sociology and the Path Dependency of Investment Treaty Design*, in RESEARCH HANDBOOK ON THE SOCIOLOGY OF INTERNATIONAL LAW 347–368 (Moshe Hirsch & Andrew Lang eds., 2018).

[109] *Id.*

[110] *See generally* Cohen, *supra* note 6, at 277 ("As a feature of legal argumentation, once a body with some authority interprets a rule, any future discussion of the rule must take that interpretation into account, even if to argue that it is wrong; further interpretations along the same lines make the burden of dismissing it even harder.").

that entrenches a judicial authority: "[t]his process becomes cumulative; the more frequently [an authority] is cited in judicial opinions, the more frequently it will be cited in subsequent ones."[111]

Second, early awards generated learning effects. In contrast to the impenetrable maze of tens of thousands of IIAs provisions, the gradual accretion of investment awards in the early 2000s provided students and practitioners of the investment regime with an opportunity to learn, in digestible increments, what core provisions might mean and how interpretive gaps could be filled.[112] Early awards also generated extensive academic attention and scrutiny. As the field of investment law grew and university programs and textbooks on the subject emerged, the early cases served as examples and authorities on how to interpret investment provisions. A generation of investment lawyers was trained with cases like *Metalclad*, further reinforcing the central role these early awards played.[113]

Third, these early awards shaped expectations on how investment treaty provisions were to be interpreted going forward—even if they got it wrong (in the eyes of the contracting states). Just like we do not second-guess the merits of QWERTY every time we type on a keyboard, lines of interpretations shaped by early awards turned into unquestioned features of the system. It thus became normal and expected for investors to rely on *Maffezini* to import more favorable treaty provisions or to cite *Pope & Talbot* on the evolution of customary law minimum standard. Early awards not only affected subsequent decisions as precedent; they framed expectations and set the terms of interpretive engagement including for contracting states. As Marc Jacob writes, precedents "lead to path-dependency by organising complex environments and creating argumentative frameworks."[114]

In combination, these factors triggered a self-reinforcing dynamic that "locked in" and entrenched interpretations adopted in early awards. That does not mean that later awards had no influence or that interpretive questions were conclusively resolved by early cases. On the contrary, the

---

[111] John Henry Merryman, *The Authority of Authority: What the California Supreme Court Cited in 1950*, 6 STAN. L. REV. 613, 618 (1954).

[112] BENTOLILA, *supra* note 68, at 235. As she points out, academic "writings identify an impressive number of specific issues that could not be identified before investment arbitration awards. The main methodology followed by these scholars is analysing, approving, criticising, comparing, and drawing common and coherent patterns among cases in order to understand and define international investment law." Differently put, awards to a large extent *constitute* the study and field of investment law.

[113] On the sociological underpinnings of precedent, *see* Harlan Grant Cohen, *Lawyers and Precedent*, 46 VAND. J. TRANSNAT'L L. 1025–1040 (2013). He notes that a "prior decision by a particular legal body is a fact, but how much weight it should be given in future debates over a particular rule is dependent on how it is perceived by the actors reading it." (p. 1034).

[114] Marc Jacob, *Precedents: Lawmaking through International Adjudication Beyond Dispute: International Judicial Institutions as Lawmakers: I. Framing the Issue*, 12 GERMAN L.J. 1005–1032, 1015 (2011).

evolution of ISDS jurisprudence remains dynamic. The point is rather that early awards played an outsized role in shaping the collective understanding of the meaning of investment treaty provisions. These awards triggered a self-reinforcing path dependency as award after award and textbook after textbook and submission after submission engaged with earlier decisions as precedent, which made it progressively more difficult to imagine investment law without them.

Crucially, then, when states began to intervene more heavily in the investment law system through more complete treaties and clarifications of original intent starting in the early 2000s, these interventions occurred against the backdrop of existing arbitral precedent. The fact that states are both contracting parties and respondents in ISDS did not help their cause. Early state interventions were then not perceived as treaty principals asserting original intent vis-à-vis their agents. Rather they were viewed as the self-serving efforts of disgruntled state respondents to opportunistically tilt interpretations in their favor.[115] Academic commentators spoke of "the Empire Strikes Back"[116] or "The Return of the State"[117] to underscore the reactive and corrective nature of states' reform efforts. Others characterized states' attempts of reform as a regression or assault on the international law rule of law, further delegitimizing their efforts.[118] In short, with early arbitral interpretations entrenched as sticky precedent, states' intervention in ISDS faced an uphill battle from the start.

IV. Breaking the Path

The question then arises how states can win that uphill battle and break the force of precedent and path dependency in order to produce change not only on paper but also in practice. Since precedent has become a systemic force, a natural place to look for answers on how to deal with it is systems research.

Donella Meadows, the intellectual mother of complex systems research, distinguishes between two types of interventions in a system that differ in their

---

[115] Cohen, *supra* note 6, at 283.

[116] Charles H. II Brower, *Investor-State Disputes under NAFTA: The Empire Strikes Back*, 40 COLUM. J. TRANSNAT'L L. 43 (2001).

[117] José E. Alvarez, *The Return of the State*, 20 MINN. J. INT'L L. 223 (2011).

[118] Charles H. Brower II, *Why the FTC Notes of Interpretation Constitute a Partial Amendment of NAFTA Article 1105*, 46 VA. J. INT'L L. 347 (2005); Stephen M. Schwebel, *The United States 2004 Model Bilateral Investment Treaty: An Exercise in the Regressive Development of International Law*, *in* JUSTICE IN INTERNATIONAL LAW (2011).

effectiveness for producing change: negative and positive feedback loops.[119] Negative feedback loops are reactive in nature. They are responses to keep the system in check when it is heading in a wrong direction. Like a thermostat, they turn up the heat when the room gets too hot. Positive feedback loops, in contrast, are proactive and self-reinforcing in nature. They deepen and further entrench change in given system. Climate change has become a positive feedback loop, whereby warmer climate disrupts processes that otherwise absorb CO_2, leading to an even warmer climate. Although negative feedback loops can help counterbalance positive ones, the latter's self-reinforcing tendencies mean that corrective interventions face an uphill battle and can easily be overpowered. Thermostats provide no relief against climate change.

The difference between positive and negative feedback loops helps explain why state-driven change has failed to dislodge precedents. States' interventions have been perceived as reactive and corrective. They work as negative feedback loops. Early awards, instead, have created positive feedback loop dynamics. The scholars and awards that continuously cite them entrench these awards further and make these precedents stick even in the face of state-driven change. Precedent not state-driven change is the default gap-filler in today's investment regime. The asymmetry between positive and negative feedback loops and between entrenched precedent and corrective states' interventions, then, is a main reason why prior case law exerts more normative pull than state-driven change. When existing precedent trumps corrective interventions new treaties are read like old ones in a path-dependent manner. Discouragingly, more corrective measures are unlikely to reverse that trend.

According to Meadows, however, there are other interventions in a system that are even more powerful than positive feedback loops, and states could make use of them to force an interpretive reset. States can change the "goals" or "paradigms" of the systems.[120] For example, by replacing ad hoc arbitrators with commercial arbitration background with a standing tribunal staffed with public international lawyers, states would likely change the self-perception of adjudicators and trigger an interpretive reset.

Aside from such major structural overhauls, however, Meadows also notes more subtle changes to the "rules of the game" whereby states could work within existing structures, but change incentives, punishments, and constraints to counter systemic self-reinforcement tendencies.[121] Applied to ISDS, states should thus police precedent directly.

---

[119] DONELLA MEADOWS, THINKING IN SYSTEMS: A PRIMER 153–156 (Diana Wright ed., illustrated ed. 2008). I am grateful to Anthea Roberts for pointing me to this research and to complexity theory generally.

[120] *Id.* at 161.

[121] *Id.* at 158.

A. Policing Precedent through Annulment
and Set-Aside

Within the current ISDS architecture, annulment and set-aside proceedings are the most potent correctors. The threat of voiding awards can impact the behavior of tribunals that want their decisions to survive review. States can therefore use annulment and set-aside proceedings more purposefully not only to police the retrospective correctness of the arbitration—voiding an award between the disputants for procedural shortcomings—but also its prospective correctness—voiding the precedential value of an award for future litigation. This can be done in two ways.

First, states need to assert more forcefully that relying on an annulled award is impermissible for an arbitral tribunal. Annulment negates an award's "legal force [. . .] returning the parties, as to that portion, to their original litigating positions."[122] For all intents and purposes, a voided award is erased in the eyes of the law. And for good reason. It would be shocking for any system of law if a judicial decision that suffers from one of the grave improprieties that make up the narrow grounds for annulment and set-aside such as corruption, a serious departure from a fundamental rule of procedure or a manifest excess of power, continues to taint the future development of law as precedent. Indeed, awards like *Gold Reserve* that decide that a voided passage can "be applied to the present case" arguably compound the original impropriety. Citing voided precedent could therefore by itself amount to annullable abuse of power. States could thus go after awards that cite voided passages and seek their set-aside or annulment in turn.

In a similar vein, annulment and set-aside requests could be used more forcefully to police the overreliance on precedent. Bolivia tested this strategy in *Quiborax v. Bolivia* when it applied for the annulment among others on the grounds that the tribunal had manifestly exceeded its powers by "giving precedence to incorrect and inapplicable decisions by international tribunals over the clear text of the treaty."[123] The annulment committee ultimately upheld the award without engaging in an in-depth discussion on precedent. Other annulment decisions, however, provide a road map for more successful challenges. In the *Enron v. Argentina* annulment proceedings, for example, the ad hoc committee found that "the Tribunal did not in fact apply . . . customary international law as reflected in that provision [Article 25(2)(b) of the ILC Articles on necessity] but instead applied an expert opinion on an economic issue."[124] On that

---

[122] Caron, *supra* note 54, at 24.

[123] *Quiborax S.A., Non Metallic Minerals S.A. and Allan Fosk Kaplún v. Plurinational State of Bolivia*, ICSID Case No. ARB/06/2, Decision on Annulment, May 18, 2018, para. 43 (author's translation from Spanish original).

[124] *Enron v. Argentina*, Decision on Annulment, para. 353.

basis, the committee determined that the tribunal had failed to apply the applicable law as a manifest excess of power. It furthermore stated that even if the tribunal "contrary to all appearances" had applied the customary law, the tribunal had failed to state reasons.[125] The same rationale can be applied to the awards that rely exclusively on previous awards instead of an independent assessment of state practice and *opinio juris* to determine the minimum standard of treatment. In the previously discussed *Railroad Development* award, for instance, the tribunal had stated explicitly that it "*adopts* the *Waste Management II* articulation of the minimum standard for purposes of this case."[126] The tribunal was thus applying a previous case rather than applying the applicable law, which, in turn, constitutes a ground for set-aside or annulment.

Granted that in the past most annulment committees and domestic courts have interpreted their mandate restrictively. More intrusive corrective interventions by courts and ad hoc committees attracted severe academic criticism for muddying the waters between annulment and appeal.[127] There is thus a likelihood that annulment requests aimed at policing precedent are rebuffed. At the same time, the mere threat of annulment or set-aside may prove enough to change the rules of the game by creating awareness among tribunals on the problematic use of (zombie) precedent and by deterring such practice in the future. Annulment or set-aside could thus incentivize tribunals to be more selective when it comes to their reliance on precedent.

B. Shepardizing Precedent

A more subtle way to reduce the stickiness of precedent and to push tribunals toward being more selective in their reliance on prior awards consists of "shepardizing" precedents. As Niccolò Ridi notes, "international law knows neither Shepard's Citations nor Westlaw: there are [. . .] no widely accepted tools and schemata to discover whether a case has been endorsed, distinguished, or 'overruled', so to speak, by subsequent adjudicators."[128] States, litigants, and tribunals lack basic analytics to tell them how a precedent has fared in the past. This is particularly problematic for a system like ISDS that is characterized by state-driven change where states routinely react to prior decisions. To be more

---

[125] *Id.*, para. 378.

[126] *RDC v. Guatemala*, para. 219 (emphasis added).

[127] For a review and critique of review decisions that approached their mandate expansively, *see* W. Michael Reisman, *The Breakdown of the Control Mechanism in ICSID Arbitration*, 1989 DUKE L.J. 739 (1989); Christoph Schreuer, *From ICSID Annulment to Appeal Half Way Down the Slippery Slope*, 10 L. & PRAC. OF INT'L COURTS & TRIBUNALS 211–225 (2011).

[128] Niccolò Ridi, *The Shape and Structure of the "Usable Past": An Empirical Analysis of the Use of Precedent in International Adjudication*, 10 J. INT'L DISP. SETTLEMENT 200–247, 201 (2019).

selective about their choice of appropriate precedent, tribunals and litigants need a "shepardization" of precedents in two forms.

First, tribunals and litigants need better knowledge of treaty design differences to understand whether they, if they reason on precedent, are comparing apples to apples or apples to oranges. Treaty design differences make otherwise like cases unlike. Treaties may differ in the words they use, which leads to interpretational differences that affect the persuasiveness of a precedent. Even where the same words are used, a different treaty structures can change the interpretive context in ways that shift the meaning of otherwise similar terms.[129] Condon, for example, found that different treaty structures under trade and investment rules change how adjudicators apply similar language.[130] Finally, differences in two treaties' object and purpose can affect interpretation under IIAs, too. Pauwelyn and DiMascio suggest that identical language under trade law and under investment law ought to be read very differently given that both fields pursue very different goals.[131]

Since differences in treaty design can result in differences in interpretation, different treaty designs also render different precedents more or less persuasive. In *Glamis v. United States*, for instance, the tribunal had to decide what types of arbitral awards it should consider in giving meaning to the NAFTA minimum standard of treatment contained in Article 1105. The tribunal rejected the investor's argument that it should seek guidance from arbitral awards rendered under BITs that contain an autonomous FET standard.[132] The tribunal concluded "that it may look solely to arbitral awards—including BIT awards—that seek to be understood by reference to the customary international law minimum standard of treatment, as opposed to any autonomous standard."[133]

Similarly, the *Kilic v. Turkmenistan* tribunal rejected a range of precedents cited by the claiming investors on the grounds that these cases "were concerned with different—and differently worded—provisions of other BITs. They cannot therefore be dispositive."[134] These tribunals sought to ensure, in essence, that like cases are treated alike.[135] They considered that cases cited by the claimants lacked persuasive authority because they differed in their underlying wording from the treaty at hand. This type of analysis should become standard practice and can

---

[129] Condon, *supra* note 15, at 342 ("The structure of a treaty is part of the context.").

[130] *Id.*

[131] DiMascio & Pauwelyn, *supra* note 27.

[132] *Glamis Gold, Ltd. v. The United States of America*, UNCITRAL, Final Award, June 8, 2009, para. 609.

[133] *Id.* para. 611.

[134] *Kilic Insaat Ithalat Ihracat Sanayi ve Ticaret Anonim Sirketi v. Turkmenistan*, ICSID Case No. ARB/10/1, Award, July 2, 2013, para. 7.1.3.

[135] For another example of a tribunal recognizing design differences, *see, e.g., Canadian Cattlemen for Fair Trade v. United States of America*, UNCITRAL, Award on Jurisdiction, January 28, 2008, paras. 212–215.

be scaled by systematically collecting information on treaty design differences, as done in Chapter 1 and further explained in Chapter 8. A routine scrutiny of awards based on the similarities of underlying treaties would make it easier to evaluate the appropriateness of a precedent to compare apples to apples.

Second, tribunals require better tracking of the lifecycle of an award. Has a decision been annulled or set aside? Have contracting parties issued a subsequent authoritative interpretation at odds with the award's reasoning? Have states intervened in subsequent disputes or in other forms to criticize the reasoning of the award? These types of information are vital for tribunals to assess the validity of the award and its quality in the eyes of the contracting states as masters of their treaties. It would also be helpful if tribunals could easily track how states react to arbitral interpretations in subsequent treaty making and to monitor how other tribunals perceive the quality of an award. In contrast to information on prior annulment or set-aside, these latter insights may not be dispositive for accepting or rejecting a prior case as precedent, but they make the selection of precedent more purposeful and informed.

Arbitrator Cremades once cautioned that "[t]he integrity of this interpretative process [under the Vienna Convention on the Law of Treaties] must not be compromised by the pronouncements of other arbitral tribunals in their interpretation of different treaties in wholly unrelated factual and legal contexts."[136] Unfortunately, this is exactly what is happening when new treaties are read in light of old case law. The lack of awareness of treaty differences coupled with a liberal acceptance of prior case law rendered on fundamentally different treaties risks overriding state-driven change. Shepardizing of precedent could assist states and litigants in better monitoring the use of precedent and could enable tribunals to be more informed and selective on precedent. This would break the interpretive path where it needs to be broken, ensure, as scholar and arbitrator Georgio Sacerdoti put it, that tribunals are "free from 'intellectual subordination' to previous decisions,"[137] and preserve state-driven change.

V. Conclusion

Relying on the wisdom of prior cases is common practice across legal systems and for good reason. Following precedent creates virtuous consequences from efficiency to enhanced predictability, stability, and consistency. But reasoning on

---

[136] *Fraport AG Frankfurt Airport Services Worldwide v. Republic of the Philippines*, ICSID Case No. ARB/03/25, Dissenting Opinion of Mr. Bernardo M. Cremades, August 16, 2007, para. 7.5.

[137] Giorgio Sacerdoti, *Precedent in the Settlement of International Economic Disputes: The WTO and Investment Arbitration Models, in* CONTEMPORARY ISSUES IN INTERNATIONAL ARBITRATION AND MEDIATION: THE FORDHAM PAPERS (2010) 225–246, 241 (Arthur Rovine ed., 2011).

precedent turns from virtue to vice when systems are characterized by a rapid normative evolution. By rooting the interpretation of new treaties in old case law, tribunals produce consistency where states seek change. To preserve state-driven change, tribunals need to be more selective what precedent to follow. States can win the uphill battle against sticky precedents by changing the rules of the game. Instead of focusing on substantive corrections alone, they need to police precedent directly by leveraging set-aside and annulment proceedings and by promoting a shepardization of awards and thus changing the role of precedent in ISDS. Ultimately, however, the best way to break interpretive path dependency is through an interpretive reset. Rather than forcing this reset only for new IIAs, states should aim for change across the board by reforming old treaties in light of new ones. Part III explains how this can be done.

PART III

NEW TREATIES AS ANCHOR POINTS

7
Forward-Looking Interpretation

I. Introduction

The preceding chapters showed how tribunals have rolled back state-driven change. The coexistence of old and new treaties ultimately enabled this practice. Incomplete IIAs supply the interpretive arguments via MFN, custom, and precedent that justify reading new treaties in light of old ones. Part III shows how to preserve and amplify the impact state-driven change by doing the reverse: reforming old treaties through new ones. Chapter 7 explores how states and tribunals can leverage clarifications in new, more complete treaties to fill interpretive gaps in older, incomplete treaties. Chapter 8 explains how states can go further and modify old IIAs in light of new treaties through data-driven renegotiations. Finally, Chapter 9 discusses how such interpretations and modifications can be multilateralized by modeling investment law reform on the international tax regime.

In today's investment regime, IIAs are interpreted through other IIAs all the time. This cross-IIA interpretation, however, is predominantly backward-looking and adjudicator-driven. Old treaties produce interpretive externalities through precedent that affect new agreements and tribunals generate systemic interpretations that connect dissimilar treaties (see Chapter 6). Precedent and not state-driven change is the default interpretive gap-filler. This chapter argues that cross-IIA interpretations can and should be forward-looking and state-led instead. New treaties can generate interpretive externalities that modernize old IIAs and fuel systemic interpretations informed by treaty practice rather than arbitral practice. Today's and tomorrow's state-driven change should become the default gap-filler.

Forward-looking and state-led interpretations have a bad reputation in some corners. States' efforts to clarify old agreements have been characterized as quasi-amendments aimed to free respondents from earlier commitments.[1] Similarly, the more precise language in new IIAs has been perceived as watering down

---

[1] Charles H. Brower II, *Investor-State Disputes under NAFTA: The Empire Strikes Back*, 40 COLUM. J. TRANSNAT'L L. 43 (2001); Charles H. Brower II, *Why the FTC Notes of Interpretation Constitute a Partial Amendment of NAFTA Article 1105*, 46 VA. J. INT'L L. 347 (2005).

Investment Arbitration and State-Driven Reform. Wolfgang Alschner, Oxford University Press. © Oxford University Press 2022. DOI: 10.1093/oso/9780197644386.003.0008

protections rather than clarifying them.[2] Finally, some scholars have questioned whether the rules on treaty interpretation even allow interpreters to read IIAs in light of third IIAs.[3] On balance, however, interpretive gap-filling is best understood as a gentle and modest tool to update outdated treaties.

Interpretive gap-filling is modest because it is necessarily bounded by the rules on treaty interpretation, which tribunals can police. These rules provide distinct pathways to update older agreements, either through subsequent agreements or practice that explicitly relate to the treaty in question or through overlapping IIAs that are applicable between the same parties or third IIAs that may implicitly shed light on the ordinary meaning of treaty terms. In these circumstances, interpretive gap-filling can import clarifications from subsequent, more complete treaties or practice to update vague terms of art such as "investment," "expropriation," "national treatment," or "fair and equitable treatment" that were left undefined in incomplete treaties. In contrast, these pathways do not allow incorporating wholly new treaty clauses, such as general exceptions, through interpretation. The risk for abusing interpretive gap-filling therefore remains low.

At the same time, interpretive gap-filling promises to gently update outdated treaties. In the tax regime, older bilateral treaties are routinely interpreted based on more recent treaty practice to close loopholes that facilitate treaty abuse, to clarify language to prevent misinterpretations, and to align law with evolving businesses practices (see Chapter 9). The same logic motivates the forward-looking interpretation of investment agreements. Initially, vague investment treaty clauses have been clarified over time in a path-dependent manner to curb treaty abuse, explain original intent, and respond to new developments. Some scholars claim that recent agreements are "designed to divorce interpretation from past experience with other IIAs."[4] But the opposite is true. States have explicitly designed more complete IIAs to inform the reading of earlier treaties. In the words of the United States, clarifications "for greater certainty," for example, "serve to spell out more explicitly the proper interpretation of similar provisions in *other agreements*."[5] State-driven change is meant to update old and new treaties alike.

Interpreters can draw from contract theory, introduced in Chapter 2, to guide the interpretive gap-filling of investment agreements. Interpreters need to approach

---

[2] José E. Alvarez, *The Return of the State*, 20 MINN. J. INT'L L. 223 (2011); Stephen M. Schwebel, *The United States 2004 Model Bilateral Investment Treaty: An Exercise in the Regressive Development of International Law*, *in* JUSTICE IN INTERNATIONAL LAW (2011).

[3] Andrew D. Mitchell & James Munro, *Someone Else's Deal: Interpreting International Investment Agreements in the Light of Third-Party Agreements*, 28 EUR. J. INT'L L. 669–695 (2017).

[4] *Id.* at 674. If anything, new treaties may be divorced from past arbitral interpretations.

[5] United States of America Third Non-Disputing Party Submission, *Omega Engineering LLC and Oscar Rivera v. Republic of Panama*, ICSID Case No. ARB/16/42, February 3, 2020, footnote 24 (emphasis added).

treaties with varying levels of completeness differently. When states incur the extra transaction costs of writing more precise rules, they fill gaps ex ante to limit the role of delegated gap-filling ex post. When confronted with highly complete treaties, adjudicators should therefore interpret the treaties as written and refrain from judicial gap-filling. In contrast, when states decide to leave contractual gaps open in highly incomplete treaties, they necessarily delegate gap-filling authority to adjudicators. Moreover, since recent, more complete investment agreements provide the best guess of how contracting states would have wanted to resolve contractual incompleteness, contract theory suggests that adjudicators should use their greater discretion to fill gaps in incomplete treaties in light of how states have closed corresponding gaps in recent, more complete treaties. Contract theory thereby offers a systemic approach for modernizing old IIAs via interpretation.

This chapter is structured as follows. Section II presents the theoretical foundations for using contract theory to structure interpretive discretion. Section III then shows how the Vienna Convention on the Law of Treaties (VCLT) constrains and enables the gap-filling of incomplete treaties in light of more complete ones.

II. Contract Theory and Interpretation

Like much of law and economics, contract theory is ultimately concerned with the reduction of transaction costs. It places the contractors in their drive toward efficiency center stage and assumes that they know their own preferences best.[6] Applied to the interpretation of investment treaties, contract theory yields three important insights. First, it suggests that adjudicators are best understood as agents rather than trustees when it comes to interpretation, which shifts attention to the contractors and their contracting choices. Second, contract theory links treaty interpretation to levels of contractual completeness. Third, contract theory provides explicit strategies on how adjudicators should fill gaps in incomplete treaties.

A. Arbitral Tribunals as the Interpretive Agents of the Contracting Parties

Most IIAs delegate authority over the settlement of investment disputes between host states and investors to arbitration tribunals.[7] Political scientists distinguish between two ideal types to describe the nature of such delegation: principals can

---

[6] Eric A. Posner, *Economic Analysis of Contract Law after Three Decades: Success or Failure*, 112 YALE L.J. 829, 834 (2002).

[7] Todd Allee & Clint Peinhardt, *Delegating Differences: Bilateral Investment Treaties and Bargaining Over Dispute Resolution Provisions*, 54 INT'L STUD. Q. 1–26 (2010).

delegate authority to *agents* that act in the interests of their delegators and are kept on a short leash, or they can confer power to *trustees* that enjoy independence from their delegators and often act in the interest of a wider community.[8] The two ideal types approach treaty interpretation differently. Whereas agents seek to narrowly advance an interpretation that benefits the contracting parties, trustees tend to consider interpretations that advance broader community values.[9]

In practice, this distinction matters greatly and ultimately explains much of the (lacking) impact of state-driven change. If tribunals perceive themselves as trustees of a broader investment law community, their independent lawmaking is vital for preserving community values. States' efforts to rewrite the terms of delegation through more complete IIAs are then rightly seen as illegitimate efforts to turn independent servants of the community into the serfs of the contracting states. If tribunals perceive themselves as the agents of the disputing parties to an arbitration (investor and home state), then the ongoing arbitral backlash against state-driven change can be similarly rationalized as legitimate efforts of neutral arbitrators to protect the equality of arms against respondents' attempts to tilt the field in their favor. Finally, if tribunals perceive themselves as faithful agents of the contracting states, there is little reason to resist state-driven change, and tribunals may even help propagate treaty design innovation to advance the legislative goals of the contracting states. This section argues that the third characterization best fits the structure of delegation under IIAs.

Are ISDS tribunals trustees or agents? On the one hand, ISDS tribunals fit the characteristics Karen Alter has ascribed to trustees. Arbitrators (1) are selected based on "personal reputation or professional norms," (2) enjoy "independent authority," and (3) act on behalf of a "beneficiary" (i.e., the investor).[10] On the other hand, as Anne van Aaken has pointed out, contracting parties guard against what is known in principal-agent theory as "agency slack," that is, unintended use of delegated power through several means of control such as authoritative interpretation and recontracting, which would suggest that tribunals are not as independent as trustees and closer to being agents.[11] In general, however, scholars have been reluctant to place ISDS tribunals in either category.[12]

---

[8] Karen J. Alter, *Agents or Trustees? International Courts in Their Political Context*, 14 EUR. J. INT'L REL. 33–63 (2008).

[9] That is why, according to Alec Stone-Sweet, constitutional courts are trustee courts. *See* Alec Sweet, *Investor-State Arbitration: Proportionality's New Frontier*, 4 L. & ETHICS OF HUM. RTS. 48–76 (2010). *See also* Harlan Cohen, *International Law's Erie Moment*, 34 MICH. J. INT'L L. 249–308, 281 (2013).

[10] Alter, *supra* note 8, at 35; Anne van Aaken, *Delegating Interpretative Authority in Investment Treaties: The Case of Joint Commissions*, 11 TRANSNAT'L DISP. MGMT. 10–11 (2014).

[11] Aaken, *supra* note 10, at 10.

[12] Dependence of arbitrators on ad hoc appointment and their frequent reference to "intentions of the parties" or "party autonomy" suggest agents, whereas (early) judicial activism and individual right-based interpretation point to trustees. Joost Pauwelyn & Manfred Elsig, *The Politics of Treaty*

But rather than being neither fish nor fowl, ISDS tribunals could be trustees and agents at the same time, yet with respect to different functions. As Anthea Roberts suggests:

> It is possible that a tribunal might be more trusteelike with respect to some functions (such as resolving certain kinds of disputes) and more agentlike with respect to others (such as law creation), to the extent that such separation is possible. . . . Accordingly, investment tribunals resemble trustees when resolving investor-state disputes, but they sit between agency and trusteeship when interpreting and developing the law because they share their interpretive authority with the treaty parties.[13]

Of course, in the ordinary resolution of a dispute, interpretive and adjudicatory functions are often intertwined—a tribunal will inevitably need to give meaning to the terms of a treaty before it can apply the law to the facts of the case.[14] Nevertheless, adjudication and interpretation involve processes that are legally and conceptually distinct.[15]

First, ISDS tribunals have two sets of principals that differ depending on whether questions of adjudication or interpretation are concerned. As Roberts puts it, tribunals "simultaneously act on behalf of the treaty parties in interpreting and developing investment treaty law and on behalf of the disputing parties in arbitrating investor-state disputes."[16] The terms of delegation can thus reasonably differ depending on whether tribunals interpret a treaty on behalf of the contracting parties or solve a dispute on the behest of the disputants.

Second, IIAs delegate interpretive and adjudicatory authority in different terms. While the adjudicatory mandate of arbitral tribunals is explicit, the interpretive authority is only the result of an implied power.[17] In contrast to

---

Interpretation: Variations and Explanations Across International Tribunals, in INTERDISCIPLINARY PERSPECTIVES ON INTERNATIONAL LAW AND INTERNATIONAL RELATIONS: THE STATE OF THE ART 445–473, 452, 455, 458, 466, & 463 (Jeffrey L. Dunoff & Mark A. Pollack eds., 2013).

[13] Anthea Roberts, *Power and Persuasion in Investment Treaty Interpretation*, 104 AM. J. INT'L L. 179–225, 188 (2010).

[14] Aaken, *supra* note 10, at 18 ("Interpretation of treaties with their legal and factual aspects are usually outsourced to courts and tribunals . . . [because] facts and norms are often hard to separate.")

[15] Adjudication is a fact and case-specific means of providing a binding resolution to a dispute. This can even take place *ex aequo et bono* without the need to having recourse to interpretation. In contrast, interpretation is an abstract and general means of clarifying treaty terms. It can take place even in the absence of facts, e.g., when states ask for an advisory opinion or an authoritative interpretation. Hence, in a dispute, the application and the interpretation of a legal norm are two distinct exercises and can thus be governed by two different delegation mandates. *See* Anastasios Gourgourinis, *The Distinction between Interpretation and Application of Norms in International Adjudication*, 2 J. INT'L DISP. SETTLEMENT 31–57 (2011).

[16] Roberts, *supra* note 13, at 180.

[17] *Id.* at 189.

state-to-state arbitration clauses that specifically include disputes over "the interpretation or application" of the treaty,[18] investor-state arbitration clauses are limited to "disputes," be it "in connection with an investment,"[19] "relating to investments,"[20] or "concerning investments."[21] Abstract interpretive disputes are consistently and exclusively reserved for state-to-state dispute settlement.[22] The interpretive mandate of ISDS tribunals is thus merely ancillary.

Third, contracting states differ in the ex post controls they enjoy over ISDS tribunals in interpretation and adjudication. As "masters of their treaties,"[23] contracting states can issue authoritative interpretation under international law with retrospective effect.[24] They can do so in ongoing disputes, because covered investors are not entitled to a specific reading of a treaty.[25] Investors are, however, entitled to rely on the terms of the treaty as they stood at the time the arbitration agreement was perfected. That is because the arbitration agreement is "autonomous," that is, it exists independently of the treaty.[26] Any efforts by the contracting states to amend the substantive or procedural protection of the treaty can only apply prospectively and leave pending arbitration unaffected.[27]

The principle of party autonomy also insulates the arbitration agreement from other ex post interventions by the contracting states. Prior to the proliferation of ISDS claims, it was not uncommon for states to settle investment disputes through lump-sum agreements.[28] As a result of such an inter-state deal, the injured investors would ordinarily receive some indemnification for their losses but arguably much less than what an ISDS tribunal would have awarded. The delegation to arbitral tribunal has altered the capacity of states to settle claims over the heads of their investors.

---

[18] Germany–Bahrain BIT (2007), art. 10(1), France–Moldova BIT (1997), art. 10(1).

[19] Hungary–Russia BIT (1995), art. 8.

[20] *See, e.g.*, France–Moldova BIT (1997), art. 7.

[21] *See, e.g.*, Germany–Bahrain BIT (2007), art. 11(1). A minority of treaties is more specific and covers disputes arising out of an investment treaty, contract, or investment authorization. *See, e.g.*, USA–Uruguay BIT (2005), art. 7.

[22] *Republic of Ecuador v. United States of America*, PCA Case No. 2012-5, Expert Opinion of Prof. Christian Tomuschat, (August 24, 2012), at 11 ("the BIT itself must be the foundation of the dispute.").

[23] UNCTAD, *Interpretation of IIAs: What States Can Do*, UNCTAD IIA ISSUE NOTE, 15 (2011).

[24] Roberts, *supra* note 13, at 210.

[25] C. J. Trevino, *State-to-State Investment Treaty Arbitration and the Interplay with Investor-State Arbitration Under the Same Treaty*, 5 J. INT'L DISP. SETTLEMENT 199–233, 224 (2014).

[26] ZACHARY DOUGLAS, THE INTERNATIONAL LAW OF INVESTMENT CLAIMS 115 (2009).

[27] Roberts, *supra* note 13, at 210. Retroactive changes of the law by the contracting states would be at odds with fundamental rights of procedural fairness such as equality of arms and due process, which the arbitration agreement protects. Gabrielle Kaufmann-Kohler, *Interpretive Powers of the Free Trade Commission and the Rule of Law*, FIFTEEN YEARS OF NAFTA 175–194, 190–194 (2011).

[28] Jonathan Gimblett & O. Thomas Johnson, Jr., *From Gunboats to BITs: The Evolution of Modern International Investment Law*, in YEARBOOK ON INTERNATIONAL INVESTMENT LAW & POLICY VOL. 2010–2011 (Karl P. Sauvant ed., 2011).

The 2006 Softwood Lumber Agreement, which resolved a long-standing dispute between the United States and Canada about their bilateral lumber trade, illustrates the point. The Softwood Lumber Agreement contained a Termination of Litigation Agreement, which settled over eighteen national, NAFTA, and WTO proceedings—and three ongoing NAFTA Chapter 11 arbitrations.[29] The United States, as the respondent, negotiated with each of the three claiming Canadian investors Canfor, Terminal Forest Products, and Tembec, who agreed to terminate the litigation. The fact that the United States did not seek to "negotiate away" the Chapter 11 disputes in bilateral talks with Canada suggests that the contracting parties cannot simply abrogate an ongoing arbitration.[30] Contracting states thus enjoy significant ex post control on interpretation, but not on adjudication.

Fourth, this functional differentiation corresponds to two different rationales for delegation that scholars have identified. On the one hand, states delegate interpretive tasks to tribunals to realize efficiency gains: tribunals fill interpretive gaps ex post in order to save drafting costs ex ante.[31] On the other hand, delegation on adjudication occurs for credibility reasons: tribunals independently police compliance with treaty commitments.[32] According to Giandomenico Majone, when principals seek to realize efficiency gains, they primarily delegate to *agents* that can faithfully and more efficiently pursue a given task in the principals' best interests.[33] In contrast, when states want to enhance credibility, they will delegate to fiduciaries or *trustees*. Because trustees enjoy independence from their principals and discretion in the exercise of delegated power, they can credibly and impartially perform a function, which may involve decisions that, at least in the short term, go against the interest of one or all of their principals.[34]

In short, the different sets of principals, the different jurisdictional mandate, the varying ex post controls, and the different underlying policy problem suggest that delegation to ISDS operates differently depending on whether the

---

[29] Notification of Mutually Agreed Solution, *United States—Reviews of Countervailing Duty on Softwood Lumber from Canada*, WT/DS311/2, November 16, 2006, at Annex 2A. *Canfor Corporation v. United States of America; Terminal Forest Products Ltd. v. United States of America*, UNCITRAL (formerly *Canfor Corporation v. United States of America; Tembec et al. v. United States of America; Terminal Forest Products Ltd. v. United States of America*).

[30] Andrea K. Bjorklund, *Mandatory Rules of Law and Investment Arbitration*, 18 AM. REV. INT'L ARB. 175, 191 (2007).

[31] Aaken, *supra* note 10, at 6.

[32] *Id.* at 6. According to van Aaken, this delegation can take two forms. First, contractors can delegate to technical experts who have specialized knowledge in separating contractual and opportunistic behavior. *Renvoi* clauses referring financial policy or taxation matters raised in arbitration to expert bodies are an example of that delegation in investment law. Second, states can delegate that power to neutral third-party adjudicators.

[33] Giandomenico Majone, *Two Logics of Delegation: Agency and Fiduciary Relations in EU Governance*, 2 EUR. UNION POL. (2001).

[34] *Id.*

interpretation of the treaty or the adjudication of a dispute is at issue. ISDS tribunals are agent-like when it comes to efficiency-driven gap-filling in interpretation and trustee-like when they police treaty compliance in adjudication to make treaty commitments credible. Since investment tribunals seem closer to agents than to trustees when it comes to interpretations, contract theory, which is centered around the interests of the contracting parties, is well suited to inform the interpretation of IIAs in ISDS especially in the context of state-driven change.

B. The Degree of Contractual Completeness Determines Tribunal's Approach to Interpretation

If ISDS tribunals are agents of the contracting states, then how should tribunals interpret IIAs on the behest of their state principals? Contract theorists have an answer to that question. They link interpretation to the design of the contract to be interpreted. In contract theory, the goal of contractual interpretation is efficiency.[35] According to Richard Posner, "[t]he essential tradeoffs in analyzing the interpretation problem [is] the more the parties invest at the first stage [contract negotiation], the lower the expected costs at the second stage [adjudication]."[36] Interpretation ex post is thus intrinsically linked to the contract design ex ante. The more complete a contract, the smaller will be the margin of interpretation or gap-filling enjoyed by courts. Conversely, the more a contract is incomplete, the more freedom adjudicators enjoy in filling its gaps. As Abbot et al. explain:

> The more "rule-like" a normative prescription, the more a community decides *ex ante* which categories of behavior are unacceptable; such decisions are typically made by legislative bodies. The more "standard-like" a prescription, the more a community makes this determination *ex post*, in relation to specific sets of facts; such decisions are usually entrusted to courts.[37]

The completeness of a contract thus determines the interpretive approach taken by tribunals. Applied to ISDS, an interpretive approach inspired by contract theory will distinguish between whether an interpreter encounters a highly complete or a highly incomplete IIA. When arbitral tribunals confront a more complete IIA, they enjoy less discretion to fill contractual gaps ex post, because contracting states went to the length of filling gaps ex ante. In contrast, where

---

[35] Posner, *supra* note 6, at 834.

[36] Richard A. Posner, *The Law and Economics Contract of Interpretation*, John M. Olin Law & Economics Working Paper, No. 229, November 2004, at 5.

[37] Kenneth W. Abbott et al., *The Concept of Legalization*, 54 INT'L ORG. 401–419, 413 (2000).

contracting states left treaties vague and incomplete, tribunals will enjoy greater authority to engage in interpretive gap-filling.[38]

The lesson from contract theory is thus clear when it comes to the interpretation of more complete IIAs: investment tribunals should interpret more complete IIAs formalistically or as written. In contract theory, "the express terms of the contract are presumed to be the best approximations of the parties' intentions."[39] In contract theory, the contractors know best. When parties incur the significant ex ante costs of negotiating detailed contracts, courts are to uphold that choice by following a literal, text-intrinsic interpretation, also known as textualism, literalism, or formalism.[40] Courts, lacking the private information to reliably second-guess the contractors' intentions, should defer to the contractors' explicit choices. Applied to investment law, tribunals should refrain from judicial gap-filling and give effect to the text of more complete IIAs.

But how should interpreters deal with incomplete contracts and treaties? What considerations should guide their interpretive gap-filling? Contract scholars have advanced two alternative efficiency benchmarks that courts can use to render incomplete contracts more complete.

On the one hand, courts can strive for achieving ex ante efficiency by creating default rules.[41] Default rules are standardized terms, often inspired by common business practices or trade usages, that are read into agreements by default to close contractual gaps based on general assumptions about how similarly situated contractors would have efficiently contracted.[42] Such default rules are desirable because they codify collective wisdom into consistently applied gap-filling rules, which, in turn, promote interpretive predictability, lower transaction costs of negotiations ex ante, and allow parties to contract on or out of these well-circumscribed rules if they find it efficient to do so.[43] Ex ante efficiency thus uses *systemic* efficiency as a benchmark and creates judge-made default rules inspired by common practices.

On the other hand, scholars have proposed that courts strive for ex post efficiency.[44] Since a systemic standard is prone to disregard the uniqueness of each contract and relationship, proponents of ex post efficiency argue that courts

---

[38] Pauwelyn & Elsig, *supra* note 12, at 462 ("the more incomplete a treaty is, the bigger the mandate or temptation to fill gaps").

[39] George M. Cohen, *Implied Terms and Interpretation in Contract Law*, 3 *in* ENCYCLOPEDIA OF LAW AND ECONOMICS 78–99, 82 (2000).

[40] *Id.* at 82.; Posner, *supra* note 6, at 840–841; Robert E. Scott, *Case for Formalism in Relational Contract, The*, 94 Nw. U. L. REV. 847, 859 (1999).

[41] Scott, *supra* note 40, at 849–851; on default rules, *see generally* Ian Ayres & Robert Gertner, *Filling Gaps in Incomplete Contracts: An Economic Theory of Default Rules*, 99 YALE L.J. 87–130 (1989).

[42] Scott, *supra* note 40, at 849; Posner, *supra* note 6, at 839.

[43] Posner, *supra* note 6, at 839; Cohen, *supra* note 39, at 83–84; Scott, *supra* note 40, at 850.

[44] Scott, *supra* note 40, at 850; Posner, *supra* note 6, at 840.

should fill gaps with a view to promoting a fair and efficient solution to each case.[45] Courts are then tasked to adjust contractual risk allocation ex post, that is, with the benefit of hindsight in line with what the parties "would have wanted."[46] Ex post efficiency is justified on the basis of the "hypothetical consent" of the contracting parties to have their welfare maximized, and so "courts ought to fill the contractual gap in a way the Pareto-efficient CCC would have prescribed it."[47] Ex post efficiency is thus about using information at the time of adjudication to fill interpretive gaps so as to maximize the welfare in a particular contractual relationship.

These two approaches are emblematic of a broader dilemma in judicial gap-filling between promoting systemic consistency and achieving fairness in individual cases, which also manifests itself in investment law.[48] Some have argued that arbitral tribunals should interpret agreements "BIT-by-BIT" to emphasize the uniqueness of every treaty and every dispute.[49] Others contend that treaties ought to be read through a systemic lens and draw on the converging arbitral precedent, manifested through a *jurisprudence constante*, in order to enhance consistency and predictability across agreements.[50] The BIT-by-BIT proponents focus on ex post efficiency, deciding each case in light of the particular facts and applicable treaty in order to promote fairness for the disputing parties and to maximize the welfare of the contractual relationship; in contrast, the proponent of a *jurisprudence constante* drive for ex ante efficiency, that is, systemic predictability through arbitrator-made default rules.

So which gap-filling strategy is to be preferred? Several contract theorists have rejected the real-life application of *either* approach on the basis that courts are not sophisticated enough to perform the gap-filling exercise efficiently. Eric Posner proposes to work on the assumption "that parties lack the clairvoyance

---

[45] Scott, *supra* note 40, at 850; Posner, *supra* note 6, at 840.

[46] Ayres & Gertner, *supra* note 41, at 90; Scott, *supra* note 40, at 858.

[47] SIMON A. B. SCHROPP, TRADE POLICY FLEXIBILITY AND ENFORCEMENT IN THE WORLD TRADE ORGANIZATION: A LAW AND ECONOMICS ANALYSIS 94 (2009).

[48] Scott describes the dilemma as follows: "the process of incorporating useful defaults often leads to misinterpretation of the express terms of the contract, while seeking predictability in interpretation [i.e. literally enforcing contractual language] undercuts the process of standardization." Scott, *supra* note 40, at 854.

[49] *See, e.g., Renta 4 S.V.S.A, Ahorro Corporación Emergentes F.I., Ahorro Corporación Eurofondo F.I., Rovime Inversiones SICAV S.A., Quasar de Valors SICAV S.A., Orgor de Valores SICAV S.A., GBI 9000 SICAV S.A. v. The Russian Federation*, SCC No. 24/2007, Award on Preliminary Objections, March 20, 2009, para. 94.

[50] *See, e.g., Continental Casualty Company v. Argentina, Decision on Application for Partial Annulment*, ICSID Case No ARB/03/9, September 16, 2011, paras. 83–84. *See also* Gabrielle Kaufmann-Kohler, *Arbitral Precedent Dream, Necessity or Excuse?*, 23 ARB. INT'L 357, 377 (2007); Andrea K. Bjorklund, *Investment Treaty Arbitral Decisions as Jurisprudence Constante, in* INTERNATIONAL ECONOMIC LAW: THE STATE AND FUTURE OF THE DISCIPLINE 7 (Colin Picker, Isabella Bunn, & Douglas Arner eds., 2010); Zachary Douglas, *The MFN Clause in Investment Arbitration: Treaty Interpretation off the Rails*, 2 J. INT'L DISP. SETTLEMENT 97–113 (2011).

needed to give courts the proper guidance if a dispute arises, and courts lack the genius that would be needed to enforce contracts properly in the absence of such guidance."[51] Also, Simon Schropp is skeptical of courts' ability to "concocting a default rule that parties could have crafted themselves (and probably even better)."[52] Courts are unaware of the contractors' preferences to begin with and can thus never produce an outcome that maximizes the contractors' utility in the same way as they themselves could do.[53] That is why these contract theorists have made a case for "formalism" under the assumption that if courts stay passive and interpret contracts strictly literally, it will create incentives for the contractors, who are in a better position than the courts to make welfare-enhancing contractual adjustments, to craft better, more complete contracts over time.[54] According to these scholars, courts should thus not engage in gap-filling either to achieve predictability (*jurisprudence constante*) or fairness (BIT by BIT).

For international investment law, this is not a satisfying response, because the incompleteness of IIAs is asymmetric. While investment protections are explicit, host state flexibilities are implicit.[55] A literal interpretation of IIAs would thus skew the interpretation toward investment protection and undercut host state policy space. At the same time, the argument that adjudicators lack sophistication to achieve ex ante or ex post efficiency carries extra weight in the investment arbitration context. That is not because arbitral tribunals are less apt to perform such a function than domestic courts, but rather that their institutional context makes that task more difficult.

When it comes to ex ante efficiency, ISDS lacks the institutional underpinnings necessary to make a system of universal default rules work. While informal adherence to precedents is widespread in ISDS and the interpretation of early cases can operate like default rules applied to subsequent cases, significant inconsistencies remain.[56] More importantly, default rules are only efficient if contractors can contract out of them if they so desire. But as Chapter 6 of this book has shown in detail, states have been unable to contract out of precedential default rules as new treaties are read in light of old case law. Hence, ex ante efficiency through arbitrator-made default rules is impossible and undesirable in ISDS.

[51] Eric A. Posner, *A Theory of Contract Law under Conditions of Radical Judicial Error*, 94 Nw. U. L. Rev. 749, 754 (1999).

[52] Schropp, *supra* note 47, at 95.

[53] Joel P. Trachtman, The Economic Structure of International Law 146 (2008).

[54] Alan Schwartz, *Relational Contracts in the Courts: An Analysis of Incomplete Agreements and Judicial Strategies*, 21 J. Legal Stud. 271–318 (1992); Scott, *supra* note 40; Posner, *supra* note 51.

[55] *See* Jorge E. Vinuales, *Customary Law in Investment Regulation Symposium: International Investment Regulation: Trends and Challenges*, 23 Italian Y.B. Int'l L. 23–48 (2013) (arguing that treaties tend to explicitly regulate investment protection whereas sovereignty is only protected indirectly, e.g., through customary law).

[56] For examples of inconsistencies, *see* Gabrielle Kaufmann-Kohler, *Is Consistency a Myth?*, *in* Precedent in International Arbitration 137 (Emmanuel Gaillard & Yas Banifatemi eds., 2008).

Concerning ex post efficiency, adjusting the contractual bargain in hindsight based on what the contracting parties would have wanted is similarly challenging in investment law. In part, this is because the contracting parties are not the disputing parties since the foreign investor and the host state are embroiled in the dispute. Absent a nondisputing party intervention by the home state, the tribunal is thus exposed to a limited pool of information that makes it difficult to follow the test of what contracting parties (as opposed to the disputing parties) "would have wanted." Furthermore, even where contracting states have intervened through authoritative interpretations and nondisputing party submissions, arbitral tribunals have been reluctant to heed their guidance, in part due to concerns over an equality of arms around the dual role of states as both contractors and litigants.[57] In sum, arbitral tribunals lack the institutional setup to engage in sophisticated gap-filling based on either ex ante or ex post efficiency.

C. Reading Incomplete Treaties in Light of More Complete Ones

Fortunately, in international investment law, there exists another strategy to fill gaps in incomplete treaties that does not require tribunals to be passive and follow formalism or to engage in an impossible ex ante or ex post welfare-maximization. Since states are still engaged in lawmaking, arbitrators can refer and defer to states' evolving practice of concluding more complete treaties to close gaps in incomplete treaties. Tribunals can thereby modernize the outdated stock of incomplete treaties in light of current best practices.

Using more complete treaties to interpret incomplete ones achieves the best of both worlds. On the one hand, reading old treaties in light of new ones achieves ex post efficiency. Ex post efficiency is about filling gaps based on how the contracting states "would have wanted" it. In ISDS, tribunals do not have to second-guess parties' intentions. They can instead rely on the explicit manifestation of state preferences in recent investment agreements, which provides the best guess of how contracting states "would have wanted" to resolve contractual incompleteness in their older agreements with the benefit of hindsight. As Jennifer Radford et al. put it, "State parties are the best positioned to speak for their drafting and negotiation intentions. To determine the meaning of a treaty term, the treaty parties' collective interpretation speaks with greater weight than arbitral tribunals' interpretation of the parties' purported intention."[58] Not only

---

[57] Todd Weiler, The Interpretation of International Investment Law: Equality, Discrimination and Minimum Standards of Treatment in Historical Context 31 (2013).

[58] Jennifer Radford, Gregory Tereposky & Kun Hui, *Investment Treaty Signatories' Joint Interpretation and the Case of the NAFTA Free Trade Commission: Evolutionary Interpretation or Modification?*, in Evolutionary Interpretation and International Law 283–295, 285 (Georges Abi-Saab et al. eds., 2019).

does this strategy avoid judicial error, it also aligns incomplete treaties with more complete ones.

On the other hand, using more complete treaties to interpret incomplete treaties also produces ex ante efficiency. Ex ante efficiency is about creating predictability through default rules. Instead of risking judicial error by relying on judge-made default rules derived from precedent, tribunals can defer to the gap-filling strategies used by the contracting parties in more recent agreements. This mirrors what courts do in domestic law when they craft default rules around business best practices and current trade usages. Where global IIA practice is converging, as is the case in relation to many of the American-style clarification of core investment treaty standards, tribunals could indirectly tap into state-made global default rules when they fill gaps in incomplete treaties. The detailed language in more complete treaties, then, not only better reflects the intentions of the contracting parties of how to maximize their welfare in IIA relations but also leads to consistency and predictability in the interpretation of investment treaties as old treaties are read in light of today's best global practices.

In short, interpreting incomplete treaties based on more complete treaties achieves the best of both worlds (ex ante and ex post efficiency) by relying on recent practice as an interpretive guidepost and the best guess on how contracting parties "would have wanted" their incomplete treaties to be interpreted with the benefit of hindsight. Moreover, it produces default rules and predictability not based arbitrator-made precedent but based on a convergence around best practices embodied in recent, more complete treaties and state-driven innovation.

In conclusion, the theoretical grounds for using contract theory as a meta-approach to treaty interpretation in ISDS are sound. The agent-like nature of ISDS tribunals on interpretation as well as the structure of the IIA universe make it possible and desirable to read incomplete treaties in light of recent, more complete ones. The question remains to what extent the rules of treaty interpretation in the VCLT permit such an approach and where the limits of reading old treaties via new ones lie.

III. Using Subsequent Agreements and Practice to Modernize Incomplete IIAs

The VCLT governs the interpretation of international treaties. Its rules on interpretation seek to discern the intentions of the contracting parties.[59] Under VCLT Article 31, interpreters must construct these intentions objectively by

---

[59] RICHARD GARDINER, TREATY INTERPRETATION 6 (2nd ed. 2015).

looking at the text, the treaty's object and purpose and context, which includes subsequent agreements and practice of the contracting states. The VCLT, however, provides little guidance on how to weigh the different elements.[60] Rather, as the International Law Commission's (ILC's) Commentary to the Convention famously put it, the listed factors are to "be thrown into the crucible, and their interaction would give rise to the legally relevant interpretation."[61] As Petros Mavroidis pointedly observed, an interpreter "is requested to complete an incomplete and often ambiguous contract [the treaty] by using yet another incomplete contract [the VCLT] to honour its mission."[62] The VCLT thus leaves considerable discretion to interpreters, which they can use by approaching interpretation through the lens of contract theory.

At the same time, the VCLT structures the interpretive exercise and sets its outer bounds. For example, subsidiary means of interpretations under VCLT Article 32, which includes a treaty's negotiating history, may only be considered if the application of Article 31 leaves the meaning ambiguous, absurd, or unreasonable.[63] Furthermore, the importance of the text of the treaty and its ordinary meaning anchor interpretations in the wording of a treaty. Therefore, entirely new provisions, such as general exception clauses, cannot be read into an incomplete IIA that lacks the corresponding wording. Interpretive gap-filling inspired by contract theory is confined to importing clarifications from more complete agreements. More extensive modifications of incomplete treaties, like the inclusion of general exceptions, require renegotiation (see Chapter 8).

VCLT Article 31 allows interpreters to use more complete treaties and other subsequent practice to modernize incomplete IIAs and draws a distinction between two pathways. On the one hand, it directs interpreters toward subsequent agreements and practice that *explicitly* relate to the treaty being interpreted. On the other hand, it also considers the *implicit* influence of subsequent agreements and practice. While joint, authoritative interpretations and concordant disputing submissions fall into the first category, subsequent IIAs almost exclusively need to be considered under the second category. Finally, as a fallback, subsequent agreements and practice may be considered under Article 32 if the investigation under Article 31 leaves the meaning ambiguous.

---

[60] Michael Waibel, *Demystifying the Art of Interpretation*, 22 EUR. J. INT'L L. 571–588, 573 (2011) ("[the VCLT] left substantial leeway for idiosyncratic approaches to interpretation within the bounds staked out by the VCLT's broad interpretive principles.").

[61] ILC, *Yearbook of the International Law Commission*, 1966, vol. II, at 220, para. 8.

[62] Petros Mavroidis, *Legal Eagles? A Look Into 10 Years of AB Case-Law*, Discussion Paper No. 49, May 2007, at 7.

[63] On VCLT art. 32 in the investment law context, *see generally* Mahnoush H. Arsanjani & W. Michael Reisman, *Interpreting Treaties for the Benefit of Third Parties: The "Salvors" Doctrine" and the Use of Legislative History in Investment Treaties*, 104 AM. J. INT'L L. 597 (2010).

A. Explicit Interpretative Gap-Filling Ex Post—VCLT Article 31(3)a) and Article (3)(b)

Inspired by more complete treaty practice, states can fill interpretive gaps in incomplete agreements by issuing either authoritative interpretations or unilateral submissions that explicitly relate to incomplete treaties.

1. "Subsequent Agreement" VCLT Article 31(3)a)—Issuing Authentic Interpretations

The binding legal effect of joint interpretations adopted by the contracting parties is well established under international law. The ICJ in the *Kasikili/Sedudu Island* dispute noted that "an authentic interpretation by the parties [. . .] must be read into the treaty for purposes of its interpretation."[64] Similarly, the VCLT asks interpreters in Article 31(3)a) to consider "any subsequent agreement between the parties regarding the interpretation of the treaty or the application of its provisions." Moreover, many IIAs explicit provide for a mechanism to issue binding interpretations.[65] These authentic interpretations can correct prior arbitral misinterpretations and reassert original intent. As the arbitral tribunal in *Methanex* stated:

> If a legislature, having enacted a statute, feels that the courts implementing it have misconstrued the legislature's intention, it is perfectly proper for the legislature to clarify its intention. In a democratic and representative system in which legislation expresses the will of the people, legislative clarification in this sort of case would appear to be obligatory. The Tribunal sees no reason why the same analysis should not apply to international law.[66]

Contracting states are making increasing use of their interpretive authority to address arbitral misinterpretations. The 2001 NAFTA FTC interpretation discussed in Chapter 5 is the most well-known example of a joint interpretation, but it is not the only one. Argentina and Panama agreed on an authoritative interpretation following the *National Grid v. Argentina* award. After the tribunal found that MFN encompasses dispute settlement provisions, the state parties clarified through an exchange of notes that the MFN clause in their treaty does not extend

---

[64] ILC, *Yearbook of the International Law Commission*, 1966, vol. II, at 221, para. 14. Quoted by the International Court of Justice in the *Kasikili/Sedudu Island (Botswana/Namibia)*, 1999 ICJ Rep. 1045, Judgement, December 13, 1999, para. 49.

[65] UNCTAD, *supra* note 23.

[66] *Methanex v. USA*, UNCITRAL, Partial Award, August 7. 2002, pt. IV, ch. C, at 10, para. 22.

to dispute settlement.[67] Joint interpretation can even affect an award after it was rendered. In *Sanum Investments v. Laos*, the respondent sought to deny jurisdiction to an investor from Macau on the basis that the China–Laos BIT (1993) did not extend to Macau.[68] After the arbitrators upheld jurisdiction, Laos was able to produce an exchange of notes with the Chinese embassy confirming its interpretation and initiated setting aside proceedings in Singapore.[69] The Singaporean courts then set aside the award for a lack of jurisdiction and found that the exchange of letters constituted a subsequent agreement by the parties as to the treaty's interpretation in the meaning of VCLT Article 31(3)a).[70] UNCTAD has documented that such authoritative interpretations are becoming more frequent.[71] Hence, joint interpretations are emerging as important tools for contracting states to correct misinterpretations.

At the same time, arbitral tribunals retain the delegated power to verify whether an authoritative interpretation is made in accordance with the treaty and the VCLT thereby guarding against the mechanism's abuse. The tribunal in *Gas Natural v. Argentina*, for instance, found that submissions by the home state as respondent in a different arbitration did not infer a common intention between the parties as to the interpretation of similar provisions in the arbitration at issue.[72] Similarly, in *Aguas del Tunari v. Bolivia*, the tribunal rejected Bolivia's attempt to invoke Dutch parliamentary debate records to demonstrate a common interpretation of the Bolivia–Netherlands BIT, reasoning that "[t]he coincidence of several statements does not make them a joint statement."[73] Finally, even if an interpretation is made jointly by the contracting states yet lacks

---

[67] Yannick Radi, *The Application of the Most-Favoured-Nation Clause to the Dispute Settlement Provisions of Bilateral Investment Treaties: Domesticating the "Trojan Horse,"* 18 Eur. J. Int'l L. 757–774, 769 (2007).

[68] *Sanum Investments Limited v. Lao People's Democratic Republic*, UNCITRAL, PCA Case No. 2013-13, Award on Jurisdiction, December 13, 2013.

[69] *Experts Line Up in China-Laos Bit Set-Aside Case*, IA Reporter, November 4, 2014, available at http://www.iareporter.com/articles/20141104_2 (last accessed March 10, 2015).

[70] *Government of the Lao People's Democratic Republic v. Sanum Investments Ltd* [2015] SGHC 15, January 20, 2015, paras. 70–78. *See also Singapore Court Rejects Arbitrators' Extension of Chinese Investment Treaty to Macao*, IA Reporter, January 20, 2015, available at http://www.iareporter.com/articles/20150121_1 (last accessed March 10, 2015).

[71] Colombia and France clarified their 2014 BIT in a joint interpretation in 2017. In the same year, India and Bangladesh issued an authoritative reading of their 2009 BIT. Finally, in 2018, Colombia and India signed an interpretive declaration relating to their 2009 BIT; *see* UNCTAD, World Investment Report 2019: Special Economic Zones 109–110 (2019).

[72] *Gas Natural SDG, S.A. v. The Argentine Republic*, ICSID Case No. ARB/03/10, Decision of the Tribunal on Preliminary Questions on Jurisdiction, June 17, 2005, para. 47, footnote 12. ("[w]e do not believe, however, that an argument made by a party in the context of an arbitration reflects practice establishing agreement between the parties to a treaty within the meaning of Article 31(3)(b) of the Vienna Convention on the Law of Treaties.").

[73] *Aguas del Tunari, S.A. v. Bolivia*, ICSID Case No. ARB/02/3, Decision on Respondent's Objections to Jurisdiction, October 21, 2005, para. 251. ("And, it is clear that in the present case, there was no intent that these statements be regarded as an agreement.").

textual grounding, then it may actually be an amendment, in which case the contracting states would have to follow the respective treaty-based procedures in order to make it effective.[74] Tribunals can therefore ensure that interpretations are not abused.

2. "Subsequent Practice" VCLT Article 31(3)b—Nondisputing Party Submissions

A second route to explicitly consider recent practice in the interpretation of incomplete treaties rests on the notion of "subsequent practice in the application of the treaty which establishes the agreement of the parties regarding its interpretation" in VCLT Article 31(3)b). In contrast to a joint agreement by the parties covered by VCLT Article 31(3)a), "subsequent practice" implies a set of unilateral acts by the contracting states, which, if taken together, signal a common understanding of the treaty's interpretation.[75] As the WTO Appellate Body explained in *Japan-Alcohol*,

> in international law, the essence of subsequent practice in interpreting a treaty has been recognized as a "concordant, common and consistent" sequence of acts or pronouncements which is sufficient to establish a discernable pattern implying the agreement of the parties regarding its interpretation.[76]

The Ontario Court of Appeal similarly characterized "subsequent practice" as "a clear, well-understood, agreed common position" adopted by the parties.[77] Like subsequent agreements, this subsequent practice needs to be explicitly directed toward the interpretation of the treaty at issue.

In ISDS, it is now increasingly accepted that unilateral acts as well as litigation submissions by the contracting states can amount to a subsequent practice under Article 31(3)b). Early on, the *Telefonica v. Argentina* tribunal had rejected the argument that the submissions made by Spain and Argentina as defendants in separate disputes could constitute relevant "practice" for the interpretation of

---

[74] One way to tell the difference between interpreting and amending a treaty is whether an interpreter could have reasonably arrived at the interpreted reading or whether such a reading cannot be reasonably accommodated by the language of the text.

[75] Underscoring the unitary nature of practice, the ILC commentary clarifies that not "every party must individually have engaged in the practice where it suffices that it should have accepted the practice." *See* ILC, *Yearbook of the International Law Commission*, 1966, vol. II, at 222, para. 15. *See generally* Julian Arato, *Subsequent Practice and Evolutive Interpretation: Techniques of Treaty Interpretation over Time and Their Diverse Consequences*, 9 L. & PRAC. INT'L COURTS & TRIBUNALS 443–494 (2010).

[76] Appellate Body Report, *Japan–Taxes on Alcoholic Beverages*, WT/DS8/AB/R, WT/DS10/AB/R, WT/DS11/AB/R, October 4, 1996, at 11.

[77] Ontario Court of Appeal, Decision on the Application to set aside award, October 4, 2011, para. 84.

whether the MFN clause in the Spain–Argentina BIT (1991) extended to the incorporation of more favorable pre-arbitral waiting periods.[78] It found that these submissions did not amount to conduct or performance by Spain and Argentina under the treaty and merely "indicate[d] their views set forth in those litigations for purposes of arguing as respondents therein."[79] Moreover, the submissions were "not directed towards each other" and thus could not produce an agreement or meeting of minds.[80]

However, since then several tribunals under NAFTA have accepted that submissions in litigation can give rise to state practice. In part, this conclusion has been aided by the fact that under NAFTA nondisputing party submissions allow contracting states to voice their interpretive views outside the respondent context. In *Canadian Cattlemen v. USA*, the tribunal accepted that the individual acts of the three NAFTA states, including their submissions in litigation, could amount to a "concordant, common, and consistent" practice on the interpretation of NAFTA.[81] In *Mobil v. Canada*, the tribunal acknowledged generally that "subsequent practice of the parties to a treaty, if it establishes the agreement of the parties regarding the interpretation of the treaty, is entitled to be accorded considerable weight."[82] The Ontario Court of Appeal went further in a set-aside proceeding, finding that if submissions amount to subsequent practice under VCLT Article 31(3)b), "it would be an error of jurisdiction for the tribunal to fail to give effect to that interpretation."[83]

The question then becomes when concordant state interventions meet the threshold of a consistent and intentional common position that implies an agreement of the contracting parties.[84] In the set-aside proceedings of the *Cargill* case, for example, the Ontario Court of Appeal found that the submissions by the contracting parties were not clear enough to embody a subsequent practice.[85] In the *B-Mex* set-aside proceedings before the Ontario Superior Court, the court found that unanimous submissions, if unrepeated, do not yet amount to a subsequent practice indicating agreement.[86] Hence, contracting states striving for

---

[78] *Telefónica S.A. v. The Argentine Republic*, ICSID Case No. ARB/03/20, Decision of the Tribunal on Objections to Jurisdiction, May 25, 2006.

[79] *Id.*, para. 119.

[80] *Id.*

[81] *The Canadian Cattlemen for Fair Trade v. United States of America*, Award on Jurisdiction, January 28, 2008, para. 189.

[82] *Mobil Investments Canada Inc. v. Canada*, ICSID Case No. ARB/15/6, Decision on Jurisdiction, July 13, 2018, para. 158.

[83] Ontario Court of Appeal, Decision on the Application to set aside award, October 4, 2011, para. 84.

[84] Arato, *supra* note 75, at 459.

[85] Ontario Court of Appeal, Decision on the Application to set aside award, 4 October 2011, paras. 83–84.

[86] *B-Mex, LLC and Others v. United Mexican States*, ICSID Case No. ARB(AF)/16/3, Judgment of the Ontario Supreme Court, July 20, 2020, at para. 217.

establishing subsequent practice under Article 31(3)b) should not only ensure that their individual pronouncements are concordant but also that they are clear, intentional, and done repeatedly.

B. Implicit Interpretative Gap-Filling Ex Post—VCLT Article 31(3)c) and Article (1)

In contrast to subsequent agreements and submissions that explicitly clarify a treaty's interpretation, more complete third IIAs can only constitute an implicit view on how the contracting states would have wanted their earlier agreements to be interpreted. As Andrew Mitchell and James Munro rightly point out, per se, "third-party IIAs are not related to the application of the IIA in question and do not establish the agreement of the parties to that IIA regarding its interpretation."[87] Third IIAs therefore do not ordinarily amount to a "subsequent agreement" or "subsequent practice," but they can nevertheless affect the interpretation of earlier agreements through other routes.

1. "Relevant Rules of International Law" VCLT Article 31(3)c)— Overlapping IIAs

In the 2016 *Windstream Energy v. Canada* ISDS proceedings, Canada's counsel argued that the Trans-Pacific Partnership (TPP), which had been concluded in 2015 and included the three NAFTA parties, was relevant for the interpretation of NAFTA's investment chapter as "the NAFTA parties' subsequent agreement."[88] According to Canada's counsel, "the NAFTA parties' understanding of what constitutes indirect expropriation under [NAFTA] Article 1110 . . . is reflected in subsequent practice, for example, in the recently concluded TPP Agreement."[89] While the TPP arguably neither amounted to "subsequent agreement" or "subsequent practice" of NAFTA in VCLT parlance, because it did not explicitly seek to interpret NAFTA, it could still matter as a relevant set of rules that applies between the same parties.

Other IIAs overlapping with the IIA that is being interpreted qualify as interpretive context under VCLT Article 31(3)c). The provision asks interpreters to consider "any relevant rules of international law applicable in the relations between the parties." The subject matter of the parallel IIAs is "relevant" insofar as

---

[87] Mitchell & Munro, *supra* note 3, at 688.

[88] *Windstream Energy LLC v. Government of Canada*, PCA Case No. 2013-22, Transcript of Hearing, Day 1, Remarks by Ms. Tabet, Counsel of Canada, February 15, 2016, at 148. https://www.italaw.com/sites/default/files/case-documents/italaw7361.pdf. Note that this argument was made before President Donald Trump withdrew the United States from the TPP in January 2017.

[89] *Id.*, at 147.

these treaties also protect investors. Furthermore, as long as the later treaty is in force between the same or a broader subset of contracting parties compared to the earlier IIA being interpreted, it is also "applicable in the relations between the parties."[90] Hence, overlapping, more complete IIAs can guide gap-filling in earlier, parallel BITs and free trade agreements (FTAs).

Successive investment treaties that exist in parallel between overlapping sets of contracting state parties are extremely common. In fact, every fourth bilateral inter-state relationship governed by investment treaty disciplines involves more than one investment agreement.[91] Typically, this involves either an early BIT coexisting with a later regional investment treaty or a later FTA with investment chapter. For instance, investments between Indonesia and Thailand are protected both by a BIT (1998) and the ASEAN Comprehensive Investment Agreement (ASEAN CIA) (2009), and investments between China and Laos are governed both by a BIT (1993) and the ASEAN–China FTA (2009). In addition, with the rise of mega-regional IIAs, it becomes increasingly frequent that successive regional FTAs with differing memberships overlap. For example, the investment relationship between Japan and Australia is governed by the CPTPP as well as RCEP. It is thus common that highly complete and more incomplete IIAs overlap between the same set of parties.

Andrew Mitchell and James Munro doubt whether Article 31(3)c) can make such third IIAs relevant. According to them, the reference "between the parties" in Article 31(3)c) may mean "parties to the dispute" and, given the nature of ISDS, the investor is party to the dispute but never party to an international treaty.[92] This reading of the VCLT is unconvincing. It would rule out the interpretive significance of any international treaty whenever individuals ligate against states, be it in ISDS, tax, or human rights dispute settlement. Moreover, the VCLT deals with treaty interpretation generally and not only interpretation in relations to disputes. The reference to "the parties" in Article 31(3)c) is thus best understood to mean "contracting parties" rather than "disputing parties." Finally, Article 31(3)c) does not require the international law rule to have been "created" by the parties; it must merely be "applicable." Since a second, overlapping IIA protecting investment is "applicable in the relations between" the host state and the investor just like the original treaty, it falls under the realm of Article 31(3)c). In cases

---

[90] The TPP is a special case insofar as it was later unsigned and never entered into force for the United States. Most overlapping mega-regional IIAs, however, once entered into force, encompass a broader membership than the earlier agreements they are overlapping with. To what extent a later agreement with more limited membership can affect the interpretation of an earlier treaty under Article VCLT Article 31(3)c) is less clear and beyond the scope of this chapter.

[91] Wolfgang Alschner, *Regionalism and Overlap in Investment Treaty Law: Towards Consolidation or Contradiction?*, 17 J. INT'L ECON. L. 271–298, 276 (2014).

[92] Mitchell & Munro, *supra* note 3, at 689.

of overlapping IIAs between the same contracting states, the VCLT thus directs interpreters to use the more complete IIA to fill gaps in the more incomplete IIA.

Consider a concrete scenario. Imagine the Indonesian government passes an environmental law that prohibits the clearing of tropical rain forest for commercial use. A Thai investor in the logging sector, having previously acquired a large parcel of rain forest land in Indonesia, considers the law an indirect expropriation and brings a claim against Indonesia based on the Indonesia–Thailand BIT (1998). Article VI of the BIT stipulates that the contracting parties "shall not take any measures of expropriation, nationalization or any other dispossession, having effect equivalent to nationalization or expropriation against the investments of an investor of the other Contracting Party." Recall from Chapter 5 that the concept of expropriation has been derived from customary law, as made explicit in the commentary to the 1967 OECD Draft Convention, but that this textual link was lost in subsequent agreements on which the Indonesia–Thailand BIT was modeled. Recent, more complete agreements, like the ASEAN CIA (2009), which overlaps with the Indonesia–Thailand BIT, have brought back that explicit link to custom and clarified that measures falling under the customary police powers doctrine are carved out from the scope of expropriation.[93]

In this situation, an ISDS tribunal guided by VCLT Article 31(3)c) should interpret Article VI of the BIT in light of the clarification provided in the later ASEAN CIA. The tribunal would recognize that Article VI contains a gap on whether a general, nondiscriminatory public purpose measure constitutes an expropriation, which the contracting parties left open. The tribunal would then seek to fill the gap based on what the parties "would have wanted" using their subsequent contracting as the best illustration of their preferences. Relying on VCLT Article 31(3)c), the tribunal would thus interpret the notion of expropriation in light of the subsequent ASEAN CIA and find that a general, nondiscriminatory public purpose does not constitute expropriation under the Indonesia–Thailand BIT.[94]

Using treaty overlap to update incomplete IIAs via interpretation holds immense promise. Given that about twenty-five percent of bilateral investment treaty relationships are governed by multiple IIAs, a sizable minority of incomplete IIAs could thus be modernized.[95] Such an interpretive alignment would furthermore prevent incomplete treaties from diverting claims away from

---

[93] The ASEAN CIA states in Article 14 read in conjunction with Annex 2(4) that "[n]ondiscriminatory measures of a Member State that are designed and applied to protect legitimate public welfare objectives, such as public health, safety and the environment, do not constitute an expropriation."

[94] This opportunity to interpret incomplete IIAs through a more complete IIA is contingent on both agreements being "applicable" between the two contracting parties.

[95] Alschner, *supra* note 91.

parallel more complete agreements. The gaps in older IIAs, if filled with investor-friendly precedent, make incomplete IIAs more attractive for investors. Yet by reading the incomplete IIAs in light of the parallel, more complete IIA, substantive protections converge, thereby lowering incentives for investors to favor incomplete treaties when it comes to litigation.

2. "Ordinary Meaning" VCLT Article 31(1)—Third IIAs Clarifying Earlier IIAs

More complete IIAs which the contracting states have entered into *with third states* are not "applicable in the relations between the parties" and thus fail to meet the requirements of VCLT Article 31(3)c), but they can help clarify the "ordinary meaning" of treaty terms in incomplete agreements via VCLT Article 31(1). Investment treaties use domain-specific jargon that differs from everyday language. When states use words such as "prompt, adequate and effective compensation" or "fair and equitable treatment," they contract on terms of art.[96]

Dictionaries are of little help to determine ordinary meaning when it comes to legal terms of art.[97] At the same time, other agreements in the same domain can elucidate such meaning. Richard Gardiner points out that in case of "common form treaties," such as investment treaties that are derived from common templates and govern the same subject in similar terms, other treaties with coinciding language "can assist by guiding the interpreter to the ordinary meaning."[98] The clarification of a term of art in one treaty can therefore provide important insights into the understanding of the same term in another IIA.[99] In that vein, the first ISDS award, *AAPL v. Sri Lanka*, already noted that investment protection standards "have to be construed according to the 'common use which custom has affixed' to them" and went on to consider similar terms in other investment agreements.[100]

The more challenging question is whether the relevance of third treaties is limited to those in existence at the time of the treaty's conclusion or comprises subsequent agreements. According to Mitchell and Munro, only IIAs concluded

---

[96] *See* K. Scott Gudgeon, *Valuation of Nationalized Property under United States and Other Bilateral Investment Treaties Contemporary United States Practice: Chapter III, in* 4 THE VALUATION OF NATIONALIZED PROPERTY IN INTERNATIONAL LAW 101–132, 104 (Richard B. Lillich ed., 1987). Recall that Judge Higgens referred to FET, for example, as a legal term of art. Oil Platforms, Separate Opinion Judge Higgens, para. 39, [1996] ICJ Rep. 847.

[97] In the words of the *Saluka v. Czech Republic* tribunal: "The 'ordinary meaning' of the 'fair and equitable treatment' standard can only be defined by terms of almost equal vagueness." *Saluka Investments B.V. v. Czech Republic*, UNCITRAL, Partial Award, March 17, 2006, para. 297.

[98] GARDINER, *supra* note 59, at 324.

[99] Maria Hilling & Ulf Linderfalk, *The Use of OECD Commentaries as Interpretative Aids—The Static/Ambulatory-Approaches Debate Considered from the Perspective of International Law*, 2015 NORDIC TAX J. 34–59, 44 (2015).

[100] *Asian Agricultural Products Ltd. v. Republic of Sri Lanka*, Award, June 27, 1990, ICSID Case No. ARB/87/3, para. 47.

prior to the agreement that is being interpreted can shed light on ordinary meaning, because IIAs often use language with established meaning grounded in earlier practice.[101] However, that reading seems unduly restrictive. If only material available at the time of a treaty's conclusion is permissible, interpreters would need to use historical rather than contemporaneous dictionaries to establish ordinary meaning, which is clearly not the case. Furthermore, the use of later materials, including international agreements, to interpret the ordinary meaning of terms in earlier treaties is widely accepted. International courts and tribunals have routinely accepted an evolutionary reading of treaty terms and have used subsequent treaties to characterize such an evolving meaning.[102] In some fields, such as international taxation, an evolutionary interpretation of older agreements via new treaties is in fact common practice (see Chapter 9).[103]

The real question, then, is whether the contracting parties' intention is to freeze the treaty's ordinary meaning in time or to see treaty terms evolve and be clarified through later practice. In *Dispute Regarding Navigational and Related Rights*, the ICJ suggested that "where the parties have used generic terms in a treaty, the parties necessarily having been aware that the meaning of the terms was likely to evolve over time, and where the treaty has been entered into for a very long period or is 'of continuing duration', the parties must be presumed, as a general rule, to have intended those terms to have an evolving meaning."[104] Investment agreements with their generic, path-dependent terms of art and their long duration neatly fit that pattern. Therefore, clarifications in subsequent IIAs can a priori inform the ordinary meaning of the terms of art that were only vaguely defined in earlier agreements.

In that vein, many gap-filling clarifications in more recent complete IIAs are explicitly designed to affect the reading of other, earlier agreements.[105] In most cases, this does not amount to an evolutionary interpretation but rather affirms original intent. As discussed in Chapter 5, clarifications that link FET and expropriation to custom, for example, date back to at least the 1967 OECD Draft

---

[101] Mitchell & Munro, *supra* note 3, at 682.

[102] Famously, the WTO Appellate Body, used subsequent environmental conventions to interpret language from the GATT 1947. *See* WTO Appellate Body Report, *United States—Import Prohibition of Certain Shrimp and Shrimp Products*, WTO Doc. WT/DS58/AB/R (October 12, 1998), paras. 129–134. *See generally* GEORGES ABI-SAAB ET AL., EVOLUTIONARY INTERPRETATION AND INTERNATIONAL LAW (2019).

[103] *See generally* P. J. Wattel & O. C. R. Marres, *The Legal Status of the OECD Commentary and Static or Ambulatory Interpretation of Tax Treaties*, 7/8 EUR. TAXATION (2003); Hilling & Linderfalk, *supra* note 99.

[104] *Dispute Regarding Navigational and Related Rights* (Costa Rica v. Nicaragua), Judgment of July 13, 2009, ICJ Rep. 2009, para. 66.

[105] United States of America Third Non-Disputing Party Submission, *Omega Engineering LLC and Oscar Rivera v. Republic of Panama*, ICSID Case No. ARB/16/42, February 3, 2020, footnote 24. *See also* Jeremy Sharpe, *From Delegation to Prescription: Interpretive Authority in International Investment Agreements*, *in* BY PEACEFUL MEANS: INTERNATIONAL ADJUDICATION AND ARBITRATION (Charles H. Brower, Joan E. Donoghue, & Esme Shirlow eds., 2022).

Convention and were repeatedly affirmed by OECD members even before ISDS cases surged.

Moreover, the United States and Canada, for example, have consistently maintained that additional clarifications in newer agreements are already implied earlier texts. In May 2000, well before ISDS became widespread and states were accused of a backlash against arbitration, the United States already noted in a nondisputing party submission that "for greater certainty" language was "not to create or limit a right or obligation but to reflect an understanding that the scope of a particular right or obligation is *already implied* in other provisions of the text."[106] In the same vein, Canada endorsed the statement by the head of the United States' NAFTA Arbitration Division, who explained that "[t]hese clarifications do not change the nature of the substantive obligations that existed under the United States' prior agreements; instead, they merely elucidate, for the benefit of tribunals charged with interpreting the treaty, the Parties' intent in agreeing to those obligations."[107] As long as such clarifications endorse one of a range of possible interpretations, they can validly inform ordinary meaning and do not stray into amendments territory.

In investment treaties, however, it takes (at least) two to tango. Unilateral clarifications are not enough to reveal a shared original or evolved intended meaning. When clarifications converge in third IIAs, however, they may be evidence of the intended ordinary meaning.

Consider the following example. In 1992, Japan and Turkey signed an investment agreement, which in Article 5(2) vaguely stipulates that investment "shall not be subjected to expropriation, nationalization or any other measure the effect of which would be tantamount to expropriation or nationalization" without paying compensation. It is left unclear how the clause relates to the customary international law police power doctrine. Subsequently, both Japan and Turkey have engaged in a concordant and consistent treaty practice with third states, clarifying that nondiscriminatory public interest regulation does not constitute indirect expropriation.[108] Now imagine an arbitral tribunal is tasked to interpret Article 5(2) of the Japan–Turkey BIT to determine whether a nondiscriminatory public interest regulation adopted by one of the two countries, which rendered the claimant's investment worthless, constitutes an indirect expropriation. The

---

[106] Second Submission of the United States, *Pope & Talbot Inc. v. The Government of Canada*, May 25, 2000, para. 6 (emphasis added).

[107] Andrea J. Menaker, *Benefiting from Experience: Developments in the United States' Most Recent Investment Agreements*, 12 UC DAVIS J. INT'L L. & POL'Y 121–129, 122 (2006). Quoted in *Windstream Energy LLC v. Government of Canada*, Respondent's Rejoinder, November 6, 2015, para. 92.

[108] For Turkey, *see, e.g.*, Turkey–Azerbaijan BIT (2011), art. 6(2); Turkey–Pakistan BIT (2012), art. 6(2); Turkey–Cameroon BIT (2012), art. 6(2); Turkey–Gabon BIT (2012), art. 6(2); Turkey–Bangladesh BIT (2012), art. 6(2). For Japan, *see, e.g.*, Japan–Colombia BIT (2011), Annex III; Japan–Peru BIT (2008), Annex IV; Japan–South Korea-China Investment Treaty (2012), Protocol; and, in the guise of a general public policy exception, *see, e.g.*, Japan–Mozambique BIT (2013), art. 18.

1992 BIT has a gap—it does not address the distinction between expropriation and general regulations. The arbitral tribunal can fill this gap relating to the ordinary meaning of expropriation by consulting the subsequent concordant and consistent practice of Japan and Turkey and interpret the ambiguous expropriation clause in the 1992 Japan–Turkey BIT in light of the countries' converging more recent investment treaties.

Some commentators are uncomfortable with such an approach to treaty interpretation. According to them, interpreting one contractual relationship through another contractual relationship between different parties violates the principles of privity, the *ratione personae* restrictions of interpretive material under the VCLT, and the maxim *pacta tertiis nec nocent nec prosunt* according to which a treaty only binds the contracting parties but not third parties.[109] This point, however, misunderstands the argument advanced. Where both states express converging views of a generic term's ordinary meaning that is left undefined in earlier treaties, this concordant practice provides a tribunal with the best guess on how contracting states would have wanted their earlier agreement to be interpreted with the benefit of hindsight. That the ordinary meaning happens to be revealed in a third-party IIA rather than a dictionary is secondary. Roberts has, for example, suggested that concordant model agreements can provide valid and relevant clues as to how contracting states would have wanted contractual gaps to be filled.[110] More complete subsequent treaties thus merely serve as evidence for the concordant subsequent gap-filling strategies that affirm intended meaning.

C. Supplementary Means—VCLT Article 32

As a last resort, third, more complete IIAs can inform interpretation as a supplementary means under VCLT Article 32. Supplementary means, which can include but are not limited to preparatory documents created during the treaty's negotiation, only come in when the interpretation according to Article 31 leaves the meaning of the treaty ambiguous or obscure. Given the vagueness of core obligations in incomplete IIAs, treaty terms can remain obscure even after considering the elements of VLCT Article 31.[111]

Tribunals can then consult other interpretive evidence. Rather than seeking help from case law, which roots interpretations in past practice, tribunals' first instinct, informed by contract theory, should be to look for how contracting states

---

[109] Mitchell & Munro, *supra* note 3, at 676; MĀRTIŅŠ PAPARINSKIS, THE INTERNATIONAL MINIMUM STANDARD AND FAIR AND EQUITABLE TREATMENT 126–130 (2013).

[110] Roberts, *supra* note 13, at 211.

[111] *See, e.g., Joseph C. Lemire v. Ukraine*, ICSID Case No. ARB/06/18, Decision on Jurisdiction and Liability, January 21, 2010, para. 258; *Ioan Micula, Viorel Micula and others v. Romania*, ICSID Case No. ARB/05/20, Award, December 11, 2013, para. 504.

would have wanted their agreements to be interpreted by investigating their subsequent treaty-making. Mitchell and Munro argue that evidence of an explicit link is necessary to consider third treaties as supplementary means informative of the common intentions of the parties such as a mention in the treaty's preparatory works.[112] But this is an unnecessarily restrictive reading of Article 32. Based on its text, it admits any supplementary means of interpretation, not only preparatory work.

IV. Conclusion

Contract theory can assist interpreters in reading old IIAs in light of new ones. When states incur the higher costs of filling contractual gaps by drafting more precise agreements, they expect deference from interpreters. Conversely, where the contracting states leave contractual gaps open, they delegate gap-filling by interpreters. In the ISDS context, these gaps should be filled by consulting the ongoing lawmaking efforts in new, more complete treaties that provide the best guess of how states would have wanted gaps to be closed in older, incomplete agreements with the benefit of hindsight. The rules on treaty interpretation allow interpreters to read old IIAs in light of new IIA practice. This is least controversial where contracting states issue joint interpretations, engage in concordant submissions, or sign more complete IIAs that overlap with older, incomplete ones. Later treaties may, however, also inform the "ordinary meaning" of earlier ones or serve as subsidiary means of treaty interpretation. Interpretation therefore promises to gently remedy vagueness in outdated IIAs. For more far-reaching modernizations of incomplete IIAs, however, states need to consider renegotiation, discussed in the next chapter.

---

[112] Mitchell & Munro, *supra* note 3, at 691.

8
Data-Driven Renegotiation

I. Introduction

When states want to go beyond interpretive clarifications and modify or amend old treaties in light of new ones, they have to resort to renegotiation. The renegotiation of individual investment agreements is often viewed as impractical, inefficient, and costly—a piecemeal response to a systemic problem.[1] Indeed, amending or replacing more than three thousand treaties agreement by agreement sounds like a daunting, perhaps impossible task. This perspective, however, misses three significant opportunities for targeted renegotiations below the multilateral level that have systemic impact without requiring systemic reform. In fact, renegotiations done right can be an efficient, practical, and low-cost way to protect innovation in new treaties and to consolidate and harmonize incomplete treaties around the best practices embodied in more complete ones.

First, on the national level, states increasingly deal with a bifurcated treaty network in which older, incomplete treaties coexist with recent, more complete agreements. These older agreements not only pose a problem per se because they lack the substantive and procedural clarifications and additions common to more complete agreements. They also affect the application and interpretation of more complete agreements and thus jeopardize national treaty modernization strategies more broadly. To ensure that a minority of early agreements do not undermine entire national treaty networks, states can target incomplete IIAs for reform and thereby protect the innovation in their more complete agreements.

Second, on the bilateral level, the shift by states across the globe toward more complete agreements creates new opportunities for renegotiating incomplete ones. Contracting parties whose recent practices converge around more complete agreements implicitly share a common vision for how to renegotiate their existing incomplete ones. In addition, the competency transfer over investment treaty negotiations from member states to the European Union has created additional opportunities to replace scores of incomplete treaties that EU members have signed individually with third states with a single more complete EU treaty in bilateral renegotiations as done, for example, between the European Union

---

[1] K. Gordon & J. Pohl, *Investment Treaties over Time—Treaty Practice and Interpretation in a Changing World*, OECD Working Papers on International Investment, 2015/02, at 32.

Investment Arbitration and State-Driven Reform. Wolfgang Alschner, Oxford University Press. © Oxford University Press 2022. DOI: 10.1093/oso/9780197644386.003.0009

and Canada through the Comprehensive Economic and Trade Agreement (CETA). Such bilateral renegotiations can furthermore produce systemic ripple effects when investment powerhouses update their investment relations inspiring corresponding lawmaking and rule-updating elsewhere.

Third, on the regional level, the creation of investment protection rules through supranational organizations like the European Union or through regional agreements such as the Comprehensive and Progressive Agreement for Trans-Pacific Partnership (CPTPP) create opportunities to consolidate and harmonize IIAs around more complete treaty practices. Some ongoing regional renegotiations promise to be game changing. Efforts to revise the Energy Charter Treaty (ECT) currently underway could, if successful, indirectly affect the reading of more than six hundred overlapping investment treaties involving country pairs as far afield as Japan and Australia or Switzerland and Turkmenistan. Yet not all regional (re)negotiation efforts are used as opportunities to update the outdated stock of agreements. While the assertion of primacy of EU internal marked rules has prompted a termination of outdated intra-EU investment treaties, the CPTPP, for example, coexists and overlaps with highly incomplete agreements.

If states were to seriously pursue renegotiation and consolidation opportunities at the national, bilateral, and regional level, then a small number of transactions—relative to the more than three thousand IIAs in existence—would have significant impact on the global IIA landscape. As in the case of EU agreements with third states, these renegotiations could replace a large percentage of existing older IIAs and entice other countries and regions to follow suit. Similarly, the updating of the ECT could produce an interpretive substantive modernization of a large portion of the global treaty stock. Hence, even absent a grand multilateral bargain, targeted renegotiations could thus reshape the investment law system in profound and systemic ways.

For these efforts to be successful, renegotiations should be data-driven. Existing data on treaty content and treaty overlaps allows states to quickly spot where they get the most bang for their buck. Moreover, data on the normative convergence of national or regional treaty practices enables states to swiftly map commonalities across IIA networks to identify promising targets for renegotiations where states already share similar preferences. Technology can even provide renegotiating states with a first compromise text draft that seeks to consolidate their respective treaty practices. A data-driven approach to renegotiations can thus overcome practical obstacles relating to inefficiency and state capacity that currently hold back more ambitious renegotiation efforts.

This chapter starts by showing that IIA renegotiations are a giant missed opportunity. They are rarely used, employed for the wrong reasons, and concentrated in a few states. While legitimate concerns hold renegotiations back, at least some of these concerns can be addressed by leveraging data and technology. A data-driven approach can help identify candidates for renegotiations and prepare and structure renegotiations themselves. The final part of the chapter discusses plurilateral IIAs that are all too often layered on top of outdated IIAs rather than used to replace or modernize incomplete treaties. If done right, bilateral, and regional renegotiations can systemically reform old treaties in light of new ones without requiring systemic reform.

II. Missed Opportunities: Why Renegotiations Are Rarely and Poorly Used

The toolbox of states to deal with outdated investment treaties is limited. Interpretive interventions must work within existing wording and, in the past, have sometimes failed to sway subsequent arbitrators.[2] Unilaterally terminating investment treaties is unenticing because so-called survival clauses keep the treaty alive and lock in protection, often for decades.[3] Joint terminations can avoid such surviving effects but remove a treaty's benefits as well as its disadvantages.[4] Renegotiations either through amendments to existing agreements or through new agreements replacing old ones seem the most effective yet nuanced tool short of a multilateral reform that contracting states possess to address the shortcomings of old, incomplete IIAs. Unfortunately, renegotiations are rarely used and when employed they often fall short of producing sweeping reforms.

A. Renegotiations Are Rare, Concentrated, and Driven by the Wrong Reasons

Most negotiation resources are directed toward concluding new treaties rather than replacing old ones. A 2015 survey conducted by UNCTAD found that

---

[2] *See* Chapters 5 and 7. Developing countries have pointed to a lacking impact of joint interpretation as one of the reasons for their relatively rare usage. *See* Taylor St. John & Geoffrey Gertz, *State Interpretations of Investment Treaties: Feasible Strategies for Developing Countries*, Blavatnik School of Governance Policy Brief, June 2015, p. 4.

[3] *See generally* Tania Voon & Andrew D. Mitchell, *Denunciation, Termination and Survival: The Interplay of Treaty Law and International Investment Law*, 31 ICSID Rev. 413–433 (2016).

[4] *See* UNCTAD, *Phase 2 of IIA Reform: Modernizing the Existing Stock of Old-Generation Treaties*, IIA Issue Note, Issue 2, June 2017, at 19. While survival clauses are typically only triggered by unilateral denunciation, some scholars have argued that third-party investor rights may also survive joint termination under specific circumstances; *see* James Harrison, *The Life and Death of BITs: Legal Issues Concerning Survival Clauses and the Termination of Investment Treaties*, 13 J. World Investment & Trade 928–950 (2012).

"relatively few countries are renegotiating, amending or interpreting existing IIAs."[5] Similarly, a 2015 OECD study concluded that "treaty amendments [and] treaty replacements have not been a major channel used by countries seeking to change the way their treaties are interpreted."[6] As a result, renegotiations remain rare. Broude et al. count a total of 226 renegotiations of BITs up to 2018 either through new a BIT replacing an old one (around 52%), amendments (around 38%) or replacement of a BIT with an FTA with investment chapter (around 10%).[7] Renegotiations became more frequent between 2004 and 2010, reaching around 20 renegotiations per year,[8] but have since slowed down (Figure 8.1). UNCTAD reported only twenty-seven instances where newer IIAs replace older ones between 2012 and 2017.[9]

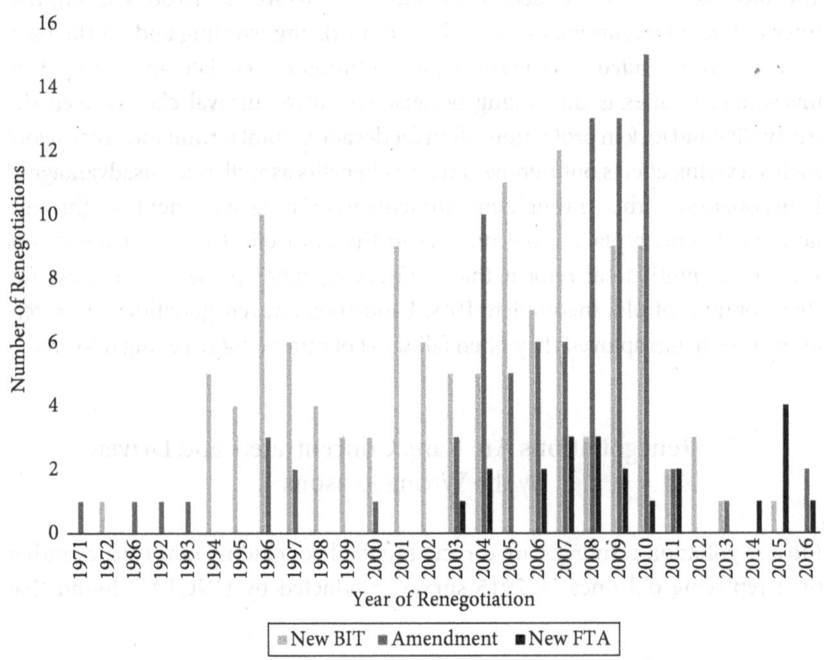

Figure 8.1 Renegotiations by year and type (data: Broude et al.)

[5] UNCTAD, WORLD INVESTMENT REPORT 2016. INVESTOR NATIONALITY: POLICY CHALLENGES 111 (2016).

[6] Gordon & Pohl, *supra* note 1, at 36.

[7] Tomer Broude, Yoram Haftel, & Alexander Thompson, *Legitimation Through Renegotiation: Do States Seek More Regulatory Space in Their BITs?* 5 (2016), https://papers.ssrn.com/abstract=2845297 (last accessed February 17, 2021). The OECD reported similar figures, at 34–35.

[8] Yoram Z. Haftel & Alexander Thompson, *When Do States Renegotiate Investment Agreements? The Impact of Arbitration*, 13 REV. INT'L ORG. 25–48, 33 (2018).

[9] UNCTAD, WORLD INVESTMENT REPORT 2018: INVESTMENT AND NEW INDUSTRIAL POLICIES 100 (2018).

Table 8.1 Number and type of BIT renegotiations by top five parties

Country	Replaced by BIT	Country	Amended	Country	Replaced by FTA
Germany	17	Romania	26	Peru	4
Romania	15	Czech Republic	21	China	3
China	13	Bulgaria	11	Australia	3
Egypt	13	Slovak Republic	10	Chile	3
Switzerland	10	United States	8	Taiwan	3

In addition, renegotiations have been concentrated among a subset of particularly active states as can be seen in Table 8.1.[10] Of the 226 renegotiations, Romania alone accounts for roughly a fifth or 41 renegotiations. States with large but dated treaty networks, such as Germany, China, Egypt, and Switzerland, have frequently concluded new BITs to replace old ones. Smaller Eastern European states like the Czech Republic, Slovakia, or Bulgaria lead the list of renegotiations through amendments typically prompted by their accession to the European Union. In contrast, South American and East Asian states have predominantly used FTAs to replace BITs, but the numbers remain low in comparison.

Although commentators and international organizations have identified renegotiation as a vital tool to introduce more policy space into older agreements,[11] research shows that renegotiated texts tend to produce agreements that offer *more* rather than *less* protection to investors and have little impact on policy space.[12] Broude et al., for example, find that renegotiated texts typically provide for broader investor-state arbitration clauses.[13] This is unsurprising given that frequent BIT re-negotiators such as Germany or China have primarily replaced old treaty texts that either lacked ISDS (in case of Germany) or limited ISDS to the quantification of compensation in cases of expropriation (in case of China). The 2009 renegotiation of the 1959 Germany–Pakistan BIT is a case in point: the inclusion of ISDS is the major design difference between the new and old BIT, which are otherwise highly similar in contractual completeness.

Moreover, instead of introducing sweeping reforms, many renegotiations only involve technical tweaks. In part, that is because about a third of all

---

[10] Haftel & Thompson, *supra* note 8, at 34. I am grateful to Yoram Haftel for sharing the underlying data.

[11] *See, e.g.,* UNCTAD, *supra* note 3; BROUDE, HAFTEL, & THOMPSON, *supra* note 7.

[12] *See generally* Andrew Newcombe, *Developments in IIA Treaty-Making, in* IMPROVING INTERNATIONAL INVESTMENT AGREEMENTS 18–24, 22 (Armand de Mestral & Céline Lévesque eds., 2011).

[13] BROUDE, HAFTEL, & THOMPSON, *supra* note 7.

renegotiations are linked to a country's accession to the European Union, which necessitates targeted adjustments to make IIA obligations compatible with EU law. These typically include reservations to national and most-favored-nation (MFN) treatment for privileges arising out of the country's EU membership or transfer restrictions imposed by EU law. Some scholars point to the introduction of new essential security clauses as evidence for more sweeping changes,[14] but these are also motivated by EU membership to ensure that "essential interests" include obligations deriving from EU membership, for example, in situations where the European Union seeks to comply with resolutions of the UN Security Council.[15]

A 2015 OECD study surveyed thirty-eight renegotiations to study the pairs of before-and-after treaties. It found that replacement treaties are longer than their predecessors.[16] The study also noted that agreements were becoming more homogenous insofar as core provisions such as fair and equitable treatment (FET), which were included less uniformly in the initial agreements, are becoming ubiquitous albeit in varying textual guises and that national security exceptions, rare in the original set, become more common.[17] These findings, encouragingly, reflect the evolution of IIAs traced in Chapter 1 as renegotiated treaties just like newly negotiated ones are moving toward greater contractual completeness. However, as discussed earlier, completing incomplete treaties is often only a by-product of renegotiations motivated by other reasons.

In short, renegotiations are not used to systematically update and improve the contractual completeness of old-generation IIAs and instead are driven primarily by the accession to the European Union and the inclusion of stronger ISDS provisions. Additional changes introduced through renegotiations coincide with larger trends, producing longer, more detailed treaties—the insertion of more regulatory space into renegotiated texts, however, is at best a mere byproduct.[18]

B. Reasons Why Renegotiations Remain Rarely Used

While a range of political, bureaucratic, and diplomatic obstacles may prevent states from using renegotiations more systematically to update incomplete

---

[14] Haftel & Thompson, *supra* note 8, at 33.

[15] *See, e.g.*, the Letter of Submission to the US Senate explaining the motivations behind the amendments of BITs with new EU members, which clarifies that the changed national security provisions were introduced "at the request of the European Commission" in order to confirm that security interests extend to those derived from EU membership. *See, e.g.*, the Letter relating to the amendment of the US-Czech Republic BIT, https://investmentpolicy.unctad.org/international-inv estment-agreements/treaty-files/4698/download.

[16] Gordon & Pohl, *supra* note 1, at 37–38.

[17] *Id.*

[18] Alexander Thompson, Tomer Broude, & Yoram Z. Haftel, *Once Bitten, Twice Shy? Investment Disputes, State Sovereignty, and Change in Treaty Design*, 73 INT'L ORG. 859–880 (2019).

investment agreements, several practical impediments are frequently voiced in state surveys. First and foremost, states find renegotiations (too) costly. An OECD survey found that states worry about the resources and time that are required to renegotiate IIAs.[19] A subsequent UNCTAD survey identified additional obstacles to widespread renegotiations, such as the opposition from treaty partners, insufficient state capacity, and a lack of political will.[20] Whereas a newly signed IIA makes headlines, renegotiations, even if in the country's best interest, are unlikely to generate the same attention and thus fall below radar of decision makers. A lack of capacity, consensus, and political reward are thus major obstacles to more frequent renegotiations.[21]

Add to this the daunting dimensions of the outdated IIA stock. According to UNCTAD, 95 percent of IIAs in force have been concluded prior to 2010.[22] Closing contractual gaps in incomplete agreements would take more than 2,500 individual treaty renegotiations. Moreover, the sheer size of some national treaty networks makes renegotiations look like a herculean task. Egypt alone, for example, has one hundred BITs in force as of this writing, ninety-seven of which have been signed prior to 2010, mostly in the 1990s, which would need updating.[23] Comprehensive renegotiations can thus easily appear as prohibitively costly and unrealistically ambitious, which likely stifles serious reform attempts even before they begin.

III. A Data-Driven Approach to Renegotiations

Quantitative thinking and technology can revitalize renegotiations as a tool for state-driven change. While they can do little to change the politics and diplomacy around renegotiations, they can reduce the costs and increase the benefits associated with renegotiations. They can help debunk misunderstandings about the inefficiencies of piecemeal renegotiations and overcome practical concerns related to the high costs, low capacity, and opposition from treaty partners in renegotiations.

A. What Treaties to Prioritize for Renegotiation?

It is easy to underestimate the benefits of renegotiations and to overestimate their costs. Most IIAs are incomplete and require modernization. Consequently,

---

[19] Gordon & Pohl, *supra* note 1, at 32.

[20] UNCTAD, *supra* note 9, at 103.

[21] These findings mirror the responses collected by Taylor St. John and Geoffrey Gertz justifying the rare use of joint interpretations. *See* St. John & Gertz, *supra* note 2.

[22] UNCTAD, *supra* note 3, at 3.

[23] Data retrieved from the UNCTAD Investment Policy Hub, May 21, 2021.

states, like the hosts after a dinner party, are daunted by the cleanup task they face. Where even to begin? Moreover, piecemeal renegotiations seem a poor use of scarce resources. Would it not be wiser to focus time and energy on new agreements or multilateral negotiations that promise higher returns for the same investment? This reasoning is flawed, however, because different renegotiation opportunities produce varying returns. A single targeted renegotiation can have more impact than the renegotiation of dozens of treaties. States can make efficient use of scarce resources by focusing on renegotiations that matter most.

The impact of renegotiations follows a power law distribution: few treaties matter a lot, and most treaties matter little. Consider three metrics: coverage of foreign direct investment (FDI) stock, overlap with other IIAs and ISDS litigation risk. Most IIAs cover a tiny fraction of global FDI stock, but a few IIAs cover large shares. Most IIAs overlap and interact with none or only one other parallel IIA. Yet a few IIA interact and influence many other agreements. Most IIAs have attracted no ISDS claims at all, while a few have been litigated extensively. Policymakers and negotiators can leverage this power law dynamic by focusing renegotiation efforts on those agreements that produce the biggest bang for the buck.

Take a treaty's coverage of FDI stock first. For example, between 2008 and 2017 the FDI stock of the European Union in China more than doubled and increased tenfold in the other direction, amounting to EUR 158 billion and EUR 59 billion in 2017, respectively.[24] The EU–China relationship thereby constitutes one of the most important bilateral country dyads in the world in terms of FDI stock. States can thus pick renegotiation targets by focusing on the economic relationships that matter most.

But states can also pick renegotiations based on their normative impact. Sometimes economic and normative impact align. IIA renegotiations between FDI powerhouses, as in the case of the renegotiation of NAFTA between Canada, Mexico, and the United States, attract global attention and may produce treaty design that is subsequently emulated elsewhere. The remainder of this section, however, focuses on renegotiations that develop significantly normative impact irrespective of their economic significance by homing in on treaty renegotiation candidates that (1) maximize treaty overlap, and (2) minimize ISDS litigations risks.

---

[24] European Parliament, *EU-China Trade and Investment Relations in Challenging Times*, May 2020, available at https://www.europarl.europa.eu/RegData/etudes/STUD/2020/603492/EXPO_STU(2020)603492_EN.pdf (last accessed October 21, 2021).

Table 8.2 EU treaties replacing overlapping BITs (source: EDIT)

EU Treaty	Number of replaced EU Member BITs
Canada–EU CETA (2016)	7
EU–Singapore Investment Protection Agreement (2018)	11
EU–Viet Nam Investment Protection Agreement (2019)	20
EU–China (under negotiation)	22

1. Maximizing Treaty Overlap

Most renegotiations update a single treaty, but a few renegotiation opportunities can generate broader knock-on effects either by replacing parallel treaties or by affecting their interpretations. It is worth considering each in turn.

The European Union has used its own IIA practice to phase out parallel IIAs concluded by EU member states. Each EU-led negotiation is therefore a de facto renegotiation whereby numerous outdated BITs are replaced by a more complete IIA (Table 8.2). For example, the envisaged EU–China investment protection treaty will not only cover one of the most dynamic and economically important investment relationships, but it will also replace twenty-two existing BITs that EU members have signed with China. These BITs are on average twenty-four years old, with the BIT between China and Sweden going all the way back to 1982. One renegotiation would therefore update a multitude of existing investment treaty relations.

A second way a single renegotiation can impact several parallel IIAs is through interpretation. As argued in detail in Chapter 7, a parallel treaty signed by an overlapping subset of states affects the interpretation of the original treaty as a relevant rule of international law applicable between the parties under VCLT Article 31(3)c. As documented in Table 8.3, the absolute champion in terms of IIA overlaps is the ECT (1994), which coexists alongside 609 signed BITs. Put differently, every fourth BIT currently in force applies in parallel to the Energy Charter. The potential of the ECT to affect the interpretation of these treaties is thus immense.

Renegotiations to modernize the ECT formally commenced in July 2020.[25] These efforts are important not only to align the ECT with the climate change objectives of the twenty-first century, but they matter immensely for the interpretative modernization of the IIA stock. True, the scope of the ECT is confined

---

[25] Energy Charter Secretariat, *Modernisation of the Energy Charter Treaty*, available at https://www.energychartertreaty.org/modernisation-of-the-treaty/ (last accessed May 21, 2021).

Table 8.3 Regional IIAs overlapping with concluded BITs (signed or in force) (source: EDIT, UNCTAD*)

Treaty	Number of overlapping BITs
Energy Charter Treaty (1994)	609
OIC Investment Agreement (1981)*	345
African Continental Free Trade Agreement (in negotiation)*	158
Unified Agreement for the Investment of Arab Capital in the Arab States (1980)	99
Regional Comprehensive Economic Partnership Agreement (RCEP) (2020)	34

to economic activity in the energy sector.[26] Yet the treaty's investment protection sections cover all core protective obligations, which are indistinguishable from those found in other IIAs in terms of form and substance. As a parallel IIA applicable between the contracting states, tribunals will need to take a renegotiated ECT into account when interpreting an overlapping BIT. As a result, the ECT provides relevant interpretive context for the interpretation of hundreds of investment agreements signed between ECT member states.

According to the modernization mandate adopted by the Energy Charter Conference in 2018, the renegotiations will cover all major aspects of the ECT's investment norms from the definition of investment, to protective obligations such as FET, MFN, and indirect expropriation, to exceptions and the right to regulate as well as matters surrounding dispute settlement.[27] The European Union has submitted detailed text, which mirrors its recent treaty practice.[28] The more than six hundred BITs that are overlapping with the ECT have been concluded on average in 1997, but stretch as far back as 1961. The ECT therefore has immense potential to indirectly inform the reading of a highly incomplete and outdated stock of hundreds of BITs. The ECT thus comes as close as it gets to becoming a quasi-multilateral substantive reform treaty.

The ECT epitomizes the impact a single renegotiation can have when the treaty overlaps with other IIAs. Such interpretive ripple effects are, of course, not

[26] *See* ECT Article 1: Definition.

[27] Decision of the Energy Charter Conference, CCDEC 2018 18, Brussels, November 27, 2018, available at https://www.energycharter.org/fileadmin/DocumentsMedia/CCDECS/2018/CCDEC 201818_-_STR_Modernisation_of_the_Energy_Charter_Treaty.pdf (last accessed May 21, 2021).

[28] EU text proposal for the modernisation of the Energy Charter Treaty, available at https://trade.ec.europa.eu/doclib/docs/2020/may/tradoc_158754.pdf (last accessed May 21, 2021).

limited to the ECT, but they apply to any regional IIA. Table 8.3 summarizes the regional IIAs with the highest overlap with signed BITs. While the ECT stands out, other (re)negotiation efforts could also update significant portions of the outdated IIA stock. A renegotiation of the Organization of Islamic Cooperation (OIC) Investment Agreement, for example, could help update the interpretation of 345 parallel BITs. In the same vein, negotiations of the African Continental Investment Code, ongoing at the time of this writing, could help modernize 158 overlapping BITs.

These varying regional treaties have, for the most part, complementary rather than shared sets of members. It follows that only a handful of (re)negotiated IIAs could update more than a third of the BIT stock. If one adds the phase out of intra-EU and some extra-EU BITs, then this almost obfuscates the need for a broader multilateral reform of substantive investment norms as around half of the BIT stock can be updated directly or indirectly through targeted renegotiations.

Add to this the signaling effect of such major renegotiations. As discussed in Chapter 3, states around the globe have routinely looked to leading developed states when revising their own treaty programs. EU-led renegotiations promise to spark similar emulation. In addition, the direct exposure of many states to (re)negotiations, for example, in the context of the ECT modernization, but also as part of the multilateral UNCITRAL reforms discussed in Chapter 9, will likely facilitate finding common ground in subsequent bilateral treaty reforms. Hence, a few renegotiations can generate systemic ripple effects without requiring systemic reforms.

2. Minimizing Risks of ISDS Claims

But focusing solely on the impact of renegotiations on parallel IIAs would miss another important point. Some bilateral relationships are in greater need for renegotiation than others. Incomplete treaties create heightened risks of ISDS claims because they appear more favorable to investors due to their vagueness and lack of exceptions, which helps attract litigation.[29] Moreover, as shown in Part II, incomplete IIAs indirectly also risk rolling back innovation in more complete agreements through MFN, custom, and precedent. A single incomplete IIA can undermine an otherwise entirely modern national IIA network. Renegotiation efforts need to target such weak spots to minimize the exposure to ISDS-related risks for all national IIAs.

Consider the IIA network of Canada as an example. Most of its IIAs are long, detailed, and comprehensive corresponding to today's best practices of concluding more complete IIAs. Yet the country is also still party to several

---

[29] *See, e.g.*, UNCTAD, *supra* note 3.

old-generation BITs in force that are short, simple, and lack the exceptions and qualifications that characterize later agreements.[30] Such outdated agreements can become a liability. As Patrick Dumberry notes, Article 3 of the Canada–Hungary BIT (1991) contains an open-textured FET clause without textual link to international law or custom, which could be read as offering more favorable treatment than all subsequent Canadian treaties that do contain such a link, in which case that more favorable FET clause could be read into all other Canadian treaties via their respective MFN clauses.[31] One treaty thereby jeopardizes the treaty practice of decades. Such outlier treaties should be prime targets for renegotiations, if only to mitigate their impact on more complete agreements in the same network.

On the other extreme are states with large, outdated treaty networks and few more complete agreements. Germany, for example, may have been a pioneer in the conclusion of BITs, but as a result, German investors are still protected by scores of old BITs that lack ISDS, because they were concluded in the 1960s to 1980s. As the OECD noted in 2012, "Germany, which is reputed to have favourable views on ISDS through international arbitration, is the country with the largest stock of treaties—and the largest proportion of treaties (36%)—that contain no ISDS provisions whatsoever."[32] Targeted renegotiations may thus not be an effective option for the country, and a more ambitious renegotiation agenda is required. Germany may therefore benefit disproportionately from EU-led renegotiations to overhaul its outdated IIA network as compared to other EU states whose treaty practice is of a more recent vintage.

The level of contractual incompleteness, however, is only a rough proxy for the risk of ISDS claims. States may want to go deeper into the design of specific IIAs to assess the vulnerability to investment claims and the probability of adverse rulings to select targets for renegotiation. Australia, for example, renegotiated its 1993 BIT with Hong Kong in 2019 after Philip Morris had launched a claim under the original BIT challenging the country's plain cigarette packaging legislation.[33] The 1993 BIT was the only Australian BIT to contain an unqualified umbrella

---

[30] Canada–Russian Federation BIT (1989), Canada–Poland BIT (1990), Canada–Hungary BIT (1991), Argentina–Canada BIT (1991).

[31] Patrick Dumberry, *The Importation of "Better" Fair and Equitable Treatment Standard Protection Through MFN Clauses: An Analysis of NAFTA Article 1103*, 14 TRANSNAT'L DISP. MGMT. 11–12 (2017).

[32] J. Pohl, K. Mashigo, & A. Nohen, *Dispute Settlement Provisions in International Investment Agreements: A Large Sample Survey*, OECD Working Papers on International Investment, 2012/ 02 at 44.

[33] *Philip Morris Asia Limited v. The Commonwealth of Australia*, UNCITRAL, PCA Case No. 2012-12. For background and commentary, *see* Jarrod Hepburn & Luke Nottage, *A Procedural Win for Public Health Measures: Philip Morris Asia Ltd v. Commonwealth of Australia, PCA Case No. 2012-12, Award on Jurisdiction and Admissibility, 17 December 2015 (Karl-Heinz Böckstiegel, Gabrielle Kaufmann-Kohler, Donald M. McRae)*, 18 J. WORLD INVESTMENT & TRADE 307–319 (2017).

clause, which Philip Morris had initially used as a basis for one of its claims. The replacement BIT does not contain an umbrella clause.[34] Furthermore, the fact that Australia chose not to renegotiate other older BITs, such as its 1990 BIT with Papua New Guinea, suggests that the country is engaged in a targeted effort to manage liability risks arising from an outlier treaty. This practice is worth emulating.

But how can states identify such outliers? Do countries like Australia have to wait for a claim to be launched before a BIT's litigation risk is exposed? The answer is no. Comparative data analysis on the content of agreements can easily spot outlier agreements. For example, consider the color-coded mapping of selected protection and exception clauses across Australia's BITs extracted from the EDIT database. It reveals the 1993 BIT with Hong Kong as an outlier (Figure 8.2). With an additional arbitrary measures clause (rare in other Australian BITs) and an umbrella clause (lacking in other Australian BITs), the BIT has more protective features than all other Australian BITs. Conversely, it lacks some of the flexibility elements present in at least some of Australia's BITs, such as a balance of payments exception. Together, this makes the Australia–Hong Kong BIT an unusually harsh investment protection agreement compared to other Australian BITs and a reasonable target for renegotiations.

B. How to Renegotiate?

The promise of a data-driven approach to renegotiation, however, goes beyond selecting candidates for renegotiations and has its greatest potential in the preparation and structuring of the renegotiation itself. So-called "legal analytics" applications that represent large amounts of legal information in accessible, often graphical or numerical forms ("dashboards") are beginning to be used throughout legal practice to make evidence-based decisions.[35] From the selection of arbitrators based on a comprehensive assessment of their past practice to the picking of a claim based on a prediction of its probable success in a litigation, legal analytics tools increasingly inform a broad range of legal decision-making, including in investment arbitration.[36] Armed with better data, lawyers and negotiators can make better decisions, including in IIA renegotiations.

---

[34] Text of the Australia-Hong Kong BIT (2019) available at: https://www.dfat.gov.au/trade/agreements/in-force/a-hkfta/Pages/the-investment-agreement-text.

[35] *See generally* KEVIN D. ASHLEY, ARTIFICIAL INTELLIGENCE AND LEGAL ANALYTICS (2017).

[36] Wolfgang Alschner & Damien Charlotin, *Data Mining, Text Analytics, and Investor-State Arbitration, in* INTERNATIONAL ARBITRATION AND TECHNOLOGY (Pietro Ortolani ed., forthcoming).

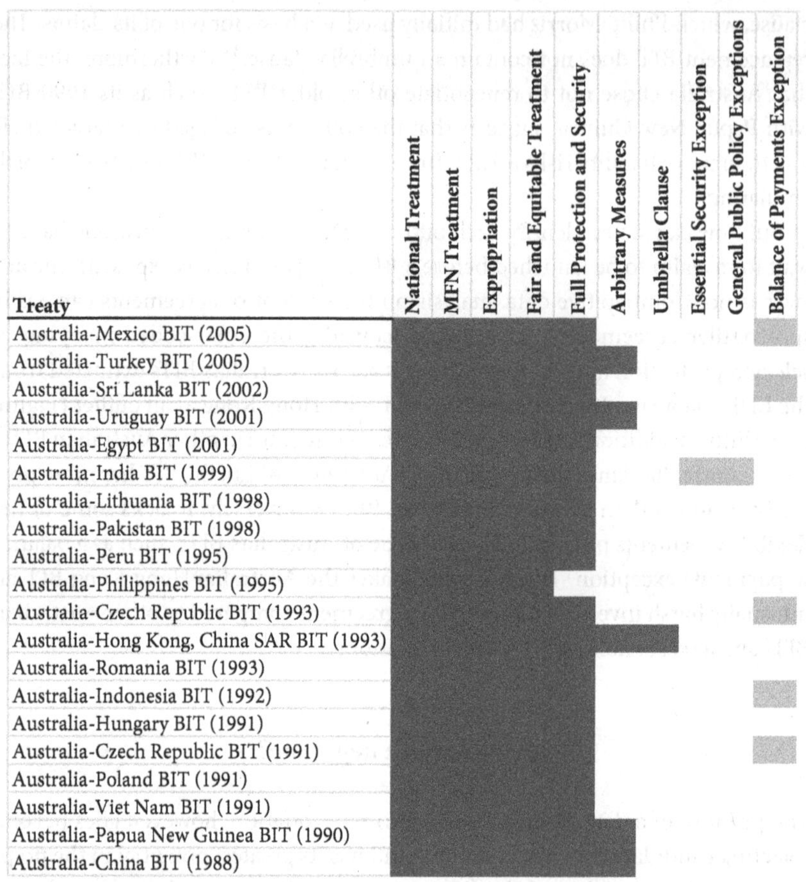

Figure 8.2 Selected content elements in Australian BITs color-coded for their presence (dark grey indicates investment protection obligations and bright grey host state flexibilities; data source: EDIT)

Capacity constraints as well as opposition from negotiation partners are core constraints preventing widespread use of renegotiations. Legal analytics can help address both issues.[37] Legal analytics applications can compensate for a lack of resources by incorporating expert knowledge. They also augment the ability of negotiators to efficiently process large amounts of complex information. For example, legal analytics allow negotiators to quickly access latest trends in treaty-making or compare national IIA practices to identify areas of normative convergence. In the future, legal analytics may go beyond descriptive insights and provide predictive solutions. Early work suggests that technology could

---

[37] At the same time, technology can also exacerbate power asymmetries; *see* Ashley Deeks, *High-Tech International Law*, 88 GEO. WASH. L. REV. 80 (2020).

autonomously generate consensus language based on an analysis of past practice to help negotiators draft the final treaty.

1. Spotting Trends: Situating Renegotiations in Global Practice

One way to alleviate capacity constraints consists of allowing negotiators to efficiently monitor trends in the IIA universe. What are current best practices? What clauses have fallen into disuse? Where is a country leading and where is it falling behind? If answering these questions requires new research every time, then it is easy to see how states find it challenging to tackle renegotiations. Legal analytics provide an alternative to efficiently monitor global practice.

In preparation for (re)negotiations, negotiators benefit from consulting recent developments in IIA practice. For example, the bar chart of Figure 8.3 compares counts of yearly concluded IIAs with umbrella clauses and public policy exceptions. Negotiators may find it useful to know that umbrella clauses have fallen into disuse while general public policy exceptions have gained traction in recent IIA practice in order to evaluate their own negotiating agenda or to anticipate expectations of their counterparts. Such knowledge can also provide evidence-based arguments for an inclusion of public policy exceptions and an exclusion of umbrella clauses.

The advantage of legal analytics platforms is that information can be adjusted and tailored almost effortlessly to new questions asked by users. Consider a hypothetical renegotiation of the 1992 Turkey–Japan BIT. The BIT ranks low in

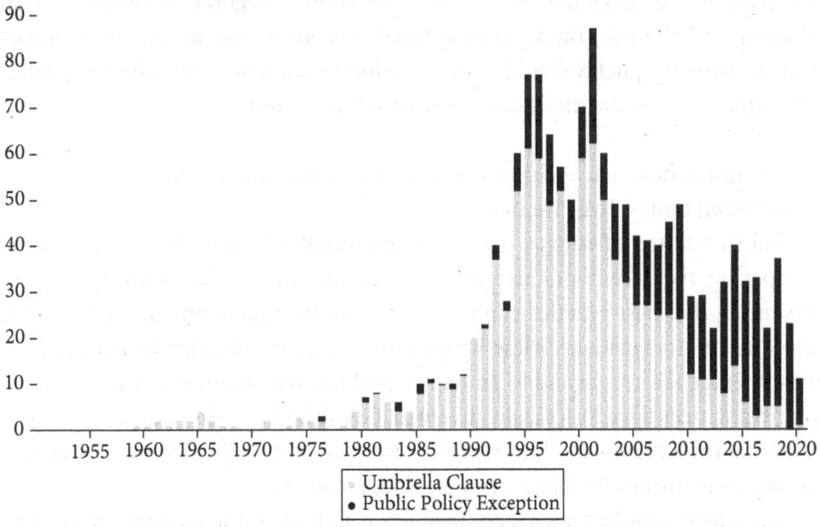

Figure 8.3 Counts of IIAs with umbrella clauses or public policy exception by year of signature (source: EDIT)

contractual completeness. The various strategies discussed in Chapter 2 that render an agreement more complete are largely absent in the treaty. Short, open-textured protective language, an absence of escape clauses (exceptions are limited to privileges arising out of tax treaties and an exclusion of some intellectual property rights), a concise ISDS clause, and a brief preamble characterize the BIT. A renegotiation would thus provide an opportunity to add detail, insert escape clauses, elaborate on the terms of delegation to ISDS, and add new relational elements to render the renegotiated agreement more complete.

Clause-specific trends can then inform the renegotiation around specific treaty elements of the 1992 Turkey–Japan BIT. For example, the 1992 BIT provides an access-to-courts provision on a national treatment and MFN basis. Such a clause is extremely rare in global practice and arguable redundant given that national and MFN treatment ordinarily encompasses treatment by all branches of governments including courts. The provision could thus be eliminated in a renegotiation. Conversely, the BIT lacks an FET provision, which (albeit in different textual guises) has since become quasi-ubiquitous in global treaty practice and could be added to align the agreement with modern practice. Other clauses absent in the original agreement, such as prohibitions on performance requirements or a national security exception, have increased drastically in relative usage and would be candidates for inclusion in a revised agreement.

While this brief comparison of the BIT's content with global practice is by no means exhaustive, it showcases how even simple analytics such as the relative global usage of specific clauses can quickly inform (re)negotiations. Legal analytics thereby does not predetermine outcomes. Negotiators remain free to swim against the tide. But legal analytics does compensate for scarce resources and expertise by quickly distilling information on current trends directing states' attention to issues that may benefit from modernization.

2. Finding Consensus: Mapping Divergence and Convergence between States' IIA Practices

Global trends are, of course, only a starting point. What matters even more is comparing the recent practice of the states involved in the (re)negotiation. Assuming that past practice can tell us about future preferences, such insights allow negotiators to identify low-hanging fruit in a renegotiation on issues where past practices converge and to anticipate and resolve disagreements on matters where practices have historically diverged. Going back to a hypothetical renegotiation of the 1992 Japan–Turkey BIT, in what areas does the recent IIA practice of Japan and Turkey diverge and where does it converge?

One way to conduct such a comparison is to look at the relative inclusion of specific treaty features in a country's recent practice. Figure 8.4 plots the share

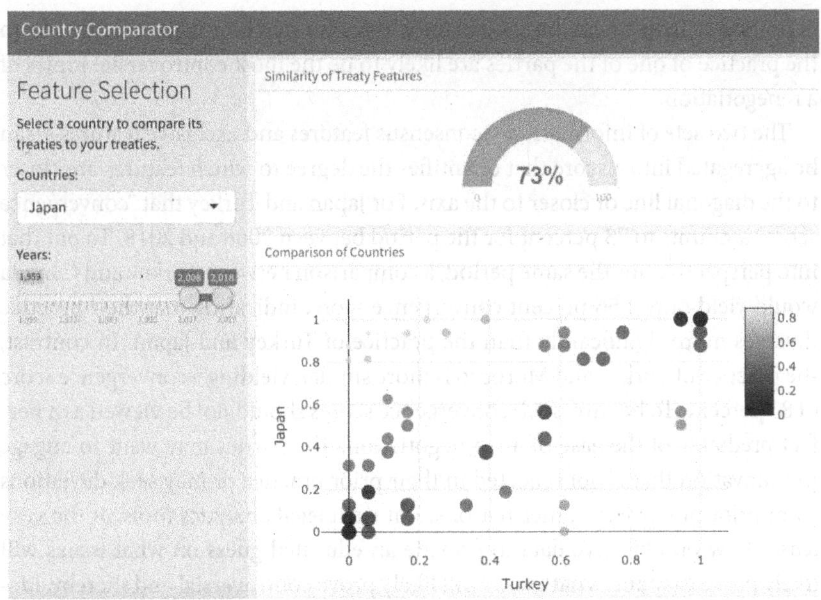

Figure 8.4 Comparison of IIA practices of Turkey and Japan (data
source: UNCTAD; analysis and dashboard by author)

of specific content features in Turkish IIAs (x-axis) and Japanese IIAs (y-axis)
signed between 2008 and 2018. If all Turkish and all Japanese IIAs possess a treaty
feature, as is the case for free transfer of fund clauses, for example, that feature
will be in the upper-right corner because 100 percent of Turkish and 100 percent
of Japanese IIAs include it. Conversely, a feature that is neither in Turkish nor in
Japanese agreements will be located on the lower-left corner because 0 percent
of Turkish and 0 percent of Japanese treaties have it. The diagonal line between
these points then represents "consensus candidates"—features that Japan and
Turkey have included in their agreements in roughly equal shares. For example,
72 percent of Turkish and 81 percent of Japanese IIAs include an essential security clause. In short, the features along the diagonal line are likely to cause little
controversy in the negotiations since Japan and Turkey have approached them
similarly in their recent practice.

The same visualization also reveals items that will likely prove controversial in
negotiations. Treaty features that are closer to the two axes are more closely associated with the practice of one of the two states. At its extreme, a feature located
on one of the axes means that only one of the states has included that clause in
its prior practice. For example, 88 percent of Japanese treaties include a prohibition of performance requirements, but none of the Turkish IIAs do. Conversely,
61 percent of Turkish agreements exclude portfolio investments from the

definition of investment, but no Japanese IIA does so. These features exclusive to the practice of one of the parties are likely to be the most controversial topics of a renegotiation.

The two sets of information—consensus features and exclusive features—can be aggregated into a score that quantifies the degree to which features are closer to the diagonal line or closer to the axis. For Japan and Turkey that "convergence score" amounts to 73 percent for the period between 2008 and 2018. To put that into perspective, for the same period, a comparison between Turkey and Canada would yield only a 56 percent convergence score, indicating that their practice diverges more significantly than the practice of Turkey and Japan. In contrast, the practice of Turkey and Morocco is more similar, yielding a convergence score of 83 percent. To be sure, such convergence scores should not be viewed as a perfect predictor of the ease of a (re)negotiation. The parties may want to engage in innovation that is not reflected in their prior practice or may seek deviations from prior practice for other reasons. But such legal analytics tools, at the very least, draw on objective data to provide an educated guess on what issues will likely prove easy and what issues will likely prove controversial and thereby, ideally, make (re)negotiations more streamlined, less contentious, and less costly.

3. The Future: Predicting Negotiated Texts

Having a snapshot of parties' prior practice is useful for preparing negotiations, to identify consensus candidates, and to anticipate controversial features. Yet it still leaves much of the actual (re)negotiation to be done as negotiators haggle over the specific language of their future agreement. But even there, the latest generation of predictive legal analytics can assist.

A (re)negotiation today is likely to start with two competing models, or at least with two competing past practices. In domestic contract negotiations, this is known as the "battle of the forms"—prospective contractors bargain over whose template or practice is to form the starting point for the negotiation. Recent advances in artificial intelligence provide an alternative. Neural networks, which have fueled recent successes from better machine translation to more accurate image recognition, have also produced another marvel: automated text generation. Recurrent neural networks (RNNs) can be trained on existing texts to generate new text.[38]

Early research has shown how this technique may be applied to automatically generate consensus drafts as a neutral starting point for IIA negotiations.[39]

---

[38] ANDREJ KARPATHY, CHAR-RNN: MULTI-LAYER RECURRENT NEURAL NETWORKS (LSTM, GRU, RNN) FOR CHARACTER-LEVEL LANGUAGE MODELS IN TORCH (2016), https://github.com/karpathy/char-rnn.

[39] Wolfgang Alschner & Dmitriy Skougarevskiy, *Can Robots Write Treaties? Using Recurrent Neural Networks to Draft International Investment Agreements*, in LEGAL KNOWLEDGE AND

Table 8.4 Computer-generated transfer of funds clause

Article 4: Transfer

Each Contracting Party shall, subject to its laws and regulations, guarantee investors
of the other Contracting Party the transfer of their investments and returns held in its
territory, including:
(a) profits, dividends, interests and other legitimate income;
(b) amounts from total or partial liquidation of investments;
(c) payments made pursuant to a loan agreement in connection with investment;
(d) royalties in paragraph 1 (d) of Article 1;
(e) payments of technical assistance or technical service fee, management fee;
(f) payments in connection with projects on contract;
(g) earnings of nationals of the other Contracting Party who work in connection with
an investment in the territory of the former Contracting Party.
1.
2. Nothing in paragraph 1 of this Article shall affect the free transfer of compensation
paid under Article 6 of this Agreement.
3. The transfer mentioned above shall be made in a freely convertible currency and
at the prevailing market rate of exchange applicable within the Contracting Party
accepting the investments and on the date of transfer.

The process consists of three steps. First, an RNN algorithm "learns to speak"
the language of IIAs. It is trained on all existing IIA articles, which are inversely
weighted by their year of creation so that recent practice matters more than older
one. Second, the RNN automatically drafts hundreds of article texts for each article category, such as expropriation or transfer of funds. Third, depending on
who the negotiating parties are, the corpus of machine-produced articles is fil-
tered to finds consensus article candidates that are equidistant, in terms of their
textual similarity, to the past practice of the negotiating states. In past research,
this technique was used to "predict" the language of a possible US–China BIT.
Table 8.4 produces an automatically generated transfer of funds clause that is
equidistant between China and the United States. Other examples are available
on an accompanying website.[40]

Admittedly, the results remain of modest quality. The current generation of
artificial intelligence excels at recognizing patterns, but it does not understand
the meaning of text. For example, RNN-produced plays sound Shakespearian,

---

INFORMATION SYSTEMS: JURIX 2016 119–124 (Floris Bex ed., 2016); Wolfgang Alschner &
Dmitriy Skougarevskiy, *Towards an Automated Production of Legal Texts Using Recurrent Neural
Networks*, 16TH INTERNATIONAL CONFERENCE ARTIFICIAL INTELLIGENCE AND LAW, CONFERENCE
PROCEEDINGS 229–332 (2017).

[40] Mapping Investment Treaties, RNN experiment, available at http://mappinginvestmenttreaties.
com/specials/rnn-experiment/.

but their plots make little sense.[41] While that means that completely autonomous text generation is still years away, it does not mean its current output is without uses. In the context of IIA negotiations, automated text generation can produce first drafts that, while far from perfect, constitute a middle ground between the negotiating parties' past divergent practice. By producing compromise text, it also helps avoid a battle of the forms.

The promise of legal analytics is thus large. In the short term, legal analytics tool can address concerns over cost and capacity constraints. Even simple analytics can help overcome opposition among contracting parties by identifying areas where global practice has moved on or by highlighting areas where the practice of contracting states provides common ground. In the longer term, the shift from descriptive to predictive analytics holds even greater potential. Negotiators ultimately care about text rather than statistics on past practice. RNN technology can significantly alleviate capacity constraints and facilitate negotiations by providing draft consensus texts. A data-driven approach therefore promises to revitalize renegotiations as a tool for investment law reform and for modernizing incomplete treaties in light of more complete ones.

IV. Plurilaterals: Replacing or Exacerbating the Spaghetti Bowl?

Renegotiations are more impactful (few renegotiations can affect many treaties) and less costly and resource-intensive (thanks to technology) than commonly assumed. But even if practical obstacles can be overcome, a policy question lingers: How far should states take the quest for renegotiation and consolidation? Regional and interregional multiparty treaties (called "plurilaterals" for convenience's sake) are quickly replacing bilaterals as the dominant medium for regulating investment protection relations. Should plurilaterals power-charge renegotiations and replace existing bilateral treaties in bulk? Or should plurilaterals add another layer on top of existing BITs?

States have pursued different strategies to manage the coexistence of old BITs and new plurilaterals. On one end of the spectrum, the European Union has used the trend toward plurilaterals to overhaul the often-outdated bilateral treaty networks of EU member states. In intra-EU relations, BITs are being phased out in favor of regional internal EU market rules.[42] In external EU relations, as noted

---

[41] Andrej Karpathy, *The Unreasonable Effectiveness of Recurrent Neural Networks*, ANDREJ KARPATHY BLOG, May 21, 2015, available at http://karpathy.github.io/2015/05/21/rnn-effectiveness/.

[42] The Agreement for the Termination of Bilateral Investment Treaties Between the Member States of the European Union entered into force in August 2020 and terminates at least 124 BITs between

earlier, new EU FTAs with investment chapters and self-standing EU investment protection agreements replace parallel BITs of EU member states. On the other end of the spectrum, plurilaterals create several additional layers on top of BITs. In Southeast Asia, for example, intra-ASEAN BITs coexist with regional ASEAN investment protection rules, and BITs or FTAs by ASEAN members with third states coexist with IIAs signed by ASEAN as a block as well as Regional Comprehensive Economic Partnership (RCEP) rules. In Africa, the future investment code of the Continental Free Trade Agreement will coexist with BITs among African countries as well as regional investment rules of COMESA or Southern African Development Community (SADC) creating three or four layers of investment protection rules.

The majority of plurilaterals are used to complement rather than replace bilaterals. The EDIT database records only thirty-five instances, in which an FTA replaces, incorporates, or suspends a BIT.[43] This compares to more than three thousand instances where FTAs coexist with BITs. Out of fifty-seven plurilaterals in EDIT that overlap with at least five other IIAs, only three plurilaterals (signed by the European Union with Canada, Vietnam, and Singapore) replace all parallel treaties. Some plurilaterals, like the CPTPP, replace some parallel BITs, but only between a small subset of its members.[44] Most other plurilaterals exist in parallel to existing IIAs. In short, as UNCTAD notes, "plurilateral IIAs have missed the opportunity for consolidation and, instead, have led to parallel application of the new and old treaties."[45]

A. The Benefits of Layering

What are the respective costs and benefits of layering? There are at least three potential advantages for using plurilaterals as complements rather than replacements to BITs: (1) treaty ambition, (2) differentiation, and (3) resilience. Ambition is perhaps the most intuitive. When more than two states are involved in negotiations, the need for compromise grows. Ambitious goals may be abandoned as negotiators are forced to settle on the lowest common denominator.

EU members. *See also* Charbel A. Moarbes, *Agreement for the Termination of Bilateral Investment Treaties Between the Member States of the European Union*, 60 Int'l Legal Materials 99–137 (2021).

[43] Similarly, Broude et al. count twenty-two instances of PTAs replacing BITs. In the same vein, UNCTAD reports only twenty-two instances of replacement of suspension by a PTA. *See* UNCTAD, *supra* note 3, at 6.

[44] Australia terminated its overlapping BITs in side letters with Vietnam, Mexico and Peru. *See* https://www.dfat.gov.au/trade/agreements/in-force/cptpp/official-documents.

[45] UNCTAD, *supra* note 3, at 13.

The logic of treaties with varying ambition drives layering in the international trade regime where the multilateral rules form a normative baseline, but states remain free to embark on more ambitious liberalization efforts through bilateral or regional free trade agreements.[46] In investment law, however, the case is less clear-cut. Even though bilaterals could, in theory, be used to entrench more ambitious investment commitments, there are only few examples in practice where that is the case.[47] In fact, plurilateral IIAs are often more rather than less ambitious than the older, shallow, and less complete bilaterals that they coexist with.[48]

What about differentiation? In negotiating plurilaterals, states may be forced to agree to a one-size-fits-all approach. That may be problematic, especially when states at very different levels of development are involved. In contrast, bilaterals, in theory, allow for careful tailoring to specific bilateral relations. In practice, however, these stylized expectations are not consistently reflected. Plurilaterals allow for a surprising amount of tailoring. Consider the United States-Mexico-Canada Agreement (USMCA) that provides for ISDS only between the United States and Mexico.[49] RCEP's investment chapter contains country-specific footnotes that carve out or clarify obligations vis-à-vis specific states.[50] The CPTPP is accompanied by side letters that tailor the agreement to the member dyads. Conversely, bilaterals typically follow model templates across negotiations with little to no tailoring to specific country relationships.[51] Hence, differentiation again seems not to be a driving force behind layering.

Resilience is a final factor driving layering. Having a "spare" bilateral in place to protect foreign investor offers a safety net in case the plurilateral is terminated. It enables states to benefit from regional efforts to protect investors, while not being dependent on them. In that sense, it appears risky not to keep overlapping bilaterals in place. Yet, there are alternatives to ensure that investment remains protected. Switzerland, for example, tends to suspend bilaterals when an overlapping plurilateral is signed.[52] If the plurilateral fails for whatever reason, the BIT is immediately reactivated. In short, while layering has potential benefits, they can be achieved without engaging in treaty layering.

---

[46] Wolfgang Alschner, *Regionalism and Overlap in Investment Treaty Law: Towards Consolidation or Contradiction?*, 17 J. Int'l Econ. L. 271–298, 286 (2014).

[47] For examples and an in-depth discussion, *see id.* at 287–88.

[48] The TPP and its successor, the CPTPP, are cases in point. They were branded as high-ambition agreements and, indeed, are firmly embedded in high-completeness-scoring American treaty practice. Wolfgang Alschner & Dmitriy Skougarevskiy, *The New Gold Standard? Empirically Situating the Trans-Pacific Partnership in the Investment Treaty Universe*, 17 J. World Investment & Trade (2016).

[49] USMCA, Annex 14-D, Mexico-United States Disputes.

[50] *See, e.g.*, RCEP, ch. 18, footnotes 1 and 2 (limiting the definition of covered investments) or footnote 18 (excluding MFN treatment for some parties).

[51] Wolfgang Alschner & Dmitriy Skougarevskiy, *Mapping the Universe of International Investment Agreements*, 19 J. Int'l Econ. L. (2016).

[52] *E.g.*, the Switzerland–Liechtenstein–Iceland–South Korea investment treaty suspends the Switzerland–South Korea BIT (1971) in Article 27 as long as the former remains in force.

B. The Costs of Layering

Whereas the benefits of layering are questionable, its costs relating to (1) litigation diversion, (2) normative conflict, and (3) unnecessary complexity are readily apparent and undermine the innovation otherwise promised by plurilaterals.

First, layered treaty levels divert claims to old bilaterals and away from new plurilaterals. Treaty shopping is a natural consequence of the availability of a variety of adjudicatory venues.[53] It can become a concern for states when litigation is diverted to unwanted treaties. Claimants are likely to bring their cases where they have the best chances of winning. The vague language and missing exceptions coupled with a poorly defined ISDS procedure tend to turn older, incomplete bilaterals into a more attractive option as compared to more complete plurilaterals.[54] Consider the newly concluded CPTPP, which incorporates the TPP and its Article 29.5, which allows parties to block ISDS claims against tobacco control measures. This new feature can easily be circumvented by launching a claim under a parallel, older BIT that lacks such a safeguard. Layering therefore dulls the practical effect of innovations in plurilaterals by diverting claims to older bilaterals.

Second, the coexistence of plurilaterals and bilaterals raises the specter of normative conflict.[55] A myriad of legal questions relating to jurisdictional treaty overlaps remain unresolved. What happens if an investor pursues the same claim under two parallel treaties, either concurrently or subsequently? Can an investor have a second bite of the apple or do principles like *lis pendens* or *res judicata* bar such claims although the underlying treaties differ slightly?[56] When it comes to the merits, largely unsettled questions on the conflicts of norms decide which of several applicable treaties prevails.[57] Would a tribunal be able to apply overlapping treaties if a claim is launched under just one of them? If so, what happens if one treaty contains a decisive exception and the other does not? In short, the overlap of parallel agreements raises a host of unresolved normative questions and complexities.

Finally, layering adds transaction costs in a system designed to reduce them. When multiple treaties apply to the same investor-state relationship, things get complex.[58] Investors have to decide what treaty is more favorable and anticipate

---

[53] *See generally* BAUMGARTNER JORUN, TREATY SHOPPING IN INTERNATIONAL INVESTMENT LAW (2017).

[54] *See* UNCTAD, *supra* note 3, at 5 (noting that "New, 'reformed' IIAs with reformed treaty clauses thus often co-exist with old, 'unreformed' IIAs containing unreformed treaty clauses.").

[55] *See* Alschner, *supra* note 46, at 288–297.

[56] On managing jurisdictional conflicts, *see* Joost Pauwelyn & Luiz Eduardo Salles, *Forum Shopping Before International Tribunals:(Real) Concerns, (Im)Possible Solutions*, 42 CORNELL INT'L L.J. (2009).

[57] *See generally* JOOST PAUWELYN, CONFLICT OF NORMS IN PUBLIC INTERNATIONAL LAW: HOW WTO LAW RELATES TO OTHER RULES OF INTERNATIONAL LAW (reprint ed. 2004).

[58] UNCTAD, WORLD INVESTMENT REPORT 2014. INVESTING IN THE SDGs: AN ACTION PLAN 121–122 (2014).

how tribunals may deal with the various normative conflicts that may arise. Host states have to manage compliance with multiple obligations and, similarly, consider possible normative conflicts between them. Since IIAs have developed, at least in part, to reduce political risk and to enhance certainty and predictability, such layering, which increases legal uncertainty and complexity, contradicts investment law's underlying goals.

C. Using Plurilaterals as Renegotiation Tools

In conclusion, states should follow the example of the European Union and use plurilaterals as renegotiation tool whenever possible. While in theory layering could have benefits, in practice these benefits can be reaped through less costly alternative legal means such side letters and footnotes that tailor commitments to specific bilateral concerns and an incorporation or suspension of parallel BITs rather their termination. At the same time, the costs of layering are real and disconcerting.

Plurilaterals are the single most effective way, short of a multilateral treaty, to modernize the stock of outdated IIAs. Of course, states negotiate or renegotiate plurilaterals for a host of political and economic reasons that often have little to do with investment protection. But when the occasion arises, each newly negotiated plurilateral is an opportunity to tidy up existing investment relations, and each renegotiation of a plurilateral is an invitation to modernize multiple parallel BITs through a single replacement agreement. Renegotiations are time- and resource-intensive even when technology is used in support. By leveraging plurilaterals as a renegotiation tool, states can make sure the invested resources are wisely spent.

V. Conclusion

A data-driven approach promises to revitalize renegotiations as a tool for IIA reform and as a vital mechanism to align outdated and incomplete IIAs with current best practices. Smart prioritization and technology can help overcome practical obstacles that thus far have held back the use of renegotiations. They ensure that the scarce resources invested in updating existing IIAs are well spent. A crucial step toward fully leveraging renegotiations consists of ending the dominant practice of layering plurilaterals on top of bilaterals. Instead, wherever possible, plurilaterals should be used to replace outdated and incomplete bilateral rules with modern and more complete intra-regional or inter-regional ones.

9

Tax-Style Multilateralization

I. Introduction

The most efficient and effective way to remedy the bifurcation of the IIA universe into old and new investment agreements is multilateral reform. Multilateralization adds scale to interpretation (Chapter 7) and renegotiation (Chapter 8) by clarifying or amending thousands of existing investment treaties in one stroke. Current multilateral efforts to update the investment regime are ongoing under the auspices of the UN Commission on International Trade Law (UNCITRAL). This final chapter explores how these multilateral negotiations can modernize IIAs in substance and procedure by modeling reforms on the international tax regime.

Tax-style multilateralism already plays a prominent role in UNCITRAL talks. Tax law's Multilateral Instrument (MLI),[1] which sweepingly updated thousands of bilateral tax treaties (BTTs) in 2018, is discussed as a potential blueprint for an opt-in convention to extend eventual UNCITRAL reforms to thousands of existing IIAs.[2] Furthermore, Colombia proposed the MLI's design, which combines mandatory minimum standards and voluntary opt-ins, as a general template for accommodating a future menu of procedural reform options.[3] Tax-style multilateralism thus increasingly informs how negotiators think about implementing eventual UNCITRAL investment reforms.

This chapter suggests that tax-style multilateralism can play an even bigger role and guide not only the implementation of UNCITRAL reforms but the reforms themselves. Like investment law, the tax regime long suffered from a legitimacy crisis that pitted corporate interests against those of states.[4] At a time when multilateralism was in retreat elsewhere, tax negotiators were able to resolve that crisis through comprehensive global reforms that modified bilateral

---

[1] OECD, Multilateral Convention to Implement Tax Treaty Related Measures to Prevent Base Erosion and Profit Sharing (MLI), June 7, 2017.

[2] *See, e.g.*, UNCITRAL, Possible reform of investor-State dispute settlement (ISDS): Multilateral instrument on ISDS reform, A/CN.9/WG.III/WP.194, January 16, 2020, para. 25.

[3] Submission from the Government of Colombia, A/CN.9/WG.III/WP.173, June 14, 2019. Conceptually similar is also the Submission from the Governments of Chile, Israel, Japan, Mexico and Peru, A/CN.9/WG.III/WP.182, October 2, 2019.

[4] Wolfgang Alschner, *The OECD Multilateral Tax Instrument: A Model for Reforming the International Investment Regime?*, 45 BROOK. J. INT'L L. 33 (2019).

Investment Arbitration and State-Driven Reform. Wolfgang Alschner, Oxford University Press. © Oxford University Press 2022. DOI: 10.1093/oso/9780197644386.003.0010

treaties in substance and procedure. These reforms offer valuable lessons for investment negotiators on how to square bilateralism with multilateralism, accommodate diversity while advancing harmonization, and promote state-driven change through ongoing informal lawmaking and creative hard law reforms.[5] Tax-style multilateralism can therefore help frame the broader UNCITRAL agenda, guide the forward-looking interpretation of IIAs at the multilateral level, and inspire hard law reforms in both substance and procedure.

Take the UNCITRAL agenda first. UNCITRAL negotiations currently prioritize procedural ISDS reforms over substantive ones out of feasibility concerns. Yet the sweeping and ambitious reforms of the tax regime illustrate that a substantive reform of thousands of IIAs—if designed right—are more realistic than many investment negotiators think. In contrast to trade negotiations where nothing is agreed until everything is agreed and talks over substance often end in deadlock, tax-style multilateralism provides a pragmatic and flexible model for states to agree on core reforms without the need to agree on everything. That approach is particularly promising for investment law, where pockets of consensus already exist around both substantive and procedural issues that could be molded into minimum standards, leaving more controversial reforms to voluntary opt-ins. Tax-style multilateralism therefore suggests a direction of travel where procedural and substantive reforms can proceed concurrently rather than sequentially to comprehensively address investment law's legitimacy crisis.

Second, tax-multilateralism provides a real-life example of how a decentralized system can multilaterally update thousands of outdated, bilateral agreements through interpretation on an ongoing basis. Tax negotiators regularly meet to revise multilateral tax soft law. This soft law embodies best practices and forms a reference point for tax official around the globe. It thereby assists states in the negotiation of new treaties and also fills gaps in existing treaties. Indeed, courts and tax administrations routinely look to the latest tax soft law for guidance on how to read old language in light of current needs and best practices. These ongoing, multilateral, and informal lawmaking efforts therefore harmonize as well as modernize the interpretation of tax treaties. Tax-multilateralism thus showcases that a forward-looking interpretation of old IIAs in light of new ones discussed in Chapter 7 is possible at a global scale.

Third, at UNCITRAL, tax law's MLI is discussed primarily as a template for implementing reforms, yet the treaty also provides broader guidance to investment negotiators on how to overcome a systemic legitimacy crisis through sweeping multilateral efforts. A deeper understanding of why the MLI succeeded and what issues it covers helps investment negotiators replicate its success. An

---

[5] Wolfgang Alschner, *Squaring Bilateralism with Multilateralism: What Investment Law Reformers Can Learn from the International Tax Regime*, 272 COLUM. FDI PERSP., February 24, 2020.

MLI-type modernization of IIAs in substance and procedure would also leverage and scale the data-driven approach to renegotiations discussed in Chapter 8 by directing efforts toward identifying areas of normative convergence and divergence as obligatory minimum standards or voluntary opt-in, respectively.

This chapter starts with a brief backgrounder on the UNCITRAL reform process and argues that the UNCITRAL mandate is flexible enough to accommodate tax-style multilateralization. The next section dissects the merits of the procedure-before-substance paradigm in UNCITRAL reforms and shows that tax-style multilateralism offers a feasible and pragmatic alternative to tackle both substantive and procedural reforms. The last section sketches out how a tax-style investment law multilateralization covering both substance and procedure could look like. It emphasizes the need for ongoing (informal) lawmaking to continuously update the interpretation of yesterday's IIAs via today's best practices and the role of hard law reforms to modify old IIAs in light of new ones.

II. The Evolving UNCITRAL Process

In July 2017, UNCITRAL mandated its Working Group III to start deliberations on a multilateral reform of ISDS.[6] The Working Group was formed to (1) identify concerns relating to ISDS, (2) consider whether reform was needed, and (3) develop reform options with the support of the UNCITRAL Secretariat.[7] The process was to be government-led, consensus-based and provide states with a forum for open discussion.[8] Input was to be sought from a broad range of stakeholders and proceedings were to be conducted transparently.[9]

The mandate of Working Group III was initially limited to procedural reforms of investor-state dispute settlement. This decision was contentious with some states advocating for a broader approach that included substantive issues.[10] At the end, however, substantive reform was relegated to future or parallel efforts or bilateral renegotiations.[11] At the same time, the mandate of Working Group III was not set in stone. The Working Group was given broad powers to "cover the widest range of issues and possible solutions."[12] Moreover, the Working Group

---

[6] Report of the United Nations Commission on International Trade Law (UNCITRAL), Official Records of the General Assembly, Seventy-Second Session, Supplement No. 17. (A/72/17), July 3–21, 2017, para. 264.

[7] *Id. See also* UNCITRAL, *Annotated Provisional Agenda, Working Group III (Investor-State Dispute Settlement Reform),* Thirty-fourth session, U.N. Doc. A/CN.9/WG.III/WP.141, September 15, 2017, para. 10.

[8] *Supra* note 6, paras. 250, 264.

[9] *Id.,* paras. 251, 264.

[10] *Id.,* para. 257.

[11] *Id.*

[12] *Id.,* para. 252.

enjoys considerable discretion to set its own agenda and to consider new issues.[13] Built into the Working Group's mandate is therefore an inherent flexibility.

Indeed, over time, the Working Group has incrementally widened its purview to consider concerns not originally envisaged.[14] New issues such as shareholder claims, reflective losses, third-party funding, and an advisory center to help developing states defend against ISDS claims were added to the list of points under deliberation.[15] Moreover, additional matters are under consideration, such as the calculation of damages.[16] These "grey issues," not quite substantive, but not purely procedural either, attest to the gradual widening of the UNCITRAL reform agenda.

Although the procedure-versus-substance divide has thus far prevented purely substantive discussions, the expanding mandate has begun to blur the boundaries between substance and procedure. In that vein, Indonesia raised concerns about the dichotomy becoming artificial and unhelpful. It noted that "procedural law is inherently substantive and vice versa [given that] [s]ubstantive and procedural provisions in the international investment agreements (IIAs) are intertwined in nature."[17] Clinging to a hard separation between procedure and substance would "defeat the purpose of having a meaningful ISDS [reform]."[18] As Working Group III considers issues that have a more direct bearing on substance, such as reflective loss, damages, or interpretive instruments, it will become increasingly difficult to maintain a strict dividing line between substantive and procedural issues. Over time, it is thus likely that states will start considering substantive alongside procedural concerns either as part of the evolving UNCITRAL mandate or through parallel efforts at the WTO, UNCTAD, or the OECD.[19]

In short, the UNCITRAL mandate is flexible, and substantive considerations increasingly arise out of practical necessity as states deliberate a comprehensive reform of ISDS. Rather than perceiving the growing role of substantive issues as

---

[13] *Id.*, paras. 254, 264.

[14] Anthea Roberts & Taylor St John, *UNCITRAL and ISDS Reforms: Agenda-Widening and Paradigm-Shifting*, EJIL TALK!, September 20, 2019.

[15] Report of Working Group III (Investor-State Dispute Settlement Reform) on the work of its thirty-seventh session, A/CN.9/970, 37th session, April 1–5, 2019, para. 84.

[16] *See* Jonathan Bonnitcha et al., *Damages and ISDS Reform: Between Procedure and Substance*, ISDS Academic Forum Working Group Paper, August 7, 2021, at 2–4.

[17] ISDS Reform: a brief perspective from Indonesia, October 29, 2018, A/CN.9/WG.III/WP.156 Annex, UNCITRAL, Working Group III (Investor-State Dispute Settlement Reform), Thirty-seventh session, New York, April 1–5, 2019, para. 2.

[18] *Id.*, para. 1.

[19] At the time of this writing, all three organizations have an active investment law mandate. Investment facilitations talks are ongoing at the WTO. UNCTAD has played a long-standing role in providing reporting, technical assistance, and convening meetings on investment treaty reform. Finally, the OECD, similarly to UNCTAD, has provided research and a forum for states to informally deliberate on investment law reform.

an unwelcomed intrusion jeopardizing the feasibility of negotiations, states are better off to embrace them as part and parcel of an overarching reform to comprehensively remedy investment law's legitimacy crisis. Negotiators can look to the tax regime for creative and pragmatic ways to include substantive reforms alongside procedural ones in multilateral investment law reform efforts.

III. Molding the Reform Agenda on Tax-Style Multilateralism

Tax-style multilateralism can assist negotiators in shifting from a procedure-before-substance mindset to one that considers substance and procedure concurrently. While the procedural focus of the original UNCITRAL mandate may have been motivated by political considerations to prioritize ISDS reforms, the negotiation mandate itself was justified by feasibility and effectiveness. Investment law's history and comparisons with trade may have seemingly made negotiators overly pessimistic about the feasibility of substantive investment law reform and overly optimistic about the potential for procedural solutions to fix substantive problems. Tax-style multilateralism provides an alternative framing that suggests that reforms that tackle both substance and procedure are more feasible and effective than commonly imagined.

A. Shaky Assumptions

The prioritization of procedure before substance in the UNCITRAL reform mandate reflects two shaky assumptions. First, "work on substantive standards was deemed less feasible than work on the procedural aspects."[20] Second, at least some procedural reforms were perceived to indirectly tackle substantive concerns.[21] Both assumptions prove shaky upon to closer scrutiny.

First, in investment law, substantive reforms are not per se more controversial or less feasible than procedural ones. If anything, reforming ISDS appears harder than reforming substance, because the consequences of different enforcement options are so drastic. The inclusion of a private right to claim is ultimately what makes IIAs so potent and so controversial. Take that away and few would lose sleep over the interpretation of fair and equitable treatment (FET). It is thus not surprising that UNCITRAL talks on ISDS reforms have since become highly

---

[20] *Supra* note 6, para. 257.
[21] *Id.*, para. 244.

contentious.[22] In short, procedural reforms are not more feasible per se. Rather, *some* substantive reforms as well as *some* procedural reforms are controversial while others are not.[23]

Second, procedural fixes alone are unlikely to alleviate substantive concerns. At its first substantive session in April 2018, Working Group III identified a lack of correctness and consistency as main motivations for a reform of ISDS.[24] States noted that procedural reforms could lead to greater consistency in the interpretation and application of diverse treaties.[25] In the same vein, the European Union has suggested that changing the current ISDS architecture by replacing ad hoc arbitration with a two-tier standing court goes a long way in addressing not only procedural concerns but substantive ones, such as consistency and correctness.[26] However, if states concluded that substantive reform were not feasible, they should not expect adjudicators to succeed where they failed.

In a universe of varying treaty design even the best-intentioned adjudicators will struggle to determine what interpretation is correct and justifiably consistent without additional substantive guidance from states. Future tribunals that read too little into treaty design differences risk ignoring instances where contracting parties purposefully chose different language to produce different outcomes. Conversely, reading too much into treaty design variation risks elevating vagueness and the absence of clarificatory language to a conscious design choice to impose unlimited investment protection obligations.[27] A century ago, Hersch Lauterpacht accurately summarized the challenge of international adjudicators as "steering between the Scylla of the complacent assumption of the completeness of the law and the Charybdis of the attempt at fulfilling the function of an

---

[22] States fundamentally disagree on whether domestic courts, arbitration, a standing international tribunal, or state-to-state arbitration should settle disputes. *See generally* Anthea Roberts, *Incremental, Systemic, and Paradigmatic Reform of Investor-State Arbitration*, 112 Am. J. Int'l L. 410–432 (2018); Anthea Roberts, *Investment Treaties: The Reform Matrix*, 112 AJIL Unbound 191–196 (2018).

[23] *See* discussion *infra* in Section IV.B.2. Reporting on the January 2020 rounds of negotiations, Anthea Roberts and Taylor St. John note that wider "support coalitions" had emerged around some issues, but not others making some reform options seem more feasible than others. Anthea Roberts & Taylor St. John, *UNCITRAL and ISDS Reforms: What Makes Something Fly?*, EJIL Talk!, February 11, 2020.

[24] UNCITRAL, Report of Working Group III (Investor-State Dispute Settlement Reform) on the work of its thirty-fifth session, 35th Session, April 23–27, 2018, New York, A/CN.9/935, paras. 20–38. *See also* Anthea Roberts & Zeineb Bouraoui, *UNCITRAL and ISDS Reforms: Concerns about Consistency, Predictability and Correctness*, EJIL Talk!, June 5, 2018.

[25] *Supra* note 6, para. 257.

[26] European Commission, Submission of the European Union and its Member States to UNCITRAL Working Group III, Establishing a standing mechanism for the settlement of international investment disputes, January 18, 2019, available at https://trade.ec.europa.eu/doclib/docs/2019/january/tradoc_157631.pdf (last accessed July 6, 2021).

[27] As will be discussed in the last section, the tax regime discourages the use of *a contrario* arguments that use the absence of clarificatory language to suggest a difference in intended meaning in older agreements.

international legislature."[28] Adjudicators tasked with finding a balance between these two minefields are invariably accused of being either overly textualist or overly activist.

If states ask or expect tribunals to accomplish substantive reforms through procedural means, they are thus setting up adjudicators for failure. As discussed in Chapter 7, adjudicators are poor gap-fillers and are best placed to leave that task to the contracting parties. Only states through their practice and substantive reforms can ultimately resolve issues of consistency and correctness by deciding what normative gaps need to be closed and what intended normative differences need to be preserved. In short, it would be unduly optimistic to believe that procedural reforms without accompanying substantive changes will fix substantive concerns in investment law.

B. Record of Procedural Successes and Substantive Failures Colored Perceptions

Investment treaty negotiators may have been more pessimistic about the prospect of multilaterally agreeing on substantive rules and more optimistic about agreeing on procedural ones because of history. The investment regime has a track record of successful multilateral agreements on procedure from the 1965 International Centre for Settlement of Investment Disputes (ICSID) Convention, setting up a multilateral architecture for dispute settlement,[29] to the more recent 2014 Mauritius Convention multilateralizing transparency rules in ISDS.[30] Conversely, repeated failed attempts to craft multilateral investment protection rules in the past, most notably the abandoned talks at the Organisation for Economic Co-operation and Development (OECD) in 1998 to create a Multilateral Agreement on Investment (MAI), show how difficult it has been to agree on investment law substance.[31]

The specter of the failed 1998 MAI negotiations under the auspices of the OECD looms particularly large over the UNCITRAL deliberations. Launched in the wake of the WTO's successful creation, the MAI was an attempt to add a multilateral layer on top of the existing bilateral architecture and foresaw the creation

---

[28] HERSCH LAUTERPACHT, THE FUNCTION OF LAW IN THE INTERNATIONAL COMMUNITY 84 (1933).

[29] Convention on the Settlement of Investment Disputes Between States and Nationals of Other States (ICSID) 575 UNTS 159, 1965.

[30] United Nations, United Nations Convention on Transparency in Treaty-based Investor-State Arbitration (Mauritius Convention on Transparency), 2014, available at https://uncitral.un.org/en/texts/arbitration/conventions/transparency (last accessed July 6, 2021).

[31] OECD, Multilateral Agreement on Investment (MAI), available at https://www.oecd.org/investment/internationalinvestmentagreements/multilateralagreementoninvestment.htm   (last accessed July 6, 2021).

of new substantive and procedural investment norms. In the UNCITRAL negotiations, it has come to epitomize the elusiveness of achieving a substantive
agreement.[32]

Commentators have done extensive postmortems on the MAI. They do not
attribute the failure of the MAI to the fact that agreeing on procedure was easy,
while substance was hard. They point to a lack of consensus among developed
countries, the exclusion of developing countries from negotiations, as well as
effective opposition from civil society organizations in developed countries as
major causes for abandoning the talks.[33] While states disagreed on substance,
first and foremost on the scope of investment liberalization obligations, disagreement on procedure was just as fierce. As one commentator notes, dispute
settlement provisions were "among the most controversial aspects of the MAI."[34]
Indeed, negotiations unfolded against the backdrop of *Ethyl v. Canada*, the first
ISDS case against a developed country in which the investor challenged a general environmental regulation, which prompted nongovernmental organizations and delegations to raise concerns about ISDS and its ability to chill public
interest regulations.[35] At the time when the MAI negotiations were abandoned,
key procedural questions, such as the need to exhaust domestic remedies and the
scope of ISDS, remained unresolved in the final draft text.

C. Trade Analogies Exacerbate Perceptions

Trade analogies arguably further exacerbate the view that substantive reform
would be hard and fueled the promise of solving substantive problems through
procedural means. In the absence of any comprehensive multilateral negotiations
over investment for two decades, trade negotiations provide a more immediate
experience to draw from. However, trade analogies come with significant conceptual baggage.

---

[32] The UNCTRIAL report notes, for example, that due to "well-founded differences [between
BITs], past attempts to forge a single, multilateral approach to investment treaties had failed (for ex-
ample, the negotiation of the multilateral agreement on investment under the auspices of OECD)."
Supra note 6, para. 244.

[33] UNCTAD, LESSONS FROM THE MAI (1999); Eric Neumayer, *Multilateral Agreement on
Investment: Lessons for the WTO from the Failed OECD-Negotiations*, 46 WIRTSCHAFTSPOLITISCHE
BLÄTTER 618–628 (1999); Peter T. Muchlinski, *The Rise and Fall of the Multilateral Agreement on
Investment: Where Now?*, INT'L LAW. 1033–1053 (2000); Andrew Walter, *NGOs, Business, and
International Investment: The Multilateral Agreement on Investment, Seattle, and Beyond*, 7 GLOBAL
GOVERNANCE: A REV. MULTILATERALISM & INT'L ORG. 51–73 (2001).

[34] Muchlinski, *supra* note 33, at 1045.

[35] *Id.* at 1046.

First, in WTO negotiations, famously, nothing is agreed until everything is agreed.[36] Negotiations proceed in rounds where a range of diverse issues are bundled together and traded off as a "single undertaking." States cannot opt in to or out of parts of the WTO rulebook, for example, accept rules on agriculture but not intellectual property. Every state has to agree on everything. This decision-making by consensus on all issues results in big-bang breakthroughs like the Uruguay Round that created the WTO. But it can also result in big-bang failures like the Doha Development Round, which was de facto abandoned after more than a decade of fruitless negotiations. A "single undertaking" mindset would naturally make negotiators skeptical about the prospect of reaching agreement on substance in investment law. States have continuously stressed the need to respect and preserve their purposefully varying treaty practices.[37] Agreeing on all issues seems elusive given the divergent practice in IIAs.

Second, while analogies with trade negotiations may have made negotiators pessimistic about agreeing on substance, trade dispute settlement may have made them optimistic about the use of procedural mechanisms to produce substantive reforms. The WTO dispute settlement mechanism was long heralded as the system's "jewel in the crown"[38] and the "the envy of the international law world."[39] Until recently, it had a remarkable track record of balancing and updating rules in the face of deadlocked substantive negotiations. The Appellate Body (AB), which sits on top of the WTO system, not only provided "security and predictability to the multilateral trading system"[40] by setting de facto precedents and producing a consistent jurisprudence. It also compensated for the vagueness of the initial WTO Agreements and stymied trade negotiations through its judicial gap-filling.[41] In effect, the WTO AB occasionally used its procedural powers to enact substantive reforms.

[36] WTO, *How The Negotiations Are Organized*, available at https://www.wto.org/english/tratop_e/dda_e/work_organi_e.htm (last accessed July 6, 2021).

[37] UNCITRAL, *supra* note 7, paras. 244–245, 252–253

[38] WTO Director General Pascal Lamy, *WTO Disputes Reach 400 Mark*, WTO Press Release 578, November 6, 2009.

[39] Gabrielle Marceau & Julian Wyatt, *Dispute Settlement Regimes Intermingled: Regional Trade Agreements and the WTO*, 1 J. Int'l Disp. Settlement 67–95, 68 (2010).

[40] WTO, Dispute Settlement Understanding, art. 3.2.

[41] In *US–Shrimps*, it famously subsumed animals under the definition of exhaustible natural resources widening the policy space for WTO members on environmental protection and conservation measures. Appellate Body Report, *United States–Import Prohibition of Certain Shrimp and Shrimp Products*, WT/DS58/AB/R, October 12, 1998, paras. 129–134. For commentary, *see* Manjiao Chi, *"Exhaustible Natural Resource" in WTO Law: GATT Article XX (g) Disputes and Their Implications*, 48 J. World Trade (2014). Furthermore, after rules partially exempting environmental subsidies from WTO challenge expired in 1999 without members agreeing on an extension, the Appellate Body engaged in "legal acrobatics" to read additional policy space to enact environmental subsidies into the Agreement on Subsidies in its 2014 *Canada–Feed-in Tariffs* Report. Aaron Cosbey & Petros C. Mavroidis, *A Turquoise Mess: Green Subsidies, Blue Industrial Policy and Renewable Energy: The Case for Redrafting the Subsidies Agreement of the WTO*, 17 J. Int'l Econ. L. 11–47 (2014).

The WTO AB experience, however, also showcases the dangers of using dispute settlement to update substance. Already in 2005, Joost Pauwelyn noted that the successful evolution of the multilateral trading system, which had consisted of the careful interplay of politics and law, was becoming unbalanced.[42] In his assessment, the outsized role of the AB coupled with deadlocked negotiations provided too little politics and too much law. This imbalance came to a head in July 2017 when the United States started blocking appointments to the WTO AB. The AB went defunct two years later in December 2019 when it was reduced to just one member and remains in limbo as of this writing. The main US grievances, detailed in an extensive report, included the AB's judicial overreach and activism.[43]

The UNCITRAL mandate was negotiated just before the AB crisis began in full and reflects a more optimistic reading of the WTO's dispute settlement record.[44] Rather than an ideal to emulate, the WTO experience now offers a cautionary tale that an outsized emphasis on judicial lawmaking to compensate for legislative deadlock can maneuver a system into an impasse. The AB crisis has reinforced Pauwelyn's insights that a regime's sustainability and resilience depends on getting the mix and interplay between law and politics right. Strong adjudication needs to be counterbalanced by continuous and corrective lawmaking. Otherwise, the system is out of whack. Applied to investment law reform, the message is clear: procedural and substantive change needs to proceed in tandem to produce successful and sustainable reform.

D. Switching Frames to Tax-Style Multilateralism

Negotiators should seek inspiration from the international tax regime instead. The tax regime places greater emphasis on continuous, informal rule-making to alleviate the need for ad hoc AB-style judicial gap-filling. Furthermore, it showcases how substantive and procedural reforms can go hand in hand through a creative and flexible approach to negotiations that contrasts starkly with the nothing-or-everything logic of WTO rounds.

---

[42] Joost Pauwelyn, *The Transformation of World Trade*, 104 MICH. L. REV. 1–65 (2005).

[43] USTR, *Report on the Appellate Body of the World Trade Organization*, February 2020, available at https://ustr.gov/sites/default/files/Report_on_the_Appellate_Body_of_the_World_Trade_Organ ization.pdf (last accessed July 7, 2021).

[44] Writing in 2015, barely two years before the blockage began, for example, Joost Pauwelyn notes: "Although powerful members such as China, the European Union (EU), and the United States are regularly on the losing side of WTO trade disputes, overall support for the system remains high. If anything, it has increased over time" in Joost Pauwelyn, *The Rule of Law without the Rule of Lawyers? Why Investment Arbitrators are from Mars, Trade Adjudicators from Venus*, 109 AM. J. INT'L L. 761, 761 (2015).

Historically, the tax regime, like the investment regime, has been based on thousands of bilateral treaties.[45] These BTTs allocate the right to tax over foreign income between the source state (or host state), where income is generated, and the resident state (or home state), where the investor resides or is headquartered. The main goal of BTTs has been to avoid double taxation. Yet ingenious taxpayers (and their tax lawyers) began exploiting loopholes and complexities created by BTTs. This increasingly gave rise to a practice of double *non*taxation.[46] Soon, the tax regime, not unlike the investment regime, was thrown into a legitimacy crisis that pitted the private commercial interests of foreign investors against the public interests of host states.[47]

All this came to a head during the 2008 global financial crisis when the newly formed G20 in search for new revenue tasked the OECD to work on solving the nontaxation crisis.[48] This resulted in the (tax) Base Erosion and Profit Shifting reform project (BEPS). In 2013, the BEPS reforms were distilled into a fifteen-point OECD Action Plan.[49] Point 15 foresaw the creation of a multilateral reform treaty, the Multilateral Instrument (MLI), which was to modify existing double taxation conventions in substance and procedure to curb tax evasion and tax base erosion.

The MLI entered into force on July 1, 2018, and by mid-2021, ninety-five jurisdictions had signed the MLI, including all G20 countries apart from Brazil and the United States, and sixty-five states had ratified it.[50] Moreover, at the time of this writing, the next stage of global tax reform is well underway. In June 2021, the G7 agreed to set a 15 percent global minimum corporate tax rate.[51] The reform aims to combat tax havens that drain the tax base of developing and developed states alike and to end the current race to the bottom between tax jurisdictions. If distilled into a final multilateral deal, which appears likely, the reform would constitute a major overhaul of the global tax architecture. In the span of less than a decade, the tax regime thus underwent a major transformation and

---

[45] Thomas Rixen, *Bilateralism or Multilateralism? The Political Economy of Avoiding International Double Taxation*, 16 EUR. J. INT'L REL. 589–614 (2010).

[46] Philipp Genschel & Thomas Rixen, *Settling and Unsettling the Transnational Legal Order of International Taxation*, *in* TRANSNATIONAL LEGAL ORDERS 154–184 (Terence C. Halliday & Gregory Shaffer eds., 2015).

[47] For a detailed comparison of the tax and trade regimes and their respective crises, *see* Alschner, *supra* note 4, at 33–34.

[48] Group of Twenty (G20), *London Summit Action Plan for Recovery and Reform*, para.15, April 2, 2009; *see also* G20, *Los Cabos Summit Leaders Declaration*, para. 48, June 19, 2012.

[49] OECD, ADDRESSING BASE EROSION AND PROFIT SHIFTING (2013).

[50] Signatories and parties to the Multilateral Convention to Implement Tax Treaty Related Measures to Prevent Base Erosion and Profit Shifting, Status as of June 8, 2021, http://www.oecd.org/tax/treaties/beps-mli-signatories-and-parties.pdf.

[51] Jeff Stein & Antonia Noori Farzan, *G-7 Countries Reach Agreement on 15 Percent Minimum Global Tax Rate*, WASH. POST, June 5, 2021.

multilateralization.[52] That success is especially remarkable since it occurred at a time when multilateralism elsewhere, including in trade, was in retreat.

Many factors, some of which are unique to the tax regime, help to explain its success. Most developed and developing states (apart from low-tax or no-tax jurisdictions) benefit from clawing back on corporate tax planning. Furthermore, taxing foreign companies rather than domestic taxpayers is a low-resistance strategy for boosting revenue, especially after the financial crisis and the global pandemic have drained public pockets. While these national and international political considerations created the consensus and momentum for the reform, it was the existing regime architecture and the creative and pragmatic solutions adopted that allowed for a swift transformation.

The BEPS reforms could draw on decades of collaboration and coordination between national tax experts under the auspices of OECD. Coupled with the technical expertise of the OECD Secretariat, this provided the epistemic convergence and know-how to quickly design major legal reforms.[53] While trade negotiations take decades, the time between inception and entry into force of the MLI was less than five years. The mandate by the G20 and the newly created "Inclusive Forum," which regroups 139 jurisdictions to oversee the implementation of the reforms, lent global legitimacy to the effort.[54]

Furthermore, tax negotiators leveraged flexibility and informal rule-making in ways unheard of in the trade regime.[55] A common explanation for the decline of the WTO lies in the growing divergence of interests among its members; the accessions of new states with different views, and in particular China, have made it harder to find consensus at the WTO.[56] The tax regime gets around that problem by forsaking the trade regime's nothing-is-agreed-until-everything-is-agreed negotiation style and its need for one-size-fits-all rules. Instead, tax multilateralism limits universal consensus to core areas—so-called minimum standards—and otherwise provides flexibility allowing states to opt out of or opt in to different sets of rules. The tax regime is thereby able to accommodate diverse interests while still achieving multilateral harmonization.

---

[52]   *See generally* Ruth Mason, *The Transformation of International Tax*, 114 AM. J. INT'L L. 353–402 (2020).

[53]   Alschner, *supra* note 4, at 64–71.

[54]   OCED, Members of the OECD/G20 Inclusive Framework on BEPS, February 2021, available at https://www.oecd.org/tax/beps/inclusive-framework-on-beps-composition.pdf (last accessed July 7, 2021). For a critical commentary, *see* Irma Johanna Mosquera Valderrama, *Output Legitimacy Deficits and the Inclusive Framework of the OECD/G20 Base Erosion and Profit Shifting Initiative*, 72 BULL. FOR INT'L TAXATION 11 (2018).

[55]   *See generally* Wolfgang Alschner, *Shifting Design Paradigms: Why Tomorrow's International Economic Law May Look More Like the Tax Regime than the WTO*, 114 AJIL UNBOUND 270–274 (2020).

[56]   Petros C. Mavroidis & André Sapir, *All the Tea in China: Solving the "China Problem" at the WTO*, 12 GLOBAL POL'Y 41–48 (2021).

In addition, the tax regime places more weight on informal state-driven rule-making and less weight on judicial gap-filling. The OECD Tax Model Treaty, on which most tax treaties are based, and its extensive commentary are continuously updated.[57] While some of this tax soft law makes it into hard law, through BTTs or the MLI, updates to the Model fulfill an autonomous function. The Model and Commentary serve as interpretive benchmark that reflect evolving best practices in tax governance and are extensively used by national tax authorities (and, to a lesser extent, courts) to plug interpretive gaps in BTTs.[58]

Conversely, dispute settlement plays only an ancillary role in tax. Tax disputes are settled either through diplomatic means (through a so-called mutual agreement procedure), decentralized proceedings in domestic courts, or international tax arbitration, which, unlike investment arbitration, does not result in reasoned opinions but is based on baseball arbitration whereby the arbitrators pick the best offer put forth by one of the litigants.[59] Although international tax-dispute settlement is on track to be legalized further, this remains a sideshow compared with the state-driven legislative developments underway.[60]

The tax regime thus offers an enticing alternative framework for structuring the investment law reform agenda. It provides a better fit than trade to anchor reforms since tax reformers, like their investment counterparts, have struggled with and succeeded in updating thousands of bilateral treaties to solve a legitimacy crisis that pitted commercial profit seeking against preserving public revenue. Moreover, the tax regime has thrived in the same diverse political climate that has crippled the WTO, which should inspire investment law reformers to build on those successes. Finally, the tax regime provides a better model for holistically resolving investment law's legitimacy crisis through reforms that tackle substance and procedure concurrently. The tax regime's focus on informal law-making and on flexible hard law solutions offers a pragmatic, feasible, and creative way to update and upgrade investment law.

IV. Reforming Investment Multilateralism Tax-Style

Tax-style multilateralism provides investment law reformers with two complementary routes to achieve a bulk reform of IIAs to align outdated incomplete IIAs with more complete ones in substance and procedure. First, multilateral tax

---

[57] Genschel & Rixen, *supra* note 46, at 160.

[58] Michael Lang & Florian Brugger, *The Role of the OECD Commentary in Tax Treaty Interpretation*, 23 AUSTRALIAN TAX FORUM 95–108 (2008).

[59] Hans Mooij, *Tax Treaty Arbitration*, ARB. INT'L (2018).

[60] Martin Hearson & Todd N. Tucker, *"An Unacceptable Surrender of Fiscal Sovereignty": The Neoliberal Turn to International Tax Arbitration*, PERSP. ON POL. 1–16 (2021).

soft law retroactively clarifies the interpretation of existing agreements, which, applied to investment law, would scale the forward-looking interpretation of outdated IIAs in light of more recent practice described in Chapter 7. Second, multilateral tax hard law directs investment law reformers to classify substantive and procedural reform issues into buckets (minimum standards, opt-out, opt-in) depending on their underlying state-backing and bundle them into a treaty to reform IIAs. This would appeal to the largest set of states by accommodating diversity, yet comprehensively address the regime's existing shortcomings thereby scaling renegotiations discussed in Chapter 8.

Both routes are complementary. The soft law path to bulk reform works like a software *update* fixing "bugs" in the international tax code. It clarifies unintended ambiguities and closes loopholes that were exploited by multinational companies to avoid taxation. The tax MLI works like a software *upgrade* to the international tax code by adding new features to covered treaties. Together they produce a holistic modernization of thousands of tax treaties and could form the template for comparable reforms of investment treaties.

A. Bulk Update through Soft Law: Emulating the OECD Model Convention and Commentary

1. The Practice in Tax

Barely a year after the OECD published the first version of its Draft Convention on the Protection of Foreign Property in 1962, the OECD released a Draft Double Taxation Convention on Income and Capital in 1963.[61] Both texts had been painstakingly negotiated by OECD member states' delegates and were accompanied by detailed commentaries. Furthermore, both drafts were endorsed by the OECD Council to serve as models to inspire later bilateral investment and BTTs by OECD member states.[62] But this is where similarities end. In the decades that followed, the OECD investment draft slowly fell into obscurity, and the crucial link between the terms of art it coined (such as "fair and equitable treatment") and their explanations in the commentary (such as rooting "fair and equitable treatment" in customary law) were lost, as documented in Chapter 5 of this book.

---

[61] *See* M. J. Van Emde Boas, *The O.E.C.D. Draft Convention on the Protection of Foreign Property*, 1 COMMON MARKET L. REV.265–289 (1963); Adrian A. Kragen, *Double Income Taxation Treaties: The OECD Draft*, 52 CAL. L. REV. 306 (1964).

[62] OECD, *Recommendation on the Draft Convention for the Avoidance of Double Taxation with respect to Taxes on Income and Capital* (adopted July 30, 1963), OECD/LEGAL/0056, available at https://legalinstruments.oecd.org/public/doc/405/405.en.pdf. OECD, *Resolution on Draft Convention on the Protection of Foreign Property* (adopted October 12, 1967) OECD Pub. 15637, available at http://www.oecd.org/daf/inv/internationalinvestmentagreements/39286571.pdf.

In contrast, the OECD tax draft turned into the OECD Tax Model—a living document and a guidepost for the evolutionary interpretation of BTTs.

Under the auspices of the OECD's Fiscal Committee (now Committee on Fiscal Affairs), the text of the OECD Tax Model and its Commentary were continuously revised. The first two revisions in 1977 and 1992 were adopted in fifteen-year intervals, but in 1991, the OECD Committee on Fiscal Affairs realized that in light of the rapidly evolving international business practices, "revision of the Model Convention and the Commentaries had [to] become an ongoing process."[63] The Committee on Fiscal Affairs through its Working Group 1 began updating the Model and Commentary every two to four years, producing a total of ten revisions between 1994 and 2017 while actively seeking input from non-OECD members.[64] In the process, the Model and Commentary swell from around sixty pages in 1963 to over six hundred pages in 2017.

It is difficult to overstate the importance of the OECD Model and Commentary, both for the negotiation of new tax treaties and the interpretation of old ones. Empirical research has shown that double taxation treaties are closely modeled on the OECD Model. Much in contrast to the universe of IIAs, where treaty design has become more diverse as states mix and match gap-filling strategies, tax treaties have become more similar over time. Tax treaties signed in the 1990s and 2000s on average copy between 60 to 70 percent of their text from the OECD Model, up from around 40 percent in the 1960s.[65] This includes non-OECD states, which equally tend to base their treaties on the OECD text.[66]

Even more significant for present purposes, however, is the fact that the Model and its Commentary harmonize the interpretation of diverse double taxation treaties over space and time. Tax lawyers distinguish two interpretive usages of the Model and Commentary. "Static" interpretations read BTTs in light of the Model and Commentary extant at the time of the treaty's conclusion, whereas "ambulatory" interpretations read BTTs in an evolutionary way by using *subsequent* versions of the OECD Model and Commentary to interpret *earlier* treaties.[67] The Model and the Commentary are understood to provide evidence for "ordinary meaning" and "object and purpose" under VCLT Article 31(1) as

---

[63] OECD, *Model Tax Convention on Income and on Capital: Condensed Version*, 2017, para. 9.

[64] *Id.*, para. 11.

[65] Elliott Ash & Omri Y. Marian, *The Making of International Tax Law: Empirical Evidence from Natural Language Processing*, University of California Irvine Legal Studies Research Paper Series 23 (2019).

[66] Considering its impact, the OECD, without too much exaggeration, has been dubbed the "informal World Tax Organization." Arthur J. Cockfield, *The Rise of the OECD As Informal World Tax Organization Through National Responses to E-Commerce Tax Challenges*, 8 YALE J.L. & TECH. 136 (2006).

[67] P. J. Wattel & O. C. R. Marres, *The Legal Status of the OECD Commentary and Static or Ambulatory Interpretation of Tax Treaties*, 7/8 EUR. TAXATION (2003).

well as "subsequent practice" under VCLT Article 31(3)b) (for the ambulatory use) and "subsidiary means" under VCLT Article 32 (for the static use).[68]

A prominent example for an ambulatory interpretation is a 2019 judgment by the Court of Justice of the European Union (CJEU).[69] The Court had to interpret the concept of "beneficial owner" in a preliminary ruling on a 2003 EU Directive that established a common system for taxing subsidiaries and parent companies located in different EU member states. The CJEU found that the OECD Tax Model provided relevant interpretative context to give meaning to the EU Directive, since, as the Directive's legislative history suggested, the term "beneficial owner" had initially been borrowed from Article 11 of the OECD Model.[70] Yet the Court went further, arguing that subsequent revisions of the Model and its Commentary adopted *after* the Directive entered into force also provided relevant interpretive context and read the concept of "beneficial owner" in line with the most recent OECD Commentaries.[71] In so doing, the CJEU brushed aside the concern that relying on subsequent versions of the Model and its Commentary "would lack any democratic legitimacy whatsoever," noting instead that the basis of the interpretation lies ultimately in the text of the Directive and its legislative history.[72]

In the tax regime, revisions of the Model and Commentary thus operate like a software update of double taxation conventions as well as national and supranational tax laws. The evolutionary interpretation of tax treaties using subsequent versions of the Model was explicitly intended by the OECD Committee on Fiscal Affairs from the start. The Committee noted that "existing [tax] conventions should, as far as possible, be interpreted in the spirit of the revised Commentaries, even though these conventions did not yet include the more precise wording."[73] That is because these revisions "reflect the consensus of the OECD member countries as to the proper interpretation of existing provisions."[74] Although more controversial among tax scholars and some domestic courts, the "ambulatory" interpretation of BTTs is common among tax authorities.[75] The United Kingdom's tax administration's manual, for example, states that "[a]s far

---

[68] Chapter 7 of this book discusses these grounds in depth. For an excellent overview of the academic debate on the issue and a nuanced analysis, *see* Maria Hilling & Ulf Linderfalk, *The Use of OECD Commentaries as Interpretative Aids—The Static/Ambulatory-Approaches Debate Considered from the Perspective of International Law*, 2015 NORDIC TAX J. 34–59 (2015).

[69] CJEU, *Danish Preliminary Ownership Cases* (Joined Cases C-115/16, C-118/16, C-119/16, C-299/16), February 26, 2019, available at https://curia.europa.eu/juris/document/document.jsf?text=&docid=211053&pageIndex=0&doclang=EN&mode=lst&dir=&occ=first&part=1&cid=1460614 (last accessed July 7, 2021).

[70] *Id.*, para. 90.

[71] *Id.*, para. 92.

[72] *Id.*, para. 91.

[73] OECD, *Model Tax Convention on Income and on Capital: Condensed Version 2017*, para. 33.

[74] *Id.*, para. 35.

[75] Martti Nieminen, *Dual Role of the OECD Commentaries: Part 2*, INTER TAX 23, 793 (2015).

as possible the latest Commentary should be used to interpret a double taxation agreement, even if an older version was current when it was negotiated."[76]

The OECD Committee on Fiscal Affairs adds three important provisos to the ambulator use of the Model and Commentary.[77] First, it notes that contracting states can contract out of an evolutionary interpretation. Indeed, some tax conventions endorse the relevance of subsequent Commentaries, while others exclude them.[78] Second, subsequent Commentaries are only relevant insofar as they are consistent with the wording of the treaty; additions of new provisions or substantive amendments that lack a textual basis cannot be retrofit. Third, the Committee explicitly rejects *a contrario* arguments that suggest that changes or clarification to subsequent Models or Commentaries imply that earlier agreements intended a different meaning.

Updates to the Model and Commentary ensure that the existing tax infrastructure can address new challenges. From a public policy perspective, this updating of older tax treaties via subsequent Models and Commentaries is vital. In an international cat-and-mouse chase, national tax authorities must constantly up their game to keep up with the creative practices of multinational corporations to exploit loopholes in older double taxation treaties to avoid taxation. The regular adjustments of the Model and Commentary represent a coordinated, international, and state-driven response to this challenge. Furthermore, the OECD Committee on Fiscal Affairs provides a central forum for the ongoing exchange of information among national tax experts and draws on a diverse set of inputs beyond the OECD member states to ensure that tax rules reflect international best practices.[79] This smoothens international coordination on tax, avoids disputes over treaty interpretation, and helps build consensus on emerging tax norms, which facilitates hard law reforms, like the MLI.

2. Application to Investment Law Reform

Investment lawyers can transpose this informal bulk update to the investment regime in two ways. First, states can recall the interpretive importance of past multilateral investment drafts and their commentaries. Like tax treaties, investment treaties have been inspired by model treaties, including the 1967 OECD Draft Convention. Recall that the OECD recommended the Draft Convention as model for bilateral investment treaties to its members. Furthermore, many states, both inside and outside the OECD, copied from its wording often verbatim, although less extensively than in tax.[80]

---

[76] Quoted from *id.*

[77] OECD, *Model Tax Convention on Income and on Capital: Condensed Version 2017*, paras. 33–36.

[78] Nieminen, *supra* note 75, at 791.

[79] OECD, *Model Tax Convention on Income and on Capital: Condensed Version 2017*, paras. 9–10.

[80] Wolfgang Alschner, Manfred Elsig, & Simon Wüthrich, *The Imprint of International Institutions on Bilateral Investment Treaties*, ISA Conference Paper, April 9, 2021.

OECD member states could reaffirm the basic interpretive tenants of the original commentary to that Draft Convention to underscore the continued relevance of the commentary for the interpretation of existing investment treaties. For example, as noted in Chapter 5, that commentary included the linking of FET to the customary minimum standard. While such a reaffirmation would not modernize investment treaties per se, it would clarify the original and continued meaning attributed to core investment principles. With respect to FET, it would root the clause in the customary minimum standard for existing IIAs irrespective of whether they mention "customary law" and correct arbitral misinterpretations of an autonomous reading of FET clauses.

Second, states, as part of the UNCITRAL process (or outside of it), could create a new soft law instrument to guide the conclusion of new treaties as well as the interpretation of existing ones. This could take the form of a model treaty with commentary that can be referenced as an interpretive focal point, but it could also be an interpretive declaration on the understanding of certain investment protection clauses or a list of model terms or principles.[81] To ensure the relevance of such interpretative instruments, states would ideally clarify its status. They could consider labeling it as a subsequent practice or agreement within the meaning of VCLT Article 31(3) and explicitly make it apply to all existing treaties Finally, such an instrument, similar to the OECD Tax Model, would benefit from regular revisions to turn it into a living document that can continuously update past practice through an ambulatory interpretation. In the process, such an instrument would facilitate the interpretive dialogue between states and tribunals as states could collectively react to and, if necessary, correct arbitral interpretations.

B. Bulk Upgrade through Hard Law: Emulating the OECD's MLI

1. The Practice in Tax

A major pillar of the BEPS reform was a bulk upgrade of BTTs. A revision of the OECD Model would have been insufficient to modify existing treaties via an ambulatory interpretation. Instead, a hard law track was necessary to propagate the amendments and additions of the BEPS reforms to existing double taxation

---

[81] *See, e.g.*, Lauge N. Skovgaard Poulsen & Geoffrey Gertz, *Reforming the Investment Treaty Regime: A "Backward-Looking" Approach*, Chatham House, Briefing Paper, Global Economy and Finance Programme, March 2021, available at https://www.chathamhouse.org/sites/default/files/2021-03/2021-03-10-reforming-investment-treaty-regime-poulsen-gertz.pdf (last accessed July 7, 2021).

treaties. The MLI was the means to do that, introducing novel procedural and substantive features into BTTs that went beyond clarifying existing concepts.[82]

The MLI does not create independent multilateral rules. Instead, it amends double taxation treaties in force between the signatories to the MLI. The MLI only covers agreements that have been notified to the convention by both contracting states.[83] This positive-list approach contrasts with the Mauritius Transparency Convention's negative list approach, which applies to all investment treaties by the signatories unless the treaty has been explicitly excluded.[84] Taxation treaties that already meet the BEPS standards do not have to be notified under the MLI or can be exempted even from its minimum standards.[85] The MLI modifies covered tax treaties in different ways. Some MLI clauses outright replace parallel BTT language,[86] others amend parallel clauses,[87] and again others add to them.[88] Importantly, however, other than the provisions that are being displaced by the MLI, the BTT remains unchanged, in force, and can be modified between contracting parties in the future.[89] The MLI thus presents a surgical intervention to upgrade targeted elements in double taxation treaties while otherwise leaving the bilateral structure of the tax regime in place.

The MLI contains mandatory and optional rules. First, there are the substantive minimum standards on preventing treaty abuse for tax avoidance (BEPS Action 6) and the procedural minimum standards on strengthening dispute settlement procedures (BEPS Action 14). These are mandatory modifications that apply to all covered treaties (unless the treaties already contain equivalent rules). The substantive minimum standards cover (1) new preambular language

[82] The MLI is accompanied by other BEPS reforms such as the 2017 modification of the OECD Model, changes to domestic law, and improved intergovernmental actions such as administrative cooperation in tax matters. *See* Yariv Brauner, *Treaties in the Aftermath of BEPS*, 41 BROOK. J. INT'L L. 1022–1023 (2016) (arguing that these complementary changes in domestic law and soft law may well be more significant than the MLI); Allison Christians, *BEPS and the New International Tax Order*, BYU L. REV. 46, 1621–1640 (2016); Valderrama, *supra* note 54, at 2. These efforts center around the improved exchange of tax information and the Multilateral Convention on Mutual Administrative Assistance in Tax Matters; *see* Miranda Stewart, *International Tax, the G20 and the Asia Pacific: From Competition to Cooperation?*, 1 ASIA & THE PACIFIC POL'Y STUD. 484–496, 490–492 (2014).

[83] MLI, Article 2.

[84] Nathalie Bravo, *The Multilateral Tax Instrument and Its Relationship with Tax Treaties*, WORLD TAX J. 26 (2016).

[85] *See, e.g.*, MLI art. 6(4) & art. 7(15).

[86] *Id.*, art. 4(2).

[87] *Id.* art. 5(3).

[88] *Id.* art. 16(4)(b)(i); OECD, EXPLANATORY STATEMENT TO THE MULTILATERAL CONVENTION TO IMPLEMENT TAX TREATY RELATED MEASURES TO PREVENT BASE EROSION AND PROFIT SHIFTING 6 (2016). *See also* Reuven S. Avi-Yonah & Haiyan Xu, *A Global Treaty Override? The New OECD Multilateral Tax Instrument and Its Limits*, 39 MICH. J. INT'L L. 164 (2018).

[89] MLI, art. 30. *See also* Sol Picciotto, *Indeterminacy, Complexity, Technocracy and the Reform of International Corporate Taxation*, 24 SOC. & LEGAL STUD. 165–184 (2015). He points out that tax treaties have to be interpreted in light of an increasingly growing web of soft law and hard law, which make the tax system more complex than the plain and simple language of DTTs would otherwise suggest.

to clarify that the treaty should not create opportunities for taxation avoidance or evasion;[90] (2) new denial of benefit clauses where tax treaty advantages are gained through strategic treaty shopping;[91] and finally, (3) amendments to several standard rules to close loopholes for tax evasion.[92] The procedural minimum standards enhance inter-state dispute settlement, the so-called mutual agreement procedure, by allowing taxpayers to launch the procedure in either contracting state (rather than just their tax residence) and by tightening timelines.[93]

Second, the MLI contains optional substantive and procedural modifications that signatories can opt in to or opt out of. In terms of substance, the MLI resolves so-called Hybrid Mismatch Arrangements, whereby varying rules on tax deductions in source and residence jurisdiction result in double nontaxation.[94] The MLI also clarifies when source countries can tax an entity active in their jurisdiction by expanding the definition of what counts as a permanent establishment and by closing loopholes that companies used to circumventing that designation.[95] In terms of procedure, the MLI introduces a complementary inter-state arbitration mechanism modeled on baseball arbitration for disputes that cannot be resolved through the mutual agreement procedure, whereby arbitrators select the solution proposed by one of the contracting parties.[96] Since the majority of BTTs do not contain an arbitration mechanism, this addition was seen as one of the most controversial elements of the MLI and was explicitly framed as an opt-in rather than opt-out provision.[97]

To ensure that a maximum of states would join the convention, the MLI provides contracting states with flexibility at every corner.[98] First, as noted, signatories can choose not to notify BTTs, particularly where they are seen as already corresponding to the BEPS standards.[99] Second, states can opt out of MLI provisions—other than on minimum standards—in relation to all their notified treaties.[100] Third, signatories can deviate from some of the provisions of the MLI where alternative arrangements meet the same underlying policy goal.[101] Fourth, signatories can choose from alternative versions of the same clause.[102] Finally, on

---

[90] MLI, art. 6.

[91] *Id.*, art. 7.

[92] *Id.*, arts. 8–10.

[93] *Id.*, art. 16(1).

[94] OECD, NEUTRALISING THE EFFECTS OF HYBRID MISMATCH ARRANGEMENTS, ACTION 2—2015 FINAL REPORT 11–12 (2015).

[95] Samuel Johnston, *Multilateral Tax Convention to Prevent Base Erosion and Profit Shifting Legislation Notes*, 23 AUCKLAND U. L. REV. 384–393, 389–390 (2017).

[96] MLI, arts. 20, 23.

[97] Mooij, *supra* note 59.

[98] Avi-Yonah & Xu, *supra* note 88, at 163–164.

[99] MLI, art. 2(1)(a)(ii).

[100] *Id.*, art. 11(3).

[101] *Id.*, art. 7(15)(a).

[102] *Id.*, art. 5. This follows the OECD's BEPS report, which proposed different solutions for the same nontaxation problem.

the most controversial aspect, tax arbitration, signatories not only have to explicitly opt in to the mechanism,[103] but can subsequently opt out of aspects of the procedure[104] or exclude it vis-à-vis specified BTTs.[105] The MLI therefore leaves contracting states with a great deal of flexibility without undermining the mandatory minimum standards.[106]

The main lesson to draw from the MLI for current investment law reform is that it is feasible to achieve an efficient bulk upgrade of investment treaties in both substance and procedure to align past incomplete treaties with today's best practices. The MLI's secret sauce lies in matching treaty design flexibilities with corresponding reform issue. The tax regime achieved a sweeping reform because it homed in on the core issues of treaty abuse and enforcement that were underpinned by a broad international consensus as minimum standards. More controversial issues and/or less essential ones were relegated to opt-out standards. The most controversial topic, tax arbitration, became a voluntary opt-in with much scope for additional tailoring. The MLI thus differs fundamentally from the WTO mantra where nothing-is-agreed-until-everything-is-agreed and one-size-fits-all. Instead, consensus around core issues made the deal possible, while flexibility at every corner ensured that the greatest number of states joined.

2. Application to Investment Law Reform

The MLI model provides a blueprint on how to comprehensively resolve a systemic legitimacy crisis. Tax treaties were concluded to avoid double taxation but instead facilitated nontaxation, prompting fears among states about an erosion of their tax base. Likewise, investment treaties were concluded to protect investment but risked chilling public interest regulations, prompting fears among states about an erosion of their sovereignty. The MLI, especially via its minimum standards, seeks to rectify these unintended consequences. Substantive minimum standards in tax thus tackle tax erosion, while substantive minimum standards in investment would need to tackle the erosion of sovereignty.[107]

The mandatory substantive minimum standards of an investment MLI would be an opportunity to inject regulatory flexibilities into incomplete IIAs that lacked them. New preambles could emphasize the right to regulate, police power carveouts could clarify primary obligations, and new exceptions could be inserted to add an extra layer of defense. Like in the tax MLI, more complete

---

[103] MLI, art. 18.

[104] *Id.*, art. 23(2).

[105] *Id.*, art. 26.

[106] Critics lament that the MLI does not go far enough and leaves too much discretion to states, e.g., when auto-determining whether existing DTTs already meet the BEPS minimum standard. At the same time, with ratifications still trickling in, it is too early to assess the compliance record of the MLI.

[107] Alschner, *supra* note 4.

IIAs that already contain these features or preserve sovereignty through different means could be exempted. Other mandatory elements of the tax MLI could also be emulated. For example, an investment MLI could mirror the tax MLI in limiting forum shopping by denying benefits for otherwise covered entities when they engage in corporate restructuring with the principal purpose of gaining access to treaty benefits. Table 9.1 summarizes a potential matrix for tax and corresponding investment reforms.

In addition, an investment MLI could contain optional substantive elements to close gaps in incomplete IIAs that are less crucial for protecting sovereignty but help to resolve ambiguities. Just like the tax MLI delineates the scope of covered BTTs through a more tailored definition of what constitutes a "permanent establishment," an investment MLI could refine the definition of what constitutes an "investment" in line with more complete IIAs. In addition, similarly to the streamlining of vague provisions that produce double deductions in the tax MLI, an investment MLI may clarify core protective standards like FET. Alternative versions of the same clause that states can select from (e.g., an FET clause linked to custom and one with its subelements clearly defined) and the ability to contract out entirely of optional substantive modifications (e.g., no FET) would make such substantive modifications palatable to most states.

On the procedural side, an investment MLI could rebalance dispute settlement under investment treaties. As discussed in Part II of this book, gap-filling via dispute settlement has crowded out and rolled back state-driven gap-filling strategies. The investment regime thus faces the opposite problem to tax of reining in rather than beefing up dispute settlement. As of this writing, there is no agreement on how such procedural ISDS reform should look, but there are pockets of consensus. In terms of procedural minimum standards, enhanced dispute prevention modalities, a code of conduct for adjudicators, and more efficient and streamlined proceedings could be endorsed by most states. More controversial questions, such as the role of domestic courts or the creation of an appeal instance or a standing court would probably need to be relegated to a voluntary opt-in mechanism, similarly to the MLI's add-on for tax arbitration.

In short, the MLI tax reforms rather than just their legal mechanics can provide valuable lessons to investment negotiators. A core challenge for negotiating an investment MLI remains to decide what investment law reform issues are to be addressed by what MLI design element. Aside from the core objective to comprehensively resolve investment law's legitimacy crisis, the data-driven and technology-assisted approach to renegotiations in Chapter 8 can help negotiators in matching reform issues to legal mechanics. For example, technology can quantify what clauses have been frequently included in past treaties, say over the last ten years, by the broadest set of states to paint a picture of convergence and

Table 9.1 Matrix of MLI reforms and their application in tax and investment

a. MLI mechanics

| | | **Ambition of Reform** | |
		Low	**High**
Level of Consensus	Low	Voluntary (Opt-out) *States can opt out of reform and select multiple compliance options.*	Voluntary (Opt-In) *States can opt in to reform but opt out of subelements or restrict application to specific treaties.*
	High	Mandatory (Min. Standard) *States have to accept reform but can select multiple compliance options or exempt already compliant treaties.*	Mandatory (Min. Standard) *States have to accept reform but can select multiple compliance options or exempt already compliant treaties.*

b. Tax MLI

| | | **Ambition of Reform** | |
		Low	**High**
Level of Consensus	Low	Hybrid Mismatches (MLI Part II) *Voluntary opt-out*	Tax Arbitration (MLI Part VI) *Voluntary opt-in*
	High	Preambular Change (MLI Part III, Article 6) *Mandatory Minimum Standard*	Denial of Benefits (MLI Part III, Article 7) *Mandatory Minimum Standard*

c. Possible Investment MLI

| | | **Ambition of Reform** | |
		Low	**High**
Level of Consensus	Low	Clarification of Substantive Protections, e.g., FET *Voluntary opt-out*	Standing Tribunal to Replace ad hoc ISDS *Voluntary opt-in*
	High	Preambular Change, e.g., adding right to regulate *Mandatory Minimum Standard*	Carveouts and general exceptions *Mandatory Minimum Standard*

divergence.[108] While negotiators may want to add or change that list, an empirical mapping of the state backing for each existing investment law provision in the IIAs could provide a starting point to allocate provisions to the matching MLI design elements (minimum standards, opt-in, opt-out) based on their level of support through existing practice. In any event, to emulate the MLI's success, it is worth studying its content and underlying motivations in depth to achieve a comprehensive investment law reform that covers both substance and procedure while ensuring the buy-in from most states.

V. Conclusion

Reformers of the investment law system can learn from the tax regime to achieve a multilateral update and upgrade of incomplete IIAs in light of more complete ones. Tax-style multilateralism underscores that it is feasible to embark on a concurrent substantive and procedural reform to holistically address the criticism levied against a regime in crisis. The tax regime has just achieved a sweeping multilateral reform that updates and modernizes thousands of bilateral treaties in one stroke. Investment law reformers should seize the opportunity and tap into the creative ways the tax regime uses to square diversity with harmonization and flexibility with minimum standards. Tax-style multilateralism could thereby scale forward-looking interpretation and data-driven renegotiation to read old treaties in light of new ones.

---

[108] Wolfgang Alschner & Dmitriy Skougarevskiy, *Convergence and Divergence in the Investment Treaty Universe—Scoping the Potential for Multilateral Consolidation*, 8 TRADE, L. & DEV. (2016).

Bibliography

Abbott, K.W. et al., "The Concept of Legalization" (2000) 54 International Organization 401.

Abi-Saab, G. et al., *Evolutionary Interpretation and International Law* (Bloomsbury Publishing 2019).

Abs, H. and Shawcross, H., "The Proposed Convention to Protect Private Foreign Investment—Introduction" (1960) 9 Journal of Public Law 115.

Akinkugbe, O.D., "Reverse Contributors? African State Parties, ICSID and the Development of International Investment Law" (2019) 34 ICSID Review—Foreign Investment Law Journal 434.

Allee, T. and Lugg, A., "Who Wrote the Rules for the Trans-Pacific Partnership?" (2016) 3 Research & Politics 1.

Allee, T. and Peinhardt, C., "Delegating Differences: Bilateral Investment Treaties and Bargaining Over Dispute Resolution Provisions" (2010) 54 International Studies Quarterly 1.

Alschner, W., "Regionalism and Overlap in Investment Treaty Law: Towards Consolidation or Contradiction?" (2014) 17 Journal of International Economic Law 271.

Alschner, W., "The Return of the Home State and the Rise of 'Embedded' Investor-State Arbitration," in Shaheeza Lalani and Rodrigo Polanco (eds.), *The Role of the State in Investor-State Arbitration* (Brill 2014) 293–333.

Alschner, W., "The Impact of Investment Arbitration on Investment Treaty Design: Myth Versus Reality" (2017) 42 Yale Journal of International Law 1.

Alschner, W., "Locked in Language: Historical Sociology and the Path Dependency of Investment Treaty Design," in Moshe Hirsch and Andrew Lang (eds.), *Research Handbook on the Sociology of International Law* (Edward Elgar 2018) 347–368.

Alschner, W., "The OECD Multilateral Tax Instrument: A Model for Reforming the International Investment Regime?" (2019) 45 Brooklyn Journal of International Law 1.

Alschner, W., "Shifting Design Paradigms: Why Tomorrow's International Economic Law May Look More Like the Tax Regime than the WTO" (2020) 114 AJIL Unbound 270.

Alschner, W., "Correctness of Investment Awards: Why Wrong Decisions Don't Die" (2020) 18 The Law & Practice of International Courts and Tribunals 345.

Alschner, W., "Ensuring Correctness or Promoting Consistency? Tracking Policy Priorities in Investment Arbitration through Large-Scale Citation Analysis," in Ole Kristian Fauchald, Daniel Behn, and Malcolm Langford (eds.), *The Legitimacy of Investment Arbitration Empirical Perspectives* (Cambridge University Press 2021) 230–255.

Alschner, W., "The Computational Analysis of International Law," in Rossana Deplano and Nicholas Tsagourias (eds.), *Research Methods in International Law: A Handbook* (Edward Elgar 2021) 203–227.

Alschner, W. and Charlotin, D., "Data Mining, Text Analytics, and Investor-State Arbitration," in Pietro Ortolani (ed.), *International Arbitration and Technology* (Kluwer Law International forthcoming).

Alschner, W. and Hui, K., "Missing in Action: General Public Policy Exceptions in Investment Treaties" in Lisa E. Sachs, Jesse Coleman, and Lise Johnson (eds.), *Yearbook on International Investment Law and Policy 2018* (Oxford University Press 2019) 363–393.

Alschner, W. and Skougarevskiy, D., "Consistency and Legal Innovation in the BIT Universe" [2015] Stanford Public Law Working Paper.

Alschner, W. and Skougarevskiy, D., "Can Robots Write Treaties? Using Recurrent Neural Networks to Draft International Investment Agreements," in Floris Bex (ed.), *Legal Knowledge and Information Systems: JURIX 2016* (IOS Press 2016) 119–124.

Alschner, W. and Skougarevskiy, D., "Convergence and Divergence in the Investment Treaty Universe—Scoping the Potential for Multilateral Consolidation" (2016) 8 Trade, Law and Development 152.

Alschner, W. and Skougarevskiy, D., "Mapping the Universe of International Investment Agreements" (2016) 19 Journal of International Economic Law 561.

Alschner, W. and Skougarevskiy, D., "Rule-Takers or Rule-Makers? A New Look at African Bilateral Investment Treaty Practice" (2016) Special Issue on international arbitration involving commercial and investment disputes in Africa 4 TDM.

Alschner, W. and Skougarevskiy, D., "The New Gold Standard? Empirically Situating the Trans-Pacific Partnership in the Investment Treaty Universe" (2016) 17 Journal of World Investment and Trade 339.

Alschner, W. and Skougarevskiy, D., "Towards an Automated Production of Legal Texts Using Recurrent Neural Networks" [2017] 16th International Conference Artificial Intelligence and Law, Conference Proceedings 229.

Alschner, W., Elsig, M., and Polanco, R., "Introducing the Electronic Database of Investment Treaties (EDIT): The Genesis of a New Database and Its Use" (2021) 20 World Trade Review 73.

Alschner, W., Pauwelyn, J., and Puig, S., "The Data-Driven Future of International Economic Law" (2017) 20 Journal of International Economic Law 217.

Alschner, W., Seiermann, J., and Skougarevskiy, D., "Text-as-Data Analysis of Preferential Trade Agreements: Mapping the PTA Landscape" [2017] UNCTAD Research Paper.

Alschner, W., Seiermann, J., and Skougarevskiy, D., "Text of Trade Agreements (ToTA)—A Structured Corpus for the Text-as-Data Analysis of Preferential Trade Agreements" (2018) 15 Journal of Empirical Legal Studies 648.

Alter, K.J., "Agents or Trustees? International Courts in Their Political Context" (2008) 14 European Journal of International Relations 33.

Altwicker, T., "International Legal Scholarship and the Challenge of Digitalization" (2019) 18 Chinese Journal of International Law 2017.

Alvarez, J.E., "The Evolving BIT" [2010] 1 Transnational Dispute Management.

Alvarez, J.E., "The Return of the State" (2011) 20 Minnesota Journal of International Law 223.

Arato, J., "Subsequent Practice and Evolutive Interpretation: Techniques of Treaty Interpretation over Time and Their Diverse Consequences" (2010) 9 The Law & Practice of International Courts and Tribunals 443.

Arthur, B.W., "Self-Reinforcing Mechanisms in Economics," in Philip W. Anderson (ed.), *The Economy as an Evolving Complex System* (CRC Press 1988) 9–32.

Ash, E. and Marian, O.Y., "The Making of International Tax Law: Empirical Evidence from Natural Language Processing" [2019] University of California Irvine Legal Studies Research Paper Series No. 2019-02.

Ashley, K.D., *Artificial Intelligence and Legal Analytics* (Cambridge University Press 2017)

Avi-Yonah, R.S. and Xu, H., "A Global Treaty Override? The New OECD Multilateral Tax Instrument and Its Limits" (2018) 39 Michigan Journal of International Law 155.

Ayres, I. and Gertner, R., "Filling Gaps in Incomplete Contracts: An Economic Theory of Default Rules" (1989) 99 The Yale Law Journal 87.

Banifatemi, Y., "The Emerging Jurisprudence on the Most-Favoured-Nation Treatment in Investment Arbitration," in Andrea K. Bjorklund, Ian A. Laird, and Sergey Ripinsky (eds.), *Investment Treaty Law: Current Issues. Remedies in International Investment Law Emerging Jurisprudence of International Investment Law, vol. III* (BIICL 2009) 241–273.

Batifort, S. and Heath, J.B., "The New Debate on the Interpretation of MFN Clauses in Investment Treaties: Putting the Brakes on Multilateralization" (2017) 111 American Journal of International Law 873.

Bentolila, D., *Arbitrators as Lawmakers* (Kluwer Law International BV 2017) .

Berge, T.L., "Dispute by Design? Legalization, Backlash, and the Drafting of Investment Agreements" (2020) 64 International Studies Quarterly 919.

Berger, A., "China's New Bilateral Investment Treaty Programme: Substance, Rational and Implications for International Investment Law Making," *American Society of International Economic Law Interest Group 2008 Conference: The Politics of International Economic Law: The Next Four Years, Washington, DC, November 2008* (2008) .

Berger, A., "Investment Rules in Chinese PTIAs—A Partial 'NAFTA-Ization'" (Social Science Research Network) SSRN Scholarly Paper ID 2171765 (2013).

Bergman, M.S., "Bilateral Investment Protection Treaties: An Examination of the Evolution and Significance of the US Prototype Treaty" (1983) 16

New York University Journal of International Law and Politics 1

Bjorklund, A.K., "Mandatory Rules of Law and Investment Arbitration" (2007) 18 American Review of International Arbitration 175.

Bjorklund, A.K., "Investment Treaty Arbitral Decisions as Jurisprudence Constante," in Colin Picker, Isabella Bunn, and Douglas Arner (eds.), *International Economic Law: The State and Future of the Discipline*, vol. 7 (Hart Publishing 2010) 265–280.

Boas, M.J.V.E., "The O.E.C.D. Draft Convention on the Protection of Foreign Property" (1963) 1 Common Market Law Review 265.

Borchard, E., "The 'Minimum Standard' of the Treatment of Aliens" (1939) 33 Proceedings of the American Society of International Law at Its Annual Meeting (1921–1969) 51.

Borchard, E.M., *The Diplomatic Protection of Citizens Abroad: Or, the Law of International Claims* (Banks Law Pub. Co. 1915).

Braumann, C., "Taxes and Custom: Tax Treaties as Evidence for Customary International Law" (2020) 23 Journal of International Economic Law 747.

Brauner, Y., "Treaties in the Aftermath of BEPS" (2016) 41(3) Brooklyn Journal of International Law 974.

Bravo, N., "The Multilateral Tax Instrument and Its Relationship with Tax Treaties" [2016] 26 World Tax Journal 279.

Broude, T., "Investment and Trade: The 'Lottie and Lisa' of International Economic Law?" (2011) 8 Transnational Dispute Management .

Broude, T., Haftel, Y., and Thompson, A., "Legitimation Through Renegotiation: Do States Seek More Regulatory Space in Their BITs?" (Social Science Research Network 2016) SSRN Scholarly Paper ID 2845297, https://papers.ssrn.com/abstract=2845297

Brower, C.H., "Structure, Legitimacy, and NAFTA's Investment Chapter" (2003) 36 Vanderbilt Journal of Transnational Law 37.

Brower, C.H., "Investor-State Disputes under NAFTA: The Empire Strikes Back" (2001) 40 Columbia Journal of Transnational Law 43.

Brower, C.H., "Why the FTC Notes of Interpretation Constitute a Partial Amendment of NAFTA Article 1105" (2005) 46 Virginia Journal of International Law 347.

Brower, C.N. and Steven, L.A., "Who Then Should Judge: Developing the International Rule of Law under NAFTA Chapter 11" (2001) 2 Chinese Journal of International Law 193.

Brown, C.M., "A Multilateral Mechanism for the Settlement of Investment Disputes. Some Preliminary Sketches" (2017) 32 ICSID Review 18.

Brown, J.G., "International Investment Agreements: Regulatory Chill in the Face of Litigious Heat" (2013) 3 Western Journal of Legal Studies 1.

Burke-White, W. and Von Staden, A., "Investment Protection in Extraordinary Times: The Interpretation and Application of Non-Precluded Measures Provisions in Bilateral Investment Treaties" (2007) 48 Virginia Journal of International Law 307.

Cai, C., "International Investment Treaties and the Formation, Application and Transformation of Customary International Law Rules" (2008) 7 Chinese Journal of International Law 659.

Calamita, N.J., "The Making of Europe's International Investment Policy: Uncertain First Steps" (2012) 39 Legal Issues of Economic Integration 301.

Cameron, M.A. and Tomlin, B.W., *The Making of NAFTA: How the Deal Was Done* (Cornell University Press 2002).

Caron, D.D., "Reputation and Reality in the ICSID Annulment Process: Understanding the Distinction Between Annulment and Appeal" (1992) 7 ICSID Review—Foreign Investment Law Journal 21.

Chaisse, J. and Bellak, C., "Navigating the Expanding Universe of International Treaties on Foreign Investment: Creation and Use of a Critical Index" (2015) 18 Journal of International Economic Law 79.

Chaisse, J. and Kirkwood, J., "Chinese Puzzle: Anatomy of the (Invisible) Belt and Road Investment Treaty" (2020) 23 Journal of International Economic Law 245.

Charlotin, D., "The Place of Investment Awards and WTO Decisions in International Law: A Citation Analysis" (2017) 20 Journal of International Economic Law 279.

Chi, M., "'Exhaustible Natural Resource' in WTO Law: GATT Article XX(g) Disputes and Their Implications" (2014) 48 Journal of World Trade 939.

Christians, A., "BEPS and the New International Tax Order" [2016] 46 Brigham Young University Law Review 1604.

Clodfelter, M., "US State Department Participation in International Economic Dispute Resolution" (2001) 42 South Texas Law Review 1273.

Cockfield, A.J., "The Rise of the OECD as Informal World Tax Organization through National Responses to E-Commerce Tax Challenges" (2006) 8 Yale Journal of Law & Technology. 136.

Coe, J.J.J., "Transparency in the Resolution of Investor-State Disputes—Adoption, Adaptation, and NAFTA Leadership" (2005) 54 University of Kansas Law Review 1339.

Cohen, G.M., "Implied Terms and Interpretation in Contract Law," *Encyclopedia of Law and Economics*, vol. 3 (2000) 78.

Cohen, H., "International Law's Erie Moment" (2013) 34 Michigan Journal of International Law 249.

Cohen, H.G., "Lawyers and Precedent" (2013) 46 Vanderbilt Journal of Transnational Law 1025.

Cole, T., "The Boundaries of Most Favoured Nation Treatment in International Investment Law" (2012) 33 Michigan Journal of International Law 537.

Condon, B.J., "Treaty Structure and Public Interest Regulation in International Economic Law" (2014) 17 Journal of International Economic Law 333.

Congyan, C., "China–US BIT Negotiations and the Future of Investment Treaty Regime: A Grand Bilateral Bargain with Multilateral Implications" (2009) 12 Journal of International Economic Law 457.

Constain, S., "11 ISDS Growing Pains and Responsible Adulthood," in Jean E. Kalicki and Anna Joubin-Bret (eds.), *Reshaping the Investor-State Dispute Settlement System* (Brill 2015) 344–350.

Cosbey, A. and Mavroidis, P.C., "A Turquoise Mess: Green Subsidies, Blue Industrial Policy and Renewable Energy: The Case for Redrafting the Subsidies Agreement of the WTO" (2014) 17 Journal of International Economic Law 11.

Coyle, J.F., "The Treaty of Friendship, Commerce and Navigation in the Modern Era" (2013) 51 Columbia Journal of Transnational Law 302.

Crawford, J., "Treaty and Contract in Investment Arbitration" (2008) 24 Arbitration International 351.

David, P.A., "Clio and the Economics of QWERTY" (1985) 75 The American Economic Review 332.

Deeks, A., "High-Tech International Law" (2020) 88 The George Washington Law Review 80.

Desierto, D.A., *Necessity and National Emergency Clauses: Sovereignty in Modern Treaty Interpretation* (Martinus Nijhoff Publishers 2012).

DiMascio, N. and Pauwelyn, J., "Nondiscrimination in Trade and Investment Treaties: Worlds Apart or Two Sides of the Same Coin?" (2008) 102 The American Journal of International Law 48.

Dodge, W.S., "Investor-State Dispute Settlement between Developed Countries: Reflections on the Australia–United States Free Trade Agreement" (2006) 39 Vanderbilt Journal of Transnational Law 1.

Dolzer, R., *Bilateral Investment Treaties* (M. Nijhoff 1995).

Dolzer, R., "Perspectives for Investment Arbitration: Consistency as a Policy Goal?," in Pierre Sauvé and Roberto Echandi (eds.), *New Directions and Emerging Challenges in International Investment Law and Policy* (Cambridge University Press 2012) 403.

Dolzer, R. and Schreuer, C., *Principles of International Investment Law* (2nd ed., Oxford University Press 2012).

Douglas, Z., *The International Law of Investment Claims* (Cambridge University Press 2009).

Douglas, Z., "The MFN Clause in Investment Arbitration: Treaty Interpretation Off the Rails" (2011) 2 Journal of International Dispute Settlement 97.

Dumberry, P., *The Fair and Equitable Treatment Standard: A Guide to NAFTA Case Law on Article 1105* (Kluwer Law International 2013).

Dumberry, P., "The Role and Relevance of Awards in the Formation, Identification and Evolution of Customary Rules in International Investment Law" (2016) 33 Journal of International Arbitration 270.

Dumberry, P., "The Importation of 'Better' Fair and Equitable Treatment Standard Protection Through MFN Clauses: An Analysis of NAFTA Article 1103" (2017) 14 Transnational Dispute Management, https://papers.ssrn.com/abstract=3126512.

Dumberry, P., "Has the Fair and Equitable Treatment Standard Become a Rule of Customary International Law?" (2017) 8 Journal of International Dispute Settlement 155.

Dumberry, P., "Shopping for a Better Deal: The Use of MFN Clauses to Get 'Better' Fair and Equitable Treatment Protection" (2017) 33 Arbitration International 1.

Dunoff, J.L. and Trachtman, J.P., "Economic Analysis of International Law" (1999) 24 Yale Journal of International Law 1.

Fauchald, O.K., "The Legal Reasoning of ICSID Tribunals—An Empirical Analysis" (2008) 19 European Journal of International Law 301.

Fontanelli, F. and Bianco, G., "Converging Towards NAFTA: An Analysis of FTA Investment Chapters in the European Union and the United States" (2014) 50 Stanford Journal of International Law 211.

Footer, M.E., "On the Laws of Attraction: Examining the Relationship between Foreign Investment and International Trade," in Roberto Echandi and Pierre Sauve (eds.), *Prospects in International Investment Law and Policy: World Trade Forum* (Cambridge University Press 2013) 105.

Fowler, J.H. and Jeon, S., "The Authority of Supreme Court Precedent" (2008) 30 Social Networks 16.

Franck, S.D., "The Legitimacy Crisis in Investment Treaty Arbitration: Privatizing Public International Law through Inconsistent Decisions" (2004) 73 Fordham Law Review 1521.

Gabriel, V., "The New Brazilian Cooperation and Facilitation Investment Agreement: An Analysis of the Conflict Resolution Mechanism in Light of the Theory of the Shadow of the Law" (2016) 34 Conflict Resolution Quarterly 141.

Gagne, G. and Morin, J.F., "The Evolving American Policy on Investment Protection: Evidence from Recent FTAs and the 2004 Model BIT" (2006) 9 Journal of International Economic Law 357.

Gann, P.B., "The U.S. Bilateral Investment Treaty Program" (1985) 21 Stanford Journal of International Law 373.

Gantz, D.A., "Resolution of Investment Disputes Under the North American Free Trade Agreement" (1993) 10 Arizona Journal of International & Comparative Law 335.

Gantz, D.A., "The Evolution of FTA Investment Provisions: From NAFTA to the United States–Chile Free Trade Agreement" (2003) 19 American University International Law Review 679.

García-Bolívar, O.E., "Railroad Development Corporation v Republic of Guatemala—The First CAFTA Award on the Merits" (2013) 28 ICSID Review 27.

Gardiner, R., *Treaty Interpretation* (2nd ed., Oxford University Press 2015).

Garibaldi, O.M., "Carlos Calvo Redivivus: The Rediscovery of the Calvo Doctrine in the Era of Investment Treaties" (2006) 3 Transnational Dispute Management . .

Gaukrodger, D., "Investment Treaties and Shareholder Claims for Reflective Loss: Insights from Advanced Systems of Corporate Law" [2014] OECD Working Papers on International Investment, OECD Investment Division. http://dx.doi.org/10.1787/5jz0xvgngmr3-en

Gaukrodger, D., "Addressing the Balance of Interests in Investment Treaties: The Limitation of Fair and Equitable Treatment Provisions to the Minimum Standard of Treatment under Customary International Law." [2017] OECD Working Papers on International Investment, OECD Investment Division.

Gazzani, T., "The Role of Customary International Law in the Field of Foreign Investment" (2007) 8 Journal of World Investment & Trade 691.

Gazzini, T., *Interpretation of International Investment Treaties* (Hart Publishing 2016).

Gazzini, T. and Tanzi, A., "Handle with Care: Umbrella Clauses and MFN Treatment in Investment Arbitration" (2013) 14 Journal of World Investment & Trade 978.

Genschel, P. and Rixen, T., "Settling and Unsettling the Transnational Legal Order of International Taxation," in Terence C. Halliday and Gregory Shaffer (eds.), *Transnational Legal Orders* (Cambridge University Press 2015) 154.

Gertz, G., Jandhyala, S., and Poulsen, L.N.S., "Legalization, Diplomacy, and Development: Do Investment Treaties de-Politicize Investment Disputes?" (2018) 107 World Development 239.

Gibson, C., "A Look at the Compulsory License in Investment Arbitration: The Case of Indirect Expropriation" (2010) 25 American University International Law Review 357.

Gimblett, J. and Johnson, Jr., O.T., "From Gunboats to BITs: The Evolution of Modern International Investment Law" in Karl P. Sauvant (ed.), *Yearbook on International Investment Law & Policy vol. 2010–2011* (2011) 649.

Gourgourinis, A., "The Distinction between Interpretation and Application of Norms in International Adjudication" (2011) 2 Journal of International Dispute Settlement 31.

Grimmer, J. and Stewart, B.M., "Text as Data: The Promise and Pitfalls of Automatic Content Analysis Methods for Political Texts" [2013] Political Analysis 1.

Grisel, F. and Stone Sweet, A., "Transnational Investment Arbitration: From Delegation to Constitutionalization?," in Pierre-Marie Dupuy, Ernst-Ulrich Petersmann, and Francesco Francioni (eds.), *Human Rights in International Investment Law and Arbitration* (Oxford University Press 2009) 219.

Gudgeon, K.S., "United States Bilateral Investment Treaties: Comments on Their Origin, Purposes, and General Treatment Standards" (1986) 4 International Tax & Business Law 105.

Gudgeon, K.S., "Valuation of Nationalized Property under United States and Other Bilateral Investment Treaties Contemporary United States Practice: Chapter III" (1987) 4 Valuation of Nationalized Property in International Law 101.

Guzman, A.T., "Why LDCs Sign Treaties That Hurt Them: Explaining the Popularity of Bilateral Investment Treaties" (1997) 38 Virginia Journal of International Law 639.

Haftel, Y.Z. and Thompson, A., "When Do States Renegotiate Investment Agreements? The Impact of Arbitration" (2018) 13 The Review of International Organizations 25.

Hamamoto, S. and Nottage, L., "Foreign Investment In and Out of Japan: Economic Backdrop, Domestic Law, and International Treaty-Based Investor-State Dispute Resolution" ' Sydney Law School Legal Studies Research Paper No. 10 / 145 December 2010.

Hamilton, C.A. and Rochwerger, P.I., "Trade and Investment: Foreign Direct Investment Through Bilateral and Multilateral Treaties" (2005) 18 New York International Law Review 1.

Harrison, J., "The Life and Death of BITs: Legal Issues Concerning Survival Clauses and the Termination of Investment Treaties" (2012) 13 The Journal of World Investment & Trade 928.

Hearson, M. and Tucker, T.N., "'An Unacceptable Surrender of Fiscal Sovereignty': The Neoliberal Turn to International Tax Arbitration" [2022] Perspectives on Politics (forthcoming).

Heindl, J.A., "Toward a History of NAFTA's Chapter Eleven" (2006) 24 Berkeley Journal of International Law 672.

Henckels, C., "Protecting Regulatory Autonomy through Greater Precision in Investment Treaties: The TPP, CETA, and TTIP" (2016) 19 Journal of International Economic Law 27.

Henckels, C., "Scope Limitation or Affirmative Defence? The Purpose and Role of Investment Treaty Exception Clauses," in Lorand Bartels and Federica Paddeu (eds.), *Exceptions and Defences in International Law* (Oxford University Press 2018) 363.

Henckels, C., "Should Investment Treaties Contain Public Policy Exceptions Essays: Substantive and Procedural Reforms" (2018) 59 Boston College Law Review 2825.

Henckels, C., "Should Investment Treaties Contain Public Policy Exceptions?" (2018) 59 Boston College Law Review 2825.

Hepburn, J. and Nottage, L., "A Procedural Win for Public Health Measures: Philip Morris Asia Ltd v. Commonwealth of Australia, PCA Case No. 2012-12, Award on Jurisdiction and Admissibility, 17 December 2015 (Karl-Heinz Böckstiegel, Gabrielle Kaufmann-Kohler, Donald M. McRae)" (2017) 18 The Journal of World Investment & Trade 307.

Herranz-Surrallés, A., "'Authority Shifts' in Global Governance: Intersecting Politicizations and the Reform of Investor–State Arbitration" (2020) 8 Politics and Governance 336.

Hilling, M. and Linderfalk, U., "The Use of OECD Commentaries as Interpretative Aids—The Static/Ambulatory–Approaches Debate Considered from the Perspective of International Law" (2015) 2015 Nordic Tax Journal 34.

Hunter, M. and Barbuk, A., "Procedural Aspects of Non-Disputing Party Interventions in Chapter 11 Arbitrations" (2003) 3 Asper Review of International Business and Trade Law 151.

Ishikawa, T., "4 Keeping Interpretation in Investment Treaty Arbitration 'on Track': The Role of State Parties" [2015] Reshaping the Investor-State Dispute Settlement System 115.

Jacob, M., "Precedents: Lawmaking through International Adjudication Beyond Dispute: International Judicial Institutions as Lawmakers: I. Framing the Issue" (2011) 12 German Law Journal 1005.

Johnston, S., "Multilateral Tax Convention to Prevent Base Erosion and Profit Shifting Legislation Notes" (2017) 23 Auckland University Law Review 384.

Jorun, B., *Treaty Shopping in International Investment Law* (Oxford University Press 2017).

Karpathy, A., *Char-RNN: Multi-Layer Recurrent Neural Networks (LSTM, GRU, RNN) for Character-Level Language Models in Torch* (2016), https://github.com/karpathy/char-rnn.

Kaufmann-Kohler, G., "Arbitral Precedent Dream, Necessity or Excuse?" (2007) 23 Arbitration International 357.

Kaufmann-Kohler, G., "Is Consistency a Myth?," in Emmanuel Gaillard and Yas Banifatemi (eds.), *Precedent in International Arbitration*, vol. 137 (Juris Publishing, Inc. 2008) 137.

Kaufmann-Kohler, G., "Interpretive Powers of the Free Trade Commission and the Rule of Law," in Emmanuel Gaillard and Frédéric Bachand (eds.), Fifteen Years of NAFTA Arbitration (Juris 2011) 175.

Keene, A., "The Incorporation and Interpretation of WTO-Style Environmental Exceptions in International Investment Agreements" (2017) 18 The Journal of World Investment & Trade 62.

Kinnear, M. and Hansen, R., "The Influence of NAFTA Chapter 11 in the BIT Landscape" (2005) 12 UC Davis Journal of International Law & Policy 101.

Kinnear, M., Bjorklund, A., and Hannaford, J.F.G., *Investment Disputes under Nafta. An Annotated Guide to Nafta Chapter 11* (Kluwer Law International 2006).

Kleinheisterkamp, J., "Investment Treaty Law and the Fear for Sovereignty: Transnational Challenges and Solutions" (2015) 78 The Modern Law Review 793.

Kolo, A., "Tax Veto as a Special Jurisdictional and Substantive Issue in Investor-State Arbitration: Need for Reassessment" (2008) 32 Suffolk Transnational Law Review 475.

Kragen, A.A., "Double Income Taxation Treaties: The OECD Draft" (1964) 52 California Law Review 306.

Kurtz, J., "The MFN Standard and Foreign Investment: An Uneasy Fit?" (2004) 5 Journal of World Investment & Trade 861.

Kurtz, J., "Adjudging the Exceptional at International Law: Security, Public Order and Financial Crisis" (2010) 59 International & Comparative Law Quarterly 325.

Kurtz, J., *The WTO and International Investment Law: Converging Systems* (Cambridge University Press 2016).

Lai, H., "The Unfulfilled Promises of the Data-Driven Approach to International Economic Law" in Rossana Deplano (ed.), *Pluralising International Legal Scholarship* (Edward Elgar Publishing 2019) 173.

Lang, M. and Brugger, F., "The Role of the OECD Commentary in Tax Treaty Interpretation" (2008) 23 Australian Tax Forum 95.

Langford, M. and Behn, D., "Managing Backlash: The Evolving Investment Treaty Arbitrator?" (2018) 29 European Journal of International Law 551.

Langford, M., Behn, D., and Lie, R.H., "The Revolving Door in International Investment Arbitration" (2017) 20 Journal of International Economic Law 301.

Lavranos, N., "The New EU Investment Treaties: Convergence towards the NAFTA Model as the New Plurilateral Model BIT Text?" (2013)

Legum, B., "Defining Investment and Investor Who Is Entitled to Claim?" (2006) 22 Arbitration International 521.

Legum, B. and Petculescu, I., "GATT Article XX and International Investment Law," in Roberto Echandi and Pierre Sauve (eds.), *Prospects in International Investment Law and Policy: World Trade Forum* (Cambridge University Press 2013) 340.

Lévesque, C., "Influences on the Canadian FIPA Model and the US Model BIT: NAFTA Chapter 11 and Beyond" (2006) 44 Canadian Yearbook of International Law 249.

Lévesque, C., "The Inclusion of GATT Article XX Exceptions in IIAs: A Potentially Risky Policy," in Roberto Echandi and Pierre Sauve (eds.), *Prospects in International Investment Law and Policy: World Trade Forum* (Cambridge University Press 2013) 363.

Lipson, C., *Standing Guard: Protecting Foreign Capital in the Nineteenth and Twentieth Centuries* (University of California Press 1985).

Liu, C., "The Evolution of Chinese Approaches to IIAs," in Armand de Mestral and Céline Lévesque (eds.), *Improving International Investment Agreements* (Routledge 2011) 59.

Livermore, M. and Rockmore, D. (eds.), *Law as Data: Computation, Text, and the Future of Legal Analysis* (SFI Press 2019).

Mahoney, J., "Path Dependence in Historical Sociology" (2000) 29 Theory and Society 507

Majone, G., "Two Logics of Delegation: Agency and Fiduciary Relations in EU Governance" (2001) 2 European Union Politics 103.

Maltz, E., "The Nature of Precedent" (1987) 66 North Carolina Law Review 367.

Manger, M.S., "A Quantitative Perspective on Trends in IIA Rules," in Armand de Mestral and Céline Lévesque (eds.), *Improving International Investment Agreements* (Routledge 2011) 76.

Manger, M.S. and Peinhardt, C., "Learning and the Precision of International Investment Agreements" (2017) 43 International Interactions 6.

Mann, F.A., "British Treaties for the Promotion and Protection of Investments" (1982) 52 British Yearbook of International Law 241.

Manning, C.D., Raghavan, P., and Schütze, H., *Introduction to Information Retrieval* (1st ed., Cambridge University Press 2008).

Marceau, G. and Wyatt, J., "Dispute Settlement Regimes Intermingled: Regional Trade Agreements and the WTO" (2010) 1 Journal of International Dispute Settlement 67.

Mason, R., "The Transformation of International Tax" (2020) 114 American Journal of International Law 353.

Maupin, J.A., "MFN-Based Jurisdiction in Investor-State Arbitration: Is There Any Hope for a Consistent Approach?" (2011) 14 Journal of International Economic Law 157.

Mavroidis, P.C. and Sapir, A., "All the Tea in China: Solving the 'China Problem' at the WTO" (2021) 12 Global Policy 41.

Mayer-Schönberger, V. and Cukier, K., *Big Data: A Revolution That Will Transform How We Live, Work, and Think* (reprint ed., Eamon Dolan/Mariner Books 2014).

Mbengue, M.M., "Africa's Voice in the Formation, Shaping and Redesign of International Investment Law" (2019) 34 ICSID Review—Foreign Investment Law Journal 455.

Mbengue, M.M. and Schacherer, S., "The 'Africanization' of International Investment Law: The Pan-African Investment Code and the Reform of the International Investment Regime" (2017) 18 The Journal of World Investment & Trade 414.

McIlroy, J., "Canada's New Foreign Investment Protection and Promotion Agreement" (2004) 5 Journal of World Investment and Trade 621.

Meadows, D., *Thinking in Systems: A Primer* (Diana Wright ed., illustrated ed., Chelsea Green Publishing 2008).

Menaker, A.J., "Benefiting from Experience: Developments in the United States' Most Recent Investment Agreements" (2006) 12 UC Davis Journal of International Law and Policy 121.

Merryman, J.H., "The Authority of Authority: What the California Supreme Court Cited in 1950" (1954) 6 Stanford Law Review 613.

Metzger, S.D., "Multilateral Conventions for the Protection of Private Foreign Investment" (1960) 9 Journal of Public Law 133.

Miles, K., "International Investment Law: Origins, Imperialism and Conceptualizing the Environment" (2010) 21 Coloradi Journal of International Environmental Law & Policy 1.

Miller, J., "Title VII and the FCN Treaty: The Exemption of Japanese Branch Operations from Employment Discrimination Laws" (1984) 7 Boston College International and Comparative Law Review 67.

Mistelis, L.A. and Baltag, C.M., "Denial of Benefits and Article 17 of the Energy Charter Treaty" (2008) 113 Penn State Law Review 1301.

Mitchell, A.D. and Munro, J., "Someone Else's Deal: Interpreting International Investment Agreements in the Light of Third-Party Agreements" (2017) 28 European Journal of International Law 669.

Moarbes, C.A., "Agreement for the Termination of Bilateral Investment Treaties Between the Member States of the European Union" (2021) 60 International Legal Materials 99.

Moll, J.H., "Intergovernmental Agreements under the U. S. Investment Guaranty Programs" (1968) 43 Indiana Law Journal 34.

Montt, S., *State Liability in Investment Treaty Arbitration: Global Constitutional and Administrative Law in the BIT Generation* (Hart 2009).

Mooij, H., "Tax Treaty Arbitration" [2019] 35 Arbitration International 195.

Moretti, F., *Distant Reading* (Verso 2013).

Mostafa, B., "The Sole Effects Doctrine, Police Powers and Indirect Expropriation under International Law" (2008) 15 Australian International Law Journal 267.

Muchlinski, P., "Trends in International Investment Agreements: Calls for Reforms of Model Bilateral Investment Treaties in Norway, South Africa and the United States," *Yearbook on International Investment Law and Policy 2009–10* (2010) 411.

Muchlinski, P., "The Rise and Fall of the Multilateral Agreement on Investment: Where Now?" [2000] 34 The International Lawyer 1033.

Muchlinski, P., *Multinational Enterprises and the Law* (Oxford University Press 1995).

Neumayer, E., "Multilateral Agreement on Investment: Lessons for the WTO from the Failed OECD-Negotiations" (1999) 46 Wirtschaftspolitische Blätter 618.

Newcombe, A., "Developments in IIA Treaty-Making," in Armand de Mestral and Céline Lévesque (eds.), *Improving International Investment Agreements* (Routledge 2011) 267 .

Newcombe, A., "General Exceptions in International Investment Agreements" 12.

Newcombe, A. and Paradell, L., *Law and Practice of Investment Treaties: Standards of Treatment* (Kluwer Law International 2009).

Nieminen, M., "Dual Role of the OECD Commentaries: Part 2" [2015] 43 Inter Tax 23.

North, D.C., "Institutions" (1991) 5 The Journal of Economic Perspectives 97.

Ortino, F., "Refining the Content and Role of Investment 'Rules' and 'Standards': A New Approach to International Investment Treaty Making" (2013) 28 ICSID Review 152.

Paine, J., "Bear Creek Mining Corporation v Republic of Peru—Judging the Social License of Foreign Investments and Applying New Style Investment Treaties" (2018) 33 ICSID Review—Foreign Investment Law Journal 340.

Paparinskis, M., *The International Minimum Standard and Fair and Equitable Treatment* (Oxford University Press 2013).

Park, W.W., "Arbitration and the Fisc: NAFTA's Tax Veto" (2001) 2 Chicago Journal of International Law 231.

Parra, A.R., *The History of ICSID* (Oxford University Press 2012).

Paulsson, J., "Arbitration Without Privity" (1995) 10 ICSID Review 232.

Paulsson, J., "International Arbitration and the Generation of Legal Norms: Treaty Arbitration and International Law," in Albert Jan van den Berg (ed.), *International Arbitration 2006: Back to Basics?*, vol. 3 (Maris BV 2007), https://www.transnational-dispute-management.com/article.asp?key=883.

Paulsson, J., "The Role of Precedent in Investment Treaty Arbitration," in Katia Yannaca-Small (ed.), *Arbitration under International Investment Agreements: A Guide to the Key Issues* (2nd ed., Oxford University Press 2018) 699.

Pauwelyn, J., *Conflict of Norms in Public International Law: How WTO Law Relates to Other Rules of International Law* (reprint ed., Cambridge University Press 2004).

Pauwelyn, J., "The Transformation of World Trade" (2005) 104 Michigan Law Review 1.

Pauwelyn, J., *Optimal Protection of International Law: Navigating between European Absolutism and American Voluntarism* (Cambridge University Press 2008).

Pauwelyn, J., "At the Edge of Chaos: Foreign Investment Law as a Complex Adaptive System, How It Emerged and How It Can Be Reformed" (2014) 29 ICSID Review 372.

Pauwelyn, J., "The Rule of Law without the Rule of Lawyers? Why Investment Arbitrators Are from Mars, Trade Adjudicators from Venus" (2015) 109 The American Journal of International Law 761.

Pauwelyn, J., "Defenses and the Burden of Proof in International Law," in Lorand Bartels and Federica Paddeu (eds.), *Exceptions and Defences in International Law* (Oxford University Press 2019) 88.

Pauwelyn, J. and Elsig, M., "The Politics of Treaty Interpretation: Variations and Explanations across International Tribunals," in Jeffrey L. Dunoff and Mark A. Pollack (eds.), *Interdisciplinary Perspectives on International Law and International Relations: The State of the Art* (Cambridge University Press 2013) 445.

Pauwelyn, J. and Salles, L.E., "Forum Shopping before International Tribunals: (Real) Concerns, (Im)Possible Solutions" (2009) 42 Cornell International Law Journal 77.

Pelc, K.J., *Making and Bending International Rules: The Design of Exceptions and Escape Clauses in Trade Law* (Cambridge University Press 2016).

Pérez-Aznar, F., "The Use of Most-Favoured-Nation Clauses to Import Substantive Treaty Provisions in International Investment Agreements" (2017) 20 Journal of International Economic Law 777.

Pérez-Aznar, F., "The Fictions and Realities of MFN Clauses in International Investment Agreements" (2018) 112 AJIL Unbound 55.

Picciotto, S., "Indeterminacy, Complexity, Technocracy and the Reform of International Corporate Taxation" (2015) 24 Social & Legal Studies 165.

Pierson, P., "Increasing Returns, Path Dependence, and the Study of Politics" (2000) 94 The American Political Science Review 251.

Pierson, P. and Skocpol, T., "Historical Institutionalism in Contemporary Political Science," in I. Katznelson and H.V. Milner (eds.), *Political Science: State of the Discipline* (W.W. Norton 2002) 602.

Pinchis, M., "The Devil Is in the Details: Using Historical Methodology to Investigate 'Fair' and 'Equitable Treatment' Clauses in Post-War United States' Commercial Treaties," in Rainer Hoffmann, Stephan W. Schill, and Christian J. Tams (eds.), *International Investment Law and History* (Edward Elgar 2018) 179.

Polanco, R., *The Return of the Home State to Investor-State Disputes: Bringing Back Diplomatic Protection?* (Cambridge University Press 2019).

Porterfield, M., "A Distinction Without a Difference? The Interpretation of Fair and Equitable Treatment Under Customary International Law by Investment Tribunals— Investment Treaty News" (March 22, 2013).

Posner, E.A., "A Theory of Contract Law under Conditions of Radical Judicial Error" (1999) 94 Northwestern University Law Review 749.

Posner, E.A., "Economic Analysis of Contract Law after Three Decades: Success or Failure" (2002) 112 Yale Law Journal 829.

Posner, R.A., "The Law and Economics of Contract Interpretation" (2004) 83 Texas Law Review 1581.

Potts, A. and Kjær, A.L., "Constructing Achievement in the International Criminal Tribunal for the Former Yugoslavia (ICTY): A Corpus-Based Critical Discourse Analysis" (2016) 29 International Journal for the Semiotics of Law—Revue internationale de Sémiotique juridique 525.

Poulsen, L., *Sacrificing Sovereignty by Chance: Investment Treaties, Developing Countries, and Bounded Rationality* (London School of Economics and Political Science 2011).

Poulsen, L., "The Politics of South–South Bilateral Investment Treaties," in T. Broude, M.L. Busch, and A. Porges (eds.), *The Politics of International Economic Law* (Cambridge University Press 2011) 186.

Poulsen, L., "Bounded Rationality and the Diffusion of Modern Investment Treaties" [2014] 58 International Studies Quarterly 1.

Poulsen, L., *Bounded Rationality and Economic Diplomacy: The Politics of Investment Treaties in Developing Countries* (Cambridge University Press 2015).

Poulsen, L. and Aisbett, E., "When the Claim Hits: Bilateral Investment Treaties and Bounded Rational Learning" (2013) 65 World Politics 273.

Price, D.M., "An Overview of the NAFTA Investment Chapter: Substantive Rules and Investor-State Dispute Settlement" (1993) 27 The International Lawyer 727.

Puig, S., "Does Bureaucratic Inertia Matter in Treaty Bargaining—Or, Toward a Greater Use of Qualitative Data in Empirical Legal Inquiries" (2013) 12 Santa Clara Journal of International Law 317.

Puig, S., "Social Capital in the Arbitration Market" (2014) 25 European Journal of International Law 387.

Putnam, R.D., "Diplomacy and Domestic Politics: The Logic of Two-Level Games" (1988) 42 International Organization 427.

Raby, J., "The Investment Provisions of the Canada–United States Free Trade Agreement: A Canadian Perspective" (1990) 84 The American Journal of International Law 394.

Radford, J., Tereposky, G., and Hui, K., "Investment Treaty Signatories' Joint Interpretation and the Case of the NAFTA Free Trade Commission: Evolutionary Interpretation or Modification?," in Georges Abi-Saab et al. (eds.), *Evolutionary Interpretation and International Law* (Bloomsbury Publishing 2019) 283–296.

Radi, Y., "The Application of the Most-Favoured-Nation Clause to the Dispute Settlement Provisions of Bilateral Investment Treaties: Domesticating the 'Trojan Horse'" (2007) 18 European Journal of International Law 757–774.

Ranjan, P., "Police Powers, Indirect Expropriation in International Investment Law, and Article 31(3)© of the VCLT: A Critique of Philip Morris v. Uruguay" (2019) 9 Asian Journal of International Law 98.

Ranjan, P. and Anand, P., "The 2016 Model Indian Bilateral Investment Treaty: A Critical Deconstruction" (2017) 38 Northwestern Journal of International Law and Business 1.

Reisman, W.M., "The Breakdown of the Control Mechanism in ICSID Arbitration" (1989) 1989 Duke Law Journal 739.

Ridi, N., "The Shape and Structure of the 'Usable Past': An Empirical Analysis of the Use of Precedent in International Adjudication" (2019) 10 Journal of International Dispute Settlement 200.

Rixen, T., "Bilateralism or Multilateralism? The Political Economy of Avoiding International Double Taxation" (2010) 16 European Journal of International Relations 589.

Roberts, A., "Power and Persuasion in Investment Treaty Interpretation" (2010) 104 American Journal of International Law 179.

Roberts, A., "Incremental, Systemic, and Paradigmatic Reform of Investor-State Arbitration" (2018) 112 American Journal of International Law 410.

Roberts, A., "Investment Treaties: The Reform Matrix" (2018) 112 AJIL Unbound 191

Robin, P.M.K., "The Bit Won't Bite: The American Bilateral Investment Treaty Program" (1983) 33 American University Law Review 931.

Ruggie, J.G., "International Regimes, Transactions, and Change: Embedded Liberalism in the Postwar Economic Order" (1982) 36 International Organization 379.

Rutledge, P.B., "TRIPS and BITS: An Essay on Compulsory Licenses, Expropriation, and International Arbitration" (2012) 13 North Carolina Journal of Law and Technology 149.

Ruttenberg, V.H., "The United States Bilateral Investment Treaty Program: Variations on the Model" (1987) 9 University of Pennsylvania Journal of International Business Law 121.

Sacerdoti, G., "Precedent in the Settlement of International Economic Disputes: The WTO and Investment Arbitration Models," in Arthur Rovine (ed.), *Contemporary Issues in International Arbitration and Mediation: The Fordham Papers (2010)* (Brill Nijhoff 2011) 225.

Sachs, W., "The New U.S. Bilateral Investment Treaties" (1984) 2 International Tax & Business Lawyer 192.

Šadl, U. and Olsen, H.P., "Can Quantitative Methods Complement Doctrinal Legal Studies? Using Citation Network and Corpus Linguistic Analysis to Understand International Courts" (2017) 30 Leiden Journal of International Law 327.

Salacuse, J.W., "The Emerging Global Regime for Investment" (2010) 51 Harvard International Law Journal 427.

Salacuse, J.W., *The Law of Investment Treaties* (Oxford University Press 2010).

Salacuse, J.W. and Sullivan, N.P., "Do BITs Really Work: An Evaluation of Bilateral Investment Treaties and Their Grand Bargain" (2005) 46 Harvard International Law Journal 67.

Sasse, J.P., *An Economic Analysis of Bilateral Investment Treaties* (Gabler Research 2011)

Schelling, T.C., *The Strategy of Conflict* (Harvard University 1980).

Schill, S.W., "Do Investment Treaties Chill Unilateral State Regulation to Mitigate Climate Change?" (2007) 24 Journal of International Arbitration 469.

Schill, S.W., "Tearing Down the Great Wall: The New Generation Investment Treaties of the People's Republic of China" (2007) 15 Cardozo Journal of International & Comparative Law 73.

Schill, S.W., "Mulitilateralizing Investment Treaties through Most-Favored-Nation Clauses" (2009) 27 Berkeley Journal of International Law 496.

Schill, S.W., *The Multilateralization of International Investment Law* (Cambridge University Press 2009).

Schill, S.W., "Allocating Adjudicatory Authority: Most-Favoured-Nation Clauses as a Basis of Jurisdiction—A Reply to Zachary Douglas" (2011) 2 Journal of International Dispute Settlement 353.

Schreuer, C., "From ICSID Annulment to Appeal Half Way Down the Slippery Slope" (2011) 10 The Law & Practice of International Courts and Tribunals 211.

Schreuer, C.H., "Diversity and Harmonization of Treaty Interpretation in Investment Arbitration" (2006) 3 Transnational Dispute Management.

Schrijver, N., *Sovereignty Over Natural Resources: Balancing Rights and Duties* (Cambridge University Press 1997).

Schropp, S.A.B., *Trade Policy Flexibility and Enforcement in the World Trade Organization: A Law and Economics Analysis* (Cambridge University Press 2009).

Schultz, T, "Against Consistency in Investment Arbitration," in Zachary Douglas, Joost Pauwelyn, and Jorge E. Viñuales (eds.), *The Foundations of International Investment Law: Bringing Theory into Practice* (Oxford University Press 2014) 297.

Schwartz, A., "Relational Contracts in the Courts: An Analysis of Incomplete Agreements and Judicial Strategies" (1992) 21 The Journal of Legal Studies 271.

Schwarzenberger, G., "The Abs-Shawcross Draft Convention on Investments Abroad: A Critical Commentary" (1960) 9 Journal of Public Law 147.

Schwebel, S.M., "The Influence of Bilateral Investment Treaties on Customary International Law" (2004) 98 Proceedings of the Annual Meeting (American Society of International Law) 27.

Schwebel, S.M., "The United States 2004 Model Bilateral Investment Treaty: An Exercise in the Regressive Development of International Law," in Stephen M. Schwebel, *Justice in International Law* (Cambridge University Press 2011) 152.

Scott, R.E., "The Case for Formalism in Relational Contract" (1999) 94 Northwestern University Law Review 847.

Scott, R.E. and Stephan, P.B., *The Limits of Leviathan: Contract Theory and the Enforcement of International Law* (Cambridge University Press 2006).

Sharpe, J., "From Delegation to Prescription: Interpretive Authority in International Investment Agreements," in Charles H. Brower, Joan E. Donoghue, and Esme Shirlow (eds.), *By Peaceful Means: International Adjudication and Arbitration* (Oxford University Press forthcoming 2022).

Shenkin, T.S., "Trade-Related Investment Measures in Bilateral Investment Treaties and the GATT: Moving Toward a Multilateral Investment Treaty" (1993) 55 U. Pitt. L. Rev. 541.

Sinclair, A., "The Origins of the Umbrella Clause in the International Law of Investment Protection" (2004) 20 Arbitration International 411.

Sornarajah, M., *The International Law on Foreign Investment* (3rd ed., Cambridge University Press 2010).

Spears, S.A., "The Quest for Policy Space in a New Generation of International Investment Agreements" (2010) 13 Journal of International Economic Law 1037.

Spirling, A., "U.S. Treaty Making with American Indians: Institutional Change and Relative Power, 1784–1911" (2012) 56 American Journal of Political Science 84.

St. John, T., *The Rise of Investor-State Arbitration: Politics, Law, and Unintended Consequences* (Oxford University Press 2018).

Stewart, M., "International Tax, the G20 and the Asia Pacific: From Competition to Cooperation?" (2014) 1 Asia & the Pacific Policy Studies 484.

Subedi, S.P., *International Investment Law: Reconciling Policy and Principle*, vol. 67 (Hart 2008).

Sweet, A., "Investor-State Arbitration: Proportionality's New Frontier" (2010) 4 Law and Ethics of Human Rights 48.

Sykes, A.O., "Economic 'Necessity' in International Law" (2015) 109 The American Journal of International Law 296.

Sykes, A.O., *The WTO Agreement on Safeguards: A Commentary* (Oxford Commentaries on GATT/WTO Agreements 2006).

Tarissan, F. and Nollez-Goldbach, R., "Analysing the First Case of the International Criminal Court from a Network-Science Perspective" [2016] Journal of Complex Networks cnw002.

Ten Cate, I.M., "The Costs of Consistency: Precedent in Investment Treaty Arbitration" (2013) 51 Columbia Journal of Transnational Law 418.

Thaler, R.H. and Sunstein, C.R., *Nudge: Improving Decisions about Health, Wealth, and Happiness* (rev. & expanded ed., Penguin Books 2009).

Thompson, A., Broude, T., and Haftel, Y.Z., "Once Bitten, Twice Shy? Investment Disputes, State Sovereignty, and Change in Treaty Design" (2019) 73 International Organization 859.

Tienhaara, K., "Regulatory Chill and the Threat of Arbitration: A View from Political Science," in Chester Brown and Kate Miles (eds.), *Evolution in Investment Treaty Law and Arbitration* (Cambridge University Press 2011) 606.

Titi, C., "Book Review: Commentaries on Selected Model Investment Treaties. By Chester Brown (Ed)" (2014) 84 British Yearbook of International Law 361.

Titi, C., *The Right to Regulate in International Investment Law* (Bloomsbury Publishing 2014).

Titi, C., "International Investment Law and the Protection of Foreign Investment in Brazil" (2016) 13 Transnational Dispute Management.

Titi, C., "Police Powers Doctrine and International Investment Law," in Filippo Fontanelli, Attila Tanzi, and Andrea Gattini (eds.), *General Principles of Law and International Investment Arbitration* (Brill Nijhoff 2018) 323.

Trachtman, J.P., *The Economic Structure of International Law* (Harvard University Press 2008).

Trevino, C.J., "State-to-State Investment Treaty Arbitration and the Interplay with Investor-State Arbitration under the Same Treaty" (2014) 5 Journal of International Dispute Settlement 199.

UNCTAD, *Lessons from the MAI* (United Nations 1999).

UNCTAD, *Bilateral Investment Treaties: 1959–1999* (United Nations 2000) .

UNCTAD, *The REIO Exception in MFN Treatment Clauses* (United Nations 2004).

UNCTAD, *Investor-State Dispute Settlement and Impact on Investment Rulemaking* (United Nations 2007).

UNCTAD, *The Protection of National Security in IIAs* (United Nations 2009).

UNCTAD, *The Role of International Investment Agreements in Attracting Foreign Direct Investment to Developing Countries* (United Nations 2009).

UNCTAD, *Most-Favoured-Nation Treatment* (United Nations 2010).

UNCTAD, "Interpretation of IIAs: What States Can Do" [2011] UNCTAD IIA Issue Note No. 3.

UNCTAD (ed.), *Scope and Definition: A Sequel* (United Nations 2011).

UNCTAD, *World Investment Report 2011. Non-Equity Modes of International Production and Development* (United Nations 2011).

UNCTAD (ed.), *Fair and Equitable Treatment* (United Nations 2012).

UNCTAD, *World Investment Report 2012. Towards a New Generation of Investment Policies* (United Nations 2012).

UNCTAD, *World Investment Report 2014. Investing in the SDGs: An Action Plan* (United Nations 2014).

UNCTAD, *World Investment Report 2016. Investor Nationality: Policy Challenges* (United Nations 2016) .

UNCTAD, *World Investment Report 2018: Investment and New Industrial Policies* (United Nations 2018).

UNCTAD, *World Investment Report 2019: Special Economic Zones* (United Nations 2019).

UNCTAD, *World Investment Report 2021: Investing in Sustainable Recovery* (United Nations 2021).

Valderrama, I.J.M., "Output Legitimacy Deficits and the Inclusive Framework of the OECD/G20 Base Erosion and Profit Shifting Initiative" (2018) 72 Bulletin for International Taxation 11.

Van Aaken, A., "International Investment Law between Commitment and Flexibility: A Contract Theory Analysis" (2009) 12 Journal of International Economic Law 507.

Van Aaken, A., "Control Mechanisms in International Investment Law," in Zachary Douglas, Joost Pauwelyn, and Jorge E. Viñuales (eds.), *The Foundations of International Investment Law: Bringing Theory into Practice* (Oxford University Press 2014) 409.

Van Aaken, A., "Delegating Interpretative Authority in Investment Treaties: The Case of Joint Commissions" (2014) 11 Transnational Dispute Management.

Van Aaken, A. and Kurtz, J., "Prudence or Discrimination? Emergency Measures, the Global Financial Crisis and International Economic Law" (2009) 12 Journal of International Economic Law 859.

Van Harten, G., *Investment Treaty Arbitration and Public Law* (Oxford University Press 2007).

Van Harten, G. and Loughlin, M., "Investment Treaty Arbitration as a Species of Global Administrative Law" (2006) 17 European Journal of International Law 121.

Vandevelde, K.J., "Of Politics and Markets: The Shifting Ideology of the BITs" (1993) 11 International Tax & Business Law. 159.

Vandevelde, K.J., "Sustainable Liberalism and the International Investment Regime" (1997) 19 Michigan Journal of International Law 373.

Vandevelde, K.J., "Brief History of International Investment Agreements" (2005) 12 UC Davis Journal of International Law & Policy 157.

Vandevelde, K.J., "A Comparison of the 2004 and 1994 US Model BITs: Rebalancing Investor and Host Country Interests," in Karl P. Sauvant (ed.), *Yearbook on International Investment Law and Policy 2008–9* (Oxford University Press 2009) 283.

Vandevelde, K.J., *U.S. International Investment Agreements* (Oxford University Press 2009).

Vandevelde, K.J., *Bilateral Investment Treaties: History, Policy, and Interpretation* (Oxford University Press 2010).

Vandevelde, K.J., *The First Bilateral Investment Treaties: U.S. Postwar Friendship, Commerce and Navigation Treaties* (Oxford University Press 2017).

VanDuzer, J.A., "Investor-State Dispute Settlement under NAFTA Chapter 11: The Shape of Things to Come" (1997) 35 Canadian Yearbook of International Law 263.

VanDuzer, J.A., "Enhancing the Procedural Legitimacy of Investor-State Arbitration Through Transparency and Amicus Curiae Participation" (2007) 52 McGill Law Journal 681.

Viñuales, J.E., "Customary Law in Investment Regulation Symposium: International Investment Regulation: Trends and Challenges" (2013) 23 Italian Yearbook of International Law 23.

Viñuales, J.E., "Too Many Butterflies? The Micro-Drivers of the International Investment Law System" (2018) 9 Journal of International Dispute Settlement 628.

Viñuales, J.E., "Seven Ways of Escaping a Rule: Of Exceptions and Their Avatars in International Law," in Lorand Bartels and Federica Paddeu (eds.), *Exceptions and Defences in International Law* (Oxford University Press 2019) 65.

Voon, T. and Mitchell A.D., "Denunciation, Termination and Survival: The Interplay of Treaty Law and International Investment Law" (2016) 31 ICSID Review 413.

Voss, J., "The Protection and Promotion of Foreign Direct Investment in Developing Countries: Interests, Interdependencies, Intricacies" (1982) 31 The International and Comparative Law Quarterly 686.

Waibel, M. (ed.), *The Backlash Against Investment Arbitration: Perceptions and Reality* (Wolters Kluwer Law & Business 2010).

Waibel, M., "Demystifying the Art of Interpretation" (2011) 22 European Journal of International Law 571.

Waibel, M., "Putting the MFN Genie Back in the Bottle" (2018) 112 AJIL Unbound 60.

Walker, H., "Provisions on Companies in United States Commercial Treaties" (1956) 50 The American Journal of International Law 373.

Walker, H., "Treaties for the Encouragement and Protection of Foreign Investment: Present United States Practice" (1956) 5 The American Journal of Comparative Law 229.

Walker, H., "Modern Treaties of Friendship, Commerce and Navigation" (1957) 42 Minnesota Law Review 805.

Walter, A., "NGOs, Business, and International Investment: The Multilateral Agreement on Investment, Seattle, and Beyond" (2001) 7 Global Governance: A Review of Multilateralism and International Organizations 51.

Wattel, P.J. and Marres, O.C.R., "The Legal Status of the OECD Commentary and Static or Ambulatory Interpretation of Tax Treaties" (2003) 7/8 European Taxation 222.

Weiler, T., *The Interpretation of International Investment Law: Equality, Discrimination and Minimum Standards of Treatment in Historical Context* (Brill Nijhoff 2013).

Weiler, T., "The Ethyl Arbitration: First of Its Kind and a Harbinger of Things to Come" (2001) 11 American Journal of International Arbitration 187.

Weiler, T., "NAFTA Investment Law in 2001: As the Legal Order Starts to Settle, the Bureaucrats Strike Back" (2002) 36 International Lawyer 345.

Whalen, R. (ed.), *Computational Legal Studies: The Promise and Challenge of Data-Driven Research* (Edward Elgar Pub. 2020).

Wilson, R.R., "Property-Protection Provisions in United States Commercial Treaties" (1951) 45 American Journal of International Law 83.

Wilson, R.R., "A Decade of New Commercial Treaties" (1956) 50 The American Journal of International Law 927.

Wirth, J., "'Effective Means' Means: The Legacy of Chevron v. Ecuador" (2013) 52 Columbia Journal of Transnational Law 325.

Yackee, J.W., "Conceptual Difficulties in the Empirical Study of Bilateral Investment Treaties" (2007) 33 Brooklyn Journal of International Law 405.

Yackee, J.W., *Sacrificing Sovereignty: Bilateral Investment Treaties, International Arbitration, and the Quest for Capital* (2007) PhD Thesis submitted at the University of North Carolina at Chapel Hill.

Yackee, J.W., "Controlling the International Investment Law Agency" (2012) 53 Harvard International Law Journal 391.

Index

For the benefit of digital users, indexed terms that span two pages (e.g., 52–53) may, on occasion, appear on only one of those pages.

Abs–Shawcross Draft Convention, 89–90, 93, 166–67
agents (delegating to). *See* delegation
ambiguity (of text). *See* vagueness
Americanization of IIAs, 108–18
annulment, 161–62, 194–95, 203, 212–13
arbitrary measures clause
    brought back via MFN, 129–30, 148
phasing-out, 65–67
arbitration (other than ISDS)
    as peaceful means of settling disputes, 87–88
    State-to-State (*see* state-to-state arbitration)
    in tax, 281, 288
arbitrators
code of conduct, 290
conflicts of interest, 4
    strategic self-interests, 202
Argentina, 130, 132, 159–61
artificial intelligence, 262–64
Association of Southeast Asian Nations
    (ASEAN), 116, 238–39, 264–65
Australia, 256–57
awards
    correcting, 192–95
    creating a firewall against IIA-based
        rebalancing, 14–15, 164–65
    inconsistency, 9
    not sources of custom, 158–59
    skewed towards older IIAs, 41–42, 185

backlash
    against investment arbitration, 2
    by arbitrators, 2, 9, 14–15, 53, 164–65, 222
balance of payments, 72
balancing (investment protection and
    regulatory space)
    in FCN treaties, 91–92
    firewall against, 14–15, 164–65
    implicit versus explicit balancing, 187–89
    importance of symmetrical relations, 109–12
    need for, 4
    optimal balance, 54–55, 139

    through a multilateral instrument, 289–90
    through customary international law, 153–54
    through exceptions (*see* public policy
        exceptions)
    through new-generation IIAs, 5–6
    under old versus new treaties, 187–89
    in US and Canadian 2004 Models, 107
balkanization of caselaw, 203
Base Erosion and Profit Shifting (BEPS), 279, 280, 286–87
big data
    datafication of treaty texts, 33–34
    limits of traditional legal methods, 23
bilateral investment treaty (BIT)
    asymmetric investment relations, 89, 92, 114
    brevity of, 91
    diffusion of, 94–95
    European-style (*see* European-style BITs)
    experimentation in early BITs, 94
    first treaty, 89–90
    incompleteness explaining success of
        BITs, 91, 94
    innovations in US BITs, 95–98
    similarities and differences with FCN
        treaties, 89–92
Brazil, 14, 18, 29, 76–77, 119

Canada
    layering flexibilities in IIAs, 165–66
    litigation under Canadian IIAs, 162–65
    Model 2004, 107–8
    NAFTA-plus IIA practice, 108
    negotiations of NAFTA, 98–100
    post-NAFTA IIA practice, 102–4
    risks of claims, 255–56
    understanding of general exceptions, 164–65, 180
Chile, 116–17, 137
China, 30, 109–10, 115–16, 249
citations
    age of cited cases, 192
    between IIAs, 185–87, 214–15

citations (*cont.*)
   skewed towards older cases, 185–86
   strategic use of, 201–2
claims
   diversion of, 9–10, 239–40, 267
   lowering risks of, 255–57
   politicization through, 113–14
clarifications
   of expropriation (*see* expropriation)
   of fair and equitable treatment (*see* fair and
     equitable treatment)
   for greater certainty (*see* for greater certainty
     clause)
   importing clarifications from more complete
     IIAs, 231–44
   misunderstood as less favorable
     treatment, 128–29
   not affected by MFN, 148
   of original intent, 175–76, 178, 192–93
   risks of, 65
   through custom (*see* customary
     international law)
   through new treaties, 58–69, 195–97
   use for evolutionary interpretation,
     220, 231–44
coexistence of old and new IIAs, 40–41, 245
Colombia, 117, 163–65
colonialism, 86–87
commissions. *See* inter-state committees
common form treaties, 240
Common Market for Eastern and Southern
   Africa (COMESA), 117
complete contingency contract. *See*
   contract theory
complexity, 210–11, 267–68
complex systems, 210–11
Comprehensive Economic and Trade
   Agreement (CETA), 4, 110–11, 118, 119–
   20, 245–46
Comprehensive and Progressive Agreement
   for Trans-Pacific Partnership (CPTPP),
   110–11, 116
compulsory licenses, 72, 100
computational legal studies, 24–26
   as complement to traditional analyses, 26
   contribution, 24–25
   doctrinal research, 25–26
   shortcomings, 26
concerns with ISDS
   correctness and consistency, 9, 200–
     1, 274–75
   costs, 9
   generally, 3–4, 9

conditions precluding wrongfulness, 160–
   62, 164
conflicts of norms, 267
consistency, 9, 199–201
consolidation of IIA practice, 246, 264–68
contract theory
   complete contingency contract (CCC), 48
   contractual completeness (*see* contractual
     completeness)
   credibility and enforcement, 50–51
   efficiency, 56, 225, 227–28
   goals, 49
   injurer and victim, 49, 91–92, 111–12
   and interpretation, 220–21, 226–30
   more commitments through more
     flexibility, 50
   premise and principles, 23, 47–53
contractual completeness
   complete contingency contract as
     benchmark, 48
   effect on interpretation, 226–30
   incompleteness explaining success of
     BITs, 94
   increasing completeness through custom,
     63–65, 153–54, 176–78
   reasons for incompleteness, 48–49
   strategies to overcome incompleteness (*see*
     gap-filling strategies)
   VCLT as incomplete contract, 231–32
convergence of IIA practice, 245–46, 260–
   62, 290–92
Cooperation and Facilitation Investment
   Agreements, 18, 29, 119
corporate social responsibility
   (CSR), 74
corruption, 74
Costa Rica, 7, 44, 180
customary international law
   as baseline, 153
   codifying custom through IIAs, 166–
     69, 175–76
   contracting on custom, 63–65
   decoupling custom and IIAs, 169–72
   evolution towards more investment
     protection, 154, 156–57
   increasing commitments, 155–59
   lowering flexibility, 159–66
   minimum standard of treatment (*see*
     minimum standard of treatment)
   moderating effect, 153–54
   police powers (*see* police powers doctrine)
   precluding wrongfulness (*see* conditions
     precluding wrongfulness)

state practice and *opinio juris*, 158–59,
173, 195–98
used akin to MFN, 157–58

data science
inductive research, 24
and international law (*see* computational
legal studies)
legal analytics (*see* legal analytics)
machine learning, 262–64
scaling empirical research, 23
uncovering new relationships, 25
default rules. *See* gap-filling strategies
definition of investment, 62–63, 111, 143, 290
delegation
agency slack, 201–2, 222
agents versus trustees, 52–53, 201–2, 221–26
control mechanisms, 77–79, 192–98, 202–6
evolution of delegation in IIAs, 77–79
as gap-filling strategy, 52, 77–79
principal-agent theory, 201–2, 210, 222
states taking back control, 9, 30–31, 77, 210
states' failure to control investment tribunals,
9, 192–98
denial of benefits, 79, 287–88
design of IIAs
Americanization, 108–18
analytics, 257–64
asymmetry and symmetry, 91–92, 109–12
competition between BITs and FCN
treaties, 89–95
differences, 28, 30, 35–37
on dispute settlement, 28
effect on interpretation, 226–30
incompleteness explaining success of
BITs, 94
more commitments through more
flexibility, 54–55
optimal design, 49, 54–55
path dependency (*see* path dependency)
similarity, 27–28, 29–30
tailoring, 266
developed countries
IIAs between, 84–86, 98–99, 110–11
as rule-makers, 28, 92–93
and state-driven change, 17–18
developing countries
nationalizations, 89
and the New International Economic
Order, 88–89
as rule-takers, 28, 92
and state-driven change, 17–18
differences between IIAs, 27–31, 35–37

differences between bilaterals and
plurilaterals, 266
diffusion
BITs, 94–95
NAFTA-plus IIAs, 108, 114–18
NAFTA-style IIAs, 102–5
digital humanities. *See* computational legal
studies
dimensionality reduction. *See* principal
component analysis
diplomatic protection, 86–88
distant reading. *See* computational legal studies
duplication and overlaps of IIAs, 246, 264–68

economic coordination exceptions, 71–
73, 100–1
EDIT. *See* Electronic Database of Investment
Treaties
effective means clause
brought back via MFN, 129–30, 147–48
inclusion in early US BITs, 97
phasing-out, 67–68
ejusdem generis. See MFN
Electronic Database of Investment Treaties
(EDIT), 19, 31–32
embedded liberalism, 86
empirical analysis
crowd sourcing, 23
relationship to data science, 23
Energy Charter Treaty, 253–55
entry of personnel clause, 96
environment
exception (*see* public policy exceptions)
ISDS disputes on, 6–7, 42–45, 163–64, 174,
180, 190–92
mentions in IIAs, 74, 99, 102, 104–5, 117,
180, 190
not lowering environmental standards, 74,
102, 104–5
escape clauses, 51, 69–73
enabling more commitments, 50, 98
as gap-filling strategy, 51, 69–73
European-style BITs
design, 90, 92–93
differences with NAFTA-style IIAs, 103–4
differences with US BITs, 95–98
origins, 86–89
European Union
Court of Justice of the, 284
evolving treaty practice, 118, 119–20
multilateral investment court proposal, 9,
119–20, 290
replacing old IIAs, 253, 264–65

exceptions
  bypassing exceptions through MFN, 131–
    32, 144
  economic coordination exceptions (*see*
    economic coordination exceptions)
  as escape clauses, 54–55, 69–73
  public policy exceptions (*see* public policy
    exceptions)
  in relation to MFN clauses, 145
  security exceptions (*see* security exceptions)
exposure to ISDS claims, 255–57
expropriation
  clarifying the meaning of, 64–65, 174–75
  compulsory licenses carveout, 72
  contestation of compensation rules, 88–89
  customary law roots, 167–68
  indirect expropriation, 171, 173–74
  NAFTA practice, 173–75
  police powers carveout (*see* police power)
  sole effects doctrine, 171–72, 175

fair and equitable treatment
  autonomous interpretation, 169–71
  clarifying the meaning of, 63, 172–73
  early treaty practice, 167–69
  link to customary law, 97, 167–68, 172–73
  minimum standard of treatment (*see*
    minimum standard of treatment)
  NAFTA practice, 170, 172–73
  path-dependent interpretation, 170–71
  survival of controversial interpretations,
    192–98, 204–6
  undefined clauses understood as
    offering more favorable investment
    protection, 128–29
feedback loops, 210–11
flexibilities
  enabling more commitments, 50, 97–
    98, 131–32
  layering of, 165–66
  in the Multilateral Tax Instrument, 288–89
focal points, 206–7, 208–9, 286
foreign direct investment (FDI)
  bidirectional flows, 109–10
  flows between developed countries, 86
  perceptions, 93
  treaty coverage of, 252
  undirectional flows from North to
    South, 86–87
for greater certainty clause, 62, 175–76,
  220, 242
Free Trade Agreements (FTAs)
  differences with BITs, 29

NAFTA (*see* North American Free Trade
    Agreement)
  overlapping treaties (*see* overlapping IIAs)
Friendship, Commerce and Navigation
    treaties (FCN)
  impact on BITs, 90, 94, 95–96
  origins in symmetrical relations, 84–86
  right to regulate, 91–92
  similarities and differences with BITs, 89–92
full protection and security, 65–66, 127–28, 167

gap-filling strategies
  competition between, 14–15, 52–53
  default rules, 219, 227, 228–29, 231
  delegation, 52, 57–58, 77–79
  diverging uses, 119
  escape clauses, 51, 54–55, 69–73
  more complete contracting, 51, 55–57, 58–69
  relational contracting, 51–52, 73–77
  through customary law, 63–65, 153–
    54, 176–78
  typology of, 51–52
General Agreement on Tariffs and
    Trade (GATT)
  coexistence with IIAs, 84–85
  disputes, 99
  exceptions modeled on Article XX, 70–71,
    164, 190
General Agreement on Trade in Services
    (GATS), 72, 100
Germany
  domestic politicization, 113–14
  first BIT, 89–90
  outdated BIT stock, 256
  renegotiation of BITs, 249
government procurement, 72
growing pains of the investment regime, 8–9
gunboat diplomacy, 87

harmonization, 246
historical institutionalism, 206–10

International Centre for Settlement of
    Investment Disputes (ICSID)
  annulment under (*see* annulment)
  creation, 87–88, 275
interpretation
  versus adjudication, 223–26
  adjudicator-driven, 2, 14–15, 219
  versus amendment, 219–20, 234–35, 242
  authoritative, 79, 164–65, 172–73, 192–93,
    224, 233–35
  backward-looking, 219

correcting, 192–94
customary-law-based understanding of
    treaty terms, 177–78
evolutionary, 177–78, 240–41, 283–85
forward-looking, 220, 231–44, 283–85
harmonious, 188
path-dependent, 132–33, 177–78, 193–94
survival of controversial interpretations,
    192–98, 204–6
travaux préparatoires, 243–44
interpretive discretion, 226–30, 231–32
interpretive reset, 9, 41, 211, 215–16
inter-state committees, 75–76
investment arbitration procedure
    "embedded" investment arbitration, 77–78
    more detailed ISDS provisions in IIAs, 77
    transparency, amicus curiae and public
        participation, 77

Japan, 114–15
jurisprudence constant, 199–201, 228–29

labor standards, 74
law and economics. *See* contract theory
learning effects, 56, 207, 209
legal analytics, 257–59
legalization, 30–31
length (of IIAs), 58–60
liberalization, 29, 95–96

Mauritius Convention on Transparency in
    ISDS, 4–5, 275, 287
Mexico
    NAFTA-plus IIA practice, 108
    Negotiations of NAFTA, 98–100
    Post-NAFTA IIA practice, 102
minimum standard of treatment
    codification, 167–69
    contrasted to autonomous treaty
        standard, 155–56
    convergence with autonomously read FET, 157
    evolution towards more protection, 156–
        57, 192–95
    Neer case, 155–56
    role of state practice and *opinio
        juris*, 158–59, 173, 176–77, 195–98
    states' clarifications, 63, 172–73, 192–98
minimum standard (in tax), 280, 287–88
most favored nation (MFN) treatment
    awards accepting incorporation by reference,
        126–28, 138
    bringing back phased-out
        protections, 129–31

cherry-picking, 131–32, 148–50
ejusdem generis, 145–48
exceptions within MFN clauses, 145–46
as incorporation-by-reference, 134–
    35, 136–38
in international law, 135–36
limitations placed on MFN, 127, 142–51
as multilateralizer, 137–38
as non-discrimination, 133–34
not altering clarifications, 148
not altering definition clauses, 143
not altering exceptions, 144
not bringing back phased-out
    protections, 147–48
notion of "more favourable," 148–49
notion of "treatment," 146–47
reassessment by scholars, 140–41
reassessment by tribunals, 141
rolling back clarifications, 128–29
taking states by surprise, 139–40
in trade law, 124, 135–36
multilateralization
    via MFN (*see* Most Favored Nation [MFN]
        Treatment)
    tax-style, 269–71, 278–81
Multilateral Agreement on Investment
    (MAI), 275–76
Multilateral Instrument (MLI), 269, 270–71,
    279–80, 286–89
Multilateral Investment Court, 9, 119–20, 290
multilateral ISDS reform, 271–73

national security exceptions. *See* security
    exception
Natural Language Processing (NLP), 33–34
necessity (state of), 160–62
negotiations
    battle of the forms, 262–64
    NAFTA, 98–100
    power asymmetries, 28, 91–92
    trade, 277–78
    travaux préparatoires, 243–44
neural networks, 262–64
New International Economic Order, 88–
    89, 168–69
new-generation IIAs
    expectations around, 3–6
    investment awards decided under, 41–45
    as more complete treaties, 58–79
nonconforming measures
    bypassed, 131–32
    interdependence with commitments, 98
    in US BITs, 97–98

nondiscrimination, 133–34
nondisputing party interventions, 78, 146, 193–
94, 235–37
North American Free Trade Agreement
(NAFTA)
authoritative interpretation, 172–
73, 192–93
Free Trade Commission (FTC), 76, 79
innovations in Chapter 11, 72, 73, 74, 76,
77–79, 98–105
NAFTA-plus IIAs, 107–8
negotiation, 98–100
rapprochement between trade and
investment, 100
rise of investment claims, 101–2
state efforts to correct misinterpretations,
172–73, 192–94
subsequent practice, 236
not lowering standards clause, 74

opportunism (curbing), 49, 50, 51, 54, 56, 91–92
ordinary meaning, 177, 240–43
organic self-correction of the investment
regime, 8–9
Organisation for Economic Co-operation and
Development (OECD)
1967 Draft Convention on Foreign Property,
85–86, 167, 285–86
early codification work, 85–86
tax model, 281, 282–85
tax regime, 279, 280, 282–85
original intent, 175–76, 178, 241–42
outlier IIAs, 256–57
overlapping IIAs
consolidation versus duplication, 264–68
IIAs with most overlap, 253–55
use in interpretation, 237–40, 253

party autonomy, 224
path dependency
of case law, 184, 208–9
and precedent, 208–10
and precision, 56–57
self-reinforcement producing, 207–8
of treaty design, 16, 29–30, 208
performance requirements
inclusion in US BITs, 97
TRIMs, 100
permanent establishment, 288, 290
plurilateral IIAs, 264–68
police powers doctrine
carveout from expropriation, 64–65,
171, 174–75

conflation with autonomous exceptions,
42–44, 162–65
as source of flexibility, 64, 69–70, 159
policy space
quest for, 30–31, 54–55
through custom (*see* customary
international law)
through exceptions (*see* public policy
exceptions)
through police powers (*see* police powers
doctrine)
through precision (*see* precision)
politicization
of IIAs, 4
through investment disputes, 105–6, 112–14
of treaty negotiations, 91
preambles, 12–13, 73–74, 129, 148, 192, 289–90
precedent
arguments weighing against following, 200–
1, 214–15
average age of, 192
becoming outdated, 183–84, 192
challenges to monitor, 206, 213–15
jurisprudence constant, 199–201, 228–29
lifecycle of, 215
path dependency, 208–10
policing, 202–6, 212–13
reasons for following, 199–201
rejected based on treaty design
differences, 214–15
reliance on, 183
self-reinforcement, 208–10
shepardization of, 213–15
states correcting or contracting out of, 45,
107, 183–84, 192, 210
stickiness of, 184, 198–210
strategic use of, 201–2
tension with state-driven change, 183–84,
192–93, 210, 211
precision
for greater certainty (*see* for greater certainty
clause)
more detailed language in IIAs, 60–63
path dependency, 56–57
as strategy to overcome incompleteness,
51, 55–57
trend toward greater, 30–31, 55–56
predictive analytics, 258–59, 262–64
pre-establishment. *See* liberalization
principal-agent theory. *See* delegation
principal component analysis, 34–35
prudential financial measures, 73
public policy exceptions

additive to custom, 165–66, 178–79
versus balancing under primary obligations,
187–89, 190–91
conflation with custom, 7, 162–65
expectations, 6
as final safety net, 165
increased use, 69–71
interpretive debates around, 179–80
missing in action, 6, 42–44, 180
recent cases on, 42–44, 162–64

QWERTY, 207

reforms of investment law
insufficiency of procedural reforms, 9–
10, 273–75
types of, 4–5
UNCITRAL (*see* UNCITRAL ISDS
Negotiations)
regionalization, 246
regret (to seize), 49, 50, 51, 54, 56, 69–
73, 91–92
renegotiation
exposure to claims, 255–57
impact, 252
motivations, 249–50
obstacles, 250–51
targets, 251–57
trends, 247–50
using legal analytics in support, 257–64
Renvoi to expert bodies of the contracting
states, 78–79
resilience, 266
right to regulate
bargaining away, 93
in early US BITs, 97–98
in FCN treaties, 91–92
through custom (*see* customary
international law)
through exceptions (*see* public policy
exceptions)
through police powers (*see* police powers
doctrine)
through precision (*see* precision)
rule-makers and rule-takers, 28

Safeguards Agreement (WTO), 50
scalability of research methods, 23
security exceptions
bypassed via MFN, 132
confused with customary law, 159–62
increased use, 69–71
self-reinforcement, 206–7

similarity of treaties
IIAs, 27–28, 29–30
tax treaties, 283
Softwood Lumber Agreement, 225
state-to-state arbitration, 223–24
State Responsibility (Articles of), 160–62, 164
subsequent practice, 235–37
subsidies, 72
systems theory, 210–11

taxation
ambulatory interpretation, 220, 282–85
Base Erosion and Profit Shifting (BEPS),
279, 280
carveout in IIAs, 72
regime, 278–81
renvoi to tax authorities, 78–79
tax-style multilateralism, 269–71, 278–81
technology supporting negotiations, 251–
64, 290–92
text-as-data analysis
datafication of treaty texts, 33–34
principles, 24–25
text preprocessing, 34
word-frequency representations of text, 33–34
trade law
interaction with investment rules, 100–1
politicization, 113
regionalism, 265–66
Trade-Related Aspects of Intellectual Property
Rights (TRIPS), 72
Trade-Related Investment Measures (TRIMS), 100
transaction costs, 48–49, 54, 220–21, 227, 267–68
treaty-shopping, 267
trustees (delegating to). *See* delegation

umbrella clause
brought back via MFN, 130, 147–48
phasing-out, 68–69
surviving controversy, 203–5
UNCITRAL ISDS Negotiations
mandate, 271–73
procedure before substance, 273
tax analogies, 269
trade analogies, 277–78
UNCTAD
mapping project data, 37–38
proposed reforms, 1
United States
BIT program, 95–98
experience with FCN treaties, 84–85
Model 2004, 107–8
NAFTA-plus IIA practice, 108

United States (*cont.*)
  negotiation of NAFTA, 98–100
  post-NAFTA IIA practice, 104–5
  Trade Promotion Authority Act 2002, 106

vagueness
  countering vagueness through detailed
    drafting, 128
  as incompleteness (*see* contractual
    completeness)
  overcoming vagueness through forward-
    looking interpretation, 220
  understood as offering more investor
    protection, 129

Venezuela, 190–91
Vienna Convention on the Law of
    Treaties (VCLT)
  as incomplete contract, 231–32
  rules of interpretation, 231–44

WTO Agreements
  dispute settlement, 277–78
  as incomplete contracts, 50
  interactions with investment
    treaties, 72
  negotiations, 277

Zombie precedents, 195